s is a revisionist history of press censorship
he rapidly expanding print culture of the six-
th century. Professor Clegg establishes the
ure and source of the controls, and evaluates
ir means and effectiveness. The state wanted
ontrol the burgeoning press, but there were
iculties in practice because of the competing
often contradictory interests of the Crown,
Church, and the printing trade. By consider-
the literary and bibliographical evidence of
ks actually censored and placing them in the
ary, religious, economic and political culture
e time, Clegg concludes that press control
not a routine nor a consistent mechanism
an individual response to particular texts
the state perceived as dangerous. This will
he standard reference work on Elizabethan
s censorship, and is also a history of the
abethan state's principal crises.

This is a revisionist history of press censorship in the rapidly expanding print culture of the sixteenth century. Professor Clegg establishes the nature and source of the controls, and evaluates their means and effectiveness. The state wanted to control the burgeoning press, but there were difficulties in practice because of the competing and often contradictory interests of the Crown, the Church, and the printing trade. By considering the literary and bibliographical evidence of books actually censored and placing them in the literary, religious, economic, and political culture of the time, Clegg concludes that press control was not a routine nor a consistent mechanism but an individual response to particular texts that the state perceived as dangerous. This will be the standard reference work on Elizabethan press censorship, and is also a history of the Elizabethan state's principal crises.

PRESS CENSORSHIP IN ELIZABETHAN ENGLAND

PRESS CENSORSHIP IN ELIZABETHAN ENGLAND

CYNDIA SUSAN CLEGG

Professor of English, Pepperdine University, Malibu

CAMBRIDGE
UNIVERSITY PRESS

PUBLISHED BY THE PRESS SYNDICATE OF THE UNIVERSITY OF CAMBRIDGE
The Pitt Building, Trumpington Street, Cambridge CB2 1RP, United Kingdom

CAMBRIDGE UNIVERSITY PRESS
The Edinburgh Building, Cambridge CB2 1RU, United Kingdom
40 West 20th Street, New York, NY 10011–4211, USA
10 Stamford Road, Oakleigh, Melbourne 3166, Australia

First published 1997

Printed in the United Kingdom at the University Press, Cambridge

Typeset in Baskerville 11/12½ pt

A catalogue record for this book is available from the British Library

Library of Congress cataloguing in publication data
Clegg, Cyndia Susan.
Press censorship in Elizabethan England / Cyndia Susan Clegg.
p. cm.
ISBN 0 521 57312 2 (hardback)
1. Freedom of the press – Great Britain.
2. Censorship – Great Britain.
3. Great Britain – History – Elizabeth – 1558–1603.
1. Title.
PN4748.G7C48 1997
323.44'5'0941–dc20 96–36670 CIP

ISBN 0 521 57312 2 hardback

To
Caitlin Wheeler
and
Michael Wheeler

Contents

Preface

Renaissance literary studies have been engaged of late in a lively reappraisal of the interrelationships of literature, politics, and culture in early modern England. At the same time that this enterprise has embraced the new by grounding its rereading of early modern texts in postmodern theory, it has been remarkably remiss in failing to reconsider those "old" assumptions that shaped political and historical studies – particularly with regard to print culture. This methodological dichotomy has yielded an interesting conundrum. We have come to accept literature as highly political and the political system governing press control as highly repressive. This would hardly be problematic except for the widely accepted premise that the principal end of press control in early modern England was to rout out discourse that did not uphold the state's religio-political hegemony. In *Censorship and Interpretation,* Annabel Patterson has proposed an appealing way out of this contradiction – functional ambiguity, that is, a code of discourse accepted by both authors and the state that allowed religio-political discourse to be contained by linguistic indeterminacy. Ironically, Patterson's work has served as fundamental to new historicist and cultural materialist studies at the same time that these studies have collapsed the notion of literature that enables Patterson's hermeneutics of censorship. Functional ambiguity works best for what Renaissance writers called "poesy," but historicist/cultural studies have exploded our concepts of literature to include a vast array of texts. This expanded notion of text and intertextuality, confronting us as it does with so many more of those "puzzling incidents of noncensorship" noted by Patterson than poesy, springs the lock of prevailing assumptions about press control.

This study, which rehistoricizes the study of press censorship, began by casting aside the dearly held assumptions about press controls and replacing them with questions. What were the mechan-

isms of press control in early modern England? How were they
instituted? What kind of legal theory governed the controls? How
were controls enforced? For answers I turned to historical archives –
Star Chamber records, State Papers, records and manuscripts in
the library of the Church of England at Lambeth Palace Library,
historical manuscripts in collections of the British Library and the
Huntington Library, records of the printing trade, and early modern
printed books – particularly censored texts. Approaching the historical record with the first three questions took me in the same path
that Frederick Siebert had followed in his history of censorship,
Freedom of the Press in England, 1476–1776, but the fourth led me in an
entirely different direction. The first three enabled a description of
how censorship should work – a theory of censorship. Looking at
how controls were enforced moved me from a consideration of
theory to one of practice. The historical record makes those incidents
of noncensorship far less puzzling by revealing the distance between
enacting mechanisms for control and regularly and systematically
employing those mechanisms. Indeed, actual practices in government
and the printing trade reveal multiple religious, political, economic,
and social interests competing for expression and control. Book
production and controls were not a whole cloth of state authority.
Despite these often contradictory and competing practices, however,
censorship did occur. If the motive for this censorship could not be
located in the efficient practice of government censorship, what
then? My study turned to censored texts themselves to consider what
protocols, what ideologies, what kinds of language invoked censorship. Over and over again, the highly allusive language of censored
texts demanded that the texts themselves be historicized, that is, read
as fully as possible within the political, religious, economic, and
literary contexts that produced them. This book, then, is principally
a history of press censorship. The texts and contexts of censorship,
however, have determined that it should be more than an "acts and
monuments" of censorship (a book of martyrs?). Since each censorship "event" is actually a complex locus in which multiple issues and
interests are represented, this is a book about books (the material
objects and the authors, patrons, printers, and authorizers), and the
political, religious, and literary culture that produced them. It is a
book that bears testimony to the degree to which print culture
became a compelling force in England in the late sixteenth-century –
compelling enough that the central religious, political, literary, and

aesthetic issues of the day received consideration in print. It also bears testimony to the anxieties that the growth in printed texts produced – certainly in the Church and state, but also in the printing trade and among writers. Church, state, and individuals were anxious about how they were represented in print and how these representations might destabilize their authority. Printers and publishers were anxious about adequate employment and their rights to copy. Writers were anxious about how print would affect their reception. Efforts to control the press were measures taken to alleviate anxieties.

Lest we judge these early modern efforts to quell anxiety too harshly, we should be reminded that print culture was as new to people in the sixteenth century as electronic media is to us today. The United States Congress in February 1996 passed the Communications Decency Act to outlaw "indecent" communications on the Internet as part of the Telecommunications Reform Act. Those economic forces – including publishers, film studios, recording companies, and software developers – which would reap economic benefits by extending copyright to electronic media have repeatedly pressed for congressional support to make it a felony to distribute any licensed material beyond its initial authorized use. The language in these matters – "authorized use," "license," "copyright," "decency" – echoes the language present throughout this book used in the late sixteenth century in relationship to controlling print. It is perplexing that efforts to control the press in early modern England have produced more indignation in recent years than V-chips, digital rights, and internet censorship – or commercial control of American television programming. Indignation, however, has too often been the point of studying censorship. We can gain far more by recognizing that by studying censorship in any culture at a given time we can locate not only where power resides but what instabilities exist in the grounding of that authority.

The shape this book has taken follows in part the structure that emerged from my questions, in part the objects and methods of my consideration. The first three chapters focus on the mechanisms of control; the last seven on censorship practices. What began as a study of early modern press censorship, however, has become a book about England during the reign of Elizabeth I. This limitation does not mean that Elizabethan censorship is representative of early modern censorship practices – quite the contrary. Censorship resulted from (and responded to) particular and local events and personalities, and it (theory and practice) altered with changes in state affairs. Since the death of a monarch was one of the most significant events in early modern national histories, the deaths of Mary and Elizabeth offer convenient margins for a book that easily could have doubled or tripled in size had it considered all of early modern England. The book's organization, besides growing out of the kinds of questions I asked, emerged from the dichotomy in my sources. Several years ago in a seminar at the Huntington Library, Patrick Collinson remarked that the difference between historians and people who work in literature is that historians study documents and literature people study texts. Since earlier studies of press censorship considering either texts or documents have proven insufficient, I have considered both. I have tried to employ the methodology of both a literary scholar and a historian, but without a distinct divide. Though the first three chapters may appear to be traditionally historical and the last seven traditionally literary, I have throughout subjected historical evidence to the kind of subtle textual reading literary scholars employ. Likewise, books, their texts, and their production, have formed a very important part of my historical evidence.

Fairly representing historical and textual evidence has been my principal concern. Since most of the early printed books and manuscripts exist only in archives and rare book libraries, I often quote rather than merely cite. I perhaps err in the direction of over quotation and citation but do so because so many former assumptions about censorship have grown out of misquotation, inference, and misinformation. Early printed texts are represented here without spelling modernization, though early modern printing house conventions of using "u" and "v" and "i" and "j" interchangeably are abandoned, as are "vv" for "w," the long s, ligatures, accents on doubled letters, contractions using "~," and "y" for thorn (for which modern "th" is employed). Obvious typographical errors such as inverted letters or arbitrary font substitutions have been corrected.

Research for this project was largely enabled by the resources of the Huntington Library – certainly their collection but also their outstanding staff, especially curators Tom Lange and Alan Jutzi, and Steve Tabor, who assisted me with searches of the *English Short Title Catalogue* at University of California at Riverside's cataloguing terminal at the Huntington. My research at the Huntington and in England received funding from the Andrew K. Mellon Foundation and the British Academy Scholars Exchange Program. The Seaver College Dean's Office of Pepperdine University provided me with travel funding. For training my historical eye, I am indebted to members of the Tudor Stuart Seminar at the Huntington Library, particularly Mary Robertson and Eleanor Searle, who have been very helpful readers along the way. Kevin Sharpe and Mark Kishlansky offered excellent tutelage on doing historical research. I genuinely appreciate the efforts of my colleagues in literature who read chapters and made helpful comments, particularly, Peter Blayney, Jean R. Brink, Elizabeth Story Donno, Alan H. Nelson, James Riddell, and Stanley Stewart. To H. E. Igoe, for making his copy of the 1587 Holinshed's *Chronicles* available to me, I am especially grateful. For their efforts in seeing this work through publication at Cambridge University Press, I am grateful to Sarah Stanton, editorial manager, Humanities, and Lindeth Vasey. Richard Dutton and Christopher Haigh, readers for Cambridge, engaged in painstaking reading and offered invaluable counsel (and encouragement) that brought this book to its final form. Finally, I acknowledge the *Ben Jonson Journal* for giving me permission to include in chapter 2 the section on the 1586 Star Chamber Decree, which appeared in a somewhat different form as "The 1586 Decrees for Order in Printing and the Practice of Censorship."

PART I

The practice of censorship

CHAPTER I

Privilege, license, and authority
the Crown and the press

What a grieffe it is to the bodie to lose one of his membres you
all knowe . . . I ame sorie for the losse of my haund, and more
sorie to lose it by judgment . . .

> Mr. John Stubbes his Wordes upon the Scaffolde, when
> he lost his Haund, on Tewsdaie, 3 Novembre 1579[1]

There as they entred at the Scriene, they saw
Some one, whose tongue was for his trespasse vyle
Nayld to a post, adjudged so by law . . .

> Edmund Spenser, *The Faerie Queene*, V. IX, 25, 1–3 (1596)

Who kills a man kills a reasonable creature, God's image; but
he who destroys a good book, kills reason itself, kills the image
of God as it were, in the eye.

> John Milton, *Areopagitica* (1644)

The recurrent images of violence in these early modern representations of censorship, conjoined with post-enlightenment privileging of
individual freedom, have deeply colored the modern and postmodern construction of the cultural practice of press censorship in early
modern England. Whether their perspective is essentialist, new-
historicist, or cultural materialist, modern and postmodern studies of
early modern culture have followed Stubbs, Spenser, and Milton in
juxtaposing the interests of liberty and authority. Glynn Wickham
envisioned in the Tudor state a "whole machinery of censorship and
control"[2] whose evolution Frederick Siebert traces in *Freedom of the
Press in England, 1476–1776*. According to Siebert, "The rapid rise of
the government control of printing took place during the reigns of
Henry VIII and Elizabeth" with Elizabeth I's reign serving as "the
high point of the entire three hundred-year period in the average
pattern of the three factors, number and variety of controls, strin-
gency of enforcement, and general compliance with regulations."[3]

3

Even though Annabel Patterson notes "those famous puzzling incidents of *noncensorship*" (like Elizabeth I's recognition of topicality in *Richard II*) that suggest a chink in the monolithic structures described by Wickham and Siebert, her notion of functional ambiguity depends not only upon the machinery being intact but upon its operation shaping discourses whose intentions were understood equally well by authors and authorities.[4]

Such a clearly intentioned and efficient censorship system has in recent years come under scrutiny, especially with regard to Stuart monarchs. Philip Finkelpearl has observed that, "An efficient system of censorship depends upon a monolithic government with a clear sense of purpose, hence a sharp definition of what is permissible and impermissible."[5] Such a monolithic government, at least with regard to dramatic censorship, Finkelpearl, Richard Dutton, and Richard Burt, among others,[6] have found wanting. Instead Finkelpearl found in dramatic censorship "violations of nearly unbelievable magnitude"; Dutton found in the Revels Office licensing practices that engendered more freedom than control; and Burt found court licensing practices so contradictory that notions of censorship, he maintains, require redefinition. The contradictions, violations, and liberties these writers have found in the censorship of Stuart drama, Sheila Lambert has similarly discovered in the Jacobean press.[7] Lambert locates the increased licensing regulations called for by the 1637 Star Chamber Decree not in escalating attempts of Charles I's government to reinforce censorship controls but in the continuing demands on the government by the Stationers' Company to reform abuses in the printing trade. Lambert joins recent studies of the drama, not in repudiating ideas of state censorship altogether, but in demonstrating that censorship (in Stuart England, at least) is not the whole cloth spun and woven in the high chambers of government posited by Wickham, and, to some degree, Siebert.

If this is the case in Stuart England, where such "puzzling incidents of noncensorship" as Thomas Middleton's *A Game at Chess* (1625) can be located, as Dutton does, in contemporary politics and Revels Office practices, is it not possible that far more complex interests – political, economic, and religious, both within the printing trade and the government – contributed more to the "puzzling incidents of noncensorship" (and censorship) during Elizabeth I's reign? According to Blair Worden, the "breadth of political exploration which did secure interloped presentation on the stage" suggests "that the government lacked not merely the power, but the inclination, to impose conditions of writing that can helpfully be called 'repressive.'"[8] Less repressive conditions can likewise be found for print culture than have been formerly acknowledged. This does not mean that the press in England between 1558 and 1603 enjoyed unrestricted freedom. Press control existed, but neither its ends nor means correspond to the overwhelming systemization found by Wickham, Siebert, or Patterson. When the encounters between Elizabethan government and the press are taken individually and understood in their economic, legal, political, and religious contexts, press censorship appears less as a product of prescriptive (and proscriptive) Tudor *policy* than a pragmatic situational response to an extraordinary variety of particular events. As such, government enactments affecting printing, as well as practices in the printing trade, are often contradictory and idiosyncratic: the fabric of Elizabethan press censorship and control is a crazy quilt of proclamations, patents, trade regulations, judicial decrees, and privy council and parliamentary actions patched together by the sometimes common and sometimes competing threads of religious, economic, political, and private interests. Press censorship and the culture that produced it can best be understood by recontextualizing these acts of control and understanding the multiple factors influencing the contexts.

The tendency in literary and historical studies to generalize censorship practices throughout the early modern period in England has contributed significantly to misunderstanding Elizabethan press censorship. While recent theoretical approaches discrediting both periodicization and regnal approaches to history support this kind of generalization, in matters regarding the press, where the monarch and his or her immediate advisers had considerable influence, failure to establish difference along with continuity distorts historical understanding. To understand press control in Elizabethan England, then, requires establishing not only those practices and institutions related to the press that Elizabeth's government continued and modified, but also those that her predecessors employed and that her government abjured. The greatest continuity in Tudor England existed in the practice of extending royal privileges – or monopolies. The greatest diversity existed in censorship practices – both pre-print allowance (licensing) and acts taken to suppress transgressive texts. This chapter establishes the practices, both in the government and among the printers, which emerged in the early years of English printing that shaped Elizabethan policy and practices.

CROWN INTERESTS IN PRINTING

Elizabeth's regime, like those of earlier Tudor monarchs, recognizing the printed word's extraordinary power to achieve religious, political, and cultural ends, engaged with the press at many levels. From printing's earliest years at the end of the fifteenth century, English government concerned itself with printing and the book trade. Henry VII demonstrated his own interest in printing by appointing the first printer to the crown in 1504, giving political authority a text that could be widely disseminated.[9] Beyond appropriating a new technology for its own uses, much of the government's early interest in the press was in passing measures to encourage and protect the English printing trade. In its early years English printing was dominated by Continental craftsmen who had brought their expertise to London, encouraged by a parliamentary act.[10] By 1534, English booksellers, binders, and printers dominated the English book trade but suffered enough from foreign competition that Parliament passed a statute for their economic relief by restricting foreign competition. Even though regulating trade practices that affected the economic well-being of English printers, booksellers, and binders fell within the jurisdiction of the Company of Stationers after it received its charter in 1557, the Tudor state repeatedly followed these early parliamentary precedents and intervened, often at the request of the Stationers' Company, to protect the economic interests of the English book trade.

Besides employing trade protection measures, Tudor monarchs patronized printing through bestowing these privileges. By granting royal privileges to printers, booksellers, and writers, the monarchs could exercise considerable influence on print culture both by extending benefits to particular printers and by ensuring that certain books or classes of books found their way into print. However well the printing privilege may have served the ends of patronage, it was primarily economic and legal in nature; it granted to its recipient the right to enjoy the economic benefits derived from printing (or in a few rare instances authorship), and because it was extended by the Crown, it gave the privilege holder recourse in the monarch's conciliar courts against anyone who infringed it.[11]

Printing privileges were granted through royal prerogative – the same authority by which Tudor monarchs appointed officers and commissions to enact policy and law, administered economic policy to control trade, wages, prices, and commodity production, and extended patronage through grants of offices, lands, incomes, annuities, and other "privileges" (special conditions, exemptions, benefits not otherwise guaranteed by the common law). The sixteenth-century jurist William Stafford identifies prerogative with property in his assessment that "prerogative doth not only extend to his own person but also to all other his possessions, goods and chattels."[12] Hence when a Tudor monarch granted a privilege – for printing or anything else – the monarch essentially transferred to the subject those property interests that by feudal rights belonged to the Crown. In this respect, printing privileges were like the Crown's grant of licenses to acquire or alienate lands, to enter upon lands, to export (ashes, beer, cloth, grain, hides, wool), to hold fairs and markets, to import (felt hats, jewels, furs, wine, wood, wool), to keep taverns, tennis courts, and bowling alleys, and to sell herring and raw hides. Indeed, most printing privileges entered in the patent rolls are entered as "licenses" and the words "license" and "privilege" are used interchangeably.

That Tudor monarchs should extend privileges for printing, then, is rather unremarkable. The status of particular privileges, however, deserves some consideration. During the reign of Elizabeth, printing privileges were regularly entered in the patent rolls under either the Privy Seal or the great seal of England.[13] The great seal was essential to all royal grants, and its use distinguished the importance of a grant like the license to Christopher Saxton "to be the sole printer and seller of all maps of England or Wales."[14] Printing privileges, including the appointment of the royal printer, regularly appear during Elizabeth's reign under the Privy Seal. During the reign of Henry VIII, however, privileges do not appear to have been issued in such a consistent manner. While some were granted as patents under the Privy Seal, others appeared in royal proclamations; some grants have probably been lost, and some may well have been issued orally. During the reign of Henry VIII, title pages and colophons bear testimony that several works were printed with privilege, even though records of only a few official grants survive.

Royal printers enjoyed some of the earliest privileges extended by the Crown. No actual record exists of the appointment of the first official printer to the Crown, the Frenchman William Faques, but between 1504 and 1507 he probably served as "printer at the King's command," as he styled himself in his earliest official printed works extant: a proclamation on the coinage, a Latin Psalter, and Statutes (all 1504).[15] Faques's successor, Richard Pynson signed a 1508 edition of the Magna Carta "Regis impressor expertissim" [sic] on 3 September 1508, and although he did not sign himself as the king's printer, he printed a Sarum Missal in 1504[16] at Henry VII's command and expense ("mandata & impensa") for which the Privy Purse accounts record payment. Even though these early works printed with Crown support can be associated with grants of royal privilege, none of these works carries the title page or colophon imprint which we have come to identify as a clear demarcation of that status, *cum privilegio*, nor do official payments to the king's printer appear until 1515.[17] The earliest extant work carrying a printed notation of privilege to a royal printer was in 1518 for *Oratio Richardi Pacei in pace nuperime composita*; the notation reads, "Impressa Londini. Anno Verbi incarnati. MDxviii. Nonis Decembris per Richardum Pynson regium impressorem cum privilegio a rege indulto," that is, printed by Richard Pynson the king's printer with privilege from the king's grace. Royal printers received not only a stipend for their office but the sole right to print government documents for which they billed the Crown, some of which were vendible as well.[18] Royal printers after Pynson generally printed all their texts with some form of the notation *cum privilegio regali*. Each Tudor monarch appointed a new royal printer upon succession to the throne: Edward VI appointed Richard Grafton (1547–53) to succeed Thomas Berthelet (printer to Henry VIII);[19] Queen Mary appointed John Cawood (1553–8).[20] Elizabeth appointed Richard Jugge and Cawood (1559, for life), and though their patent did not specify the office of "Queen's printer," it extended to them the same privilege to print statutes, acts of parliament, proclamations, and injunctions, and added service books and other books printed by authority of Parliament.[21]

Outside of the office of printer to the Crown the status of royal privilege among Elizabeth's predecessors is less clear. A few distinct records exist of explicit monopolies granted under the Privy Seal, like the one extended to Grafton and Edward Whitchurch on 28 January 1543 to print liturgical books for church use. This monopoly was important enough that its existence was announced by a royal proclamation on 28 May 1545.[22] It appears, however, that most printing privileges were recorded only in the books themselves. A July 1539 letter to Thomas Cromwell regarding one of the privileged books, a primer printed by John Mayler for John Wayland, indicates that at least some privileges were granted verbally, with the imprint serving as the record of privilege.[23] As Henry VIII's chief minister and Lord Privy Seal, Cromwell possessed full authority to grant such privileges.[24] An increase in privileged books corresponds to both Henry VIII's break with Rome and Cromwell's rise to power. For the 2,233 extant titles printed during the reign of Henry VIII, 302 were printed with privilege.[25] Of the 135 extant works that were printed with privilege before a 1538 proclamation called for the uniform notation of privilege (*cum privilegio ad imprimendum solum*), the king's printers printed 73, just over half (55 percent). Of the remaining 62 extant works, 16 were legal, and 3 were liturgical (not including the Bible, Psalms, or catechisms). The remaining 43 extant works, including translations of the works of Erasmus, chronicles, prognostications, sermons, dictionaries, and grammars were printed "cum privilegio regia majestate," "cum privilegio regis," and simply "cum privilegio," all indicating some kind of special status, usually, of the printer's sole right to print the particular work for a specified period.

The royal printing privilege extended to its owner economic and legal benefits. This is made clear by a 1533 register of "such specialties as now, 15 May 25 Henry VIII, remain in my master Thomas Cromwell's hands, concerning the appearance of certain persons before the [Privy] Council." Cromwell held a bond "of Rob. Redman in 500 m. that he shall not sell the book called 'The Division of Spirituality and the Temporalty,' nor any other book privileged by the King." [26] The holder of a privilege (printers at this time were also booksellers) had recourse to the Privy Council should his privilege be violated, and the Privy Council could, if it chose, enforce the privilege holder's benefits – in this case the right to sell the work – against the interloper.

The nature of printing privileges has sometimes been misunderstood by later students of Tudor history. The words *cum privilegio* printed on a title page have often been understood as the mark of official permission or approval (license), implying a process of review and implicit censorship. Some of this confusion derives from the 16 November 1538 Henrician proclamation that called for official licensing and directed "not to put these words *cum privilegio regali*, without adding *ad imprimendum solum*, and that the whole copy."[27] This proclamation, one of several Henrician enactments directed at controlling the press, has elicited considerable scholarly debate that has centered around whether *cum privilegio ad imprimendum solum* indicates official approbation (license) or right to copy (privilege). This discussion has overburdened *ad imprimendum solum* to suggest among other things that the language was instituted to absolve the King of responsibility for indiscriminate use of his privilege to being a defining statement of copyright.[28] This proclamation's clear end was to institute pre-print censorship of scripture and other religious texts and to prevent the printing of objectionable texts "set forth with privilege, containing annotations and additions in the margins, prologues, and calendars, imagined and invented as well by the makers, devisers and printers of the same books, as by sundry strange persons called Anabaptists and Sacramentaries."[29] By calling for the addition of *ad imprimendum solum*, the proclamation sought a printed notation that would allow discrimination between those objectionable books printed *cum privilegio* with offensive addenda and those books to which authentic royal privilege had been conferred.[30] From December 1538 until the end of Henry VIII's reign, any work printed *cum privilegio* included *ad imprimendum solum*. The books so privileged shared the same categories as texts that had previously received royal printing privileges. After the proclamation, of the 166 extant works printed with privilege, Berthelet, the King's printer, printed 90 (54 percent). Of those remaining, 12 were legal and 8 liturgical. The liturgical works included two editions of the *Orarium* printed by Grafton "per regiam majestatem & clerum"; two editions of Grafton's English primer, "set foorth by the kynges majestie and his clergie," whose preparation the King supervised; and a Whitchurch Sarum rite *Portiforium*.[31] Grafton and Whitchurch's "Great" Bible accounts for another 7, but only one of these editions received ecclesiastical review and approval. Two-thirds of the works printed *cum privilegio ad imprimendum solum*, then, were of some significance to the King and his administration of Church and state.

Perhaps the reason three small Latin words have posed such a problem for scholars is that, contrary to widely respected views from their earliest years, all privileges to print were not the same. As we have seen, some were those exercised by the King's printers that were related to both the privilege of their office and the interests of government. Others were special privileges granted, like the ones to Grafton and Whitchurch, and Cromwell, to ensure that certain kinds of works were printed. Still another had to do with assuring that a particular book was printed – like those extended for Palsgrave's French language book or Lily's English and Latin grammars. The remainder – those to which only title pages and colophons bear testimony – reflect the government's effort to extend support to the printing trade. Despite the differences, during the reign of Henry VIII, all privileges shared two common characteristics. First, a royal privilege protected the holder's right to print exclusively the privileged title, or titles. This of course did not prevent infringement of the privilege, but it did give the patent holder legal recourse in the Privy Council – a recourse that was widely exercised, as we shall see, during the reign of Elizabeth. Second, despite Pollard's claim that "the one word 'privilegium' seems to have been used as a Latin equivalent"[32] for both privilege (the protection from copyright infringement) and licence (the permission to print granted once a work received official scrutiny), being printed *cum privilegio* did not mean that a privileged work had necessarily received the official scrutiny called for by royal proclamation or parliamentary statute.

That the distinction between license and privilege was maintained into and during the reign of Elizabeth can be seen in the wording of Elizabethan printing patents, which were regularly entered under the Privy Seal in the patent rolls. Elizabethan printers enjoyed privileges for individual works, classes of works, and even for all works they printed for a limited time, but these privileges differed in their licensing requirements. Elizabeth called for ecclesiastical licensing in her 1559 Injunctions.[33] The first patent she issued was to John Day the same year. It specified not only a lifetime privilege to print William Cuningham's *The Cosmographicall Glasse*, but a privilege for seven years to print other books compiled at Day's expense. It restricted his other publications: "so that they be not repugnant to Holy Scripture or the law; none of the books to be copies belonging by office to the queen's printers or derogatory books already printed by former licensees; the books to be perused and allowed before printing, according to the late injunctions."[34] Day printed part of this patent in *The Cosmographicall Glasse* in place of any form of the legend *cum privilegio*[35] but did not include the requirement for allowance, presumably since that was required only for the other

books. The licensing statement in *The Cosmographicall Glasse* begins,
"AN EXTRACTE OF THE QUENES highnes gracious Priviledge,
& Licence," reflecting the increasingly complicated language of
privilege and licensing. In the case of Grafton and Whitchurch's
Bible, privilege was distinct from license. In the case of Day's patent,
privilege and license were the same thing (*The Cosmographicall Glasse*
was both licensed and privileged), but perusal and allowance was an
added requirement for the other texts he printed.

That license and privilege are synonymous in Elizabethan patents
– and that they are distinct from "perusal" and "allowance" – is
apparent throughout the grants. William Seres received privilege in
1559 to print "all authorised books of private prayers, called primers
[and] psalters."[36] This required no further "allowance" because
these books were official. In 1571 this patent was extended both to
include Seres's son Richard and to include "all other books which
they have printed or shall print, set forth by any learned man of the
realm, whether in English or Latin" but without any stipulation of
allowance.[37] Richard Tottell's 1559 "licence" to be the "sole printer
of books on common law," granted "so long as he shall behave in
using the licence," required no perusal or allowance.[38] Day's 1567
license for ten years to print the metrical Psalms and the ABCs with
the little catechism includes a renewal of his 1559 license with its
stipulations for perusal and allowance.[39] Similarly Day's 1574 license
to print Alexander Nowell's Latin catechisms, as well as "all other
books in English or Latin made by Nowell and appointed by him to
be printed by Daye," required that "all books printed and sold by
virtue of the present privilege to be perused and allowed before
printing."[40] After Elizabeth's government became anxious about
prophecies and prognostications foretelling the Queen's deposing
and death, Richard Watkyns and James Roberts received a 1578
license to print for ten years "all such almanacks and prognostications as being allowed by any of the commisioners for causes
ecclesiasticall."[41] This privilege, only to "allowed" books, still
distinguished between license and allowance. Thomas Marshe, who
received his 1572 patent for Latin schoolbooks in consideration of his
great cost in procuring "more proporcionable and apt lettres than
heretofore hath been occupied" and to encourage the use of the
schoolbooks no longer available from the Continent because of
import restrictions, received the license without any stipulations for
perusal or allowance.[42] Neither of Thomas Vautrollier's patents for

specified books in Latin (1573 and 1574) require allowance, though the 1574 patent contained the proviso that "none be repugnant to scripture or to the laws of the realm."[43] Henry Bynneman's 1584 license "for all dictionaries and chronicles whatsoever" required no perusal or allowance.[44]

Besides confirming that printing privileges, unless clearly specified, were not generally the means by which Tudor monarchs censored the press, the Elizabethan patents explain her use of privileges. The patents to Marsh, Vautrollier, and Bynnemann reflect her regime's interest in fostering education and classical learning and, in the case of chronicles, in fostering knowledge of England's past. Privileges exist as well for particular works in which Elizabeth's government had a vested interest: John Bodeleigh's 1561 license to print an annotated English Bible dedicated to the Queen,[45] for example, or Christopher Saxton's atlas, or Nowell's catechisms. Like Cromwell's Bible patent, the almanac patent reflects the Crown's use of privilege to restrict unacceptable versions of a work that was otherwise acceptable. Finally, some of Elizabeth's patents, such as those awarded to Day, and possibly William Seres, demonstrate their value as a tool of patronage. Day's initial patent clearly ensures personal printing privileges rather than an interest in a particular work or particular works, with the exception of Cuningham's book. *The Cosmographicall Glasse* is itself dedicated to Robert Dudley, and John Day received patronage from Archbishop Matthew Parker.[46] William Seres had held a patent to print primers from Edward VI, but that he was deprived by Mary "to his utter undoing" is offered, in part, as justification for his Elizabethan privilege. All privileges were not patronage, as Tottell's Elizabethan law book patent's provision – "so long as he shall behave well in using the license" – seems to suggest.[47]

With all these different uses, printing privileges during Elizabeth's reign were still more clearly defined than they had been during her predecessors'. All privileges appear in the patent rolls under the Privy Seal, and the purposes of each privilege are more clearly delineated in their grants. What has disappeared is the plethora of privileges issued to protect printers' rights to copy. These had become unnecessary, as we shall see, by the chartering of the Company of Stationers, which assumed central responsibility between 1557 and 1603 for the operation and control of the book trade. The Stationers' Company Charter was itself a grant of royal privilege by Queen Mary – a privilege that was affirmed by Elizabeth when she came to the throne.

THE LONDON COMPANY OF STATIONERS

Receiving its charter in 1557, the Company of Stationers appeared quite late in the life of London guilds, many of which were in decline by the mid-sixteenth century.[48] Although its formal incorporation came late, printers, booksellers, and binders had practiced their trade in London since the end of the fifteenth century, and by the early sixteenth century evidently enjoyed guild status. On 24 October 1525 the London Court of Aldermen with the approval of the "Wardens of the Stationers" agreed to the translation of a Richard Nele from the craft of Stationers to that of Ironmongers.[49] A 12 September 1538 letter to Thomas Cromwell, Myles Coverdale, and Richard Grafton referring to the Company of Booksellers of London preventing their French host from selling his wares in England indicates that the Company could act to restrict participants in the trade, particularly in the interest of controlling "inferior" products.[50] Although royal privileges offered some printers valuable protection for their copy, Cyprian Blagden indicates that among the early articles by which the Company governed itself was an ordinance securing the right of a printer to the work he printed (an early form of copyright) through recording the title with his name in a register book.[51] Although the Stationers clearly possessed status as a craft, with the ability both to restrict foreigners and to regulate the craft, the grant of their charter, which had been formally requested of the Court of Aldermen in London on 3 June 1557, assured them a status in the City of London comparable to other companies and guilds.

This charter conferred on the Company of Stationers privileges and practices common among the older guilds: rights of property ownership, self-regulation, keeping apprentices, and engaging in searches to protect the trade from "foreigners" (nonmembers) and poor workmanship.[52] It allowed the Stationers to petition the City for the right to have a livery (granted in 1560), which assured the Company voting rights in London and parliamentary elections, participation in London governance, and status among London livery companies. Further, the Charter specified that the Company would be governed by a Master and two Wardens, appointed three men to the offices, and provided for subsequent annual elections for these positions. Beside the Master and Wardens, the Stationers' Company was governed by its Court of Assistants. The regular membership of the Company were its yeomen (those members who had served their apprenticeship to the Company or been "translated," transferred, from another company) – both journeymen who performed the trade's labor and young masters.[53] In these respects, the Stationers were no different from other city companies. One benefit procured by the Stationers in their 1557 charter, however, assured them a privilege beyond those of other companies: while the custom of the City allowed men free of one company to engage in the trade of another, the Stationers' Company charter reserved to members of the Company the exclusive practice of the trade of printing.

By 1562 the Company had drafted ordinances to consolidate the Court of Assistants' power: to require that members obtain from the Wardens the Company's license to print a particular copy, to require entrance of that license in the Company's Register, and to order the regular life of the guild.[54] While no copy of these ordinances is extant, the records of the Court of Assistants indicate that outside of matters of guild life, the principal business of the Company was protecting members' rights to copy. This was accomplished first by requiring Company licenses, and then by bringing those who printed against license before the Court of Assistants, which would decide a case's merit and, where warranted, impose fines. Among the earliest records of the Company of Stationers, besides the register of licenses, is a register of "fynes for defautes for pryntynge withoute lycense."[55]

With so much invested in assuring and protecting its members' rights to their copy, the integrity of the Company license was central to the Stationers' authority. It is not surprising, then, that regulations requiring licensing and recording licenses were an important part of the early ordinances. And since these ordinances no longer exist, understanding the Company licensing has over the years posed considerable difficulties. Some of this confusion has derived from identifying Company licensing with the efforts before 1557 of Tudor monarchs to control heresy and sedition by imposing government licensing contingent upon official authorization. Company licensing becomes much clearer if we maintain the distinction between license and authorization. Henry VIII, Edward VI, and Mary required that printers obtain a license from the Crown to print any book, but that license was contingent upon the approval of specified officials.[56] A license could have been required without approval or authorization as it was for importing wines. (The Crown could likewise have granted a wine import license with a condition, say, for example, that the wines were not sold above a certain price, or that they be certain varieties.) The Stationers' Company, having been granted the privilege to exist by letters patent, assumed the position of the Crown in requiring licensing. In essence, it extended to its members the privilege to print, and then required that members obtain the Company's permission/right/license for each book that they wished to print. The Company clerk recorded the license in the company books or Register. Each Register entry records the copy's title, the name of the Stationer holding the license, the entry date, and the entrance fee. If an equation must be made, the Company's license was more like a printing "privilege" granting the holder the sole right to print than it was a "license" granted upon the premise of official approval. In situations where a work also received "authorization" or approval by a government or ecclesiastical official, the entry generally specifies this.

In the early years, the notice of entrance (entry) in the Company Register simply records the license to print and the fee paid to obtain it. "John Judson ys lycensed to prynte *the Compendious treates or manuall of prayers* . . . iiij^d" or "Lycensed to William Seris to prynte *the Image of idelnes* and *psalmes in mytre noted* and *proverbis in mytre* . . . xii^d."[57] Between 1576 and 1578 most Register entries note payment of a fee and add the words "and a copie," reflecting enforcement of the ordinance that the Company should receive a copy of any book it licensed. After 1578 mention of a copy appears less frequently, though entries begin to note the Master's or Wardens' approval: 13 February 1578/9 "master Norton. Lycenced unto him under th[e h]andes of the wardens. A booke intituled. *An easie entrance into the principal pointes of christian Religion verie short and plaine for the simpler sorte* . . . vi^d."[58] It may be that the license holder could either obtain the Wardens' permission to print or submit a copy once the text was printed. That the Company license is distinct from a license contingent upon official approval is made clear in the Register by identifying the outside authorizer if there is one; for example, one of a group of Register entries dated between 4 September and 27 October 1565 reads "Receaved of Henry Rocheforth for his lycense for pryntinge *an almanacke and a prognostication* of his own makynge *for the yere of our lorde god 1565* auctorysshed by my lorde of LONDON

. . . viii^{d}."^{59} Even after 1586, when a Star Chamber Decree called for ecclesiastical authorization, the Stationers' Register distinguishes between the Company's license (sometimes referred to simply as "his Copie") and the ecclesiastical "allowance." An 8 February 1589 entry reads:

William Wright Entered for his Copie *a farewell entituled to the famous and [fortunate] generall[s] of our Englishe forces, Sir JOHN NORREYS and Sir FRAUNCIS DRAKE knightes &c.* donne by GEORGE PEELE, And aucthorised Under the Bishop of LONDONS hand, and master Coldockes [Warden] hande beinge to the Copie . . . vi^{d}.^{60}

While the Stationers' Register is accurate, it offers an incomplete record of everything printed. The Company license, in establishing copy ownership, was required only for first editions, so subsequent issues and editions usually went unentered. Further, since the royal printing privilege assured copy ownership, Crown printers almost never entered their titles in the Register, and privilege holders (patentees) did so rarely. Only works printed by Company members were entered, and some works which were apparently licensed were not entered. Peter Blayney believes that company licensing entailed two parts: the license, actually procured by showing copy to the Wardens (which entailed one fee), and the record of the license or entrance (entailing a second fee).^{61} Evidence exists to support Blayney's view. For example the Register for 1558–9 contains the entry: "John Daye ys lycensed to prynte a boke of phisycke called the treasury of [Philiatres Evonymus] translated out of laten and hath not payed for the sayd boke but only the entraunce which he payd iiij^{d}."^{62} Further Blayney's explanation conforms with other Tudor record-keeping practices. Archbishop Whitgift's 1597 book specifying the fees that could be charged for ecclesiastical services^{63} indicates two fees for each service – one for performing the service and one for entering a record of the service performed in the ecclesiastical registers. It also seems feasible that for some titles at least – works such as civic entertainments or guild records which might not have invited much competition among the printers – the printers may have made a special verbal agreement with the Company Wardens.

Comparing entries in the Stationers' Register with extant works recorded in the on-line *English Short Title Catalogue* offers some evidence of both the Register's accuracy and its importance to the

Stationers. For the 1560s the Stationers' Register records 1,005 works and the *ESTC* has 1,014. While not every work entered in the Stationers' Register survived, and not all works were entered, these numbers are remarkably close.[64] Similarly, extrapolating entrance for the five years missing for the 1570s from the 672 recorded entries and comparing this with the 1,375 recorded by the *ESTC* reveals a similar correlation, with well over ninety percent of the works being entered. In the 1580s, however, entrance dropped below sixty percent. The actual percentage of works entered in the Register decreased from sixty percent in 1590–9 to fifty percent in 1600–9. Some of the decline can be attributed to a large number of works that were issued in multiple editions subsequent to their initial entry, and hence did not require entrance. A substantial decline, however, must be attributed to works that were apparently "licensed" but not entered. Many of these works were printed "legally" since their title pages reflect no effort to conceal the printers' and publishers' identities or the locations of their presses. Blayney offers the most credible explanation for these omissions from the Stationers' Register: they were motivated by the desire to save money. A Stationer could pay the sixpence fee for obtaining his license from the Company, but he could save the fourpence fee paid to the Company clerk for recording the license's entrance in the Register.[65]

While one might conclude that avoiding entrance and authorization was done to avoid censorship, in most instances this seems highly unlikely. In the *Short Title Catalogue of English Books, 1475–1640* (hereafter *STC*), unentered titles appear along with entered titles in the record of works by most sixteenth-century authors (with the exception of those authors who were working from underground presses). A correlation of Register entries with the *STC* affords no consistent rationale for unentered works, outside of works printed on the Continent or by presses concealing their identity by using a Continental imprint. Some groups of works, civic pageants or masques for example, are less likely to be entered than plays – though some plays are not entered and some pageants and masques are. Most, but not all, sermons, are entered; but not all the sermons by one preacher may be entered. Foreign newsbooks are largely entered; local news may not be. Some poetry is entered, some not. Despite these vagaries, the Company's license (distinct here from Register entrance) was important enough that the Company imposed substantial fines for printing without license and for violating another printer's copy. The recurrence in the Register and court records of fines for violating Company licensing ordinances has dual and conflicting implications. On the one hand, the diligence of the Company officials in imposing fines indicates the perceived importance to the trade of legally establishing right to copy. On the other hand, the frequency of such violations suggests that even within the closed community of London printers, effective print control was impracticable. The benefits to be derived from printing – economic or ideological – outweighed the risks, even for some of the most established printers. The record of Elizabethan press control and censorship, as the next chapters will show, bears testimony not only to the difficulties the government encountered against writers and printers willing to take risks for ideological and economic reasons but to the efforts of the Stationers' Company to reserve to its members the economic benefits to be derived from the rapidly emerging print culture.

The chartering of the Stationers' Company has been seen variously as a draconian measure on the part of Tudor hegemony to control the printed word, as the means by which the government could achieve its end of controlling sedition and heresy, and as a triumph for Stationers who "obtained their Charter on their own terms," albeit "at a time when it suited the Crown to make use of their organization for other purposes."[66] In response to assertions that Mary created the Stationers' Company "in order to exercise a more effectual control over all English printed books," Edward Arber answers that "it was the printing and publishing trade which had been long organized as a City Craft that sought the royal incorporation and the civic livery for its own greater honour and importance." Arber also raises the important distinction, that as a civic guild, the Stationers were more "directly amenable to the Lord Mayor and the Court of Aldermen" than to the monarchy.[67] That the Company was formed at the height of Queen Mary's censorship campaign as a "suitable remedy" to seditious and heretical printing,[68] however, counters Arber's confidence in its independence. We do know that the Company had in 1542 sought a Charter and failed.[69] Why was 1557 different from 1542? Blagden speculates that Henry VIII may have rejected the initial charter because the powers the Stationers sought were too wide.[70] This is probably true, but it may also have been because he feared reform sentiments in many of the printers. By 1542 Cromwell had fallen, and Henry VIII was withdrawing from the religious reforms Cromwell had initiated. To surrender any control of the printed word would have been to risk empowering the very voices the King needed to silence. 1542 was too late for the printers.

During the reign of Edward VI printers flourished, but during Mary's regime their numbers diminished by nearly half, with many fleeing to the Continent.[71] Those who remained in London may have felt it necessary to appeal to the Crown to protect their trade, and to accomplish this, created a compromise document. That the Master of the Company at the time of the Charter, Thomas Dockwray, was neither a printer nor bookseller, but an ecclesiastical lawyer – and probably a Catholic according to Arber[72] – certainly suggests that the Company was employing some bargaining tactics. Whatever the Stationers' may have conceded in the preamble to their Charter and a Master acceptable to the Crown, they would gain in their privileged status.

Considering the Charter within its legal context, that is, as a grant of privilege extended through a patent under the Privy Seal,[73] further explains the Company's status. As we have seen, the Privy Seal was used as part of the regular administrative machinery of Tudor government, and patents issued thereby were in a sense "routine" business – confirmation of a previously arbitrated document. Further, since such grants and privileges were related to feudal property rights – the Crown was transferring property interests to a subject – the Stationers' Charter must be seen in terms of what precisely it transferred. The Charter not only granted the Stationers' Company its corporate right to exist and assigned to the company the power to govern itself and the trade, it also conferred on its members *in perpetuity* the sole economic benefits of printing. Except for the right reserved to the Crown to issue patents (privileges), the Stationers' Company charter transferred authority over printing from the Crown to the Company. The principal relationship, then, between the Crown and the Stationers, as between the Crown and the recipients of patent privileges, was a relationship of property, albeit one which derived from the feudal relationship of Crown and subject where the Crown bestowed economic benefit in return for a subject's loyalty. With regard to the book trade this feudal legacy meant that Stationers, as "privileged" printers, could enjoy the economic benefits conferred to them by the Crown as long as they did not engage in printing works which the laws of the realm defined as treasonous or seditious; beyond that the Charter does not indicate substantial controls.

One aspect of the Charter that has probably led to some misunderstanding is the grant of the right to search for and seize materials printed "illegally." From the perspective of hegemony and control, such a grant has been understood to indicate that the Stationers served as the agents of government censorship. The government ruled works illegal; the Stationers searched for these illegal works and seized them. The record of the Charter in the *Calendar of the Patent Rolls* supports such an interpretation. It reads,

The master and wardens shall make search in any place, shop or building of any printer, binder or seller of books for any books printed contrary to statute or proclamation and shall size, burn or convert the same to the uses of the commonalty.[74]

The full patent, printed in Arber, says that the Crown "will, grant, ordain, and appoint . . . that it shall be lawfull for the Masters and Keepers or Wardens aforesaid and their successors for the time being to make search."[75] The distinction here is between the Charter requiring the Stationers to serve government interests and the Charter making it lawful for Stationers to search for materials "contrary to the form of any statute, act, or proclamation." Search is not required, but legalized. Furthermore, legal searches may be made of printers, binders, and booksellers only, not of the general citizenry. To the degree that the Stationers' officers employed searches to confiscate printed materials declared illegal by the state, they participated in government censorship. Between 1558 and 1603, as we shall see, records indicate that the Stationers did perform searches, but the majority of these were not for treasonous and seditious literature. The latter were largely carried out by non-Stationers. It is not altogether clear, either, that Mary had employed the Stationers as her agents. The ecclesiastical commissions Mary created to search out sedition and heresy in the private chambers of her subjects possessed far more power to achieve her religious and political ends than the Stationers did.

Mary's ends, which understandably found their way into the language of the Stationers' Charter, were quite clear: suppressing "detestable heresies against the faith and sound catholic doctrine of Holy Mother Church."[76] Only one year later, Elizabeth's accession returned England to Protestantism. Her subsequent confirmation of the Company's charter in November 1559 was a rather perfunctory document which neither repudiated Philip and Mary's goals for using the Stationers to eradicate anti-Catholic doctrine in England nor advanced her own interests in a reformed English church. The Charter appears in the Conformation Roll followed by Elizabeth's confirmation:

We have inspected the letters patent of Lord Philip King, and Lady Mary, late Queen of England . . . holding firm and agreeable the foresaid letters and all and several the contents of the same, for ourselves, our heirs and successors, as far as in us lies accept and approve of them, and ratify and confirm them to our beloved Reginald Wolfe, now Mastr of the Mistery . . .[77]

"As far as in us lies" appears as an extraordinary qualification in such a confirmation, but probably a useful one since Elizabeth I justifiably found the Charter legal ("firm and agreeable"), but must have required some equivocation to confirm her approval of those parts of the "all and several" contents upholding "Holy Mother Church." Elizabeth I's confirmation is dated 10 November 1559; earlier by 19 July the Queen had appointed the first Ecclesiastical Commission, authorized by the 1559 Act of Uniformity, to "put in execution" that act's provision for the reform of the English Church.[78]

That Elizabeth could have so readily confirmed an organization supposedly formed to effect the censorship of Protestant heresy and sedition evokes some skepticism about the rhetoric of authority, and calls for the examination of the economic, social, and political issues that, along with religion, actually shaped the government's working relationship with the London press. How these issues, caught up in the radical political and religious reversals of the mid-sixteenth century, affected the Stationers may be understood by looking at the career of one man, Reyner (Reginald) Wolfe, who was seventh in the Company charter's mention of Mary's "Beloved and faithful lieges"[79] and the first Company Master ("our beloved Reginald Wolfe") under Elizabeth I. According to Sidney Lee, the Strasburg native Wolfe was "a man of learning and a devoted Protestant" who "settled in England, apparently at Archbishop Cranmer's invitation" in 1537.[80] In 1530, during a trip to Frankfurt, presumably to the book market there, Wolfe served as courier between Thomas Tebold and the Earl of Wiltshire, and Tebold in a letter to the Earl identified Wolfe as "bookseller, of St. Paul's Churchyard, London."[81]

According to Anne Boleyn's biographer, E. W. Ives, Tebold was circulating among German and French religious reformers and "spreading the idea that Thomas Boleyn was a promising patron of works, theological and other."[82] Wolfe subsequently established his printing house in Paul's Cross churchyard on land he obtained from Henry VIII.[83] According to Elizabethan chronicler John Stow, Wolfe built his dwelling, identified by the sign of the Brazen Serpent, "from the ground out of the old chapel which he purchased of the king at the dissolution of the monasteries; on the same ground he had several other tenements, and afterwards purchased several leases of the dean and chapter of St. Paul's."[84] During the reign of Edward VI, in 1549, after removing the bones, Wolfe apparently expanded his operation into the former charnel house. Peter Blayney's *The Bookshops in Paul's Cross Churchyard*, confirms Stow:

By 1543 he had set up the first (and only) printing house known to have existed in the Cross Yard, and was printing, publishing and selling books in a large property rented from the Bishop of London. By the time he died in 1573, Wolfe not only owned the shops on the site of the charnel chapel, but also held leases for (at least) all the properties between those shops and the Bishop's Head. All told, his known holdings formed a continuous stretch of more than 120 feet of the best bookselling frontage in England.[85]

Wolfe and his printing business flourished during the reigns of four Tudor monarchs. He received in 1547, shortly after Edward VI ascended the throne, a patent for the "office of the kings typographer and bookseller in Latin, Greek and Hebrew."[86] Though Mary granted the reversion of this patent to John Cawood to be received upon Wolfe's death, she also upheld the patent for Wolfe on 17 July 1558 when she granted to him and his deputies the right "to search the shops and houses of booksellers, typographers or others in the city and suburbs of London or elsewhere within the realm and to seize all such books as they shall find printed or put to sale without his license."[87] Wolfe also obtained another grant from Mary, this for an assignment to himself and to John Gawyn of "the king and queen's estate and interest" in the "manor or site of the dissolved monastery of Kyrstall *alias* Kyrkestall and Arthington and of land belonging thereto" – a property which had been seized from Wolfe's former patron Cranmer "before he was attainted of high treason and afterwards burned for heresy."[88] While it might be tempting to suspect that Wolfe found favor with Mary by subscribing to her religious agenda, this is most unlikely. A year after she became

Queen, Elizabeth granted to Thomas Cranmer, the son of the
Archbishop, rent from the "crown interest in the manor of Kyrstall,"
which had been "reserved under a grant to John Gawin and
Reginald Woulfe" during the reign of Philip and Mary."[89] However
much Wolfe's allegiances may have been shaped by patronage and,
presumably, religion, he was able to enlist Crown support – Catholic
and Protestant – to preserve and protect his own economic interests.

Reyner Wolfe's experience foregrounds the complex issues affecting printing. First, as we have seen, Tudor monarchs, regardless
of their religious allegiances, recognized the printed word's potential
power to achieve their religious, political, and cultural ends. In this
respect they employed their prerogative to grant both authority and
economic benefits to the printers. In the case of Mary's grant to
Wolfe of the power to search and seize works printed against his
patent, the Crown was actually assigning its right of governance.

Wolfe's affairs call attention to a second important factor affecting
printing – patronage. He almost certainly was able to achieve his
early preeminence in London's printing community – not to mention
his extraordinarily valuable real estate – because of Cranmer's
patronage, a favor he returned in "reserving" rents from Cranmer's
seized property for Cranmer's son. Patronage made possible by royal
prerogative seems to be forthright – a "Protestant" archbishop
patronizing a Protestant printer. The issue of patronage becomes
increasingly more complicated if we consider that Mary would have
preferred that Cawood enjoy the benefits of Wolfe's Latin patent,
but she could extend that privilege to him only in reversion upon
Wolfe's death. Obviously, too, the patronage system could be
employed to serve ends not immediately evident – such as Wolfe's
"reservation" of Crown rights for Cranmer's son. While prerogative
itself, the rights it could confer, and the means by which it conferred
those rights can be found in legal documents, patronage is more
elusive. In the complex web of human relationships, patronage
produced competing and often contradictory interests and practices,
often subverting more official interests.

Wolfe's experiences, while they tell much about royal interest in
printing, prerogative, and patronage, say little about early modern
England's most volatile issue – religion. Wolfe was almost certainly a
Protestant, receiving and returning Cranmer's favor, yet he wielded
some influence with Mary. His position in the printing community
was recognized – indeed supported – by the Company Charter, the

same document that stated the Company's purpose was to remedy printed affronts to Holy Mother Church. The contradictions inherent in Wolfe's experience confirm the degree to which the relationship between the Crown and a patentee was primarily one of property, and only secondarily one of allegiance. In terms of religion, this meant that printers like Reyner Wolfe would adjust the religious materials they chose to print according to the dictates of the Crown – especially since, as I will prove later, for Tudor monarchs the central end of press censorship and licensing was controlling opposition to their regimes' religious reforms. Beyond that, Wolfe's experiences suggest the relative independence exercised by individual London Stationers.

PRESS CONTROL PRIOR TO 1558

While Tudor monarchs, including Elizabeth, were fairly consistent in the practice of extending royal privileges to the print trade – both individually and corporately – licensing policies and censorship practices differed significantly. In 1414 Parliament passed the first censorship measure by confirming the legal right of ecclesiastical officers to take action against the authors of heresy and their books.[90] This, despite David Loades's claim that the roots of censorship lay in the treason laws,[91] provided the foundation for early Tudor censorship practice. The principal measures taken to control the press during the reigns of Henry VIII, Edward VI, and Mary related directly or indirectly to the Crown's interest in ensuring a particular religious settlement.

In Henry VIII's earliest efforts to control the press he defended the Catholic Church against the heretical writings of Martin Luther and other reformers. In the most dramatic of these efforts, Henry issued two royal proclamations, in 1529 and 1530, that together outlawed the possession and importation of nineteen heretical books printed in English on the Continent and the printing of any book concerning Holy Scripture without ecclesiastical examination and approval.[92] The effect of the proclamations was to provide a tangible touchstone for prosecuting heresy. Countless records of heresy proceedings rely not only upon knowledge of the ideas of Luther, Tyndale, and others but possession of the books proscribed by these proclamations.[93]

Once Henry VIII broke with Rome, suppressing the kinds of "heresies" that had been the object of the two proclamations was no longer the government's central concern. Ironically, it is to the ideas of reformers such as Luther and Tyndale that the architects of Henry VIII's royal supremacy turned for their justification of the English Church's claims against papal supremacy and the King's claims of authority over the Church.[94] According to John Guy, during the 1530s, Thomas Cromwell's "emphasis on faith, the primacy of the Bible and the value of preaching put him firmly in the 'reformed' camp," and as the King's vice-regent in spiritual matters, his patronage of Richard Taverner's translations of Luther, Erasmus, and the Bible went a long way towards instilling ideas of reform in English thinking.[95] Despite Cromwell's personal power and reforms, events occurred on the Continent and in England that led in 1538 to the King's distancing himself from religious reforms and renewing efforts to suppress reform writing.

Increasingly, as religious reforms abroad became associated with political anarchy, Henry feared the open actions of reformers at home.[96] His fears were fed by a political faction led by Cuthbert Tunstal that sought to reverse Cromwell's reforms. Henry's November 1538 proclamation, which instituted press licensing, responded to conservative fears by suppressing any debate on transubstantiation, exiling Anabaptists, and depriving married clergy.[97] Frederick Siebert says that the "Proclamation of 1538," representing a "new system of control" instituted once Henry had "concluded the church Settlement," was the "first attempt to establish a regular censorship and licensing over all kinds of printing."[98] While it does offer the first instance of licensing for "any book in the English tongue," to assume that it institutes a "new system of control" is mistaken. As we have seen, its requirement to indicate privilege by *cum privilegio ad imprimendum solum* seeks to remedy a particular problem. The entire proclamation likewise addresses specific historical contingencies. Although licensing all books may be new, the intent of licensing – suppressing religious heresy – is consistent with earlier measures to control oppositional religious texts.

As the highest law of the land, the Statutes passed in 1540 and 1542–3, rather than the 1538 proclamation, articulate the core of Henrician licensing and censorship.[99] The 1539 statutory enactment for religious uniformity[100] gave to ecclesiastical authorities acting as a Commission the right to confiscate offensive texts. The 1542–3 act abolished any books contrary to the Henrician articles of faith that espoused traditional Catholic doctrine without papal authority. Although the act strictly controlled religious printing, it allowed unrestricted possession of certain books printed before 1540, including proclamations and law books, chronicles, biographies, and books by Chaucer and Gower, and permitted plays, songs, and interludes that "meddle not with interpretations of Scripture, contrarye to the doctrine set foorth."[101]

That licensing and censorship measures appeared in statutes and proclamations directed at achieving religious uniformity indicates that Henry's end was not uniform control of print culture but rather preventing both the Protestant reform of the English Church and the political disruptions associated with the radical reformers.[102] Henrician press control ended in 1547 at the accession of Edward VI. His government repealed all of the Henrician censorship measures directed at Protestant reform,[103] and for five years the press enjoyed extraordinary freedom. In 1551, however, Edward called for press licensing far more intrusive than any Henry had instituted: a 28 April 1551 proclamation required pre-print licensing by the king or six of his privy councillors for any text – not just religious works – prior to printing.[104] This proclamation expressed concern that the liberty of printers, booksellers, and players to produce "whatsoever any light and fantastical head listeth to invent and devise" was provoking the King's subjects to abuse "the most precious jewel, the word of Godd" and engage in "vicious livings and corrupt conversations . . . licentious behavior, lewd and seditious talks." This proclamation, with its peculiar association of political sedition and Protestant morality belonged to the efforts of John Dudley, Duke of Northumberland, who, according to Guy "promulgated undiluted Protestantism" as a means for achieving social order in the midst of economic distress. This proclamation sought to send "light and fantastical" books the way of maypoles and alehouses – other objects of Northumberland's restrictions – as a means of securing an orderly society.[105]

Mary's accession was marked by the repeal of Edwardian religious reforms and a return to pre-Tudor treason laws. Since the pre-Tudor laws made no mention of printed treason, Parliament passed a statute that extended the definition of treason to include writing "any false Matter Clause or Sentence of Sclander Reproche and Dishonor of the King and Queenes Majesties."[106] Beyond this, Mary's censorship efforts were directed against Protestant writing, which she regarded as heretical and seditious. On 18 August 1553, she issued a proclamation extending "freedom of conscience" to her subjects but that prohibited any printing without the Queen's express written license.[107] Two years later on 13 June, Mary prohibited and ordered burnt "any works by any protestants" and authorized bishops and local civic officials "to inquire and search out the said books, writings, and works, and for this purpose enter into the house or houses, closets, and secret places of every person whatsoever degree."[108] On 25 April 1556 she issued letters patent to establish a special commission to "inquire concerning all heresies, heretical and seditious books" and "to seize all such books and writings in printers' houses or shops or elsewhere."[109] Finally on 6 June 1558, Mary issued a proclamation that by proclaiming martial law, exempted censorship from the due process provisions of English common law, and ordered that anyone possessing "wicked and seditious books" should be "taken for a rebel, and . . . without delay be executed for that offense."[110] Mary's was not a mere program of licensing, but an all-out attack on religious and political opposition waged through censorship. This escalating censorship campaign testifies to the strength both on the Continent and at home of the opposition to her regime's religious and political policies. The Marian war against heretics forced English Protestants into exile on the Continent, where they produced a powerful propaganda campaign that even drastic censorship measures could not suppress.[111] Their effectiveness underscores the difficulty Tudor monarchs had in employing government licensing to eliminate opposition literature. At "best," through statutory licensing Henry VIII's government prevented English printers from producing unauthorized religious books. Licensing requirements instituted by proclamations that provided ineffective means for their enforcement were less successful. No licensing, however, eliminated books from the Continent, or books that English printers would risk printing under false imprints. Further, because the objects of control altered with changes in the weathercock religion of the sixteenth century, government press control lacked both continuity and uniformity from one Tudor monarch to the next. Tudor monarchs did not pass on a legacy of licensing and press controls from one regime to the next; their only legacy was the general precedent for controlling the press. Like her predecessors, Elizabeth would act upon this precedent, but the policy and practice that resulted were distinctively Elizabethan because the complex of political, economic, and religious pressures belonged to the years between 1558 and 1603 – years marked by an increasing momentum of Protestant reform on the Continent, a more clearly articulated Catholic response, Elizabeth's own religious settlement, and an increasingly vital English book trade.

CHAPTER 2

Elizabethan press controls
"in a more calme and quiet reigne"

> But as in tempest or winter one course and garment is
> convenient . . . in cawlme or warme weather a more liberall
> rase or lighter garment bothe maye and ought to be followed
> and used, so we have seen divers streight and sore lawes, made
> in one parliament the tyme so requiringe, in a more calme and
> quiet reigne of a nother Prynce by like aucthoritie and parlia-
> ment repealed and taken awaie.[1]

No Tudor monarch can truly be said to have inherited the government of his or her predecessor; shifting religious priorities made this
impossible, especially in matters of press control and censorship.
When Elizabeth came to the throne in 1558 heralded by the City of
London as the Protestant Deborah, "the judge and restorer of
Israel,"[2] she faced the task of revoking her predecessor's political and
religious "reforms" and changing the clothes of government.[3] In its
first year Elizabeth's government took several actions that had
significant implications for press control. Among these were two
measures that continued institutions and policies established by her
predecessors: Parliament retained the Marian statute on seditious
rumor, and Elizabeth issued letters patent to confirm the Stationers'
Company's 1557 charter. The overwhelming changes came in the
legislation that has come to be known as the Elizabethan Settlement
– the 1559 Parliamentary Acts of Supremacy and Uniformity. These
measures that defined the Queen's role as head of both Church and
state laid the foundation for Elizabeth's government's control of the
press. All later definitions of seditious and treasonous writing derived
from the royal authority established by the Act of Supremacy. The
Acts of Supremacy and Uniformity together gave Elizabeth the
authority to enact the reformation, which she did in part by
establishing the High Commission – a body to which she also gave
authority to approve texts for print. The principal means thus

established for exerting controls over print culture were sedition and treason statutes, ecclesiastical licensing (authorization), and trade controls. The administration and enforcement of these controls rested in the law courts (including the Court of Star Chamber), the High Commission, and the Stationers' Company. These controls, their enactment, and the bodies that administered them look very much like the "whole machinery of censorship and control" that scholars have repeatedly found in studies of Elizabethan press censorship. The routine business of Parliament, the law courts, the High Commission, and the Stationers, however, regularly took precedence over assuring cultural hegemony. Indeed, the mechanisms for press control (outside of the Stationers' efforts to protect members' rights to their copies) were usually invoked only in response to particular events. In practice, then, press control was largely reactive rather than proactive even though its mechanisms were well defined. This chapter examines the "whole machinery of . . . control" instituted in Elizabethan England and evaluates its administration and effectiveness.

PARLIAMENT AND PRESS CONTROL

Between 1558 and 1603 Parliament passed no statutes with the express purpose of controlling the English press. While bills related to the press were read during the Parliament of 1584–5, they represented special interests rather than government policy.[4] Such efforts, although instructive of wider cultural attitudes toward the press, tell us less about actual censorship than the statutes that could be invoked to "lay hold" on "bookes sclanderous to the stat" – the treason statutes. During Elizabeth's reign Parliament passed eleven statutes addressing treason and sedition that included in their definitions some form of the phrase "by Wryting Pryntinge Preachinge Speache expresse Wordes or Sayinges." The 1559 Act of Supremacy formed the theoretical grounds of Elizabethan treason and sedition. The Oath of Supremacy called for by the Act defined the limits of loyalty to the monarchy: "that the Quenes Highnes is thonelye supreme Governour of the Realme . . . as well in all Spirituall or Ecclesiasticall Thinges or Causes as Temporall" and that "no forreine Prince Person Prelate Stat or Potentate hathe or oughte to have any Jurisdiction Power Superioritee Preheminence or Auchtoritee Ecclesiasticall or Spiritual within this Realme."[5] While universal subscription was not requisite, all subjects were held to its standards by sanctions for violating the Oath's provisions "by writing printing teaching preaching expres woordes dede or acte."[6] A second act in 1559 added to the definition of treason, to "compas or imagyn to depryve the Quenes Majestie that now is, or theire of her Body to bee . . . from the Stile Honour and Kingly Name of Thimperiall Crowne of this Realme" and to deny the Queen's right to the Crown.[7] In 1571 Parliament strengthened the 1559 treason laws both by increasing the penalties and extending the definition.[8] It now became treason to "compas or imagyn" bodily harm against the Queen, to stir foreigners to invade England, or to declare in words or writing that Elizabeth was a heretic, schismatic, tyrant, infidel, or usurper. Furthermore, it mandated a year's imprisonment for writing about the succession to the English Crown.[9] In the 1570s and 1580s a group of recusancy laws further classified as treason withdrawing English subjects from their obedience to the Queen, converting them to Roman Catholicism with the intent of turning them against the Crown, and harboring anyone committing these offenses.

What the Elizabethan treason laws did not address, her rumor and sedition statutes did. During Elizabeth's first Parliament, the Marian statute against rumor and libel was extended to her. It specified that anyone found guilty of writing anything "containing anie false matter, clause, or sentence of slaunder, reproach and dishonour of the king and Queenes Majesties . . . or to the incouraging, stirring, or moving of any insurrection or rebellion" would for their first offence "in some Market place . . . have his or their right hand stricken off."[10] In 1581 Parliament replaced this with a statute mandating the death penalty for anyone found guilty of "devising, writing, printing, or setting forth" or "procuring or publishing" any text "containing any false, seditious, and slanderous matter to the defamation of the Queenes Majesty, that now is, or to the incouraging, stirring or moving of any insurrection or rebellion."[11]

The statutory grounds for press censorship are clear. Writing or printing texts denying Elizabeth's ecclesiastical and temporal authority, advocating the rights of anyone else to that authority, advocating rebellion, calling the Queen a heretic or usurper, "compassing" bodily harm to the Queen, or slandering or defaming her – that is, attacks on the Queen's authority – came within the definition of high treason. Possessing books which did any of these things, however, often became part of the evidence rather than the cause itself in treason trials. Writing, publishing, or printing texts with rumors, libels, or slanders against the Queen – that is, attacks on her dignity – were felonies that invoked increasingly more rigorous sanctions. To be accused of high treason during Elizabeth's reign was no small matter, for as John Bellamy has demonstrated, it was in these matters that the government often resorted to torture to secure either a confession or information about conspirators.[12] Trials for high treason (conspiracy to overthrow the Queen or participating in actual rebellion) were held before special commissions of oyer and terminer called for the express occasion.[13] According to Bellamy – and contrary to common belief – the evidence presented in these trials appears to have been fairly accurate, though the government in its indictments and evidence often took advantage of an excellent propaganda opportunity.[14] Other treason cases were tried at the assizes.

The notorious treason trials of the Duke of Norfolk, Anthony Babington, Edmund Campion, Mary, Queen of Scots, and the Earl of Essex fill the annals of Elizabethan political and legal history. Only a few cases of treason, however, related directly to press censorship. On 20 January 1584 London printer William Carter was executed for treason for printing a London edition of Gregory Martin's *A Treatise of Schism* (Douay, 1578) that contained passages inciting the women of the court to assassinate the Queen.[15] Carter had earlier been arrested for maintaining a secret press and for selling a French book identified in English as *The Innocency of the Scottysche Queene* (1572), a book supporting the Stuart claim to the English throne, praising the Duke of Norfolk, defending the Northern Rebellion, and attacking Burghley – but he had been released.[16] Carter's relative treatment in these two matters marks the difference between malicious libel (the book on Mary) and treason in advocating rebellion (*Treatise of Schism*). But even malicious libel required considerable evidence for conviction. In 1584, a presentment was brought against Robert Sutton of Aylesham before the Norfolk assizes for publishing a book containing the words "Not to be with the Pope is to be with Antichrist," but the indictment was held to be insufficient.[17]

Many Catholic books appeared in England as objectionable as Gregory Martin's, and while their Continental authors and printers remained beyond the pale of English law, their distributors and owners in England did not. William Cardinal Allen and Robert Parsons engaged in a prolific print war to win Englishmen to Catholicism. Some of their apologetics, though suppressed by proclamation, lay outside the bounds of treason. Some, however, provoked enforcement under the treason laws. Allen's *A True, Sincere and Modest Defence, of English Catholiques that Suffer For their faith* (1584) attacked English practices against recusants, painted Burghley as a relentless persecutor and villain, and justified military action to overthrow a heretical ruler. On 5 July 1585 an English missionary priest, Thomas Alfield, who had also written a defense of Campion, was found guilty under 23 Eliz., ca. 2 of "publishing of books containing false, seditious, and slaunderous matter, to the defamation of our Soveraygne lady the Quene."[18] Alfield's indictment had accused him of importing and dispensing Allen's *A True, Sincere and Modest Defence*.

The statutes against treasonous writing and printing also provided the legal grounds to proceed against the Protestant left; Henry Barrow, John Greenwood, John Penry, and John Udall were all prosecuted under them. Their prosecutions and convictions reflect a general anxiety about reformers provoked both by William Hacket and by frustration over the government's inability to discover and prosecute the author(s) and printers of the Marprelate pamphlets. Around Easter 1591 Hacket and a few credulous disciples believing in Hacket's immortality and heavenly mission to inaugurate a new era on earth, caused a considerable tumult in the London streets as they preached their gospel of reform.[19] They planned to dethrone the Queen, set Hacket on the throne, abolish the episcopacy, and establish an eldership in every congregation. The bishops made good use of Hacket's "mission" to demonstrate the political implications of radical Protestantism.[20] While it has been argued that in their writings Barrow, Greenwood, Penry, and Udall maintained their loyalty to the Queen, their texts received an unusually narrow reading by bishops whose authority had suffered at the hands of Martin Marprelate and who likened the political implications of these earnest reformers to the efforts of Hacket. Moreover, each of these men's association with Martin Marprelate had been rumored, but the bishops could not gather sufficient evidence to indict them for Martin's writings.[21]

The most remarkable aspect of statutory press control is that it did not go beyond protecting the authority and dignity of Elizabeth.[22] For measures more restrictive on the press than those that would protect the authority and dignity of the Queen, Parliament was largely uninterested, but this does not, however, mean that Parliament never concerned itself with suppressing the printed word. In 1581 the House of Commons censured one of its members, Arthur Hall, and censored his book, *A Letter sent by F. A., touching the Proceedings in a private Quarrell and Unkindnesse, between Arthur Hall and Melchisidech Mallerie* (1579), because Hall had abused the privilege of Parliament in claiming immunity to Mallerie's litigation, and also because the book disparaged the current Speaker of the House.[23] Furthermore, bills for press control were either prepared or presented four times during Elizabeth's reign (1577, 1580, and twice in 1584). In 1584, according to Neale, two bills were read in Commons and met with instant hostility. The first reflected the Stationers' attempts to secure statutory control over the printing trade.[24] The second, concerned with slanderous books and libel, Neale considered a response to Catholic propaganda, particularly *Leicester's Commonwealth*. Whatever the interests of these two bills, according to Neale, opposition came from the puritan constituency in the Commons which would oppose any "measure which could weight the scales more heavily against the clandestine Puritan Press."[25]

As an anonymous speech prepared for the 1584 session of Parliament indicates, puritans were not adverse to press control, only to that which did not meet their interest in suppressing "Idell pamphletts & dire leud & wanton discourse of love of all languages leud . . . ballads [and] lying historyes."[26] The religious reform movements' interest in controlling the press may be identified with the draft for a parliamentary licensing act made first in 1577 and revised in 1580 by W. Lambarde.[27] This draft has been regarded as representative of the government's growing interest in press control in the 1580s.[28] The draft's preamble, however, suggests that it represents the same puritan interests reflected in the anonymous speech. The 1580 preamble expresses the desire to suppress books serving "to let in a mayne Sea of wickednesse, and to set up an arte of making lascivious and ungodly love, to the highe displeasure of GOD, whose guiftes and graces bee pitifully misused thereby."[29] While the reformers may have desired to control the "Sea of wickednesse" emanating from the English press, they never presented their bill – probably because they understood that statutory licensing may have instituted more effective measures for silencing the godly than were already in place.[30]

PRESS CONTROL AND THE ELIZABETHAN CHURCH
SETTLEMENT

While the 1559 Act of Supremacy had laid the foundation for later statutes governing treasonous and seditious writing, it also gave to the Queen the title of "Supreme Governor of the Church" and articulated means by which the Queen could assure the Reformation of the English Church. The Act of Uniformity gave shape to that Reformation by reinstituting the use of the Book of Common Prayer (the central product of Edward VI's religious reforms) and specifying penalties for those ministers who did not use it or who spoke against its use, and by ordering attendance at church on Sundays and holy days.[31] According to Norman L. Jones, "much of the government's effort in 1559 was devoted to the establishment of the reformed Church mandated by Parliament."[32] Elizabethan measures to control the press by instituting official authorization belong to these efforts to secure the Reformation.

The Act of Supremacy lies at the center of press control because it gave to the Queen both the authority to visit and reform the "ecclesiastical state" and the means to execute this authority. The Act authorized the Queen to employ royal letters patent to create an ecclesiastical commission to:

visite, reforme, redressse, order, correct and amend all such errors, heresies, schismes, abuses, offences, contempts and enormities whatsoever, which by any maner Spiritual or Ecclesiasticall power, authority or jurisdiction, can or may lawfully be reformed, ordered, redressed, corrected, restrained or amended, to the pleasure of Almighty God, the increase of vertue, and the conservation of the Peace and unity of this Realme . . .[33]

Sometime before 19 July 1559, authorized by this Act, Elizabeth I issued letters patent for an Ecclesiastical Commission for London, which came to be known as the High Commission. The letters patent name Matthew Parker, "bishoppe" of Canterbury designate, and Edmund Grindall, bishop of London designate, first among the Commission's seventeen members, six of whom must act together, "to put in execution throughout the realm the Acts (1 Elizabeth) of Uniformity and Supremacy and to inquire touching all heretical opinions, seditious books, contempts, false rumours and the like and hear and determine the same."[34] While these powers appear all-encompassing, visitation and reform were restricted by the Act of Supremacy to "the Visitation of the Ecclesiastical state and persons, and for reformation, order and correction of the same."[35] An Ecclesiastical Commission was likewise established at York for the northern province.

The task of visitation and reformation that would shape the High Commissions' work received definition from the Queen's 1559 Injunctions, issued by royal proclamation on 19 July 1559 and printed by the Queen's printer. The Injunctions set forth to the clergy the form and substance of the Elizabethan Church and the means by which it should be reformed and governed. One of those means, as item 14 specifies, was that the clergy should "once every quarter of the yeare reade these Injunctions given unto them."[36] Besides calling deans, archdeacons, parsons, vicars, and other ecclesiastical persons to "faithfully keep and observe . . . all and singular laws and statutes made for the restoryng to the crown and ancient jurisdiction over the state ecclesiastical and abolishing of all foreign power repugnat to the same" (A2r), the Injunctions call for educated and licensed preachers to teach the Word of God, and, in their absence, for the reading of homilies; the removal of Catholic trappings from the churches; tithing; the use of parish funds to support both the poor and scholars; and the placement in churches of Bibles and Erasmus's *Paraphrases*.[37] Item 50 recognized that alterations in religious rites and ceremonies bred discord and called upon the Queen's subjects to live in charity, but particularly not to use words like *papist, papistical heretic, schismatic, or sacramentary* as words of reproach.

The next item (51) likewise treating of words, called for licensing printed works.[38] It required licensing for print of "any manner of boke or paper, of what sort, nature, or in what language soever it be" by the allowance of the Queen (in writing), by six privy councillors, the chancellors of the universities, or by ecclesiastical authorities specified in the Injunctions. To indicate this "allowaunce," "the names of such as shal allowe the same" should "be added in thende of every such worke." "Any manner of boke or paper" appears to be so inclusive that the subsequent provisions not only seem to be superfluous, but raise the possibility that "any manner of boke or paper" must be read within the religious context of the entire set of Injunctions. One subsequent provision calls for licensing by three Ecclesiastical Commissioners of "pampheletes, playes and balletes" and another for the High Commission ("saide commyssyoners within the Cytie of London") to decide whether or not works previously printed, both in London and abroad, were acceptable. The licensing requirement, however, did not apply to all new books since it carried the caveat, "Provyded that these orders do not extend to anye prophane aucthours, and workes in any language, that hath ben heretofore commonly receyved or allowed in any the unyversities or Scholes: But the same may be prynted and used as by good order they were accustomed." Arber glosses "prophane" as classical in the selection from the Injunctions included with his *Transcript*,[39] but the word's common use after 1483 was secular or nonecclesiastical. The exclusion, then, depending entirely on how the passage is read, may apply to nonreligious works (including those by classical authors) that are schoolbooks, or to any books acceptable in the schools, including those by secular authors and those in other languages. "That hath ben heretofore commonly receyved" may be read separately from "allowed in any the unyversities or Scholes," creating two categories of books exempted rather than one. There is enough ambiguity in the language and syntax to allow – indeed to require – interpretation on the part of a printer.

How a printer would read the Injunction may be understood from the section on previously printed works: "And touchinge all other bokes of matters of religyon, or polycye, or governaunce, that hathe ben printed, eitheir on this side the Seas, or on thother side." This seems to suggest that the Injunction likewise concerned itself primarily with any manner of book or paper to be printed on matters of religion, policy, or government. Given this and the entire Injunction's context – one among fifty-three injunctions directed at achieving the Elizabethan Reformation of the English church – the end it sought to achieve was ecclesiastical scrutiny of printed texts on matters of religion and, since in the person of Elizabeth government of the Church and state were conjoined, matters of policy and government. Taken within this context, the Injunction's program of licensing appears, like so much of the rest of the document, as a desideratum, albeit one which if not respected threatened unspecified sanctions from the ecclesiastical authorities.

The 1559 Injunctions have been widely regarded as the central means by which Elizabeth established pervasive press censorship.[40] Siebert suggests that the sole purpose of the 1559 Injunctions was to devise a licensing system for the press: "The year after her accession Elizabeth paused long enough in framing the church settlement to devise a licensing system for the press."[41] He sees the licensing called for in item 51 as distinct from the Church settlement. As we have seen, the licensing provision is but one of fifty-three items in a document whose end is the Church settlement. Seeing the injunction on printing within this context, as an instrument to be used for visitation, helps to explain why, as Siebert observes, "the available evidence indicates that the licensing regulations were neither strictly obeyed nor wholly disregarded . . . Neither the minutes of the Privy Council nor the papers of the Star Chamber mention any prosecution of a printer for violation of the injunctions."[42] Prosecutions do not appear in Privy Council or Star Chamber records because the 1559 Injunctions placed printing within the jurisdiction of the Ecclesiastical Commission. In short, the press control established by the 1559 Injunctions was certainly ecclesiastical in its administration and likely ecclesiastical in its intent.

Placing licensing under ecclesiastical authority, a practice with clear historical precedents, is considerably less remarkable than the means by which the licensing requirement was mandated. As a visitation document, the clergy had to subscribe to the Injunctions. Clergy who refused to read the document, and who, likewise refused to take the Oath of Supremacy and institute the Book of Common Prayer, could be called before the Ecclesiastical Commissioners, who would "hear and determine" their offense. Such proceedings against the clergy would have had little effect on printing. That such licensing practices existed, however, and that all the clergy knew about them, might deter nonconforming clergy from using the press to voice their opposition. Printers and publishers would presumably learn of the licensing requirements at church. A copy of the Injunctions was sent to Stationers' Hall as well. Within the context of a document whose stated intent was "to plant true religion to the extirpation of all hypocrisy, enormities, and abuses" (A1v) the licensing provision (item 51!) may well have appeared to the printers as less than the highest priority – particularly since, except for religious texts, the provisions for their enforcement were ill defined. The Ecclesiastical Commissioners held authority to impose fines and imprison, and according to item 51 they could opt for such sanctions – but only against the person or persons who sold or disseminated ("uttered") unlicensed materials. Beyond that, the licensing requirement of the 1559 Injunctions, issued as they were by royal proclamation,[43] lacked the legal teeth to impose the kind of draconian book control so often credited to the Injunctions.

The injunction on printing ended with the Queen's commandment to "al manner her subjectes, and specially the wardens and company of Stationers, to be obedyent"; the High Commission's task was to secure that obedience. Licensing would be as effective and inclusive as the High Commission made it, and from all available evidence, though the High Commission did on several occasions exert its authority over printing, it never enforced invasive and inclusive licensing of *all* printed matter. Over the years, whatever jurisdiction over printing this injunction had given to the High Commission came to be exercised by the Archbishop of Canterbury and the Bishop of London. Whenever matters arose in the Privy Council regarding printing, they served as liaisons between the government and the Stationers. Furthermore, they both served, though not exclusively, as official authorizers. After 1586, the informal governance of printing that had been assumed by these ecclesiastical leaders was formalized: the Archbishop of Canterbury and the Bishop of London were designated as responsible for pre-print authorization, and the Archbishop was given authority to approve requests for establishing new printing presses.

The same year that Elizabeth issued the 1559 Injunctions, she confirmed the Stationers' Company charter. The 1557 charter had given to the Stationers the authority to regulate the printing trade and had held them accountable directly to the Queen (then Mary). In creating the High Commission and making it responsible for the contents of printed texts, Elizabeth effectively delegated to the Commissioners the task of achieving the English press's accountability for the books they printed. In the Charter, as we have seen, the monarch delegated to the Stationers' Company both the Crown's rights to govern trade and some of the Crown's economic interests, but retained the right to issue individual privileges or monopolies. In effect, then, both the High Commission and the Stationers' Company joined the Crown in exercising the Crown's authority over printing. In practice all three issued licenses to print – the Company's license and the royal privilege protected a printer's economic interests in a text, and the Commissioners' license (authorization) assured that the text would not interfere with their charge to "reforme, redressse, order, correct and amend all such errors, heresies, schisms, abuses, offences, contempts and enormities whatsoever, which by any maner Spiritual or Ecclesiasticall power, authority of jurisdiction, can or may lawfully be reformed."[44] The relationship between Elizabeth's government and the press needs to be seen as an ongoing negotiation between the economic interests of the Stationers and privilege holders and the religious interests of the High Commission. To understand this negotiation requires understanding the institutions. As we saw in Chapter 1, the London Stationers enjoyed the exclusive practice of their trade and the right to regulate any matters relating to the Company and the book trade. Similarly, by the time of Elizabeth's reign, royal printing privileges were regularly conferred and entered in the patent rolls. The High Commission's practices are less clearly understood.

Some misconceptions derive from Roland Usher's *The Rise and Fall of the High Commission* (1913). He saw the High Commission as a special "court of law, in session at London between (approximately) the years 1580 and 1641," whose judges were "about a dozen of the Ecclesiastical Commissioners appointed by royal Letters Patent."[45] Usher distinguishes between the High Commission and ordinary ecclesiastical commissions whose interest was in suppressing heresy. Philip Tyler argues that Usher was wrong, and the Elizabethan High Commission was identical in authority and purpose to pre-Reformation ecclesiastical commissions that had their origin "in the Crown's traditional right and duty to safeguard the Church."[46] Tyler makes it clear that Elizabethan ecclesiastical commissions (both provincial – the "High" Commissions – and diocesan) were properly constituted law courts from the time their patents were issued. Their procedure derived from the older church-law courts, and much of their business derived from episcopal or archepiscopal visitations. Tyler distinguishes between the royal visitation commissions formed to seek out error and abuses and the ecclesiastical commissions created to serve as sovereign criminal courts,[47] but John Guy says that the High Commissions erected at Canterbury and York under the authority of the Act of Supremacy combined judicial and visitatorial functions to deprive clergy who refused to take the oath to Elizabeth's supremacy and to conform to the Act of Uniformity and the Queen's 1559 Injunctions.[48]

Richard Cosin's *An apologie: of and for sundrie proceedings by jurisdiction ecclesiastical* establishes that by 1591 the High Commission exercised jurisdiction almost entirely over matters of conformity and uniformity among the clergy, while the regular diocesan courts exercised authority over the morals and beliefs of the faithful. According to Cosin the categories of offenses punishable by regular ecclesiastical jurisdiction were: crimes "against the Pietie of god," including "blasphemy, swearinge, idolatrie, heresie, errour in faith, schisme, apostacie from Christianitie, not frequenting publicke prayer, neglect of the Sacraments, perjurie in the Ecclesiastical Court or mater, disturbance of divine service, violating or prophaning the Sabboath";[49] acts contrary to Church offices such as simony and neglect of or disrespect for Church buildings; all acts of sexual or marital incontinence; and testamentary matters such as will and divorce. Cosin said that the specific jurisdiction of the High Commission was in "visiting, reforming, redressing, ordering, correcting, and amending all such errours, heresies, schismes, abuses, offences, contemptes."[50] Although Cosin's work was written in response to numerous challenges to the High Commission, and especially to its use of the oath *ex officio*, works on both sides of the controversy recognized the High Commission's jurisdiction over ecclesiastical conformity.[51]

The High Commission was not only distinct from the regular ecclesiastical courts, but the government clearly distinguished the High Commission's jurisdiction from its own concern for affairs of state. A 3 January 1574/5 letter from the Privy Council to the Bishop of London reserved to the state jurisdiction over treason and assigned to the High Commission jurisdiction over doctrine. This appeared in a letter from the Bishop of London informing the Council of John Willoughby's importing of "erroneous" books. The Privy Council directs that Willoughby be examined, the books perused, and the Bishop confer with the Solicitor,

. . . and if he shallbe founde culpable in any offense of Treason against her Majesties person or State for bringing in of said bookes, to procede and order him according to the lawes; if his offence shalbe but a matter of doctrine, then to be punished by the Ecclesiasticall Commissioners according to the qualitie of his offence.[52]

This distinction was not merely theoretical. The Privy Council monitored both the High Commission's jurisdiction and its procedures. A 1581 letter to Burghley from Bishop of London, John Aylmer, reveals that Burghley had rebuked the Commissioners for overstepping their jurisdiction.[53] Further, on 9 May 1594 in a letter to the London High Commission, the Privy Council offered to assist the Commissioners "in any lawfull cause against such as refuse to conforme themselfes to the Uniformitie of Religion" but rebuked the

Commission for its procedure "that men shold be so long deteyned without having the cause examined" and required them "to proceade in suche cases more spedelye hereafter, and . . . in case any be so sicke that they cannot well there continew, to suffer them to be bailed till their cause be ended."[54] While the High Commission at times may have abused the limits of its jurisdiction, Elizabeth's government clearly intended that the High Commission should concern itself only with ecclesiastical matters.

THE HIGH COMMISSION, THE STATIONERS, AND PRESS CONTROL TO 1586

From its inception in 1559, the High Commission was clearly the means by which Elizabeth's regime expected to control opposition to the religious settlement – including printed opposition. The Stationers were expected to seek approval "according to her Majesty's Injunctions," but their authority over trade matters was distinct from the High Commissions' authority over conformity. Between 1559 and 1586 both the Stationers and the High Commissioners generally functioned independently from one another, although on some occasions each relied on the other's authority to serve some mutual advantage. The relationship between them was remarkably fluid, responding to changing political and economic events.

The principal area in which the High Commissioners and Stationers had to interact was licensing. The language of the 1559 Injunctions' printing item suggests that printers would regularly seek ecclesiastical authorization for the texts they printed. During the 1560s only three percent of the entries in the Company's Registers record ecclesiastical authorization; during the 1570s this increased to seven percent, and in the 1580s to forty-two percent.[55] This increase might be attributed to better record keeping, except that during the 1580s the rate of entrance dropped by one-third. In the 1560s seventy-two percent of the books that received ecclesiastical authorization treated religious or political topics, while most of the remainder were in foreign languages or translations of contemporary Continental authors. In the 1570s sixty percent were religious or political, the remainder again being largely foreign language texts or translations. When the Stationers sought approval, they went to local clerics as often as to the heads of the High Commission, the Bishop of London and the Archbishop of Canterbury. Never do the

Stationers appear to have secured the specified approval of the ordinary *and* another ecclesiastical licenser – or of six privy councillors. This evidence suggests that the Stationers understood the requirement that books should be licensed "according to her Majesty's Injunctions" to mean that they needed to seek official approval only for religious, political, or foreign texts. Apparently the High Commissioners deemed the Stationers' conduct satisfactory since no efforts appear to have been taken to seek greater compliance.

In 1566, consistent with its charge "to inquire touching all heretical opinions, [and] seditious books," the London High Commission took action to control the flow into England of illegal books from the Continent and to define illegality for English printers and booksellers. At the Commission's request, the Privy Council sitting in the Star Chamber issued "Ordinaunces decreed for reformation of divers disorders in pryntyng and utteryng of Bookes" on 24 June. The first item reads:

That no person shall prynt, or cause to be imprynted, nor shall bring, or cause, or procure to be brought into this Realme imprynted, any Booke or copye agaynst the fourme and meanyng of any ordinaunce, prohibition, or commaundement, conteyned, or to be conteyned in any the statutes or lawes of this Realme, or in any Injunctions, Letters patentes, or ordinaunces, passed or set forth, or to be passed or set forth by the Queenes most excellent Majesties graunt, commission, or aucthoritie.[56]

The provisions following prohibit selling or binding illegal books and extend the Stationers' Company's right to search locations where imported books might be found. Further, these ordinances provided effective means to enforce their provisions by designating penalties for violating the ordinance, (book forfeitures, fines, imprisonment, and exclusion from the trade).

Cyprian Blagden says that he is "unable to say why the Ordinances were framed in 1566 rather than in 1565 or 1567," although "the general right to search, though ostensibly directed against seditious publications, was exactly what the governing body of the Company wanted for the battle which was just beginning, against the secret printing of privileged copies."[57] The ordinances were issued at a time when Catholic texts from the Continent were challenging the controls imposed by the 1559 Injunctions. Furthermore, neither the Injunctions nor the Stationers' Charter had satisfactorily defined the relationship between printing and English law by defining both legality and sanctions. The Stationers' Charter had held up the law of the land as the standard for legal printing. These ordinances defined as the source of that law statutes, injunctions, letters patents, and ordinances. This, of course, prevented printing against the Acts of Supremacy and Uniformity, and the treason laws, but it also prevented printing against royal privileges granted to the Stationers' Company and to patentees. Further, it offered protection to the London Stationers' from foreign copyright violations – something their Charter had not done – both by preventing the import and sale of "illegal" works and by extending the Stationers' right to search to include venues where these works might be kept. While this clarification shored up the Stationers' privileges, it also created a means by which Elizabeth's regime could respond to Continental literature opposing the Queen and her Church. In 1566 this was a more serious problem than Blagden admitted. Catholic presses on the Continent had mounted a formidable campaign against the English church, provoking the concern of Elizabeth's government.

This concern is made clear in a letter that went out to Lord Treasurer Winchester in January 1565/6 over Elizabeth's signature. It calls upon Winchester to inform Customs and other appropriate persons that the Bishop of London's appointees will search ships in English ports for "lewde and slanderous books" which, if found, will be brought to the Bishop for review and sanction. Conditions requiring these searches are explicit: fugitives from England living abroad "practyse continually to sende in hither certayn new books bothe slaunderous & seditious and sprede abroad the same contrary to the statutes & lawes of our realme and directly against the pollicie of the same." As "one of our comissioners for matters eccliasticall," the Bishop of London is "for sondry respects most fit to see & consider suche books as from tyme to tyme shalbe brought in from the said parts beyond the sees and therupon to Juge what books ar to be used and which not published and uttered."[58] This letter is germane to the 1566 Ordinances: it reflects first that the government was concerned over the influx of Continental imprints; second, that these books – most were Catholic in nature issuing as they did from fugitives from English law – were printed and distributed contrary to English statute and laws; and third, that searches were under the High Commission's auspices. This letter's timing suggests that the 1566 ordinances were a particular response to these "lewde and slanderous books." The ordinances provided the means by which the Bishop of London could administer the searches and "deale with the bringers or receyvours of the same" referred to in the January letter to Treasurer Winchester. The books that provoked the government's concern were Continental Catholic books in "The Great Controversy."[59] In 1565–66 alone twenty-eight books on the controversy issued from Continental Catholic presses, and all the authors whose names were specified in the search subsequent to the 1566 Ordinances were controversialists. While theological debate lay at the center of the controversy, increasingly the Catholic apologists cast the Protestant bishops as mountebanks, English law as Machiavellian policy, and the Protestant faithful as deceived fools. This might all have been tolerated except that arguments emerged denying Elizabeth's ecclesiastical authority.

Like both the Stationers' Company Charter and the printing Injunction, the 1566 Ordinances served different interests simultaneously. They provided the means by which the government could search incoming ships for Continental imprints opposing Elizabeth's religious settlement at the same time as they defined more clearly the privileges and authority of the London Stationers. Records of searches subsequent to these ordinances show how these interests were served concurrently. They also indicate the degree to which the Stationers' role as government agents has been misunderstood.

After July 1569, Hugh Singleton, one of the searchers appointed by the Stationers' Company, was paid 2s. for "taken up bokes at the Water syde."[60] This singular event, however, was not as significant as the major search in which Company searchers had been employed in 1566–7, immediately after the Ordinances were issued. Records relating to the latter demonstrate that protecting privilege was as important to the Stationers' Company as confiscating Catholic imprints. Between July 1566 and July 1567 Singleton and Thomas Purfoot "rode abroade" as Company-appointed searchers; Arber indicates that the £5 they received reflects a "long search."[61] Early in 1567 they visited booksellers in York. According to Robert Davies, they inquired first after Latin primers, portesses, missals, or ABCs in Latin, and second, after works by Thomas Harding, Thomas Dornan, Thomas Stapleton, William Allen, Nicholas Sanders, and John Rastell, all of whom had contributed to the controversy begun by Bishop Jewel, and whose books had been printed abroad in 1565.[62] Davies mistakenly concludes that the first group of works were made illegal by a statute from Edward's reign, but this had been repealed by Mary. This search provided "confessions" from the

York booksellers about primers in English and grammars and accidences that reveal some confusion about the first group of works. On 8 May 1567 Purfoot and Singleton presented to the Ecclesiastical Commissioners at York, this inventory of "unlawful" books found in the possession of the York stationers:

John Scofield, a grammar

Thomas Richardson, a portass

John Goldethwaite:

    17 primers in Latin in 8vo.

    50 Primers in English in 16 mo.

    3 accidences

    3 Geneva grammars.

    1 A.B.C. in Latin

Thomas Wraythe:

    3 primers in English in 16mo.

    1 accidence

    2 psalms of Geneva

    1 mass book, Eboracensis

    17 latter endings of grammar.

The nature of these works' "illegality" is curious. William Seres printed primers under his privilege, so any primer not printed by him or his assigns would have violated his privilege. Since Seres's patent also included psalters, the Geneva psalms would also have violated it. A Latin ABC would not have been illegal simply because it was Latin, but in 1567 Reyner Wolfe held the royal patent for all Latin printing, which also included the accidence and grammar. Many of the works the booksellers confessed to receiving and selling enjoyed the status of being the books most frequently printed against privilege during Elizabeth's reign. The York booksellers implicated London Stationers Thomas Marshe, Gerard Dewes, and John Wight, not only in providing the books listed above that they turned over to the searchers, but in books they had previously received. John Goldenwaite had received seventeen Latin primers and two ABCs from Dewes, one hundred English primers from Thomas Marshe, and twelve accidences from Gerard Dewes. Thomas Wraith had received a hundred English primers from the three London Stationers and fifty "grammars and accidences" from Dewes.[63] None of the York booksellers possessed any of the Great Controversy books on the first list. The only penalty the York booksellers incurred for trading in "illegal" texts was forfeiting those still in their possession; Marshe, Dewes, and Wight incurred heavy fines from the Company. Siebert's conclusion that these London booksellers were "the principal dealers in prohibited Catholic books" is patently wrong. Had they been, their position in the trade would have been far different: Marshe served as renter warden to the company the next year and two years later Dewes was admitted to the livery. [64]

Because both the Charter and the 1566 Ordinances gave to the Stationers the legal right to search, it has frequently been assumed that the Stationers served as the agents of government censorship on a regular and continuing basis. The 1566–7 search, besides demonstrating the nature of "illegal" books and the way in which the Stationers and the government co-opted each others' interests, indicates that Stationers' Company searches, at least before 1576, were special rather than routine events and that searchers required special authority. The Purfoot–Singleton search was a singular event for which the two men received special papers; the Stationers paid 2s. 6d. for the "wrytinge of Acctorytye."[65] The payment of £5 may rather have been for a "far" search than a necessarily "long" one as Arber suggests. Both Singleton and Purfoot were in London until late November 1566,[66] and Purfoot had returned by May 1567.[67] Purfoot appears to have taken little time away from his printing business, although he did not enter copies in the Company's Register in 1567 before July. Singleton's printing business was at a low ebb during 1566–7. Although he did enter ballads and broadsides in the Company Register nothing printed by Singleton between 1566 and 1574 is extant. Singleton appears to have continued in the position of searcher during this time, although he is mentioned only twice in the records of payments.[68] No records exist revealing subsequent zealous searches like the one in 1567. In 1576 the Stationers' Company appointed twenty-four searchers (including the Master, William Seres, and three other privilege holders) to carry out weekly searches, but the object of their interest was Company business rather than heretical and seditious texts.[69]

While "illegal" religious writing continued to concern the Ecclesiastical Commissioners and the Crown, and while both on a few notable occasions employed the Stationers to discover illegal presses and confiscate illegal texts, for the most part, Stationers' Company searchers were not the High Commissions' primary tool of control.[70] Indeed, even the Commission concerned itself less and less with Catholic texts. Once the 1570 Papal Decree excommunicated

Elizabeth and released her Catholic subjects from obedience to her, and the Jesuits escalated their mission to England in the 1580s, Catholic matters became the object of Parliamentary and Privy Council control. The Privy Council employed its own searchers and informers, independent from both the Stationers and the High Commission, to seek out Catholic books.[71] The High Commission was left to contend with radical Protestant opposition.

While the Privy Council assumed authority over Catholic matters, the High Commission served as the principal court of inquiry into conformity among the English clergy. In both the Vestiarian Controversy in the 1560s and the Admonition Controversy in the early 1570s, clerical nonconformists put their opposition into print. When a radical reform agenda appeared in print, the High Commission found additional grounds on which to question and challenge the dissenting ministers who authored and printed oppositional texts.[72] At issue among the most radical reformers was a civil magistrate's authority over the ecclesiastical state, church polity, and the "popish" practices prescribed by the Book of Common Prayer. Refusal by clergy to affirm the Queen's authority as Supreme Governor or to accept the Book of Common Prayer afforded the ecclesiastical commissions grounds for depriving clergy of their benefices. Radical Protestant opposition culminated in the late 1580s in the Martin Marprelate pamphlets, which personally attacked the ecclesiastical establishment and advocated dismantling the episcopal governance of the Church. In this case the High Commission was joined by the Crown, the Privy Council, and the entire ecclesiastical establishment to discover Marprelate and his printers.

Establishing the actions of the High Commission regarding the puritan press is difficult – in part because of the absence of records for the London High Commission,[73] and in part because previous writing on the matter has been colored by assumptions regarding the oppositional nature of puritanism and the absolute suppression of the puritan press.[74] Undeniably, the Commission examined puritan ministers to establish their conformity. Their methods indeed may have been abusive: they allowed their examinees to languish in prison before their hearings; they administered the oath *ex officio mero* before they read charges and indictments; and they legally required imprisonment to enforce conformity. They likewise called in and examined authors and printers of some of the most radical puritan manifestos – particularly the pamphlets in the Vestiarian and

Admonition controversies and the Marprelate tracts. Both the Admonition and the Marprelate pamphlets' attacks on the bishops in general and the Ecclesiastical Commissioners in particular have provided often unquestioned evidence of High Commission abuses. Texts that came from Martin Marprelate and the "puritan press" receive full consideration in a later chapter. Here, we need to consider whether or not in its treatment of the "Puritan Press" the High Commission exercised the tyrannous inquisition that Martin Marprelate alleged in his *Epistle*.[75]

In the Vestiarian dispute in the 1560s, that the High Commission appears to have been more concerned with conformity than censorship is evidenced by the experiences of Robert Crowley and the London Stationers who printed his works. Crowley, a clergyman and the "first English printer of Puritan doctrine,"[76] was appointed to the archdeaconry of Hereford and served as vicar of St. Giles Cripplegate, rector of St. Peter-le-Poer, and prebendary of St. Paul's. According to Greg, he was "one of the 'ministers of this towne' whose advice the Master and Wardens were in the habit of seeking concerning copies of importance touching divinity," even though Crowley was one of the most outspoken reformers among the London ministers.[77] Patrick Collinson describes Robert Crowley as the leader and organizer of "the more intransigent nonconformists" in the Vestiarian dispute.[78] In 1566 Crowley, along with other obdurate reformers, was deprived by the High Commission of his London benefice and sent out of London into the custody of the Bishop of Ely, but returned to become Vicar of St. Lawrence Jewry nine years later. In 1578, he became a freeman of the Stationers' Company, and in subsequent years took apprentices in his bookselling business. In 1588 Archbishop of Canterbury, John Whitgift, appointed Crowley to the official board of ecclesiastical licensers he established that year.[79] During his career, Crowley penned several treatises which engaged in contemporary religious debate. In 1566 London Stationer Henry Bynneman entered Crowley's defense of predestination, *An apologie, or defence, of those Englishe writers which Cerberus chargeth wyth false doctrine* (printed by Henry Denham) in the Register without authorization, and Bynneman entered likewise Crowley's *The opening of the wordes of the prophet Joell*. In 1566 Henry Denham, another member of the Stationers' Company, printed Crowley's *Briefe discourse against the outwarde apparell of the popish church* (the manifesto of the London reforming clergy in the Vestiarian

Controversy),[80] clearly without a Company license, since he was fined 20s. for its printing.[81] Both Crowley and Denham must have recognized that open opposition to the Church and Crown was dangerous enough that the pamphlet should be printed without either the author's or the printer's name, but Denham also must not have feared harsh sanctions. His actions did not bring him before the High Commission; he was not the object of a Company search for "illegal" printing; his involvement in the pamphlet was well enough known by fellow Stationers that they could fine him for printing a book without obtaining the Company's license. As for Crowley, his open opposition to the religious establishment and not his religious views cost him one ecclesiastical living; even so, he gained another one. Furthermore, he continued to confer ecclesiastical authorizations for the Stationers, and evidently, was well enough respected in this capacity to be appointed officially. Crowley, Bynneman, and Denham point to the far greater liberty (within limits) for radical reform ideas within the printing establishment and the Church than earlier studies of print culture have allowed.

At the end of June 1572, *An Admonition to Parliament*, ascribed to two radical Protestant ministers, John Field and Thomas Wilcox, issued from the secret (and illegal) press at Hemel Hempstead of John Stroud, minister cum printer. Within weeks Field and Wilcox were committed to Newgate prison. Three months later, when Archbishop Parker's chaplain met with them, Wilcox said it was about time that someone came to see them since no one had sought to convince them of their error. Field maintained that they were unjustly imprisoned for having done nothing other than write "a boke in the parliament tyme (which should be a free tyme of speaking or wrytinge), justly cravinge a redresse and reformation of many abuses."[82] During the course of the interview with Mr. Pearson, the ministers made clear the reforms they sought in the English church. In October Field and Wilcox were brought before the Lord Mayor and the Court of Aldermen and charged under the Act of Uniformity, and they were sentenced to one year's imprisonment. The *Admonition* appeared in three editions during 1572. In 1572 two other works issued from Stroud's secret press, *An Exhortation to the Bishops*, attacking the church hierarchy for not answering the *Admonition*, and *The Second Admonition*. Before the end of the year John Whitgift's *An answere to a certen libel intituled An Admonition* reprinted the original *Admonition* with his responses to the assertions. In 1573 Thomas Cartwright responded to

Whitgift with *A Reply to An Answere made of M. Doctor Whitgifte* (also printed at Hemel Hempstead).

John Stroud, the *Admonition* pamphlets' printer, like Crowley, was a clergyman, and like Crowley, his nonconformity led to losing his benefice. Stroud, however, was not part of the London printing establishment. Even so, it is not altogether clear that he suffered for printing books that were not only suspect to the High Commission but banned by royal proclamation. Archbishop Parker's 1571 letter to Burghley regarding the efforts to discover the underground press printing the *Admonition* suggests that in policing radical Protestant presses, the High Commission was not an entirely effective tool. Parker wrote:

For all the devices that we can make to the contrary, yet some good fellows still labour to print out the vain "Admonition to the Parliament." Since the first printing it hath been twice printed, and now with additions, whereof I send your honour one of them. We wrote letters to the Mayor and some aldermen of London to lay in wait for the charects, printer, and correcter, but I fear they deceive us. They are not willing to disclose this matter.[83]

W. H. Frere and C. E. Douglas conclude that "the secret press was skilfully shielded, for the puritans had long held a powerful position in the book trade."[84] Parker's letter, however, suggests that the London printing establishment was not alone in aiding the concealment of puritans; "They" who were unwilling "to help" were the Mayor and Aldermen, who Parker reported "deceive us." The High Commission finally discovered the press in Hemel Hempstead and sent their pursuivant, accompanied by the Stationers' Company warden, to confiscate the press and secure the printer's arrest.[85]

Stroud appeared before the High Commission on 25 November 1573 where he was questioned regarding Cartwright's books.[86] They asked where the remaining copies were, to which he replied that "he had deliverd 34 of them to the B. of Lond. in one bundell, more he said he had, but his wife had burned them, as she was told. And for the rest, they were dispersed abroad, he knew not where, for they never came to his hands, for he was an 100 miles of[f]." The Commission then asked why he dared print a second edition "seeing the queenes proclamation was against them," and he answered that they had been printed before, "and herein he confessed himself to have offended the lawe." The High Commission further examined Stroud regarding his conformity – receiving the sacraments and accepting the Book of Common Prayer and its prescribed rites. He was called upon to subscribe to the following – which he did:

1. that thou has offended the lawe in printinge Cartw. books.
2. that cartw. booke is nether godly nor lawfull.
[3.] that thou does not condemne the booke of common prayer, but wilt receave the Sacram. of the L. Supper accordinge to the order prescribed.

This apparently satisfied the Commission, and, for the time being at least, he returned to his ministry, though this time printing was not part of it, his press having been confiscated and sold.[87]

John Stroud's experience fixes quite clearly the issues most troublesome to the High Commission: acceptance of the Book of Common Prayer and celebrating the Lord's Supper according to its prescribed order. When he appeared for printing Cartwright's books, the Commissioners showed far more interest in his conformity than in his illegal press. His confession to having printed Cartwright's books and his admission of their error appears to have been all that was required of him. When he subscribed, the Commissioners revoked a 1567/8 deprivation, and he became vicar in Yalding the next year. Stroud may have been fortunate in his encounter with the High Commission since the *Admonition* pamphlets held a high enough priority with Archbishop Parker that he was spared some of the worst circumstances concomitant with the Commission's investigations: other religious reformers called before its intensified scrutiny of both clergy and laity in 1573 languished in miserable, crowded London prisons awaiting the Commission's inquiry.[88]

Stroud's experiences belie the Marprelate tracts' harsh indictment of the High Commission's relationship with puritan printers. So, too, do the experiences of Robert Waldegrave, the Marprelate printer. Despite Marprelate's claims to the contrary, Waldegrave appears to have had good relations with the Stationers' Company and to have enjoyed relative freedom to print puritan texts for several years.[89] But as the puritan attack on the Bishops escalated in the mid-1580s, Waldegrave's press and its products became a thorn in the Archbishop of Canterbury's side. In 1588 Waldegrave lost his press, most likely at the High Commission's behest, for illegally printing Udall's radical anti-episcopal tract *Diotrephes* (that is, for printing without license or authority). In the next few months Waldegrave secretly printed the first four Marprelate tracts on a movable secret press, but when opposition to the pamphlets (official and otherwise) escalated, he fled to Scotland by way of the Continent. In 1590 King James VI appointed Waldegrave to the position of King's Printer.

The High Commission's efforts to control radical religious writing – both from the right and the left – underscore the degree to which its position as an effective control on the press has been overstated. Like so many other sixteenth-century institutions, what looks like hegemony in conception, in practice emerges riddled with contradictions shaped by competing interests. At its best the High Commission appears to have done what it was intended to do, authorizing books, ordering searches for Catholic presses and books, and pursuing the likes of Crowley, Stroud, and Waldegrave. But when we recognize that puritan texts were regularly entered in the Stationers' Registers without authorization, that authors and printers of oppositional texts were prosecuted in the civil courts, and that Crowley regained his benefice, Stroud returned to preaching, and Waldegrave found royal favor in Scotland, the Commission's tight reign of authority looks more like a frayed rope lead. Even when the Commissioners acted as literary censors in calling in George Gascoigne's *Poesies* in 1576,[90] the meager fifty copies taken out of circulation the year after they had been printed points to a considerably less resolute Commission in censorship matters than has generally been assumed. All in all, the London High Commission was largely ineffectual against the Continental Catholic press, and their interest in achieving clerical conformity commanded far more of their attention than censoring the products of English presses – religious or literary.

THE 1586 STAR CHAMBER DECREES FOR ORDER IN PRINTING

Robert Waldegrave's 1588 conviction by the Stationers' Court of Assistants "accordinge to the late decrees of ye Starre chamber and by vertue thereof"[91] for printing *Diotrephes* points to a new dimension in the relationship between the Crown and the Elizabethan press. According to Siebert, the Star Chamber Decrees of 23 June 1586, "the most comprehensive regulation of the press of the entire Tudor period," were Elizabeth's answer to "insufficient efforts" of "government officials, ecclesiastical licensers, and Stationers' Company searchers" to suppress opposition literature.[92] Following Martin Marprelate and relying on John Strype, many scholars, including Patrick Collinson, have credited the Archbishop of Canterbury, John

Whitgift, with originating the 1586 Star Chamber Decrees. Strype indicates that at Whitgift's request, the decrees were made "by the Queen's special order."[93] Neither did the Queen issue the order, nor was Whitgift its principal initiator.[94] That Whitgift was interested in church censorship of the press can correctly be inferred from the articles he proposed in 1583 to enforce laws against Catholic recusants, which included an ecclesiastical licensing requirement.[95] These articles, however, were primarily directed against Catholic recusants.[96] Whatever interest Whitgift may have had in censorship, the 1586 Star Chamber Decrees were not the Queen's response to that interest, but rather a legal decision rendered by the Court of Star Chamber resolving nine years of conflict in the printing trade over royal privileges and the authority of the Stationers' Company.

Some of the confusion that arises about the Star Chamber Decrees for Order in Printing derives from the long-held view that the Tudor Star Chamber often engaged in draconian measures to achieve civil order, and thus the 1586 Decrees were likewise draconian since they issued from the Star Chamber. According to Elton, the Star Chamber, the Privy Council sitting as a court, "was simply one of the courts of the realm, dealing largely with cases between parties . . . It was highly regarded and very popular with litigants because it was relatively speedy, flexible and complete in its work."[97] The court's procedure was similar to Chancery, commencing with a plaintiff's bill, the defendant's answer, and the usual succession of written pleadings and witness examinations. It usually punished with fines or ordered the loser to comply with an earlier decision, frequently an earlier Star Chamber decree.[98] According to Elton, some orders, like the 1586 Decrees for Order in Printing, "look like Orders in Council or proclamations. In truth, however, these, (if issued by Star Chamber) were always the outcome of a law-suit involving larger principles and worth embodiment in a formal and public pronouncement because they might affect both policy and other suits."[99] The papers of Sir Thomas Egerton, Lord Keeper and subsequently Lord Chancellor from 1596 to 1617, include summaries of the kinds of cases that historically came within Star Chamber jurisdiction and "disorders in printing and uttering of books" are among them.[100] Since the Court of Star Chamber was the regular venue for printing disputes, it was not at all unusual that it should have heard a number of printing cases between 1577 and 1586 that arose from a challenge posed not only to the Stationers' Company's powers but to the printing privileges extended by the Queen. The 1586 Star Chamber Decrees for Order in Printing responded to these matters.

In 1577 journeymen printers filed a complaint with the Council against abuses by holders of printing privileges. In 1582 they presented two further petitions complaining to the Privy Council that their grievances had not been addressed, and a commission that had been formed to hear their concerns was inattentive to their pleas. In 1583 the Privy Council appointed an expanded commission to address the printers' concerns, and the Council's letter makes it clear that members of the printing trade were concerned about "the proliferation of printers, incompetent printing, inconsistent book pricing, and abuses of printing privileges," as well as the effect of privileges on printers of the "poorer sort."[101]

Besides the journeymen's petitions, John Wolfe, a member of the Fishmonger's Company, led an all-out attack against printing patents and the privileges of the Stationers' Company.[102] In 1581 Wolfe set up his printing business in London and shortly thereafter applied for a printing privilege that was denied because of its general nature. He proceeded to print copy belonging to other printers, particularly Christopher Barker, the Queen's printer. Barker attempted to dissuade Wolfe from printing privileged copies by offering to provide him with business and translate his freedom from the Fishmongers' to the Stationers' Company. Wolfe declined and continued to print privileged books, including Francis Flower's Latin grammar – an action that brought him before the Privy Council.[103] By 1582 Wolfe became identified as the leader of the whole movement against privileges. With other protestors, he was summoned to appear before the Privy Council, and when he refused, was committed to prison. Once released, Wolfe appealed first to the Stationers' Company and later to the Privy Council for a redress of grievances against printing patent holders.[104] The commission on printing privilege sought a compromise between the patentees and the journeyman printers that failed to satisfy Wolfe, who continued his outspoken opposition to privileges.[105] In 1583 he reached his own compromise with the Stationers and accepted Barker's promise of work and Company membership,[106] but the larger issues remained for the Commission and the Crown to decide.

At the same time, privilege holders appealed to the Privy Council for protection of their patents. Beginning in 1577 Christopher Barker complained that other members of the Company were printing against his patent, and the Privy Council reiterated his privilege to the Master and Wardens of the Company.[107] Between 7 and 10 February 1581/2, John Day brought a bill of complaint in the Court of Star Chamber against Roger Ward and William Holmes for their failure to comply with the 1566, which had affirmed both Stationers' Company authority and printers' privileges "set forth by the Queenes most excellent Majesties graunte."[108] The extensive documentation of this in Arber points to the rights and privileges of the Stationers, rather than censorship, as the legal concern. In the early 1580s several other cases of printing-privilege violations, again well documented in Arber, were brought before the Court of Star Chamber.[109] (Ironically, Wolfe, who had finally received a patent as an assign of Day, even brought legal action for violation of his privilege.) All of these cases appeal to the precedent established by the 1566 Star Chamber Ordinances in designating the Court of Star Chamber's venue in matters relating to printing-trade regulation and privilege violations. (None concerns itself with government suppression of religiously or politically unacceptable printed materials – that is, with materials traditionally considered likely candidates for censorship.) Any one of these cases (or all of them) may have been the issue which finally led in 1586 to the Decrees for Order in Printing.

In 1583 the expanded commission on printing presented its report to the Privy Council. It recommended restricting the number of presses, requiring licensing of new presses by either the Stationers' Wardens or the High Commission, restricting the number of apprentices, punishing incompetent printing, controlling book prices, upholding royal privileges and company licenses, and providing for the Company's poor by having patentees yield up some of their privileges to the Company.[110] According to Greg, "the report throughout envisages a prospective decree of the Star Chamber."[111] Such a decree, however, was not immediately forthcoming, and pressures continued to mount. In 1585–6 three cases came before the Star Chamber, all regarding privilege violations. In May 1586 the Privy Council called for Ward's presses to be seized for printing against privilege, and also in May 1586 the Queen's patentees petitioned the Council for the reformation of disorders and the punishment of privilege infringers.

On 23 June 1586 the Court of Star Chamber issued its Decrees for

Orders in Printing.[112] According to Elton, this "so-called order concerning printers arose out of a judgment in a case based on a breach of the proclamation of 1566."[113] Which particular breach forced the Decrees is unrecorded, but they resolved most of the cases presently before the Star Chamber by upholding royal privileges, Company authority, and the 1566 Ordinances. The Decrees were clearly framed in response to all the disruptions in the printing trade and not just the matters before the Court of Star Chamber: they incorporated many of the recommendations made in 1583 by the commission on printing and they upheld the rights of Oxford and Cambridge universities to have printing presses.[114]

A genuine triumph for the Stationers' Company and the privileged printers, the 1586 Decrees were extraordinarily conservative. Only Stationers and privileged printers could print; printing was confined to London and the two universities; search and seizure was affirmed as the means of enforcing this right; restrictions were placed on the numbers of printers and apprentices; and outside authority "accordinge to th[e] order appoynted by the Queenes maiesties *Iniunctyons*" was requisite. It unequivocally upheld the rights and prerogatives of the Company and the privileged printers in the face of the recent challenges and sought to ensure both adequate work and adequate employment within the Company. Measures to restrict the proliferation of presses were expected to provide adequate work for the existing presses while limiting the number of apprentices, which would restrict future numbers of journeyman printers and create fuller employment. The Decrees specify the period of time for registering presses, the means of doing so, the means of being admitted as a printer, the official authorizers, and the punishments for violating the Orders. Finally, as an alternative to the Court of Star Chamber, they gave to the Commissioners for Causes Ecclesiastical (one of whom was to be either the Archbishop of Canterbury or the Bishop of London) jurisdiction to resolve those disorders in the printing trade that lay beyond the jurisdiction of the Stationers' Court of Assistants because they involved non-Stationers.

Viewing the 1586 Star Chamber Decrees from the perspective of trade interests rather than censorship challenges the predominant vein of past historical arguments about Tudor government. As Ian Archer has pointed out, "Historians of Tudor government have tended to write about the relationship between rulers and ruled in terms of the ability of central government to impose on the localities things which they did not want."[115] Recent revisionist arguments – Ian Archer's among them – have demonstrated the degree to which local interests pursued redress of their grievances through a variety of tactics including "passive resistance by individuals, petitions to the privy council, the enlistment of the support of the aldermen, litigation in the courts, and complaints in parliament."[116] Indeed, according to Archer, in the late sixteenth century, London livery companies generally used these means to lobby the government in order to gain control over their trades, tighten restriction on competition, and maximize employment within their trade. Like the Stationers, the other companies "aimed to extend their control over those pursuing the trade who were not free of the company . . . to give statutory sanction to the search, and to give it greater definition than was provided by company ordinances . . . and to maximize employment for members" by curbing imports.[117] Parliamentary acts reflect the lobbying successes of the Coopers, the Clothworkers, the Fishmongers, and the Haberdashers. The Woolmen achieved their ends by securing royal proclamations ordering trade practices. The Stationers had mounted their campaign on several fronts: Parliament, the Privy Council, and the Court of Star Chamber. The Star Chamber Decrees demonstrate the Stationers' success at Court and in the courts where their parliamentary bill failed.[118] That neither this kind of success nor the lobbying for exclusive trade control was unique to the Stationers requires considerable revision of pervasive views that through the Decrees Elizabeth imposed press control to censor religious dissent and political opposition.

The Star Chamber Decrees, with their clearly specified provisions for ordering the printing trade, should have more greatly affected trade practices than either the 1559 Injunctions or the 1566 Ordinances. Indeed, in the years immediately following (1586–1602), the Stationers' Court Book B[119] records twelve searches for presses that were printing illegally by violating patent or copyright. Action was also taken five times against printers who operated illegal presses: once against Waldegrave for printing *Diotrephes*, twice against Catholic presses, and twice against non-Stationer Ward for printing privileged books. We also find stays issued against printers until they applied to the Archbishop for the right to operate a press, and admissions of printers who had received that right.[120]

One of the 1586 Decrees' more significant effects derived from consolidating authority over the press in the High Commission.

While little evidence suggests that the whole Commission regularly exercised this authority,[121] the Archbishop of Canterbury John Whitgift did. Perhaps one of the reasons Whitgift has been credited with enacting the 1586 Decrees derives from the increased authority he personally assumed and exercised in their wake; the actual circumstances of his personal censorship, however, argue his appropriation and not creation of the censorship authority. He assumed full authority for licensing new presses and overseeing ecclesiastical authorization. In 1588 Whitgift appointed a panel of authorizers to regularly "peruse and allow" books for the Stationers. He also served as a kind of liaison between the Privy Council and the Stationers. In 1587 the Council called upon him to see to the review and reform of Holinshed's *Chronicles*.[122] He also extended his licensing authority to exercise personal censorship. A 1587 entry in the Stationers' Register for *A Commission sent to the pope and Convenres of freres by Sathen* is crossed out with a notation that the Archbishop of Canterbury ordered the book burnt on 27 February 1587. On 15 August 1595 at Whitgift's command, five books (all apparently foreign) were burnt at Stationers' Hall[123] In 1599 Whitgift suppressed John Hayward's *Henry IV*, in 1600 Essex's *Apology*, and in 1599 together with the Bishop of London, he banned satires and called for Privy Council authorization of histories.[124]

Whitgift's panel of authorizers gave to ecclesiastical licensing the kind of bureaucratic efficiency that former licensing provisions had lacked. Obtaining an authorization from three members of the Commission for ecclesiastical causes or from six privy councillors as Elizabeth's injunction on printing had specified would have challenged any printers' resourcefulness. Even the 1586 Decrees' provision that all books be perused and allowed by the Archbishop of Canterbury or the Bishop of London would have been an administrative nightmare for these two men with the hundreds of books issuing from London presses in the late 1580s. To call upon one of eight senior or two of four junior authorizers was far easier for an author or printer.[125]

But even with this increased efficiency, the 1586 Star Chamber Decrees and the 1588 panel of authorizers did not achieve full ecclesiastical licensing of the English press. In 1580 approximately twenty percent of the books entered in the Register showed ecclesiastical or government authorization.[126] In 1584 and 1585, the Register shows twenty-four and sixteen percent authorization rates respectively. Perhaps of greater interest is that in 1584 fewer than one-quarter of the books printed appeared in the Register at all, and in 1585 less than one-fifth were entered. One year after the Star Chamber issued its printing decrees, forty-seven percent of the Register's entries carried authorization, but once Whitgift appointed the panel of authorizers, authorization increased significantly. The Register reports seventy-eight percent in 1588, eighty-five percent in 1589, and eighty-six percent in 1590. Besides affecting ecclesiastical authorization in the first few years after its enactment, the Decrees (and likely the searches they sanctioned) created greater respect for Company licensing. Entrance rose from fewer than half the books printed in 1586 to two-thirds in 1587 and 1588. Increased entrance and increased authorization meant that between 1588 and 1590, approximately half the English printed books were "seen and allowed."

After the flurry of conformity in the years immediately following 1586, both entrance and authorization declined. By 1592 although two-thirds of the entered books were "seen and allowed," only half the books printed were entered (thirty-four percent, then, received scrutiny). In 1596, less than forty percent of printed books were entered in the Register, and only forty percent of those were authorized (fifteen percent of the total were approved). These numbers tell only part of the story. Both entrance and licensing practices tell more.

The primary purpose of entering a title in the Company Register was, as we have seen, to secure the sole right to have a title manufactured. Once the text was published, the licensee retained this right through multiple editions – even editions with significant changes. The right could be assigned at any time during the licensee's life or bequeathed at death. Assignments and legacies were entered in the Register, but subsequent editions were not. Hence, any book once licensed, whether or not it was entered in the Register, could be reprinted without further Company licensing or entry. Since ecclesiastical or government perusal, when it was required, preceded the initial Company license, or a Company license was issued upon the condition that authorization be granted, only new books received scrutiny.

Spenser's *Faerie Queene* offers an instructive example of licensing and allowance practice. On 1 December 1589 Ponsonby "entered for his Copye, a booke intytuled the fayre Queene dysposed into xii.

bookes. &c. Aucthorysed vnder th[e h]andes of the Archbishop of Canterbury."[127] That the Archbishop rather than one of the panel of authorizers should have perused the text speaks to Spenser's ambition that his poem, whose title and structure complimented the Queen, should gain him preferment. Archbishop Whitgift, who sat on the Privy Council, was the only authorizer with such access to the Queen. Of course, all that the Archbishop could have perused at this point would have been Books I–III. On 20 January 1596 Ponsonby entered *The second parte of the ffaery Quene conteining the 4. 5. and 6. bookes* without ecclesiastical authorization. Technically, the 1596 *Faerie Queene* was a second edition since all six books had been previously entered and books I–III had been already printed. The entrance of books IV–VI without ecclesiastical license was well within the bounds of "legality."[128] Had he wished to (and I do not maintain that he did), Spenser easily could have kept the 1596 text from the eyes of ecclesiastical authorizers. By this same means, as P. M. Olander has pointed out, Elizabethan Calvinist catechisms and sermons continued to appear in print legally into the reigns of James I and Charles I, long after their theology encountered official disapproval.[129]

These few examples epitomize how Stationers' Company practices subverted official scrutiny and authorization. Ironically, the licensing bureaucracy itself also contributed to ineffectual authorization. Given the irregular means by which authorization proceeded, it is not surprising that several texts seen and allowed by authorizers met with subsequent censorship. One of the anomalies, Crowley's appointment to the board of authorizers, has already been considered. Another can be seen in the demands upon the authorizers themselves. While several served at any time, certain authorizers were called upon more often than others. But the numerical evidence is somewhat misleading. For example, looking at the frequency of Abraham Hartwell's authorizations, Greg observes that of the panel of correctors "he was the most active and long-abiding member."[130] This might lead one to conclude that Hartwell, as the Archbishop's secretary, took an inordinate interest in reviewing. Instead, he apparently had a close working relationship with John Wolfe, who after his translation to the Stationers, became one of London's most prolific printers. Of the 278 works Wolfe entered in the Register between 1587 and 1599 with outside authorization, Hartwell authorized 155. The Bishop of London authorized sixty-three (thirty-three in 1592 when Hartwell was doing very little licensing) and the Archbishop of Canterbury twenty. In 1588 Hartwell and the Bishop of London authorized half of all books printed, and in 1589 Hartwell and Thomas Staller authorized close to two-thirds – a sizable workload.

Authorizer Samuel Harsnett in 1600 told how authorizers proceeded in their job. His written testimony relates to Hayward's *Henry IV*, which he approved but which was suppressed by the Archbishop of Canterbury in 1599.[131] According to Harsnett, the "custom and use" was "for eny man that entended in good meaning to put a booke in print, the Author him selfe to present the booke vnto the Examiner and to acquaynt him wth his scope and purpose in the same." The situation for *Henry IV*, however, was unusual: "the author delivered his pamphlet unto a gentleman in my Lord of London his house who begged your Orator his approbation unto the same in the name of a cantel of our Englishe chronicles phrased and flourished over onlie to shew the Author his pretie Witt." In response to this appeal, Harsnett "sett to his hand sodeinlie as mooved by his freind never reading (upon his salutation) more then one page of the hedlesse pamphlett." Given the circumstances of this interrogatory, Harsnett may be overstating the uniqueness of the situation. His testimony sought to justify himself against Hayward's attempt "to excuse his publishinge the sayd pamphlett, as being allowed and approved" by Harsnett. With the pervasiveness of favoritism and patronage at the end of the sixteenth century, however, many authorizations must have been granted "upon . . . salutation," such as this one was, with the authorizer never reading "more then one page." Even for the customary situation, Harsnett's remarks are revealing. Apparently, rather than scrutinizing a text in the quiet of a library, the authorizer sat down with the author and discussed the text with him.[132] According to Greg "such converse between author and examiner, if it was really customary, carries with it a suggestion that a book might be allowed without further scrutiny upon the author's assurance regarding his motive in writing it."[133] Even when a book's motives may not have met with the authorizer's approval, authorizers and authors then worked together to "correct" the text. Daniel Featly's testimony in *Cygnea Cantio* – and here again this should be read with some skepticism since he is likewise defending his authorization of a subsequently censored text – says the authorizer "might and did alter with his [the author's] consent, what we thought fit."[134] Revealing more about the process, Featly defends his authorization on grounds that exception had never before been taken to the author's other books, and that the author was a minister in good standing, who was "meek in spirit and peaceable" (and his neighbor).[135] While both Harsnett and Featly illuminate the role personal relations played, Featly appears to have been somewhat more thorough than Harsnett, having at least read the text. The circumstances were, however, different, and this explains a great deal about ecclesiastical authorization: Featly was a minister authorizing a religious text, and Harsnett confessed himself "a poore divine unacquainted with books and arguments of state, and with consequences of that nature."

While Harsnett may protest too much his ignorance of state affairs, except in the most blatant cases, matters of religion were surely better served by the ecclesiastical authorizers than matters of state. Even so, when the initially conscientious respect for authorization requirements subsided after 1592, the Stationers' Register shows that entries for political and religious texts nearly always carried official authorization. When authorization requirements were ignored, it was for titles like: Simon Forman's *The groundes of the Longitude*, Henry Chettle's *The bayting of Dyoneses*, Charles Gower's *The School of fayre wrytinge*, Thomas Hood's *The maryners guyde*, W. Leake's translation of Boethius's *De consolatione Philosophiae*, or Nicholas Breton's *The Arbour of Amorous delights*.[136] The lapses, however, have a logic all their own. For example, Shakespeare's *Richard II*, entered to Andrew Wise on 29 August 1597, was unauthorized; *Richard III*, entered also to Wise shortly thereafter on 20 October, carried the authorization of William Barlow, Whitgift's chaplain.[137]

The order that the 1586 Decrees brought to printing, then, appeared more in the Stationers' control of the printing trade than in scrutiny and approval of printed texts. Waldegrave's loss of his press for printing "illegal" books demonstrates how effectively the Stationers could exercise their authority over a recalcitrant brother – especially at the Crown's command. The appearance of the Marprelate tracts, however, demonstrates how ineffective a tool for censorship requirements for licensing and authorization were – and how ineffectual press control was outside London confines. As they had before 1586, printed books in England (printed legally with or without authorization, or "illegally" either on hidden or Continental presses) continued to represent an extraordinary range of religious views.[138] Neither the Star Chamber Decrees' licensing requirements nor Whitgift's panel of authorizers could impose complete control on the printed word because the very institutions they employed – ecclesiastical authorization and Company licensing – were in the hands of people who acted according to independent motivations. Many of the Stationers supported religious reform; some of the authorizers did. Beyond the obvious, neither Stationers nor authorizers could always discern what should be approved and what censored – especially in matters outside their purview. This does not mean that texts went uncensored after 1586 – anymore than before. It means that the real authority to suppress transgressive texts lay outside the ecclesiastical authorizers, the Stationers, and the High Commission. For this we have to look to the Privy Council and the Crown.

CHAPTER 3

Elizabethan censorship proclamations
"to conserve her realm in an universal good peace"

Elizabethan England's tripartite licensing provisions (royal privilege, ecclesiastical imprimatur, and Stationers' Company license) motivated as they were by different and sometimes competing interests, created a porous system of press control that enabled the printing of a high proportion of texts that received either partial prepublication scrutiny or none at all. For the most part the contents of unlicensed (or under-licensed) texts printed in England did not provoke government suppression, but some did. These were joined by the enormous issue of Continental presses – Catholic and Protestant – that opposed the Elizabethan religious settlement. When such transgressive texts appeared in England and the authors and publishers could not be prosecuted under the treason statutes, the government's principal tool to oppose them was the royal proclamation. The majority of texts censored between 1559 and 1603 were censored by eleven royal proclamations. Taken together, these illustrate that government press censorship, for the most part, proceeded *ad hoc*, responding to transgressive religious and political discourses as they arose.

The effectiveness of royal proclamations as a tool of censorship was limited by the nature of proclamations themselves. Royal proclamations were restricted by English common law. Statute and common law in Tudor England, according to G. R. Elton, held the highest authority; proclamations were inferior:

They could not (and did not) touch life or member; though they might create offences with penalties, they could not create felonies or treasons. Nor could they touch common law rights of property . . . proclamations covered administrative, social, and economic matters – though they included religion, as the sphere of the supreme head's personal action – but never matters which both the judges and Parliament would regard as belonging to law and statute.[1]

Proclamations held no force in the common law courts and required for their effective administration provisions within the proclamation for their enactment. The royal proclamation was, in short, an administrative tool as effective as its own provisions made it.

The real power in a royal proclamation lay in its value as propaganda. Paul L. Hughes and James F. Larkin in *Tudor Royal Proclamations* observe that the Tudor proclamation was "a literary form psychologically gauged to elicit from the subject an obedient response, favorable to the interests of the crown."[2] As administrative tools, Elizabethan proclamations reflect the Crown's response to particular events calling for immediate government action. As propaganda, not only do they offer the government's version of the events and the rationale for its actions, but they project an image of a unified English commonwealth, its peace and stability tended by the Queen and her good subjects. Censorship, from this perspective, was a dire action for dire circumstances that endangered the commonwealth.

Of the eleven proclamations issued to censor printed texts during the reign of Elizabeth, six addressed Catholic texts issued from Continental presses, one a principally political work, and four related to texts associated with radical Protestantism.[3] Of those concerned with Catholic texts, only the first concerned itself with apologetics; the remainder address works clearly political in nature. On 1 March 1569 the Queen issued the first censorship proclamation, which responded directly to Continental Catholic texts answering Bishop Jewel's challenge for any evidence from scripture or the early Church fathers justifying transubstantiation, communion in one kind, non-vernacular service, and papal authority. The challenge made in 1559 had by 1569 produced sixty-two texts, forty-four by Catholics finally judged in 1569 to be "enemies to God's truth and the quiet government of the Queen, in maintenance of the usurped jurisdiction of the Papistical See of Rome."[4] The proclamation does not specify particular texts to be censored as Henrician proclamations had, but it calls upon the Queen's "honest and quiet subjects" to "forbear utterly from the use of dealing with any such seditious books ... derogatory to the sovereign estate of her majesty, or impugning the orders and rites established by law for Christian religion and divine service." These "good" subjects are "not to keep or read any seditious books" but should submit them to the local bishop. The tone is solicitous; its authority, much like a parent's, only *threatens* consequences for non compliance – "upon pain of her majesty's grievous indignation, and to be punished severely."

Shortly after this effort to suppress the works of Catholic controversialists, Pope Pius V issued the bull excommunicating Elizabeth and releasing her subjects from fealty to her.[5] After this the tone of censorship proclamations intensified the oppositional discourse between Continental Catholicism and England. One issued 1 July 1570 says that "certain wicked and seditious persons . . . do by secret manner contrive and scatter certain infamous scrolls and bill in some parts of her realm, and into some other parts bring in traitorous books and bulls as it were from Rome."[6] Further, in 1569–70 when the efforts of English Catholics in France to reestablish the Catholic Church in England became political, a series of books appeared supporting Mary, Queen of Scots, accused in the murder of her husband and implicated in the Northern rebellion. These books, and others like them, elicited the proclamation, issued 14 November 1570, calling upon the Queen's subjects to serve as informers: "to employ their uttermost diligence in the apprehension of such secret persuaders of disobedience and breaking of laws, and of the sowers and stirrers of sedition."[7] Since such an action requires complicity, the tone is particularly solicitous, appealing not only to the subjects' loyalty but to their patriotism:

The Queen's Majesty, considering with herself how it hath pleased Almighty God at this present to conserve her realm in an universal good peace and her subjects in a constant obedience unto her majesty, notwithstanding the sundry secret malicious solicitations of certain fugitives and rebels being fled now and remaining out of the realm, by their seditious messages and false reports sent into the same tending to provoke others to be partaker of their malicious treasons:

Cannot but first give the due thanks and praise thereof to Almighty God, and therewith commend both the loyalty of her good subjects for their obedience, and allow of this their universal constancy in the conservation of themselves together within the bond of common peace . . .[8]

The proclamation, again, does not censor specific texts, but warns against "seditious books, writings, or such like traitorous devices against the laws and government of the realm or any wise prejudicial to the royal estate of her majesty." The good subject will comply; the bad subject – one who aids the seditious persons or conceals seditious books – "shall be taken, reputed, and punished as abettors and maintainers of the principal traitors that were authors of the same."

This final section is coercive in language alone since it establishes no mechanism by which this threat can be carried out.[9] Probably the most remarkable of the proclamations is the one issued 28 September 1573 ordering the destruction of seditious books.[10] This proclamation, according to Hughes and Larkin, "was directed chiefly at *A Treatise of Treasons against Q. Elizabeth and the Crowne of England,*[11] an attempt to discredit Cecil as the author of Elizabethan religious policy in the eyes of the English people." To counteract this, it summons powerful propaganda strategies. The books in question have issued from "obstinate and irrepentant traitors" who for the "prosecuting of their rooted malice" congregate themselves "together in routs" and "contrive all the mischief they can imagine" to their native country which they "behold with deadly envy." In a state of desperation because their prior attempts have failed, these traitors

have lately caused certain seditious books and libels to be compiled and printed in divers languages, wherein their final intention appeareth to be blaspheme and as it were to accurse their native country with all manner of reproachful terms against the peaceable government thereof, condemning generally the whole policy of the present estate as having no religion, nor piety, nor justice, nor order, no good ministers at all, either for divine or human causes.[12]

It declares the books and libels to be the "works of despisers of God's true religion" devised "to ruin" her majesty's "person, and to overthrow her estate." Despite this, no order is given for the books' destruction other than the charge to "all manner of persons to despise, reject, and destroy such books." Like those before it, this proclamation better serves to set the good subject apart from the traitor than to offer an efficient means of censoring the text.

The other two proclamations directed at suppressing Continental Catholic political propaganda continue the same kind of highly polarized language constructing England as the place of "loving subjects" and "present most happy and quiet government" with the authors of the libels cast as the traitorous other residing abroad engaging in "unnatural, devilish, and traitorous practices."[13] These later proclamations, however, provide far more efficient means to suppress the objectionable texts. The first, issued 12 October 1584, appeared in response to William Allen's *A True, Sincere And Modest Defence, of English Catholiques that Suffer For their Faith* (1584), condemning the English persecution of Catholics, and two works advancing Mary Stuart's right to succession.[14] Again the proclamation does not name titles, but its description is sufficient to make clear what "the said books or libels"[15] are that should be deposited with a member of the Privy Council or the *custos rotulorum* of the shire. For those who do not comply, the proclamation calls for imprisonment. The second was issued 1 July 1588 to suppress Allen's *Admonition to the Nobility and People of England and Ireland* (1588), which attacked Elizabeth, justified the Spanish invasion of England, and admonished the people of England and Ireland to withdraw all support from her. It declares martial law and maintains that it is itself "sufficient warrant" to all public officers and "loving subjects" to "inquire and search for all such bulls, transcripts, libels, books and pamphlets, and for all such persons whatsoever as shall bring in, publish, disperse, or utter any of the same."[16]

The Catholic political pamphlets' rhetoric prompted the polarized rhetoric of the Elizabethan proclamations condemning and suppressing them. Texts on both sides relied upon a construction of otherness using language of violent agent and oppressed subject, with each merely reversing the other's oppressor and victim. While the English Channel provided Elizabeth and her Privy Council with a convenient line from which to mount their verbal assault, the effectiveness of either the geographical boundary or the censorship campaign actually to control the influx of objectional Catholic texts is doubtful. On the one hand, in their lack of specificity, successive proclamations had a cumulative effect in promulgating censorship. Each one responded to a new wave of texts, but all of them, by not naming titles, enabled the condemnation and suppression of all texts that previously had been condemned. On the other hand, such vagueness could not have enabled effective suppression of specific texts, particularly when the proclamations did not provide any means to administer their admonitions. Undoubtedly possessing "popish books" served to incriminate Jesuits, seminary priests, and recusants otherwise suspected of subversive activities. The public officer's job in suppressing unnamed texts in and of themselves, however, must have been formidable. Furthermore, that the successive proclamations employed inclusive language suggests that previous censorship efforts had proven ineffective, as indeed they had been. According to A. C. Southern in *Elizabethan Recusant Prose*, before 1580 nearly 20,000 Catholic books had been imported into England and sold, and this kind of volume continued *throughout* Elizabeth's reign.[17]

While the religious, political, and geographical divide had served Elizabeth and her Privy Council well in constructing the Catholic enemy, the distinctions among English Protestants were less clear. Even members of the Privy Council aligned themselves differently on the spectrum of religious reform. This kind of diversity in Protestant allegiance and belief undoubtedly contributed to laxness in licensing and authorizing puritan texts, many of which were printed legally during the 1570s and 1580s.[18] Indeed, as the printer Henry Bynneman pointed out in his preface to the reader in *A true and plaine report of the furious outrages in France* (1573): "The very treatises of divinitie are not al waranted that be printed" (A2r). A few texts, however, were provocative enough to elicit condemnation and suppression by proclamation.

Elizabeth and her Privy Council acted four times to suppress texts associated with radical Protestant reform and once to suppress a political book that could be associated with the interests of the Protestant left. In the last case, the proclamation issued 27 September 1579, denouncing Stubbs's *The Discovery of a Gaping Gulf*, stands alone as a government act to suppress an English book regarded as seditious on entirely political grounds. The proclamation argues that it is not Stubbs's attempt to dissuade Elizabeth's marriage to the Duke of Alençon that is at issue, but that the book is a "heap of slanders and reproaches of the said prince bolstered up with manifest lies and despiteful speeches of him, and therewith also seditiously and rebelliously stirring up all estates of her majesty's subjects to fear their own utter ruin and change of government."[19] The tone is paternalistic; the book is dangerous because it "tends to open to her majesty's subjects such fearful dangers to her majesty's person, to the cause of religion, to the whole estate of the realm, and so forth, and all by her majesty's marriage." The means of remedy is to destroy copies of the book before public officers "wheresoever they or any the like may be found." The proclamation serves far better as political propaganda to justify the French marriage and praise the Duke than to provide an effective means for calling in and destroying the offending text. The Privy Council, however, issued orders to the Lord Mayor to charge the officers of the various London companies to bring him the names of Company members possessing the book "except in cases where any person shall bring to light, to be destroyed according to the content of the said proclamation."[20] This illustrates how genuinely effective press censorship could be –

especially since John Stubbs and the distributor William Page suffered the loss of their right hands. (The printer, Hugh Singleton, however went free.)

Elizabeth's first proclamation against books of religious reform came in 1573, ordering the surrender of *An admonition to the parliament* and the pamphlets defending it.[21] The *Admonition* and its defenders advocated further reform of the Church along Calvinist lines. The *Admonition* having been printed in three editions in 1572, this proclamation represents a response from the Crown after other efforts to control the controversy had failed. In 1572 John Whitgift had written his response to the *Admonition*, which rather than quieting the Admonitionists promoted further controversy. Then in March 1573 Archbishop Parker and other bishops sought support from the Court and the Council in their efforts to resist the puritan campaign.[22] By April 1573 Thomas Cartwright's *A Replye to An Answere made of M. Doctor Whitgifte Agaynste the Admonition to the Parliament by T. C.* appeared advocating presbyterian governance and criticizing both the episcopacy and the Book of Common Prayer. So the 11 June 1573 proclamation appears more in response to this escalation and the bishops' efforts than to the original *Admonition*. Like the earliest proclamations against Catholic propaganda, the means prescribed to achieve the its ends are ineffectual. It charged:

all and every printer, stationer, bookbinder, merchant, and all other men (of what quality or condition he or they be) who hath in their custody any of the said books to bring in the same to the bishop of the diocese, or to one of her highness' Privy Council.[23]

Public response (or, rather, nonresponse) is notorious. After the twenty-day grace period had expired, Archbishop Parker complained to Burghley: "Her Majesty's proclamation took none effect: not one book brought in."[24]

Two other proclamations subordinated censorship of texts of religious reform to the larger interests of suppressing the reform sects themselves. A proclamation on 3 October 1580 outlawed the Family of Love and the texts serving as the "ground of their sect." The Familists' offense was in declaring themselves saved and all others damned, but the proclamation's language casts their practices in the language of necromancy:

there are certain persons which do secretly in corners make privy assemblies of divers simple unlearned people, and after they have craftily and hypocritically allured them to esteem them to be more holy and perfect men than others are, they do then teach them damnable heresies.[25]

To justify actions against the Familists, it makes clear that the sect is "an evil by the malice of the devil first begun and practiced in other countries to be now brought into this her realm." Such an assault from outside justifies the desire "to root them out from further infecting of her realm." The proclamation calls upon ecclesiastical officials to seek out members of the sect and proceed against them by both ecclesiastical and temporal laws and also to search

in all places suspected for the books and writings maintaining the said heresies and sects, and them to destroy and burn; and wheresoever such books shall be found after the publication hereof . . . the same persons to be attached and committed to the close prison, there to remain, or otherwise by law to be condemned, until the same be purged and cleared of the same heresies, or shall recant the same . . ."[26]

The 30 June 1583 proclamation declaring Brownist writings seditious and schismatic employs far gentler rhetoric. It returns to the language and procedures of the *Admonition* proclamation, and while it threatens those who would further print or distribute Brownist writings[27] with the full execution of laws against sedition, its central remedy is: "that all manner of persons whatsoever, who have any of the said books . . . bring in and deliver up the same unto the ordinary of the diocese."[28] With such ineffectual censorship measures, the proclamation suggests that the government was less concerned about the books than about events associated with the Brownists. On 4 June 1583, two followers of Robert Browne, Elias Thacker and John Coppin, had been brought before the assizes for denying the Queen's supremacy. The indictment included the offense of conspiring to dispose of Browne and Harrison's books. The proximity of the indictment and the proclamation suggests that the activities of Thacker and Coppin may well have caused the government to ascribe a more dangerous nature to the writings of Browne and Harrison than otherwise would have been warranted.

The final proclamation directed toward radical Protestant writings appeared 13 February 1589 to order the destruction of the Marprelate publications. The seven Marprelate pamphlets appeared between October 1588 and September 1589, and despite their illegality and the High Commission's zeal to discover their perpetrators, a veil of secrecy protected the authors and printers. Coming as it did in February 1589, the proclamation lent authority to the

Commission's campaign against Martin, and it also suggests why the pamphlets were perceived so ill by the government. The proclamation finds in the books, "doctrine very erroneous, and other matters notoriously untrue and slanderous to the state, and . . . the persons of the bishops."[29] This suggests that offense rested as much in how this was said as in what was said: "in railing sort and beyond the bounds of all good humanity." This "railing" might well have been tolerated except for its effects on the status quo:

All which books, libels, and writings tend by their scope to persuade and bring in a monstrous and apparent dangerous innovation within her dominions and countries of all manner ecclesiastical government now in use . . . with a rash and malicious purpose also to dissolve the estate of the prelacy, being one of the three ancient estates of this realm under her highness, whereof her majesty mindeth to have such a reverent regard as to their places in the church and commonwealth appertaineth.[30]

The proclamation makes it quite clear that the authorities were using the Martin Marprelate pamphlets as a scapegoat for the presbyterian polity reforms sought by the Protestant left. It followed by only a few days Richard Bancroft's 9 February Paul's Cross sermon denouncing puritan reforms. Collinson says this sermon was "a minor landmark in English church history" offering a foretaste of the "forensic ruthlessness" that would mark Bancroft's assault on the reformers: "The puritans were 'false prophets' in sinister alliance with the Arians, Donatists, anabaptists and other sectaries." The ensuing war against reform waged by Bancroft, Whitgift, and other members of the High Commission, Collinson believed reflected Elizabeth's own views and represented the dissolution following Leicester's death in September 1588 of any government support for reform sentiments.[31]

If Collinson is right about Elizabeth's views on puritanism, the Marprelate proclamation's rhetoric is particularly remarkable. It lacks entirely the polarizing language of Bancroft's sermon, language similar to that which the council had employed in the proclamation against the Family of Love. Instead, this proclamation seeks the discovery of the "enormous malefactors" and almost naively suggests that their apprehension and punishment will put an end to the reformers' demands. It prohibits further writing, printing, or possession of such texts or assistance to writers or printers, and threatens "such further pains and penalties as by the law any way may be inflicted upon the offenders." The proclamation also calls upon the people's good will to discover the "authors, writers, printers, or dispensers thereof" by assuring that informants will not be "molested or troubled."[32]

This proclamation calls for the Marprelate tracts' suppression; the means it provides are relatively benign. It authorizes no searches; it declares no martial law. The government may proceed against offenders "by the law." The proclamation's real value lay in its persuasive agenda: it declared the dangers to church and state of whatever radical reforms might be sought in the Parliament newly convened, justified the High Commission's opposition to reform, and provided for the Commission a visible means to assault the reformers. As for the Marprelate tracts themselves, according to Collinson, all but a few puritan divines joined in their censure.[33] Although their printer, Robert Waldegrave, was never discovered, four persons were tried before the Star Chamber and sentenced: Sir Richard Knightley was fined £2,000 for allowing *The Epitome* to be printed in his house;[34] John Hales was fined 1,000 marks for allowing Martin's *Hay any worke for Cooper* and John Penry's *The Supplication to Parliament [A View]* to be printed in his; Lady Wigston was fined £1,000 for allowing *Martyn Senior* and *Martyn Junior* to be printed in hers, and her husband received a fine of 500 marks for not disclosing the printing. Upon Whitgift's intercession on their behalf, all were set at liberty and their fines remitted.[35]

Elizabethan censorship proclamations, all particular measures directed toward particular texts, testify to the degree to which press censorship between 1558 and 1603 proceeded *ad hoc* rather than by unifying principle. In this they are paradigmatic of press censorship as a whole. Hence, all the following statements about the proclamations apply equally to other measures of Elizabethan press censorship (with the caveat that an exception exists for every generalization except the first). First, no single common denominator unifies all the proclamations except their reliance on the due process of English law. Where they can, they depend upon statutory definitions of sedition and treason as grounds for censorship and call for trial under the applicable statutes. Second, the principal end of censorship was suppressing religio-political texts – either Catholic writings that denied Elizabeth's supremacy and advocated placing a Catholic monarch on the English throne, or radical Protestant texts that denied the Queen's authority over religion. Third, except for *A Gaping Gulf*, the suppression of texts censored by proclamation was largely ineffective. As propaganda, however, the proclamations served their purposes, particularly those that called for the suppression of Catholic texts from the Continent. They consolidated English nationalism and constructed a benevolent relationship between Elizabeth and her subjects, with censorship represented as a desperate resort taken to ensure this relationship. The behavior of those who would threaten this bond is consistently defined in terms of deviance – terms defined by the degree of the perceived threat. To appreciate the extent to which Elizabeth's proclamations sought to consolidate the relationship between monarch and subject, they need to be measured against the divisive language of James I. For example, a 1610 censorship proclamation articulates a genuinely oppositional stance between a Divine Right King and his subjects when it finds "such an itching in the tongues and pennes of most men" that they "doe not spare to wade in all the deepest mysteries that belong to the persons or State of Kings or Princes, that are god upon Earth."[36] Here James justifies censorship to silence not the country's but the King's enemy – the meddling subject.

The censorship proclamations testify to the reluctance of Elizabeth's government to engage in a ruthless and relentless censorship campaign, but they likewise bear witness to the fact that censorship did exist. Since censorship was a response to specific texts and their local reception, to understand fully Elizabethan press censorship will require us to look at censored texts and their contexts.

PART II

Censored texts

CHAPTER 4

Catholic propagandists
"concerning the Queen's majesty or the realm without licence"

Mandating both print licensing and the High Commission within the 1559 religious settlement displayed the government's early concern over printed opposition to Elizabethan religion – a not unusual concern given the precedents. The statutory settlement, however, did not designate Catholicism as heretical, and the Queen's Injunctions deplored employing *heretic, papist*, etc. as terms of derogation. Bishop Jewel's challenge, with its clear expectation of Catholic response, suggests that government anxieties were associated with something other than discussions of dogma. Being Catholic or writing about Catholic belief – at least in the early years of Elizabeth's reign – was neither transgressive nor inherently seditious. After the Northern Rebellion and the 1570 Papal Bull excommunicating Elizabeth, Roman Catholic religion and politics became inseparable. The deaths of 160 Catholic priests and 60 Catholic laymen in England between 1558 and 1603, most after 1580, bear testimony to the government's active prosecution of perceived Catholic sedition. While the justifiability of these prosecutions has been widely debated,[1] history has maintained a consensus about government censorship of Catholic books: Catholic texts were illegal, and Elizabeth's government relentlessly sought out Catholic presses and suppressed Catholic texts. Commands existed to burn popish books and paraphenalia. Searches, midnight raids, patrols of English ports, spies and counterspies at home and abroad sought to "stifle the thought and faith of man."[2] After the 1571 parliamentary act against reconciliation prohibited importing Catholic religious objects (upon a sentence of forfeiture of property), the authorities engaged in widespread searches to discover evidence – including "popishe bookes" – of Catholic missionary activities.

The zeal with which government pursuivants sought proof of illegal Catholic activities, however, must not be confused with efforts to suppress objectionable Catholic texts. Records of government searches make it very clear that the authorities discriminated between objectionable texts – those sought in and of themselves – and devotional works that were seized as evidence of illegal Catholic practices. While popish books might be confiscated, merely possessing them did not constitute grounds for arrest. A. Throckmorton and Richard Chetwode wrote to Robert Cecil that they had searched the possessions of one Thomas Marryott and "only found certain papistical books." While they seized the books because they thought them "not fit to remain in his hands," they had no "further matter" to charge him with.[3] Here the "papistical books" were evidently incidental to another matter that prompted the search in the first place. In another instance, however, a particular book itself offered grounds for increased surveillance. The nature of the book's offense is made clear in Richard Carmarden's 19 July 1592 letter to Lord Burghley:

Having even now received from one Emanuell Allen from Dover, who serveth there under the Surveyors of the Ports by your Lordship's appointement, a book very lately brought over to that port with two more of the same, as he writeth me, wherof one more he hath; the third was, as he heareth, escaped and brought hither to London; which book I send your good Lordship herewith. I gave this man charge when the Surveyors placed him there to take care to look after all manner of books that should be brought over to that port and to seize such as might any ways touch or concern the State.[4]

However fine the line may have been between books that touched the state and less objectionable popish books, the authorities charged their searchers to discriminate and to "seize such as might any ways touch or concern the State." Books that did not touch the state not only went uncensored, but in some cases, like the devotional poetry of the Jesuit poet, Robert Southwell, were printed with ecclesiastical authorization.[5]

Some Catholic books clearly offended more than others. Besides the countless firkers of Popish books seized at the ports, or the small private libraries of nameless books taken along with *agnus dei* and vestments as evidence of Catholic worship, certain books placed printers and booksellers and owners in legal jeopardy. Their contents – more than the circumstances of their authors and disseminators, or the fate of the presses that printed them – locate Elizabeth's government's anxieties about Catholic books. Those that provoked government suppression were of three kinds: they treated the succession (a subject deemed censorable by statute), attacked members of the English government, or justified resistance to the rule of a religious heretic. In each case the texts that provoked suppression intensified stress along the fault lines that threatened to undermine the authority of Elizabeth's government – the succession, the rule of favorites, and the allegiance of her Catholic subjects.

Elizabeth's government sought to restrain perceived threats to her authority by passing Article 5 of the treason statute 13 Eliz, ca. 1, which mandated a year's imprisonment for anyone writing about the succession. While this may have deterred English authors and printers, at no time during Elizabeth's reign did it affect the Continental presses. As James E. Phillips points out, prior to her death in 1587 Mary, Queen of Scots served as the focal point of Catholic interest in the succession, and several texts issued from the Continent maintained her right to the Crown of England.[6] After her death, which followed upon the triumph of the Protestant party in Scotland, Catholic propagandists looked increasingly to the Spanish infanta. One of the most objectionable Catholic books of Elizabeth's reign, *Conference about the next succession to the Crowne of England* (1595), written under the name of R. Doleman, advanced this claim through elaborate legal and theological justifications for depriving a ruling monarch. These texts and the circumstances surrounding their production indicate that English concerns about their intentions were not altogether unwarranted. Not only did they serve to spearhead efforts to unseat Elizabeth (even when their texts supported her rule), but their arguments on law and inheritance denigrated her authority.

According to Phillips, *A defence of the honour of the right highe, mightye and noble princesse Marie quene of Scotlande* (1569) by her friend and representative John Leslie, Bishop of Ross, served as "the fountain-head of all subsequent argument" for the claims of Mary, Queen of Scots to the English succession.[7] Leslie's *Defence of the Honour* was written in three parts. The first defended Mary against accusations of immoral conduct with her secretary David Rizzio and complicity with Lord Bothwell in the murder of her husband, Lord Darnley; the second justified Mary's claims to the English crown following Elizabeth; and the third defended female rule. Sections of *Defence of the Honour* reappeared in various forms in Leslie's later books, but the later revisions and versions omitted the defense of Mary against charges of immorality and focused on the succession. All maintain "that the right heire and Successor apparent unto the Crowne of this realme of England . . . is suche a one, as for the excellente giftes of God and nature in her most princelie appearinge, is worthie to inherite either this noble realm, or any other . . . I meane the right excellente Ladie, Ladie Marie Quene of Scotlande."[8] Leslie advanced Mary's right from Margaret, eldest daughter of Henry VII, and sister of Henry VIII. He argued from English inheritance law and discredited Henry VIII's will that had set aside Margaret's successors in favor of those issuing from his younger sister Mary (the Sutton claim). All versions are reasonably argued and refrain from denying Elizabeth's authority. Indeed, all maintain the desirability of keeping "whole and sound" the authority of the prince and argue that the one branch of policy serving this end is for subjects "lovinglye and reverentlye to honour, and obedientlye to serve their Soveraigne, which for the time hath the rule and government."[9] Leslie advocated deciding the succession in favor of Mary during Elizabeth's lifetime to prevent the civil unrest that would be imminent upon the latter's death.[10]

After 1571 the Bishop of Ross's books indeed violated the law against writing on the succession, but none appears to have been particularly seditious in and of itself – all honored Elizabeth as Queen.[11] But even before the 1571 law, the 1569 *Defence of the Honour* provoked the government to stay its London printing.[12] While the text itself may not have been seditious, Lord Burghley (then Cecil) associated it with seditious activities. Two years after the 1569 edition's printing had been stayed, Burghley was brought a portmanteau "full of Englysh books printed at Lorayne" that had been brought in at Dover by Charles Bally. Burghley found "cause to mislike the books,"

for that they were the same that had been attempted to have been secretly printed at Islington by the bishop of Rosse the year before, for the which the bishop of Rosse was committed to the bishop of London, and also the books were entitled for the defence of the Queen of Scots, both for her title to the crown and for the murder of her husband Lord Darnley, and contained a great number of manifest untruths, and namely to the prejudice of her majesty's right.[13]

Recalling the events of 1569–70, Burghley suspected "that Charles had some greater matter in charge than the bringing of the said books." The "greater" matter was Bally's role in the affairs of

Norfolk and Mary, Queen of Scots. Burghley conflated Leslie's (and Bally's) seditious activities with Leslie's book and saw both as prejudicial to Elizabeth's right.

The only part of *Defence of the Honour* that could have been seen by Burghley as prejudicial to her is this passage relating to the Third Act of Succession of Henry VIII's reign and his will:

> It dothe appeare by the saide Statute of 28. of kinge Henrie the eight, that there was aucthorie geaven him by the same to declare, limitte, appointe, and assigne the succession of the crowne by hys lettres patentes, or by hys laste will signed with his owne hande. It appearethe also by the foresaide Statute made 35. of the saide kinge, that it was by the same enacted, that the crowne of this realme shoulde goe and be to the saide kinge and to the heires of his bodie lawfullie begotten, that ys to saye, unto his hyghnes firste sonne of his bodie betwene him and the Ladie Jane then hys wife, begotten: and for defaulte of suche issewe, then unto the Ladie Marie his dawghter, and to the heires of her bodie lawfullie begotten. And for defaulte of such issewe, then unto the Ladie Elizabeth his dawghter our Sovereigne Ladie the Quenes Majestie that now ys, and to the heires of her Majesties Bodie Lawfullie begotten.[14]

Leslie then argues that since the statute established the succession as it existed, the will was moot – its only use was being made by Mary's detractors to deny her right to the succession:

> To this yt ys on the behalf of the saide Ladie Marie Quene of Scotlande amonge other thinges a[n]swered that kinge Henrie the eight never signed the pretensed will with his owne hande: And that therefore the saide will can not be any whitte prejudiciall to the saide Queene.[15]

In the will Henry gave succession in the failure of his own line to his sister Mary, and thus denied it to his sister Margaret and her grand-daughter, Mary, Queen of Scots.

Leslie's contention that problems existed with Henry's will was correct. Two versions existed; neither was signed. While Elizabeth's succession was secure by statute, the messy issue of the wills, departing as they did from common law – as Leslie points out all too clearly – placed royal succession in Chancery's hands rather than God's. On the other side, to concede Leslie's point that the will was invalid in the case of Mary's succession was to invite challenges to Elizabeth's right to rule from parties who would happily argue that she was Henry's illegitimate child and therefore lacked right. Further, even if Leslie accepted that Elizabeth held statutory right to the succession, by rehearsing the proliferation of statutes successively altering the succession during Henry's reign, he assigned to Parliament authority over the Crown that Elizabeth was unwilling to recognize.

Defence of the Honour points to the complex issues that could be, and were, raised in any discussion of the succession. Burghley and Elizabeth may well have agreed with Leslie that Mary and her heirs were entitled to the English throne in the event of Elizabeth's death. To discuss the succession, however, as he demonstrated, inevitably led to privileging one line of inheritance over another, one legal principle over another, or one court – royal, chancery, or parliamentary – over another. The Tudor succession was never so unsullied – despite its propaganda to the contrary – that it could rest easily under this scrutiny. In 1569/70 Leslie's arguments must have led both Elizabeth and Cecil to realize their implications and that probably contributed to the 1571 statutory prohibition against writing about the succession.[16]

In 1569/70 Leslie's writing about the succession, however, had been nowhere as important as his acting on assumptions about a successor's rights, and in 1570 Cecil had probably been more concerned about the latter. While in 1572 Cecil aptly recalled his objections to the book, his memory of the events related to its publication, secondary as they were to the matter of Norfolk, appears flawed: the Bishop of Ross had been detained in early February 1570 at the Bishop of London's house – but not for seeking to print secretly his *Defence of the Honour*. When Mary wrote to Elizabeth to request his release, the Queen responded, "I have thought good to assure you that the restraining of the bishop of Rosse, your minister at this time has proceded of many and necessary causes."[17] Elizabeth appointed a "conference" to examine Leslie. Her ministers were concerned that he supported Mary as England's rightful queen and participated in the Northern Rebellion. Their concern about his book arose from intelligence that the book accepted Mary as the "right heir of this realm."[18] In response to their concerns Leslie replied:

He was very sorry from his heart that the Queen's majesty should "tak ony evill opinione thairof," considering that nothing was intended but a defence of her honour against so many blasphemous "treteis" and "pamflettis" as have been set abroad both in England and Scotland, which are printed at London . . . If the same might have given any occasion to offend the Queen's majesty in any sort, it should not have been printed, and although it had been printed, the same did not comprehend so manifest untruth as is reported.[19]

He convinced the Privy Councillors; on 18 May, he thanked Cecil for his liberty.[20]

Cecil's 1572 memory of Ross's 1569 offense had been colored by events subsequent to the book's suppression. Between May 1570 and April 1572, Cecil (now Burghley) had come to view Mary as a major threat to the security of Elizabeth's throne. In 1570 the Bishop of Ross had offended because he had printed a book "concerning the Queen's majesty or the realm without licence" – a relatively minor offence.[21] In 1572 Bally acted against Elizabeth's proclamation by bringing in "illegal" books on the Queen of Scots – books that now violated a statutory prohibition against writing on the succession. Even though the stakes had gone up, as long as Mary was alive, Continental Catholics issued books promoting her succession. Coupled with repeated Catholic plots against Elizabeth, the books came to look less like the defense found in Leslie's 1569 vindication and more like a rallying cry for revolution. In 1584 Leslie's *Treatise towching the right of the Most excellent Princesse Marie* (another version of *Defence of the Honour*) joined other Catholic propaganda as the object of Elizabeth's proclamation ordering that books "defacing of true religion" and endangering her title be suppressed.

After Mary's death, the Catholic cause looked elsewhere. The Elizabethan State Papers are filled with intelligence about manuscripts and books, largely Continental, advancing one Catholic line or another, principally against the claim of James, who was now clearly Protestant. A letter on 31 March 1593 reported to Burghley that Richard Verstegan was printing a book entitled *News from Spain and Holland* advancing the Spanish right to the English throne.[22] In 1595 Burghley received intelligence about a book being printed on the Spanish right of succession that included along with the report a letter written by Catholic William Gifford objecting to the book as "the most pestilent ever made,"[23] and he wrote out his own notes on this dangerous book arguing for the infanta,[24] clearly *A Conference About The Next Succession to the Crowne of Ingland* (1595), written by Robert Parsons under the pseudonym of R. Doleman. Reports of book seizures during these years reveal that such books were the object of rigorous exclusion efforts at the ports.[25] Parsons's *Conference* was objectionable on many grounds – and to many parties.

Not only did the *Conference* arouse the concerns of Burghley and other English statesmen, it offended many English Catholics, both at home and abroad, who hoped to secure toleration in exchange for their support for James. English Catholics openly denounced the Jesuit party, and their objections to the *Conference* became central to their overall objections to the Jesuits. Henry Neville brought Jesuit support for Spanish interests in England to Cecil's attention in a 27 June 1599 letter in which he claimed that the Jesuits were taking the side of the infanta "violently" especially since the publication of Parsons's book. Neville proposed that the infanta's claim advanced in the *Conference* should, in turn, be used as a litmus test for the loyalty of English Catholics. He recommended that "Priests and recusants, when apprehended, should be examined whether they have not been solicited or solicited others to subscribe to the Infanta's title."[26] Though Cecil appears not to have followed the advice (at least officially), Neville's letter suggests one reason the *Conference* was perceived as particularly dangerous; it provided, in its claims for the infanta, a new figure in whom English Catholics, prompted by the Jesuits, could place their hopes for a Catholic monarch in England. According to Parsons, William Allen had supported the *Conference* because "he hoped that on sight of the book, the wise and Catholic part of our nation would join with him, and his friends, in some good means for saving themselves and their country."[27]

While the Bishop of Ross's books had been perceived to advance Mary's claim by prejudicing, though not denying, Elizabeth's rights, Parsons's book effectively denied the validity of the entire Tudor line by asserting the primacy of the Spanish claim by way of John of Gaunt. To privilege this old direct Lancastrian line against the York claim, definitely prejudiced Elizabeth's right by maintaining that the York claim was subordinate to the Lancastrian, and her Lancastrian claim far weaker still. Parsons argued for the strength of the Lancastrian line by demonstrating that Richard II was legally deposed:

... for that al kingly authority is given them only by the comon wealth, & that with this expressse condition, that they shal be governe according to law and equity, that this is the cause of their exaltation above other men, that this is the end of their goverment, the butt of their authority, the starr and pole by which they ought to direct their sterne, to witt, the good of the people, by the weale of their subjects, by the benefite of the realme, which end being taken away or perverted, the king becommeth a tyrant, A Tigar, a fearse Lion, a ravening wolfe, a publique enimy, and a bloody murtherer, which were against al reason both natural and moral, that a comon wealth could not deliver it selfe from so eminent a distruction.[28]

The deposition itself was justified,

First for that it was done by the choise and invitation of al the realme or greater and better parte therof as hath bin said. Secondly for that it was done without slaughter, and thirdly for that the king was deposed by act of parlament, and himselfe convinced of his unworthy goverment, and brought to confesse that he was worthely deprived, and that he willingly and freely resigned the same . . . (II, p. 67)

With regard to the legitimacy of the Lancastrian succession over the York, Parsons says,

And first of al it is to be understood, that at that very tyme when king Richard was deposed, the house of Yorke had no pretence or little at al to the crowne, for that Edmond Mortimer earle of march, nephew to the lady Phillip, was then alive, with his sister Anne Mortymer marryed to Richard earle of Cambrige, by which Anne the howse of Yorke did after make their clayme, but could not do so yet, for that the said Edmond her brother was living. (II, p. 72)

Parsons here is privileging the elder brother's claim over the younger's and male inheritance over female. Henry IV claimed his right to the Crown through his father, John of Gaunt, Duke of Lancaster. Any York claim was subordinate to this: first, because the Duke of York was younger than the Duke of Lancaster, and second, because his actual heirs made the York claim by marriage through the female to the rights of the elder brother, the Duke of Clarence.[29] Whatever his objectivity in discussing the York claim, Parsons finally concludes that York kings proceeded to the throne by bloodshed and enjoyed violent reigns while Lancastrians were good kings. Since he identifies Henry VIII as a York king who "passed al the rest in crueltie, toward his owne kynred" (II, p. 101), he doubled his affront to Elizabeth.

The nature of the *Conference*'s offense is complex. Parsons refrains from directly attacking Elizabeth's personal right to rule at the same time that he discredits the entire Tudor succession. Furthermore, its rhetorical restraint, particularly its disinterested and objective tone, lends credibility to arguments entirely untenable to her. It purports to report on a 1593 conference in Amsterdam convened to discuss the succession. Among the speakers are two "Gentlemen Lawyers" who address the question from two perspectives: the civil lawyer examines the legal premises of kingship, while the "temporal" lawyer examines the history of the succession, focusing finally on the divide relevant to the matter at hand – the conflicting claims of the Houses of Lancaster and York. To a reader not extremely well versed in the nuances of political theory and blood inheritance, the argument is authoritative and substantive. The first part argues that kingship derives both from succession (propinquity and priority of blood) *and* admission by the commonwealth, but

it is the coronation and admission, that maketh a perfect and true king, whatsoever the title by succession be otherwise, & that except the admission of the common wealth be joyned to succession, it is not sufficient to make a lawful king, and of the two the second is of far more importance, to wit the concent and admission of the realme, then nearnes of blood by succession alone. (Liv mispaginated "i")

The lawyer cites as evidence, historical matters familiar to England:

after the deposition of king Richard the second, depended of this authority of the common wealth, for that as the people were affected and the greater parte prevailed, so were their titles ether allowed confirmed altered or disanulled by parlaments, and yet may not we wel affirme, but that ether part when they were in possession and confirmed therin by thes parlaments, were lawful kings, and that God concurred with them as with true princes for goverment of their people . . . (I, p. 195)

This example – here appearing to be merely illustrative – provides the foundation of Part II, which "indifferently" reviews current claims to and details the history of the succession, debates the relative merits of the claims of Lancaster and York, and then one by one eliminates claimants to the succession, using as the principal criterion distance from the legitimate Lancastrian blood. Only the Spanish line stands the test of the last, best claimant.

J. E. Neale judges Parsons's *Conference* to be "an important and disturbing book" for "repudiating the doctrine of divine hereditary right, placing election alongside birth as a way to succession, and by implication arguing that Parliament could take away the King of Scots' right to the English throne."[30] While these aspects may well have sent out warning signals to Burghley, it actually supports the King of Scots' hereditary right, though it rejects him personally as England's potential king. The significant issue is not Parliament's right to affirm, but the grounds on which a blood successor ought to be be rejected by the commonwealth. According to Parsons,

. . . nothing in the world can so justly exclude an heyre apparent from his succession, as want of religion, nor any cause what so-ever jusitifie and cleare the conscience of the common wealth, or of particuler men, that in this case should resist his entrance . . . (I, p. 212)

From a Catholic perspective, James was utterly unacceptable, and for a Catholic to support his succession was a sin:

And now to apply al this to our purpose for Ingland, and for the matter we have in hand, I affirme and hold, that for any man to give his helpe, consent or assistance towards the making of a king, whom he judgeth or beleveth to be faultie in religion, & consequently would advance either no religion, or the wrong, if he were in authority, is a most grevous and damnable sinne to him that doth it, of what side soever the truth be, or how good or bad so ever the party be, that is preferred. (I, p. 216)

Burghley's notes do not suggest that he found the book seditious because of its arguments on the nature of kingship – or Parliament – but because it argued against the King of Scots and for the King of Spain.[31] Any book about the succession was objectionable,[32] but a book supporting the Spanish succession that could potentially raise support for another Armada was seriously seditious – and potentially more dangerous than anything Leslie had written supporting Mary.

The question of the succession was never very far from the focus of Catholic books, even when their central concern lay elsewhere. Another genre of Catholic propaganda that met with rigorous suppression still had something to say about the succession, but these works were far more objectionable for what they said about the current government of England. Two of these, *A Treatise of Treasons* and *Leicester's Commonwealth*, provoked proclamations suppressing them. Since both of these books address the succession, they offended statute, but in both cases, as the proclamations' language makes clear, their greater offense lay in their treatment of the Queen's ministers.

A Treatise of Treasons Against Q. Elizabeth and the Croune of England (1572) followed Cecil's attack in *Salutem in Christo* (1571) on the Duke of Norfolk and those associated with the Northern Rebellion. *A Treatise of Treasons* has been assigned with reservation to John Leslie, probably because, like *Defence of the Honour*, it defends Mary and advocates the Stuart succession.[33] The proclamation makes entirely clear that the

Crown's principal objection to the *Treatise of Treasons* was for spreading libels of treason against the Queen's councilors, "specially aginst two, who be certainly known to have always been most studiously and faithfully careful of her majesty's prosperous estate."[34] The *Treatise of Treasons'* 182 pages condemn the "two Machiavelles" Cecil and Nicholas Bacon, who "for their own private advancement" and to secure their power by advancing their own family (the Suffolk line) to the succession have diverted England from its proper "course, race, and line" established by law. They circumvented the Queen, "indangered her State, steined her honour, oppressed her people, impoverished the Realme, and procured infinite perils to depende over the same."[35] As evidence of their betrayal, the *Treatise of Treasons* assigns virtually every disturbance during her reign – national or international – to their hands. They have engineered foreign wars, bred faction at home, spread heresy and atheism, and perverted the succession by preventing the Queen from marrying. Even without its objectionable attack on Elizabeth's ministers, its treatment of her would have brought it within the purview of the treason statutes; it denied the legitimacy of the Queen's ecclesiastical supremacy – though it mitigates the tone by arguing that Cecil seduced the unwary Eve to usurp this jurisdiction.

Ordering the *Treatise of Treasons'* destruction did little to prevent it appearing in another form. *L'Innocence de la tresillustre tres-chaste, et debonnaire Princesse, Madame Marie Royne d'Escosse* (1572)[36] contained all of the attack on Cecil and Bacon. This apparently made its way to England and was being distributed for several years before the printer William Carter was arrested for selling it from his shop. In 1579, the Bishop of London John Aylmer wrote to Burghley:

. . . I have founde out a presse of printyng with one Carter, a verye Lewed fellow, who hath byne dyvers tymes before in prison for printing of Lewd pamphlettes. But nowe in searche of his Howse amongst other naughtye papystycall Books, ̄wee have found one wrytten in Ffrenche intytled the innosency of the Scottishe Queene, a very dangerous Book wherein he calleth her *the heir Apparant of this crowne*: he enveyth agaynste the faction of the Duck of Norfolk, defendeth the rebellion in the north, and dyscourseth agaynst you and the Late Lord keper. I doubt not that your L. Shipp hath seene it nevertheless I thought good to furnishe this muche unto your Lordshippe that you maye deale with the fellowe who is nowe neare you in the Gatehowse as so your wysdom shall seme good. I can get nothing of him for he did denye to answere upon his othe . . .[37]

Consistent with the 1572 proclamation's order to destroy the *Treatise of Treasons*, Carter's press and books were confiscated, but he escaped prosecution, at least in this case and for the time being.[38]

The copie of a leter, wryten by a master of arte of Cambrige to his friend in London (1584), known as *Leicester's Commonwealth*, also occasioned a proclamation to suppress it, followed a year later by a letter from the Privy Council to officials in London and the provinces to make better efforts for its suppression.[39] While the proclamation was directed towards other texts as well – all objectionable because they "traitorously and injuriously" slandered the present government and in doing so, they touched the Queen "as making choice of men of want both of justice, care, and other sufficiency to serve her Highness and the commonweal," the letter names "one most infamous, containing slanderous and hateful matter against our very good lord the Earl of Leicester" (p. 72). Like the *Treatise of Treasons*, *Leicester's Commonwealth* treated the succession and other political issues important to the Catholic party. D. C. Peck is, however, misleading in saying, "The book is widely known for the rhetorical flights of its railing upon Leicester, and to be sure these are memorable, but elsewhere within it one encounters exploration of serious political ideas . . . " (p. 32). *Leicester's Commonwealth*'s consideration of political matters, arguments for religious toleration and the Marian succession, frame – but are clearly subordinated to – the attack on Leicester. The book's organizational device, a seemingly "indifferent" conversation among three Englishmen – a lawyer, a scholar, and a gentleman, requires that their discussion of Leicester's abuses belong to the wider political landscape. The talk settles periodically on contemporary events – the persecution of Catholic priests and recusants, events in the universities, a parliamentary statute on the succession – as a springboard to Leicester. The real events lend authenticity to the discussion of his misconduct that makes up nearly eighty percent of the text. Even those parts that are seemingly unrelated to Leicester, such as the twenty pages discrediting any successors besides Mary, exist to demonstrate the utter depravity of his ambitious schemes.

Leicester's Commonwealth's initial reflections on the need for religious toleration digress to Leicester by observing that in the current state of English religious affairs the papist, puritan, and religious Protestant are all being exploited for private gain by "the fellow being of neither" – Leicester (p. 72). The gentleman summarizes the charges against him, the ensuing conversation offers the evidence to prove the charges, and the conclusion restates the charges and appeals to the Queen to take action against him, and if not her, then God. Leicester is indicted as a man of,

extreme ambition pride, falsehood and treachery; so born, so bred up, so nuzzled in treason from his infancy; descended of a tribe of traitors, and fleshed in conspiracy against the royal blood of King Henry's children in his tender years, and exercised ever since in drifts against the same by the blood and ruin of divers others; a man so well known to bear secret malice against her Majesty for causes irreconcilable and most deadly rancor against the best and wisest counsellors of her Highness . . . hateful to god and man and so markable to the simplest subject of this land by the public ensigns of his tryannous purpose . . . that nothing wanteth in him but only his pleasure, and the day already conceived in his mind to dispose as he list both of prince, crown, realm, and religion. (p. 73)

Leicester's Commonwealth argues that Leicester has the motive (ambition and revenge against the Queen for not marrying him), the means (a personal history of murderous acts, a knowledge of poison, and political cronies in places of power), and the opportunity (constant access to the Queen) to effect his ends. The *Commonwealth* is even more pernicious than the *Treatise of Treasons* because it depends on detailed reference to actual people and specific events (rumored or true), and thereby slanders not only Leicester but other members of the government. Furthermore, while it ostensibly argues that he is capable of accomplishing a coup, it effectively demonstrates that "Leicester's Commonwealth" already exists in his tremendous wealth, the extent of his control over local politics, and his influence on the Queen.

Leicester's Commonwealth differed from most Catholic propaganda: with its focus on Leicester and its intimate knowledge of patronage politics and administrative practices, it appears to have been directed towards building a conservative consensus within the government against Leicester. It appealed not for the reestablishment of the Catholic religion in England, but for religious toleration for Catholics. Most Catholic propaganda offered perfunctory compliment to Elizabeth; *Leicester's Commonwealth* offers a warning to her to preserve herself and her kingdom from her minister. These differences undoubtedly derive from its authorship. The *Commonwealth* has often been attributed to Robert Parsons, but Peck maintains that "the tract is not at all the book Parsons would have written" (p. 27); instead, "the *Commonwealth* seems very much a desperate *pis aller* of the conservative old nobility, whose members found themselves being replaced in power and influence by the left-Protestant 'new men,'" that is, of the Paris circle of the Howard Court party.[40] Secretary of State Walsingham clearly understood the book's effort to influence the Queen against Leicester and suggested that if she happened to be drawn in so far even as to allow its circulation, "the mischief like to ensue thereby will in the end reach to herself."[41] *Leicester's Commonwealth*, however, posed particularly difficult problems for Elizabeth's government because it played in the international arena. Walsingham saw the book as part of the international Catholic conspiracy that had become suspect at Court in the 1580s. Further, he viewed the book as an effort to discredit the Queen and undermine her government both at home and abroad. Besides clearly violating statutory constraints against libel and writing on the succession, *Leicester's Commonwealth* contained adequate sedition and potential treason to provoke the government.

While books on the succession and libels against the Queen's ministers clearly violated English law, the last class of Catholic texts inhabited more disputed territory. Most of these, the Catholic cause maintained, were for the spiritual nourishment of English Catholics. Elizabeth's government, however, found treason in them. A most notorious example was *De Schismate* or *A Treatise of Schism*, written by Gregory Martin in 1578. According to Peter Milward, it addressed the practical question of outward conformity facing English Catholics and offered a full explanation of the Catholic position that required church attendance savored of heresy or, at the very least, schism.[42] In 1584, William Carter, from whom copies of *L'innocence de . . . Marie* had been seized in 1579, was tried and convicted of treason for reprinting *Treatise of Schism*. In his 1584 *A True, Sincere and Modest Defence of English Catholiques*, William Allen offers Carter as a martyr to the Catholic cause, his trial and execution as evidence that the English justice system prosecuted Catholics for their religion and not for their politics. According to Allen, Carter was "a poore innocent artisan":

who was made away onelie for printing a catholique booke *De schismate*: in which no worde was found against the state, the quarel onelie most unjustlie being made, upon a certaine clause, which by no likelie honest construction could apperteine to the Q. person: *viz.* that the Catholike religion should once have the upperhand of heresie, and *Judith* cutt of the head of *Holophernes*: which they in their extreame jelousie and fear of all thinges wold needs wreast against her Maiestie.[43]

The passage regarding Judith illustrates the complex problem of reception. It follows several pages on the English church's heretical nature, and for English Catholics to communicate with heretics, *Treatise of Schism* maintains, is sinful. Judith's story is one among several Biblical exempla justifying civil disobedience.

Judith foloweth, whose godlye and constant wisedome if our Catholike gentlewomen would folowe, they might destroye Holofernes, the master heretike, and amase al his retinew, and never defile their religion by communicating with them in anye smal poynt.[44]

Judith outwardly sought to please Holofernes, but because she would concede no matter that would compromise her religious practice, she gained liberty once a day to "goe in & out the gate" for her devotions:

Which her constance (a wonderful thing to tel) was the very means afterward, wherby she carried away his head safely, the porters presupposing that she went (as before) to pray to her God.[45]

Allen found nothing objectionable in the passage, and A. C. Southern concurs: "Quite clearly Judith is being held up to the 'Catholike gentlewomen' for her steadfastness of religion, and of course she provides an excellent example for those whom the writer is exhorting 'to abstaine altogether from heretical Conventricles.'"[46] Neither takes into account the body of Catholic propaganda that followed the 1570 papal bull characterizing Elizabeth as the ultimate heretic. Nor does either consider that though copies of Martin's book had been around for some time, it was not until 1584, when Carter engaged in reprinting the book, that a problem arose.

Allen's and Southern's judgment that Martin intended nothing more than the spiritual sustenance of English Catholics may have been justified in 1579, but by 1584 conspiracy and treason were in the air. October 1583 had seen Walsingham's discovery of an elaborate conspiracy including Mary, Queen of Scots, the King of Spain, the Guise party in France, and the Pope to mount a Catholic invasion, reestablish Catholicism, and, if necessary, assassinate Elizabeth. The Spanish Ambassador Bernardino de Mendoza and the Englishman Francis Throckmorton were the principal conspirators in England. When Throckmorton was arrested, a search of his house produced a list of English Catholics who were prepared to aid in any rebellious schemes against the Queen.[47] Such a list, together with the discovery of a conspiracy, offered clear evidence to the state that Catholics – English Catholics – were practicing treason in the name of religion.

So the reprinting of Martin's text offered the government an opportunity not only to eradicate a piece of propaganda that they could justifiably argue advocated assassination to secure religious freedom, but also to eliminate a principal source of Catholic propaganda – Carter's press (and shop).

The case of William Carter points to the highly contested nature of Catholic discourse in the 1580s. With the English government's increased restraints against Catholic recusants and its prohibition against Continental missionaries, Catholic propagandists held a highly vested interest in casting the government as unjustifiably prosecuting Catholics for religion and not for politics. In doing so they could mount international pressure for toleration and solicit international military action. As the climate of conspiracy heightened, the English government increasingly blamed the Jesuits, missionary priests, and Catholic exiles for orchestrating political action. Any historic assessment of the validity of the opposing viewpoints had been distorted by the lenses of religious, political, and even philosophical bias. While the debate cannot be resolved here, one extraordinary document, an annotated copy in the Huntington Library of Allen's *A True, Sincere and Modest Defence*, offers not only a clear articulation of the Catholic position that Catholics in England were dying for their religion, but undeniable evidence that the authorities received the book as "A false, seditious, & Immodest offense."[48]

The death of Edmund Campion and his companions on Tyburn Hill, 1 December 1581, for conspiracy elicited a wave of texts written not merely to defend but to venerate him and other victims of English justice as Catholic martyrs. These texts, according to MacCaffrey, "celebrated both the innocence and the courage of the priests, while painting a very ugly picture of a hypocritical government which, while claiming to leave men's consciences free, sent them to their death for exercising that freedom."[49] While few of the texts engaging in the martyrology were specifically culled out for extraordinary measures of suppression, it is clear that these books provoked Elizabeth's government. In December 1583 an anonymous text, since attributed to Burghley, *The execution of justice in England* issued from the press of the Queen's printer, Christopher Barker.[50] Burghley's book defended the English justice system by recounting the rebellions against Elizabeth "animated" by the Pope and by contending that the 1570 papal bull "commanding all her subjects, to depart from their natural alleageances" provoked and authorized "all persons of al degrees" in her realms to rebel.[51] The end of the Jesuit mission was "to perswade the people to allowe of the *Popes* foresaid Bulles and warrantes, and of his absolute authoritie over all Princes and Countries" and to engage in conspiracy.

And therefore as manifest traitours in maintayning and adhearing to the capitall enemy of her Majestie and her Crowne, who hath not only bene the cause of two rebellions alredie passed in *England* and *Ireland*, but in that of *Ireland* did mainfestly wage and maintaine his owne people Captaines and Souldiours under the Banner of *Rome*, against her Majestie . . . These I say have justly suffered death not by force or forme of any newe lawes established, either for religion or against the *Popes* supremacie, as the slanderous libellers would have it seeme to be, but by the auncient temporall lawes of the realme, and namely by the lawes of Parliament made in King Edward the thirds time . . . these persons were justly condemned of treason, and lawfully executed by the auncient lawes temporall of the Realme, without any other matter then for their practizes and conspiracies both abroad and at home against the Queene and the realme, and for maintaining of the *Popes* forewaid authoritie and Bull, published to deprive her Majestie of her crowne . . . [52]

Allen's *A True, Sincere and Modest Defence* articulately counters Burghley by likening *The execution of justice in England*'s author to the heretic Julian the Apostate, who, in the name of politics, deprived Catholic martyrs of the honors due them for dying for their religion.

S. Gregorie NaZian Zene livelie expresseth the condition of al Heretiques, in the behaviour of *Julianus the Apostata*, thus writing of him: *He openlie and boldlie professing impietie, yet by coulor of clemencie covered his crueltie; and lest we should atteine to the honours done customablie to Martirs (which he disdeined to the Christians) he used namelie this fraude and deceipt, that such as he caused to be tormented for Christs cause, should be thought and reported to be punished not for their faith, but as malefactours.*[53]

The first eighty-five pages of Allen's book maintain that any charges of treason brought against Catholics were unfounded since they were not brought under the old treason laws in place under Catholic monarchs, and further, that since all acts by Catholics were governed by the Church and directed by conscience, they were religious and not within the domain of civil law. With regard to the papal bull, Allen replies that it caused problems that he and others sought to mitigate – basically by praying that the Queen should return to the Church – but that papal actions against heretics did not constitute treason. Had Allen stopped here, English authorities may not have found his text any more objectionable than countless other Catholic texts.

Peter Milward identifies Allen's *A True, Sincere and Modest Defence* as the "principal controversial work from the Catholic side during the whole period," which purported "to demonstrate that the priests and laymen who had been executed in England in the past few years were not traitors to the country, but martyrs for the Catholic faith."[54] MacCaffrey more accurately describes *A True, Sincere and Modest Defence* as "the Catholic case against the Elizabethan regime," but even he does not go far enough to ascribe to the work the genuine threat that the government found.[55]

Handwritten marginal annotations in the Huntington copy of Allen's *A True, Sincere and Modest Defence* demonstrate that someone in the service of the state viewed the book as a program for rebellion: that it justified all of Burghley's claims in *The Execution of Justice*. The marginalia[56] are marked with silk string double sewn from the edge of the page through the margin to the printed text and then back to the edge and knotted, leaving a tab to mark and enable quick reference to the annotated passages. The first string tab (now torn out) appeared about one centimeter from the top of the page, and each successive tab is located about one centimeter below the previous one. The marginalia are all in the same highly stylized Italic hand as the title-page annotation that reads: "To bee redd & used for ye Service of God, Q Elizabethe, & the peace of Englande, & for No othe^r purpose, Or Cause." This inscription on a text censored by proclamation suggests that this particular copy was reserved to use by members of the government, and its possession was exempted from any legal action. Further, it dates the annotations within Elizabeth's reign, probably before 1587, since one note characterizes Mary, Queen of Scots' succession as the "feares of all present treasons."[57] The markings do not appear to be directed toward determining whether or not Allen's text is treasonous. Instead they turn this copy into a kind of reference work – a catalogue of Catholic seditions and treasons to be used for God, Queen, and country.[58] It provided a measure of the clear and present danger of the Catholic political agenda: Catholics who subscribed to Allen's views were not religious but political offenders.

The theme of the annotator's concern – the justifiable grounds for relieving a ruling monarch of his or her authority – is made clear at the first string marking a passage in Allen's text on the Lateran Council. The annotation reads "The decree of that Counsell in what cayse a Sovereigne Lords subje[ct] be discharg^d of the^r Duty & ther

Lands to be possess[d] by Catholiks."[59] The second string marks a passage on historical and biblical precedents for ecclesiastical judgment on rulers.[60] The marginalia reads: "That kk[s] may bee deposed by preests & proffits as judges." When this is read together with the marginalia at the next string – "{Warre} for Ro: {for the Catholique religion both lauful & honorable.} warranted by y[e] supreame preests"[61] – the annotator's concern over Catholic political motives becomes clear. The priest's role in such political action is illustrated on the next page by Allen's Old Testament exemplar: "*Phinees* the Priest of God by sleaing a cheefe captaine with his owne handes deserved eternal praise, and the perpetuitie of his Priesthood."[62] The handwritten marginalia on that page aptly summarize the passage and articulate the Biblical lesson's import: "Mary the preests must direct the murderers for y[e] Cause & Action" emphasizes the text, "Marry in al this . . . the Prophet and Priests must direct them for the cause and action . . . "[63] As the annotations clearly demonstrate, Allen has provided considerable ground for the government position that the seminary priests and Jesuits were engaged in a political mission.

The argument marked by the next string moves to justifying the deposing of a ruling monarch. The annotation summarizing the marked passage reads: "kk[s] may bee & have beene deposed for Crymes tẽdĩg to y[e] perĩcon of y[e] people the[r] subjects As weel as for injurys done to Gods Churche."[64] Allen's text goes on to maintain that such an action is not treason, as the next annotation makes clear: "No traterous opynyo[n] that a p[r]ince Anoÿted may bee deposed for herezy whe[r] A traito[r] is Judge."[65] The annotator understands that the judge in this case is the Pope, whom he regards as traitorous: "a Prince (otherwise lauful and annointed) may be excommunicated, deposed, forsaken or resisted by the warrant of holie Churches judgement and Censure."[66] The remaining annotations follow Allen's argument that deposing apostate princes is justifiable first, because if it were not, it would appear that God had not sufficiently provided for man's salvation, and second, because as a wife cannot live with an infidel, so Christian men cannot live with an apostate prince. These invite the annotator's Protestant outrage. On the first he comments, "heryzye, for the[m] y[e] deathe of Christ is not suficiẽt for o[ur] Salvation," and of the second, "Agenst S[t] Pauls doctry[n] & y[e] Scriptu[re]."[67]

The annotator's response to Allen's summary of this justification crystallizes the reception of the book. To Allen's:

Therfore let no man marvel that in case of Heresy the Soveraigne loseth his superioritie and right over his people and kingdome . . . No anie one person being simplie necessarie for the preservation of the same; as some one (being an Heretique and enimie to Religion) . . .

The annotator responds: "Treason to God & to kk^s & QQ^s."[68] This illuminates the irreconcilable differences between the radical Catholic and the state positions. To the first, Elizabeth was a heretic, who thereby lost her temporal authority, but under English law any effort to deprive the ruling monarch was an act of treason. To the first, action taken to deprive an apostate ruler was an act of religious duty – martyrdom came from losing one's life in such an act; but under English law treason in the name of religion was still treason.[69] While Allen and other Catholic propagandists saw the presence of Jesuits and priests in England as a religious mission, those in the "Service of God, Q Elizabethe, & the peace of Englande" – as the annotations to Allen's *True, Sincere and Modest Defence* demonstrate – found Catholic religious justification for political action suspect as "Treason to God and kings and Queens." Allen's *Defence* fed their suspicions.

Evidence that these suspicions were well founded came in 1588 with the Spanish Armada. While this may be viewed as an inevitable playing out of the pressures of international power politics, Allen did not miss the opportunity to emphasize the Armada's religious implications. In 1588, sometime between the end of April and early June (i.e. prior to the Spanish invasion), he wrote *Admonition to the Nobility and People of England and Ireland*. A printed broadside summarizing it, *A Declaration of the Sentence and deposition of Elizabeth, the usurper and pretensed Quene of Englande*, appeared at the same time. Allen's work appealed to the Catholic nobility of England to support the upcoming invasion. Both book and declaration restate Elizabeth's crimes against true religion and affirm that King Philip of Spain, with the Pope's blessing, is carrying out the "chastisment of that wicked woman; the bane of Christendome."[70] Allen assures the English nobility that the Spanish invasion's end is not destruction but the "restitution and preservation of the Catholike religion." He admonishes the people of England and Ireland to withdraw all support from Elizabeth and her forces and to join with the "Catholike army."[71] Both the book and the declaration deem it lawful "for any person publike or private" to capture Elizabeth or any of her army and promise liberal payment for any English effort to provide food or munitions to the Catholic army.[72]

On 12 June 1588 Burghley sent a copy of Allen's *Admonition* to Walsingham and recommended that it be suppressed "under pain of treason" and that an answer be written "as if from the Catholics of England." His assessment of English reception of the book was that "The Cardinal [William Allen] is deceived if he thinks that any nobleman or gentleman of possessions will favor the invasion of the realm. The Cardinal's book may give cause of danger to all Catholics and Recusants."[73] Rather than pen a response, the Privy Council drafted a proclamation informing England of the imminent Spanish invasion and warning against Allen's book "which, although but a blast or puff of a beggarly scholar and traitor, was intended as a traitorous trumpet to wake up all robbers and Catholics in England against their sovereign."[74] It closed with an appeal to pray for the protection of England. Evidently the Privy Council thought better of this approach. Warned by Allen's writings, Walsingham explored places in which recusants might be confined,[75] and the Privy Council made a drastic effort to prevent the circulation of *Admonition to the Nobility* and *Declaration of the Sentence*. On 1 July 1588, just as the English fleet departed from Plymouth, the Privy Council declared martial law against possessors of the offensive works.[76]

If Allen's *True, Sincere and Modest Defence* had been found subtly seditious by a far from disinterested party, the 1588 texts openly offended every statutory effort to preserve the Queen's authority, dignity, and person. *Admonition to the Nobility* describes her as a "wicked Jesabell" who presumes to be "the verie cheefe spirituall governesse under God."[77] It calls her the "pretensed Queen," a woman sinful from birth, the product of "incestuous copulation with usurped Anne Bolen" who sins by profaning the sacraments, seizing sacred persons, engaging in licentious conduct, murdering the Scottish Queen, and endangering her country.[78] Like the 1570 papal bull, the "new bull" Allen described was particularly threatening because it absolved English Catholics of any actions they might take against the Queen. Only this time the danger was not imagined; the invasion was imminent. Walsingham's intelligence network had long warned of Catholic conspiracy, and the shape it had assumed in the minds of Walsingham and Burghley corresponded to what they now saw. They had believed the Pope would raise an army among Catholic nations to invade England. They had suspected that invading forces would find waiting for them a Catholic political underground, bred and fed by the Jesuits and seminary priests, which would turn plowshares into swords and rise up against the Queen. Allen's texts offered the final watering to force the fruits. The censorship of Allen's *Admonition to the Nobility* and *Declaration of the Sentence* belonged to England's effort to turn back the Spanish invasion and prevent the deposition of Elizabeth.

Most appraisals of English censorship of Catholic writing have not discriminated adequately between what Leona Rostenberg describes as "the zeal of the devout"[79] and what Elizabeth's minister saw as "false, seditious, and immodest offense." Excellent as they are in their own ways, Thomas H. Clancy's *Papist Pamphleteers* and Peter Milward's *Religious Controversies of the Elizabethan Age* are largely blind to what Elizabeth's government found offensive in the texts it took extraordinary efforts to suppress. Technically, of course, the High Commission, port patrols, and government searches of private homes were interested in Catholic books, but in most instances those books were sought as evidence of this practice, and Catholic practice interested the authorities principally because it engaged the dreaded priests and Jesuits. From the perspective of four hundred years, the English authorities' offenses against private property and individual liberty are egregious indeed. Today, "paranoia" seems too mild a word to describe the position of Elizabeth's government against Catholics in the 1580s and 1590s, but then, as an investigation of those texts that the government deemed truly objectionable shows, the Catholic propagandists were engaging in a war against her and against English institutions. Catholic writers directly and indirectly discredited Elizabeth's rule. Furthermore, the writings that issued from the Continent flagrantly violated English statutes that forbade writing about the succession, libel (particularly against members of the government), and treasonous writing. Considering these violations, Leona Rostenberg's widely accepted assessment of Elizabethan censorship of the Catholic press looks remarkably naive:

The zeal of the devout was not to be crushed. The books, expounding his tenets, continued to be printed on the Continent and within the homeland. Neither persecution, conflagration, search nor sequestration could diminish the dedication of the Catholic – his conviction, a burning taper held aloft, a votive candle to his God, a soaring flame of faith! His was the true religion not to be vanquished by the state and its instruments of destruction.[80]

What would have happened if Catholics had not been participants in efforts to put the Scottish Queen on the throne? Or if William Allen and Robert Parsons had not engaged in political activism? Burghley's comment that "The Cardinal's book may give cause of danger to all Catholics and Recusants" suggests that the political "zeal of the devout" may itself have guaranteed that those who subscribed to the zealots' tenets were *"punished not for their faith, but as malefactours."*[81]

CHAPTER 5

George Gascoigne and the rhetoric of censorship
A Hundreth Sundrie Flowres *(1573)* and
The Posies *(1575)*

Literary historians have spoken with some confidence about what appears to have been one of the Elizabethan state's first suppressions of a nonreligious printed text: George Gascoigne's *A Hundreth Sundrie Flowres* and its revised version, *The Posies*. *The Posies'* prefatory letter "To the reverende Divines," apologizing for the *Flowres* and claiming that this new edition, *The Posies*, would be "gelded from all filthie phrases, corrected in all erronious places, and beautified with addition of many moral examples,"[1] has led generations of scholars like Gascoigne's biographer C. T. Prouty to conclude that "If Gascoigne is writing an apology to the Queen's Commissioners, it seems evident that the book defended had been banned."[2] They have read Gascoigne's dedicatory letter to *The Posies* with uncommon confidence given they have rejected the claims of preliminaries in the *Flowres*. Adrian Weiss's more recent work demonstrating *all* the *Flowres'* prefatory materials to be an elaborate fiction constructed to serve Gascoigne's personal end of distancing himself from the printed text[3] invites a reconsideration of Gascoigne's claims in the prefatory materials to *The Posies*. Such a reconsideration argues that just as the preliminaries of *A Hundreth Sundrie Flowres* sought to shape its reception, *The Posies'* preliminaries were an elaborate "devise"[4] that sought to depoliticize its reception. Despite the 1575 text's prefatory claims that the revisions produced a substantially more moral text to please the censors, a close study of the revisions reveals a rhetorical strategy that sought to deflect reception away from political and personal slander. Complicit in this strategy, the *Posies'* prefatory materials actually draw the reader's attention to its sexualized discourse. Although the 1573 *Flowres* may have been censured for its slander, it was probably not censored for its sexuality. *The Posies* was not so fortunate; a 1576 entry in the Stationers' Court Book, Register B indicates that it was called in.[5] The explanation for this censorship

– as well as the noncensorship of the *Flowres* – rests in Gascoigne's subtle negotiations between the rhetoric of his text and its contexts.

The preliminaries to *A Hundreth Sundrie Flowres* reveal that Gascoigne was capable of constructing an elaborate fiction to conceal both himself as author and his own involvement with the text's publication. In "H. W. to the Reader," H. W. includes a letter from "G. T." describing how he obtained "sundry copies of these sundry matters" which he found to be of some merit and thus sends on to his friend "H. W." with the admonition to "by no meanes make the same common."[6] G. T.'s initial letter is dated August 1572. H. W.'s "to the Reader," dated 20 January 1572/3, explains:

In August last passed my familiar friend Master *G. T.* bestowed uppon me the reading of a written Booke, wherin he had collected divers discourses & verses, invented uppon sundrie occasions, by sundrie gentlemen (in mine opinion) right commendable for their capacitie. And herewithal my said friend charged me, that I should use them onely for mine owne particuler commoditie, and eftsones safely deliver the originall copie to him againe, wherein I must confesse my selfe but halfe a marchant, for the copie unto him I have safely redelivered. But the worke (for I thought it worthy to be publilished) [sic] I have entreated my friend *A. B.* to emprint: . . . And I must confesse that . . . I have contrary to the chardge of my said friend *G. T.* procured for these trifles this day of publication. (A1r–A1v, pp. 201–2)

The "Printer to the Reader" offers this history of the text:

Master .H.W. in the beginning of this worke, hath in his letter (written to the Readers) cunningly discharged himselfe of any such misliking, as the graver sort of greyheared judgers mighte (perhaps) conceive in the publication of these pleasant Pamphlets. And nexte unto that learned preamble, the letter of .G.T. (by whome as seemeth, the first coppie hereof was unto the same .H.W. delivered, doth with no lesse clerkly cunning seeke to perswade the readers, that he (also) woulde by no meanes have it published. Now I feare very muche (all these words notwithstanding) that these two gentlemen were of one assent compact to have it imprinted: And yet, finding by experience that nothing is so wel handled now adayes, but that some malicious minds may either take occasion to mislike it themselves, or else finde meanes to make it odious unto others: They have therefore (each of them) politiquely prevented the daunger of misreport, and suffered me the poore Printer to runne away with the palme of so perillous a victorie. (A2v)[7]

These prefatory materials misled William Hazlitt to conclude in his 1869 edition that the 1573 *Flowres* was a "spurious and unsanctioned impression."[8] Likewise, the *Dictionary of National Biography* essay on

Gascoigne notes that the *Flowres*, "a collected volume of his verse," was published in 1572 during Gascoigne's absence in the Netherlands without the author's authority.[9] In his 1942 edition of *Flowres*, Prouty acknowledges that Gascoigne perpetrates a ruse in the prefatory letters, but he accepts their dates (used to indicate publication) and the "Printer to the Reader" as authentic.

Adrian Weiss, relying on bibliographical evidence of shared printing and print font fouling, has demonstrated that "The Printer to the Reader" and the publication dates are part of the fiction. According to Weiss, "the bibliographical evidence reveals that copy was delivered to Bynneman in at least six separate manuscript segments" and that the printing took place over at least eight months.[10] The false dates were employed "to allow for a credible passage of time for H.W. to have decided upon publication, produced a fair-copy for the printer, made arrangements with the fictitious publisher A.B,' and gotten the project underway by 'the xx. of January.1572[/3].'" Weiss's arguments about *Flowres* are important not only because they demonstrate Gascoigne's ability to create an elaborate fiction about publication to serve his personal ends,[11] but because he establishes that Gascoigne wrote "The Printer to the Reader," which became separated from its intended location in *Flowres*. It was intended to precede "The Adventures of Master F. J." Thus, according to Weiss, "Gascoigne intended that 'the adventures of master F. J.' appear first in the book. Moreover, his references in the letter to *Supposes* and *Jocasta* leave absolutely no doubt that the two plays were to be printed along with 'F. J.' but *after* it."[12] *A Hundreth Sundrie Flowres* should have begun with "The Printer to the Reader" followed by the letters indicating surreptitious printing. These would have led into the four parts of *Flowres* in this order: "The Adventures of Master F. J.", "The devises of sundry Gentlemen," "certayne excellent devises of Master Gascoyne" and the incomplete "Dan Bartholmew."[13] All of this would have been followed by *Supposes* and *Jocasta*.[14] The 1573 text, thus, would have privileged "The Adventures of Master F. J." as the principal part of the virtuoso fiction of G. T.'s "found" English poetry lent credibility by its inclusion with plays by Euripides and Ariosto in a literary miscellany.

That the organization of the 1573 text of *A Hundreth Sundrie Flowres*, published by Richard Smith and printed by Henry Bynneman, departed from Gascoigne's original intent would itself have been grounds for the 1575 edition of *The Posies*, which, according to its title page, was "Corrected, perfected and augmented by the Authour." In the later edition he added fifty-four stanzas to "Dan Bartholmew" and separated it from the other three components of *Flowres*. Beyond that, as modern editors and scholars have frequently remarked, the contents changed very little. According to Prouty, *The Posies*,

contained, with four exceptions, all the poems and prose passages contained in *A Hundreth Sundrie Flowres*. Although few poems were omitted, the order of all poems was greatly altered by grouping them under three main headings: "Flowres," "Hearbes," and "Weedes." Gascoigne also added three poems dealing with the greene Knight, and three introductory epistles.[15]

Despite the Italianization of "The Adventures of Master F. J." with its changes from "F. J." to "Ferdinando Jeronimi," "Lady *Elynor*" (or "Dame Elynor") to "Elinora de Valasco" and England to Italy, modern commentators have often remarked how little Gascoigne actually changed despite his admission prefacing *The Poesies* "that sundrie well disposed mindes have taken offence at certaine wanton wordes and sentences passed in the fable of *Ferdinando Jeronimi*, and the Ladie *Elinora de Valasco*, the which in the first edition was termed The adventures of master F. J." (2¶r).

Any attempts to explain the differences between the *Flowres* and *The Posies* (beyond comments about their unremarkable nature) have begun with the premise that the first was censored and Gascoigne was thereby discredited. The 1575 edition accordingly represents his effort, however gratuitous, to redeem himself and his reputation. Commentators generally assent that Gascoigne wrote *A Hundreth Sundrie Flowres* to curry favor. Richard McCoy argues that *Flowres'* appeal for patronage made a "case for poetry's rhetorical virtuosity" both by displaying wit and eluding conventionality.[16] Presumably this freedom and the censorship it purportedly engendered has led commentators to conclude that the book was for Gascoigne "a professional disaster."[17] According to Prouty, Gascoigne returned from his service in the Netherlands to learn that "his book, *A Hundreth Sundrie Flowres*, had raised a storm of objection . . . Gascoigne was in trouble over his *Flowres* and became further involved . . . with the supposedly revised text."[18] According to McCoy, "through this show of submission" of the revised *Posies*, Gascoigne "hoped to retain his poetic autonomy," but in "the book which he saw as his best means to literary fame and patronage . . . once again his efforts failed" to gain him the patronage he sought.[19]

However strongly Prouty and McCoy argue for the failure of Gascoigne's career, the evidence is curiously contrary. In 1575 he appears to have been employed by Robert Dudley, the Earl of Leicester, in writing entertainments for the Queen's visit to his newly acquired house at Kenilworth. Such employment looks like the end Gascoigne sought in both the *Flowres* and the *Posies*. Further, according to Prouty,

on August 22, 1576, shortly after the publication of *A delicate Diet*, Gascoigne received what he had so long desired – royal employment. His strenuous literary efforts or his friends, Bedford, Grey, and Gilbert had proved to the world that "the ydle poett" was no more . . . the poet was sent by the government to observe affairs in the Low Countries.[20]

Interestingly, this royal favor came just nine days after fifty copies of *The Posies* were "Receyved into the [Stationers'] hall by appointment of the Q.M. Commissioners."[21] This censorship, following as it does in the wake of Gascoigne's apparent success, suggests that we have misread both the relationship between Gascoigne's political career and his texts – and the censorship of those texts.

The Posies' letter "To the reverende Divines" serves as the foundation for existing arguments about the *Flowres'* censorship, and thus must serve as a starting point for reassessing the censorship. Since it also provides a key to understanding the revisions Gascoigne made in the *Posies*, it represents a key to the 1576 suppression. The part of his letter "To the reverende Divines" most frequently considered is his recognition that the earlier work had been ill received:

It is verie neare two yeares past, since (I beeing in Hollande in service with the vertuous Prince of Orenge) the most parte of these Posies were imprinted, and now at my returne, I find that some of them have not onely bene offensive for sundrie wanton speeches and lascivious phrases, but further I heare that the same have beene doubtfully construed, and (therefore) scandalous. (¶2r)

The usual importance gleaned from the letter is that the earlier work offended principally because it was "wanton" and "lascivious," and that the "reverende Divines" "hathe thought requysite that all ydle Bookes or wanton Pamphlettes shoulde bee forbidden" (¶2v). The conclusion has been that since some of the *Flowres* offended in their "wantonness," they were forbidden. Nothing in the letter actually says that the 1573 text was suppressed, only that it offended. Further, the cause of that offense is skillfully both revealed and concealed by Gascoigne's elaborate justification of the "considerations" that "did first move me to consent that these Poemes shoulde passe in print" (¶4r). Articulated in circuitous arguments, these, rather than apologizing for the lascivious 1573 text, argue the poet's unsullied motives: because in all ages poetry "hath beene thought a right good and excellent qualitie," he has written poetry – English poetry, at that – to "content the learned and Godlye Reader," to offer "a myrrour for unbrydled youth," and to gain "preferment, and to the profite of my Countrey" (¶3r–¶4r). Throughout this apology and answer to anticipated responses to it, Gascoigne maintains the fiction that the *Flowres* had been the poems of his youth. He indicates that he desires a new edition (still the poems of his youth) be printed for the same reasons that he "consented" to have them printed before, but that this corrected edition will provide moral examples and restrain from linguistic license. As in the "Printer to the Reader" and the introductory letters in the *Flowres*, Gascoigne has here constructed an elaborate artifice. We know from Weiss that Gascoigne was writing the *Flowres* in 1573; hence, neither the *Flowres* nor *The Posies* represent a youthful effort. Furthermore, in reiterating his absence during the *Flowres*'s printing and in using the notion of "consent" with regard to their publication, Gascoigne perpetuates the fiction that his poems had been sought out (by G. T. and H. W.?) and that he neither initiated their printing nor benefited financially from it. These persistent fictions call into question all of *The Posies*' prefatory materials and suggest that as Gascoigne's creation, they must be read as skeptically as those to the *Flowres*.

Since the *Flowres*' prefatory materials had deliberately misled by their dates, the dates of the prefatory materials in *The Posies* become suspect. The letter to the divines concludes "From my poore house at Waltamstow in the Forest, this last day of Januarie. 1574" (¶21v). The letter "To al yong Gentlemen, and generally to the youth of England" ends "From my poore house at Waltamstow in the Forest the second of Januarie. 1575" ([2¶2r, 2¶4v]). This represents an attempt to separate the two letters, suggesting that the first letter accompanied the manuscript to the official reviewers and some time passed between its submission, their approval, and the book's printing. The discrepancy in dates, of course, may be credited to printer error, but even if such an error is allowed, the presence of a letter to the ecclesiastical authorizers in a printed book bears a strange relationship to authorization practices. Ecclesiastical authorization preceded printing, hence *The Posies* would have already been approved. Rather than a letter of explanation seeking official approval, Gascoigne's letter "To the reverende Divines" looks like another device – but for what purpose?

The letter to the "divines" must be read alongside the other prefatory letter – "To al yong gentlemen" – and the address "To the Readers generally" (3¶1r). The letter to young gentlemen also reiterates the notion that Gascoigne "permitted" the *Flowres* to be published, and that they were misconstrued. It emphasizes too that the *Flowres* were misunderstood for their wantonness and lasciviousness, and were therefore disapproved by "grave Philosophers . . . finding just fault in my doings at the common infection of love":

They wysely considering that wee are all in youth more apt to delight in harmefull pleasures, then to digest wholesome and sounde advice, have thought meete to forbid the publishing of any ryming tryfles which may serve as whetstones to sharpen youth unto vanities.

And for this cause, finding by experience also, how the first Copie of these my Posies hath beene verie much inquired for by the yonger sort: and hearing likewise that (in the same) the greater part hath beene written in pursute of amorous enterpryses, they have justly conceyved that the continuance thereof hath beene more likely to stirre in all yong Readers a venemous desire of vanitie, than to serve as a common myrrour of greene and youthfull imperfections . . .

To speake English, it is your using (my lustie Gallants) or misusing of these Posies that may make me praysed or dispraysed for publishing of the same. (2¶3r–2¶3v)

At the same time that this cautions the young readers not to "misuse" *The Posies*, it refers to them as "my lustie Gallants" and reminds them that the *Flowres* were sought by "the yonger sort" – implicitly for their "pursute of amorous enterpryses." At the same time that this furthers the fiction that the poems were the product of his youth and their publication is cautionary ("that because I have [to mine owne great detriment] mispent my golden time, I may serve as ensample to the youthfull Gentlemen of England, that they runne not upon the rocks which have brought me to shipwracke," 2¶4v), it says nothing about the verses that have been "gelded" as the letter to the divines. In the *Posies*, "reformed" into "*Floures, Hearbes,* and *Weedes,*" the weeds are unpurged (2¶4r). Nor does the final address "To the Readers generally" make any mention of reforming the *Flowres'* wantonness; instead it offers the excuse that certain objectionable passages derive from other men's commissions and not the author's interests and intents.

Each of these preliminaries envisions a different kind of reader: a learned scholar, a young gentleman, a common reader – (precisely the same categories of readers Gascoigne refers to in the letter to the young men). Each speaks to the respective interests of its audience. The first, with its arguments for English poetry, its references to the ancients, and its allusion to the Calvinist theologian Theodore Beza, addresses the learned (and reverend) reader; the second, with its insistence on the presence of immorality for moral purposes, the "lustie Gallants"; and the third, with its implicit message that the wanton still remains, everyone who would admit to misreading the moral intent as illicit. While men might acknowledge the misreading of youth (and of their youth), few would want to be the worst sort of readers – those who, being diverted by wanton words, missed the moral purpose. In short, the three letters serve to "advertise" that *The Posies* still contain the weeds "inquired for by the younger sort" (presumably, maintaining their worth in the marketplace) at the same time that they condemn as "general" (common) those readers who misread the weeds as immoral.

This unmistakable moral emphasis that simultaneously invokes and condemns a sexualized reading of *The Posies* has misled modern readers like McCoy to believe that Gascoigne was predominantly concerned about moral objections and thus reformed (or pretended to reform) his work to respond to them. On the contrary, Gascoigne, reformed his text and contributed the preliminaries to engage his readers in speculation about morality in order to deflect their interest from the more dangerous objections that had been raised about *A Hundreth Sundrie Flowres* – those misreadings that had tended to slander. This can be seen both in the letter to the divines and in the actual revisions Gascoigne made.

If the letter to the divines is read omitting the extended rhetoric defending *Flowres*, the objections become much clearer. The author returned from abroad not only to discover that his poems had offended in their language but further they had been "doubtfully construed, and (therefore) scandalous." In particular "busie conjectures have presumed" that "The Adventures of Master F. J." was "written to the scandalizing of some worthie personages, whom they woulde seeme therby to know." (2¶1r) The offending matter is clear: "wanton speeches and lascivious phrases . . . doubtfully construed" – particularly those in "The Adventures of Master F. J."[22] Gascoigne's use of "wanton" and "lascivious" (like his claims of surreptitious publishing) are deliberately misleading. The Domestic State Papers and Acts of the Privy Council are filled with the Council's attention to "lewd" words and "wanton" reports, but inevitably the libels and slanders are character assassinations. Thus, the words Gascoigne selects to indicate transgressive language in his texts can refer to either sexualized discourse or personal attack – or both.

The *Flowres* offended not merely in its "wanton" words, but in the offense conceived when "wanton speeches and lascivious phrases" were misconstrued as applying to worthy personages and were therefore read as scandalous. The revisions removed very few offensive words (indeed, as we have seen, they call attention to them), but they did try to reform the ways the readers construed them.

The Posies' reorganization of *Flowres* does two things: like the preliminaries, it invokes a moral reading of the text, and it directs attention away from the most offensive text, "The Adventures of Master F. J." The creation of the subsections of "*Floures, Hearbes*, and *Weedes*," particularly with their introduction in the preliminaries, emphasizes *The Posies'* moral focus. This, like the *Flowres'* letter to the divines, seeks to disengage the reader's attention from the kind of suppositional reading that created scandal. The *Flowres* text may well have invited far greater speculation than Gascoigne had intended if Weiss is correct: had the printers been working from a completed text, the plays, *Supposes* and *Jocasta*, would have followed "The Adventures of Master F. J." Lorna Hutson has suggested that by giving "pride of place" to the *Supposes*, Gascoigne invited the kind of speculative reading that would have demonstrated the rhetorical skill which would have gained him patronage.[23] Undoubtedly, the text of "Master F. J.," suggestive as it was of events at court, would itself have invited this kind of reading, its misfortune was to be preceded by the *Supposes* in the 1573 edition, inviting not merely "busie conjectures" but the kind of overreading that invoked charges of scandal. The 1575 edition removed "Master F. J." from any "pride of place" and sought, by placing it among the immoral "weeds," a moral/immoral reading rather than a suppositional one.

Gascoigne's revisions of "Master F. J." were also directed to changing the way in which the text was read. That he would shift the setting from England to Italy, and the characters Elinor and F. J. to Elinora and Ferdinando are strikingly transparent for the kind of sophistication Gascoigne has demonstrated elsewhere. More than simply saying, "Do not read these characters as known English people," it says, "Do read this as a sexualized narrative." Early modern English literature frequently stereotyped Italians as idle, wanton, and lascivious. In thus shifting the nationality, Gascoigne is not offering a transparent excuse for "Master F. J." 's sexuality; he is calling attention to it. Despite this, to lend credability to his assertions that he has purged his text, the 1575 version does remove one explicitly sexual scene. That Gascoigne did make this change might well lend credence to the case that *Flowres* was censored for being "wanton" and "lascivious," except that this passage (like so much of "Master F. J.") differs little in kind from Chaucer's "Merchant's Tale" or the tales of Ovid that were the mainstay of every schoolboy's Latin. More likely, this passage, like others changed between the 1573 and 1575 texts, invited more speculation about particular personages than the aspiring author could stand.

Such minor changes in the actual content, particularly to "Master F. J.," suggest that *A Hundreth Sundrie Flowres*'s text did not meet with actual official suppression but with too "busie conjectures" and censure. Had it actually been suppressed, it seems likely that Gascoigne – a man using his writing to seek political advancement – would have been far more circumspect and the revisions far more drastic. The 1575 text still reveals the free range of his wit and art in courtship. Its literary sophistication still invites reading on multiple levels – at the same time that it discourages *too* much conjecture.

If Gascoigne's employment by Leicester in 1575 and his political position in the Low Countries in 1576 represent, as they appear to, political advancement, *The Posies* achieved Gascoigne's goal. What then are we to make of their censorship – which, unlike that of the *Flowres*, is clearly documented? The answer, if any exists at all, lies in his revisions – what he did not change, what he did, and what he must not have changed enough. Understanding these changes and their implications requires looking rather closely at the 1573 "Master F. J."

"The Adventures of Master F. J." narrates in prose a story that both accounts for and links a group of courtly love poems that are integrated into it. The narrative begins with letters linking the poems and story to the epistolary frame of the *Flowres* as a "found" object. This rhetorical strategy serves to suggest the authenticity of the ensuing narrative of courtship, seduction, and rejection.

And to begin with this his history that ensueth, it was (as he declared unto me) written uppon this occasion. The said *F.J.* chaunced once in the north partes of this Realme to fall in company of a very fayre gentlewoman whose name was Mistresse *Elinor*, unto whom bearinge a hotte affection, he first adventured to write this letter following. (A3r, p. 205)

F. J.'s letter, written in Petrarchan oxymorons of frosty fire, establishes him as the amorous lover. The correspondence that ensues, and the poetry it produces, employ courtly conventions of devoted swain and disdainful mistress (Elinor's part penned by her secretary).

Later, courtly love conventions are exchanged for dangerous liaisons when Elinor's secretary departs for a time, and she succumbs to an illness. F. J.'s bedside cure of her nosebleed segues into a nighttime assignation:

And when he thought aswell his servaunt, as the rest of the houshold to be safe, he arose again, & taking his night gowne, did under the same covey his naked sword, and so walked to the gallerie, where he found his good Mistresse walking in hir night gowne and attending his comming. (E1r, p. 233)

They embrace and the lady shrieks at discovering his sword, saying, "Alas servaunt what have I deserved, that you come aginst me with naked sword as against an open enimie." F. J. quiets her by maintaining that he brought the sword for her defense:

The Ladie being therwith som what apeased, they began with more comfortable gesture to expell the dread of the said late affright, and sithens to become bolder of behaviour, more familier in speech, & most kind in accomplishing of comon comfort. (E1r–E1v, p. 233–4)

Complications threaten because Elinor's sister Fraunces spied F. J. returning to his chamber afterwards, naked sword still apparent under his nightshirt. She engages in an intrigue of her own (and a bit of sisterly rivalry) by stealing F. J.'s sword from his chamber and teasing him with her secret knowledge.[24] He fears discovery, and taking Elinor aside, confesses that his sword was taken, "and that he dreaded much by the wordes of the Lady *Fraunces*, that she had some understanding of the matter" (F1r, p. 241). Lady Elinor secures the sword's secret return, and "Many dayes passed these two lovers with great delight, their affayres being no lesse politikely governed, than happely atchived . . . in which time *F. J.* did compyle very many verses according to sundrie occasions proffred" (F1v, F3v, pp. 242, 246).

The dalliance of Elinor and F. J. survives her husband's return, but falls victim to F. J.'s jealousy of her secretary. F. J. "found

meanes so to ensignuate himselfe" with the husband, "that familiar-
itie tooke deepe roote betwene them," and the two passed time
hunting, only to have the husband lose his "horn" (F4v, p. 248).
When the secretary returned, F. J. "fel into a great passion of mynd"
and withdrew to his chamber (G1r, p. 249). To speed his recovery,
the gentlewomen of the household entertained him with stories of
disappointed love. Following such an evening Elinor returned alone
to minister to her lover's illness, and F. J. "could no lesse do, than of
his curteous nature receyve his Mistresse into his bed" (I3r, p. 269).
Emboldened by this renewed affection, he confessed that he had
recently seen a change in her affections: "Yea and (that more was) he
playnly expressed with whom, of whom, by whom, and too whom
shee bent hir better liking" (I3v, p. 270). In response, Elinor
developed a "disdayneful moode" against F. J. and returned to her
secretary (I4v, p. 272).

Now genuinely rejected by Elinor, F. J.'s illness returned, and once
again the gentlewomen, except Elinor, went to his chamber and
engaged in storytelling. This time they tell "a straunge historie, not
fayned, neither borowed out of any olde aucthoritie, but a thing
done in deede of late daies" (K3v, p. 278). It is a story of a beautiful
gentlewoman Besse who, though happily married for four or five
years, was so wooed by a "lustie younge gentleman" that "he woon
so much in hir affections, that forgetting both hir owne dutie and hir
husbandes kindnes, she yeelded hir body at the commaundement of
this lover, in which pastime they passed long time by their polliticke
governement." (K3v, p. 278). The lady's friends, "and especially
three sisters which she had," seeing the familiarity counseled Besse to
cease her attentions. She did not, and the sisters spied on the lovers
and reported the affair to her husband, who continued his kindness
to the young man but took his revenge against Besse by leaving
money every time he "had knowledge of hir" (L1r, p. 281). When the
wife asked about this, her husband revealed that he knew everything,
but still he forgave her indiscretions, and she being reconciled with
her husband, spurned the lover. The lover appealed to Besse, and
she, confessing her grief, gained his oath that he "should never
attempt to break hir constant determination" (L2v, p. 284).

Misreading the story's moral import, F. J. recovers from his illness
and acknowledges the offense of his jealousy: "concluding further,
[that] if his mistres wer not faulty, then had he committed a foule
offence in needlesse jelousie, & that if she were faulty (especially with

the *Secretary*) then no persuasion could amend hir" (L3v, p. 286). F. J. continues his courtship in poetry but then discovers Elinor dallying with the secretary. He confronts her; she denies the relationship; and F. J. takes his leave. The narrative reaches an indeterminate conclusion with a final F. J. poem followed by the narrator's abrupt intrusion, "I will trouble you no more with such a barbarous style in prose, but will onely recite unto you sundry verses written by sundry gentlemen . . ." (M3r, p. 293). "The Adventures of Master F. J." thus ends as it began, woven into the fiction of the *Flowres*' wider frame.

Despite Gascoigne's claims of having reformed "Master F. J." for *The Posies*, "The pleasant Fable of *Ferdinando Jeronomi* and *Leonora de Valasco*, translated out of the Italian riding tales of *Bartello*" contains virtually all the plot recounted above (N1r, p. 193). except "Leonora" (Englished throughout as "Elinor") is not married. (In one passage she becomes a "mery" woman, not a married woman [*Flowres*, D4v, p. 216; *Posies*, D3v, p. 230].) Since she is unmarried, the entire sequence about the husband's return, the camaraderie between him and F. J., the hunting, and the horn jokes disappear. Further, all initials used for naming and identifying characters in the 1573 edition become names in the 1575. For example, two gentlemen,. H. D. and H. K., in the 1573 text (D3r, p. 229) become *Hercule Donaty* and *Haniball de Cosmis* in the 1575 (O4r–O4v, pp. 215–16). Further, one particular name is changed entirely. In the final interior story, the name of the unfaithful wife, Besse ("for so in deede was hir name," 1573: K4r, p. 279; 1575: K3v, p. 262), becomes Lamia, and the parenthetical comment calling attention to the name shared with Elizabeth becomes meaningless. These revisions, hardly striking for providing a less lascivious narrative, epitomize the changes generally made that distance the work from England and from English people.

By changing Elinor's marital status, the 1575 version effects a secondary revision that affects the way the entire narrative is read. In the 1573 version the interior tale of Besse, her husband, and her lover parallels the circumstances of Elinor and F. J. Besse's is a story of adultery discovered by righteous sisters. The good husband well-disposed to his wife's lover is like Elinor's husband. Just as Besse's three sisters spy on the lovers, Fraunces spies on F. J. and Elinor. Although the 1575 version retains the inner tale of adultery and discovery, its moral significance for Ferdinando is not quite so pointedly referential to his circumstances. The effect is to suggest to F. J. – as the entire 1575 revision does to its readers – that he should read for moral significance but *not* for parallels to personal circumstances.

As for "purging," Gascoigne leaves both the assignation scene with its naked sword and the bed scene. He does, however, abbreviate the narrator's comments about the assignation. In the 1573 version, the narrator comments:

But why hold I so long discourse in discribing the joyes which (for lacke of like experience) I cannot set out to [the] ful? Were it not that I knowe to whom I write, I would the more beware what I write. *F. J.* was a man, and neither of us are sencelesse, and therfore I shold slaunder him, (over and besides a greater obloquie to the whole genealogie of *Enæas*) if I should imagine that of tender hart he would forbeare to expresse hir more tender limbes against the hard floore. Suffised that of hir curteouse nature she was content to accept bords for a bead of downe, mattes for Camerike sheetes, and the night gowne of *F. J.* for a counterpoynt to cover them, and thus with calme content, in steede of quiet sleepe, they beguiled the night, untill the proudest sterre began to abandon the fyrmament, when *F. J.* and his Mistresse, were constrayned also to abandon their delightes, and with ten thousand sweet kisses and straight embracings, did frame themselves to play loth to depart. (E iv, p. 234)

The 1575 version stops with the first sentence (O6v, p. 220).

Such Chaucerian specificity as the 1573 text has may well have been judged inappropriate in an Elizabethan courtly romance, but I suspect the offense lay more in the presence of such specificity in a story about "Ladies" and "Gentlemen" – particularly one that ends with the rather peculiar apology that closes the 1573 version:

It is time now to make an end of this thriftlesse Historie, wherein although I could wade much further . . . Yet I will cease, as one that had rather leave it unperfect than make it to plaine. I have past it over with quod he, and quod she, after my homely manner of writing, using sundry names for one person, as the Dame, the Lady, Mistresse, &c. The Lorde of the Castle, the Master of the house, and the hoste: neverthelesse for that I have seene good aucthors terme every gentlewoman a Lady, and every gentleman *domine*, I have thought it no greater faulte then pettie treason thus to entermyngle them, nothing doubting but you will easely, understand my meaning . . . (M2v–M3r, pp. 292–3)

The 1575 omission of this ending is particularly telling. Instead of inviting judgment about the behavior of ladies and gentlemen generally, or inviting particular names to be conjoined with *Flowres*' "sundry names for one person," it provides narrative closure and a moral:

Notwithstanding al which occurements the Lady *Elinor* lived long in [the] continuance of hir acustomed change: & thus we see that where wicked lust doeth beare the name of love, it doth not onelye infecte the lyght minded, but it maye also become confusion to others which are vowed to constancie. (S2v, p. 276)

This kind of closure is appropriate for a story entitled (on the running head) "The fable of Ferdinando Jeronimy" that begins, "In the pleasant Countrie of *Lombardie*, (and not farre from the Citie of *Florence*) there was dwelling sometimes a Lorde of many riche Seignories . . ." (N1r, p. 193). The beginning and ending of Ferdinando's story, regardless of the thinly veiled changes, make the story into a story – a fiction safe in its geographical and narrative distance from the English reader – particularly the courtly English reader. This differs significantly from the narrative bridges in to and out of the 1573 text, which, by opening the narrative to the "reality" of arranging and publishing the text, render it as "history" rather than story, leaving the reader to perform the "pettie treason" of naming every "Lady" and "*domine.*"

Clearly, then, the most substantial revisions between the two versions of Gascoigne's book – the revisions in the F. J. narrative, the altered structure, and the demand on the reader to read morally (or immorally) rather than conjecturally – indicate that the 1573 text aroused problems because of the way it had been read. It is a mistake, however, to read the 1573 F. J. piece as a roman à clef; Gascoigne had, in his own words, "entermyngled" his narrative. His was a fiction – but with referentiality – that invited speculation. What that might have been can be surmised by looking at events at Elizabeth's court in 1572–73. Particularly useful in this regard is a letter written home from the court by Gilbert Talbot to his father, the Earl of Shrewsbury, dated 11 May 1573:

My Lord Leicester is very much with her Majesty, and she sheweth the same great good affection to him that she was wont: of late, he hath endeavoured to please her more than heretofore. There are two sisters now in the Court that are very far in love with him, as they have been long, my Lady Sheffield and Frances Howard: they of like striving who shall love him better are at great wars together, and the Queen thinketh not well of them, and not the better of him; by this means ther is spies over him . . . My Lord of Oxford is lately grown into great credit; for the Queen's Majesty delighteth more in his personage, and his dancing and valiantness, than any other . . . My Lady Burghley unwisely has declared herself (as it were) jealous, which is come to the Queen's ear; wherat she hath been not a little offended with her, but now she is reconciled again. At all these love matters my Lord Treasurer winketh, and will not meddle any way. Hatton is sick still; it is thought he will very hardly recover his disease, for it is doubted it is in his kidneys: the Queen goeth almost every day to see how he doth. Now is there devices, chiefly by Leicester (as I suppose), and not without Burghley's knowledge, how to make Mr. Edward Dyer as great as ever Hatton; for now, in this time of Hatton's sickness, the time is convenient. It is brought thus to pass: Dyer lately was sick of a consumption, in great danger; and, as your lordship knoweth, he hath been in displeasure these two years: it was made the Queen believe that his sickness came because of the continuance of her displeasure towards him, that, unless she would forgive him, he was like not to recover; and hereupon her Majesty hath forgiven him, and sent unto him a very comfortable message: now he is recovered again, and this is the beginning of this device.[25]

Waxing and waning in royal favor, rivalries, jealousy, sickness at heart for loss of favor, special royal attention at a sickbed – this is the material of F. J.'s world. Furthermore, the Queen herself had been ill with smallpox in the fall of 1572. Sir Christopher Hatton fell ill shortly after. Operating as it did, in a climate of rumor and innuendo, Elizabeth's court invited Gascoigne's kind of writing; his did not need to be a roman à clef, particularly given the kind of "secret" reading the opening and closing to "The Adventures of Master F. J." invited. His courtly readers "easely" understanding his meaning could perform the "pettie treason" of naming every "Lady" and "*domine.*"

What further scandals Gascoigne's courtly readers may have seen in his 1573 text are suggested by the kinds of rumors circulating in London in the 1570s. Many of these were associated with Hatton and Leicester – both the Queen's creations. In January 1572 a man named Mather, being examined in an effort to release the imprisoned Duke of Norfolk, said Hatton "had more recourse unto her Majesty in her Privy Chamber than reason would suffer . . ."[26] Hatton's letters to the Queen, affectionate as they were, lend some credibility to such gossip that he was her paramour.[27] Gabriel Harvey's marginalia on his copy of *The Posies* identifies the motto "*Si fortunatus infoelix*," which appears after the poem following "Master F. J.," as "lately the posie of Sir Christopher Hatton."[28] Besides rumors about his relationship with the Queen, according to his biographer Eric Brooks, when on the Queen's business at Sheffield Castle in 1572, Hatton had an affair with Elizabeth Cavendish. Brooks concludes, "If Sheffield Castle was the scene of Hatton's brief wooing, it would fit the passage in the story that Master F. I. [F. J.] met his lady in the north parts of the realm . . . Elinor had a sister Fraunces and . . . Elizabeth had a sister Frances Pierrepont."[29]

Even more than Hatton, Leicester was the subject of scandalous rumors. In his introduction to *Leicester's Commonwealth*, one of the most outspoken pieces of libel against an Elizabethan courtier, D. C. Peck remarks that the "Anti-Dudley propaganda . . . accumulating throughout Leicester's life and beyond it, make up a whole body of 'secret lore.'" Further, "attacks upon him were more comprehensive, *ad hominem*, and scurrilous because curtailing his authority was less a matter of argument or voting than of altering the Queen's affection for him."[30] In December 1574 Antonio de Guaras, the Spanish merchant and intermediary, reported home of a plot to marry the Earl of Hertford to "a daughter of Leicester and the queen of England, who, it is said, is kept hidden, although there are bishops to witness that she is legitimate."[31] Of another scandal regarding Leicester, Prouty remarks,

> One notorious scandal was the Earl of Leicester's seduction of Douglas Sheffield, which took place in 1568 on the occasion of Queen Elizabeth's progress to Belvoir Castle. The story, as told by Sir Gervase Holles . . . contains similarities as striking to us as they must have been to Gascoigne's contemporaries.[32]

Actually, the story Holles related in his 1658 account of his family, much more closely resembled the interior story told to entertain F. J. – a happy marriage is disturbed by a sudden passion between the visiting young man and the beautiful wife, and a sister discloses the relationship to the husband, who then seeks revenge.[33] Written nearly ninety years later, Holles's story suggests the persistence of gossip and scandal about Leicester.[34]

The pervasiveness and longevity of such court rumors tell why Gascoigne's *A Hundreth Sundrie Flowres* might have incited censure, but they do not assure that the book was censored. Since libel frequently was the cause of legal action during Elizabeth's reign, that Gascoigne was free in 1574–5 to revise the book indicates that his strategy of "entermyngling" lords and ladies served to protect him from serious libel actions (and censorship). His strategy sought to deflect further all but the most general kinds of contemporary associations without sacrificing his witty representation of courtly love. It must have been a success since Gascoigne received preferment, and since *The Posies'* apparently enjoyed commercial success. (Only 50 copies still remained in Smith's shop in 1576 when they were seized.)[35]

That *The Posies* was ultimately called in, I suspect, has less to do with the success or failure of Gascoigne's revision strategy than with a new round of rumors and slander and with Gascoigne's rising stature.

In December 1575 De Guaras wrote,

As the thing is publicly talked about in the streets there is no objection to my writing openly about the great enmity which exists between the earl of Leicester and the earl of Essex, in consequence, it is said, of the fact that whilst Essex was in Ireland his wife had two children by Leicester. She is the daughter of Sir Francis Knollys, a near relative of the Queen, and a member of the Council, and a great discord is expected in consequence.[36]

This report was just rumor, but it was part of a heightened environment of scandal that included the Colchester libels and those circulating against the Queen, and the latter produced enough concern at Court to warrant a royal proclamation against libels in March 1576.[37] Such a milieu may well have revived speculative reading of Gascoigne's work, leading to the suppression of the remaining copies.

But assigning such a political motivation to *The Posies* appears to run counter to the circumstances of their suppression. A 13 August 1576 entry in the Stationers' Company Court Book records that 50 copies of *The Posies* were called in with two other books: 225 copies of *A handfull of Delight[s]*, printed by Richard Jones, and 200 copies of *Restorities to love*, printed by Henry Kyrkham. The order was "by appointment of the Q. M. Commissioners." Richard McCoy has identified these texts' common denominator – their amatory nature – as the cause for their censorship. He ignores, however, the problematic nature of this suppression – Jones and Kyrkham were returned their books the following year. Furthermore, there is some question of whether or not the Commissioners were ecclesiastical.[38] I suspect they were, but they may not have been the London High Commission for on 1 August 1575 letters patent had created an ecclesiastical commission "to inquire concerning offences against the Acts (I Eliz) of Uniformity and Supremacy and of all heretical opinions, seditious books, contempts, conspiracies, false rumours, seditious misbehaviours, slanderous words and sayings . . ." in the diocese of Lincoln.[39] This was a distinguished commission headed by Burghley, which included the Earl of Bedford and Lord Grey, two of Gascoigne's patrons. Three members constituted a panel of inquiry, and though its principal object of concern was the Diocese of Lincoln, it would not have been impossible for this commission to stay the sales of Gascoigne's book. But what of the other two texts? Could the commissioners have been uncertain of the title? Or the searchers? The three shops from which the books were seized were adjacent to each other in Paul's Cross Churchyard.[40] Whatever the motivation for this suppression, or whoever the commissioners were, Gascoigne undoubtedly benefited more by having his "wanton . . . and lascivious" words out of the limelight and out of circulation, especially if parallels might be drawn between *The Posies'* remaining story of marital infidelity and the Earl of Leicester. In August 1576 Gascoigne could stand no "battery to the ramparts" of his credit (*Posies*, 2¶4r).

Gascoigne's *Hundreth Sundrie Flowres* and *Posies* challenge prevailing understanding of the mechanisms of early modern press censorship. That either of these works later found offensive should have been printed at all discounts any notion of effective pre-print review and licensing of literary works. One might argue that the printers may not have sought review for the *Flowres*, which, given authorization practices in the 1570s, may well have been the case. Arguing the same for *The Posies*, depending as it does on a rhetoric of censorship, poses a problem. If Gascoigne's *Posies* received pre-print review, as "To the reverende Divines" indicates, its censorship a year after its printing argues a defect in the machinery of control. On the other hand, if the book did not receive pre-print scrutiny, Gascoigne appears to have exercised extraordinary liberty in combining his letter to the reviewers with his meager revisions. The suppression might look like a constraint imposed for such liberty except that it occurred when he was reaping the political reward that *The Posies* had sown.

A Hundreth Sundrie Flowres and *The Posies* also raise some problems in relation to Annabel Patterson's hermeneutics of censorship. According to her, early modern writers, operating in a "culture governed by censorship . . . fully and knowingly exploited . . . the indeterminacy inveterate to language."[41] In this culture "the prevailing codes of communication, the implicit social contract between authors and authorities" were "intelligible to all parties at the time, as being a fully deliberate and conscious arrangement."[42] Official suppression was a sign that "the codes governing sociopolitical communication had broken down, that one side or the other had broken the rules."[43] Gascoigne undeniably exploits "the indeterminacy inveterate to language" in promising in his *Posies* a text purged of the lewd and lascivious but providing a repackaging of the *Flowres'* contents that sought more reform in his readers than he provided in his text. Whether or not this exploitation was within the bounds of understood codes, however, is not altogether clear. Few printed texts in Elizabethan England articulate the codes governing writing as fully as "To the reverende Divines," and few violate them as directly as *The Posies*. Gascoigne articulates a code of morality but sexualizes his discourse. He scorns suppositional reading but employs a strategy of revision to deflect too "busie conjectures." This appears to argue that the codes were so well understood that Gascoigne could manipulate them with considerable sophistication – indeed, so much that he could curry political favor – except that *The Posies* was suppressed. Did Gascoigne break the rules? Or, did the commissioners? Patterson does admit that "the analogic potential" of a text changes with the "reader's historical circumstances."[44] I would suggest, however, that the codes themselves changed with historical circumstances. This can be seen with the *Flowres/ The Posies* in two respects. First, if indeed a code regarding sexuality existed, it appears to have been unstable. (Explicit sexual encounters were acceptable in Chaucer and Ovid but not in Gascoigne.) If, as I have argued, the *Flowres'* moral lewdness and lasciviousness was a red herring, and the real issue rested in offense to members of the Court, then *The Posies'* changing reception argues an unstable political code. Undoubtedly, writers understood that they could not name the Queen and her courtiers, but also understood that some measure of ambiguous representation was acceptable (otherwise there could have been no *Faerie Queene*). What that "measure" was, rather than existing in socio-political codes, rested in the text's reception – and that depended on patronage, personalities, historical events, and policital conditions. With regard to Gascoigne's *Flowres/ The Posies* this means that what was censurable in 1573 was revised and became acceptable in 1575, and what was acceptable in 1575 became censorable in 1576. As we have seen, the text changed minimally, but Gascoigne's status and the climate of reception changed substantially.

CHAPTER 6

John Stubbs's The Discovery of
a Gaping Gulf *and Realpolitik*
"The kings sin striketh the land"
but *"God Save the Queen"*

The 1579 suppression of John Stubbs's *The Discovery of A Gaping Gulf* is often taken as an exemplary instance of Elizabethan press censorship. An outspoken attack on Elizabeth's intended marriage with Francis, Duke of Alençon and Anjou, *A Gaping Gulf* appeared in August 1579. On 27 September, she issued a proclamation ordering the destruction of the book before a public officer. Letters to the Lord Mayor and to England's principal bishops sought swift and effective compliance. At the same time that the proclamation's lively propaganda defended "Monsieur" and justified the marriage, it laid the groundwork for a government legal case against the author, printer, and disseminator of the "libel" by describing *A Gaping Gulf* as "a lewd, seditious book" containing "a heap of slanders and reproaches of the said prince bolstered up with manifest lies . . . and therewith also seditiously and rebelliously stirring up all estates of her majesty's subjects."[1] On 30 October 1579, the book's author, John Stubbs, its printer, Hugh Singleton, and its distributor William Page[2] were tried before the King's Bench under the Statute against "seditious libel" passed by Parliament under Mary (ca. 3) and extended to Elizabeth. The jury found them guilty; Stubbs and Page, according to the statute's designated punishment, lost their right hands on 4 November 1579. Singleton was apparently pardoned.

The effective means called upon to suppress the text and the swift and efficient justice met by the libel's perpetrators point to the degree of the government's dissatisfaction with *A Gaping Gulf* – one that has been widely misread. Instead of accepting the censorship as a serious local political action, it has been read as a measure of wider socio-political practices. That Stubbs was tried and lost his hand, Annabel Patterson takes as illustrative of a typical official response to broken codes of sociopolitical communication.[3] Frederick Siebert understands it as an instance of arbitrary Tudor government:

"Elizabeth was furious" that anyone would "discuss in public print any matter of state policy!"[4] J. A. Froude sees it as a mark of Elizabeth's ineffectual government and believes that the trial grasped at legal straws: "Elizabeth, when she stooped to strike, preferred to choose a humble quarry" who was then "indicted for conspiracy to excite sedition under an Act which had been passed in the late reign for the protection of the Queen's husband. 'The Queen's husband' was construed liberally to cover the Queen's suitor."[5] Froude and Siebert followed Camden's report that "Her Majestie likewise burned with choller that there was a booke published in print, inveighing sharply against the mariage," though Camden credited her concern with increasing hostility against the Puritans:

Since that, shee begunne to bee the more displeased with Puritans then she had been before time, perswading her selfe that such a thing had not passed without their privitie: and within a few dayes after, *John Stubbes* of Lincolnes Inne, a zealous professor of Religion, the Author of this Ralative Pamphlet (whose Sister *Thomas Cartwright* the Arch-Puritan had maried) *William Page* the disperser of the Copies, and *Singleton* the Printer were apprehended: against whom sentence was given that their right hands should be cut off by a law in the time of *Philip* and MARIE, against the Authors of *Seditious Writings*, and those that disperse them. Some Lawyers storming hereat, said the judgement was erroneous, and fetcht from a false observation of the time, wherin the Statute was made, that it was onely temporarie, and that (Queene MARIE dying) it dyed with her. Of the which Lawyers, one *Dalton* for his clamorous speeches was committed to prison, and *Monson* a Judge of the *Common-pleas*, was sharply rebuked, and his place taken from him, after that *Sir Chr. Wray* chiefe Justice of *England* had made it manifest by Law, that in that Statute there was no errour of time, but the Act was made against such as should put forth, or divulge any seditious writing against the King . . . yea, that Statute likewise in the first yeare of Queene ELIZABETH was revived againe to the Queene . . .[6]

(Camden, unlike historians who followed him, at least got the legal matters correct.) This report indelibly etched in history the image of Stubbs, one hand bloody, the other removing his hat, proclaiming, "God save the Queen."[7] This utterance, taken together with contemporary accusations of "erronious" judgment, has muddied historical understanding of the circumstances of *A Gaping Gulf*'s production and censorship. A closer examination of the event, the French marriage and English response to it, and the way the text addressed it gives a clearer sense of why this particular book was received by the government as "seditious" and not simply bothersome. At home the

French marriage was widely regarded as grounds for popular rebellion. Stubbs's book not only fanned this fire, but its international dissemination threatened an international incident. It is no wonder, then, that this book was not simply called in, but was censored by proclamation and its perpetrators tried under statutory law – by jury.[8]

Like other marriage negotiations undertaken by Elizabeth, those for the French marriage were motivated primarily by political interests. In 1578 the European political picture was complex. England's principal concern was in deterring both Spain's direct aggression and its support for Catholic rebellion against England, led either from Scotland or Ireland. The Protestant Low Countries were seeking to throw off the yoke of Catholic Spain, and while a war would serve England by distracting Spanish resources from England, for England to support directly the Low Countries would have been costly both economically and politically. An alliance between England and France could serve as a formidable deterrent to Spanish aggression, but if it were not well conceived and executed, England increased her vulnerability to the machinations of the Catholic League (the Guise faction whose influence England so greatly feared in their claims on Mary, Queen of Scots). Against France's complex partisan politics – the strongly Catholic Guise faction, the "politique" but Catholic Valois court, and the Protestant interests of Henry of Navarre – the Duke of Alençon appeared remarkably independent. He had escaped the French court, condemned the St. Bartholomew's Day massacre, and come to the aid of Protestant interests in the Low Countries, even though he was himself a Catholic. The faction of Elizabeth's court led by Burghley saw a marriage to Alençon as (in the words of *A Gaping Gulf*), "a bridle to the French king, a snaffle to Spain, and a stop-gambol to all practices of competition of Popery or any other traitorous attempt at home or abroad."[9] From the perspective of realpolitik, even if the marriage were not effected, its pursuit opened up political dialogue with France for a defensive alliance.

Historical perspective, benefiting from hindsight, has generally regarded the French marriage negotiations as a political exercise, albeit one that may have personally interested the Queen for a short time. John Guy best epitomizes this view when he comments:

. . . the negotiations proved to be Elizabeth's winning card for a decade: Alençon was deployed whenever an English reaction was required abroad. He was used to bind England with France against Spain; to protect the

Huguenots and *politiques* against the French Catholic League; to fight Elizabeth's battles in the Netherlands; and even in a short-lived final attempt to recover Calais. He was manipulated to curtail Guise intrigue in France, Scotland, and England; and to persuade Philip II to compromise with the Dutch . . . So Alençon visited England in August 1579 and October 1581 to forward his marriage suit . . . During his first visit Elizabeth seriously contemplated marrying him; but she shook off sentiment for diplomatic dividends – at his second departure she privately rejoiced to see him leave.[10]

Even Camden, himself so near to the events he wrote about, remarks that Elizabeth "excellently put . . . off" Jean Simier's negotiations on Francis's behalf in 1579 and ultimately placed considerations for her people above the marriage when he visited again in 1581.[11]

While these assessments are probably correct, they neglect the genuine turmoil that the prospective French marriage produced. The letters of the Spanish ambassador, Bernardino de Mendoza, offer a useful barometer of public sentiment.[12] Talks of a French alliance had begun in 1572 but subsided in the wake of the St. Bartholomew's Day massacre of French Protestants;[13] they resumed late in 1578 and their momentum accelerated when Simier and other French negotiators appeared at Elizabeth's court in January 1579, and at their first appearance, the Spanish Ambassador reported that "the people at large show no joy at their coming" (vol. II, p. 542). By the end of January "books in french & others" appeared in the Queen's chamber, "admonishing her to avoid attaching herself to the French or having doings with them" (vol. II, p. 547). Even though by the end of February it was generally perceived that the Queen would marry, opponents persisted in their opposition. The Spanish Ambassador reported on 31 March that,

In the sermons preached before the Queen they speak very violently about this marriage. The preacher on the first Sunday in Lent said that marriages with foreigners would only result in ruin to the country, as was proved by what happened when the sainted King Edward died and was succeeded by Mary, who married a foreigner, and caused the martyrdom of so many persons, who were burnt all over the country. When the preacher finished the subject, but not the sermon, the Queen rose, which was considered a great innovation. They are also attaching much importance to the fact that preachers are constantly saying this to the Queen and that she takes no steps, from which it may be inferred that they are inspired from high quarters. (vol. II, p. 563)

If some in "high quarters" opposed the marriage, others, particularly Sussex and Burghley, favored it, and by May conflict emerged at court (vol. II, p. 571). Hoping to gain support, Elizabeth called upon the Privy Council to discuss the marriage, but her efforts failed.

The new councillor as first speaker, pointed out how bad this talk of marriage was both for the Queen and the nation, since no succession could be hoped from it, and great confusion might be caused by the coming hither of Catholics, and above all Frenchmen, who were their ancient enemies. He pointed out many other great objections, and the rest of them all agreed with him except Sussex. (vol. II, p. 576)

The Council went so far as to approach Simier and express their dissatisfaction with the proposed terms, after which the Queen apologized to Simier "that they opposed what she so much desired" (vol. II, p. 576).

Though she favored the marriage, she did insist that she should see Alençon, and plans began for his visit. On 24 June de Mendoza wrote that the Queen was "burning with impatience for his coming," although her councillors pointed out to her that her subjects so opposed the marriage – indeed hated it – that "some are of opinion here that Alençons coming may cause disturbances in this country" (vol. II, p. 581). By August some of the councillors judged that the only way to prevent political disturbance was for Parliament to sanction the marriage (vol. II, p. 590). Elaborate efforts were taken to conceal Alençon's August visit, suggesting that Elizabeth must have felt some concern about disturbances. The greatest problem was rumor and silent opposition:

The Queen was very angry at the gossip that was going about Alençon's coming, and she formally ordered that the matter should not be spoken of . . . The councillors themselves deny that Alençon is here, and in order not to offend the Queen they shut their eyes and avoid going to Court, so as not to appear to stand in the way of her interviews with him . . . It is said that if she married without consulting her people she may repent it . . . The people at large are so displeased, that, if Alençon stays here, they say it is very likely trouble will come of it, above all if they are urged to it by others. (vol. II, p. 592)

De Mendoza's report hints at what was to become the prevailing condition at court in the coming months – the Queen's obstinate pursuit of the marriage amidst equally obstinate opposition from her Council. Of reaction to the marriage in the world beyond the court, de Mendoza comments: "The people in general seem to threaten revolution about it" (vol. II, p. 593).

John Stubbs's *The Discoverie Of a Gaping Gulf Whereunto England Is Like To Be Swallowed by an other French mariage, if the Lord forbid not the banes, by letting her Majestie see the sin and punishment thereof* was conceived in anticipation of the planned visit of the Duke of Alençon, sometime after the end of June 1579. Most of the tract was written before the visit, as the author clearly refers to the anticipated visit conditionally:

And if he should come in which that honorable show becoming his greatness, and as any other such man will come that wooeth with good meaning and feareth not any detection of hidden treacheries, his voyage hither would be mightily chargeable, a thing ill becoming him, who is already drawn dry to the bottom and extremely indebted . . . And if he should speed (which God forspeak), yet must he come to a people that loves him not nor his train . . . (pp. 84–5)

But judging from an addition made at the end that refers to the actual visit, the book was clearly in press (or just printed) at the time of Alençon's visit. Stubbs's initial closing builds through an appeal to each of the classes and orders of English society indicating the course they should take to prevent the marriage, ending with a request for the prayers of the "meaner sort . . . To solicit the Lord for his church, for this commonweal, and for the Queen that of his great mercy he will turn away this plague of a stranger in Christian Israel and foreign Frenchmen in England." Without even a paragraph demarcation, the text shifts to acknowledge that the feared visit has occurred:

The only noise of whose making hithertoward gave all these causes of fear, and wrong thus much hitherto said to be written, as it were, with the tears of an English heart. And his sudden arrival here with all the manner and circumstances thereof would yield new arguments of a much longer discourse. For, first, his coming hither, as it were, in a mask betrays a strange melancholic nature in himself . . . Then it shows his extreme want of ability to defray the expense of wooing in a bountiful show fitting such a prince as cometh to obtain our Queen. This his secret coming and departing discovers a mistrustfulness in him towards our people, and therefore no love, which must needs come from his own ill conscience of fearing French measure in England . . . (pp. 92–3)

This indicates that the book was born *at the particular moment* when the Queen had pursued the marriage against the recommendations of all her councillors (except Sussex and Burghley), when rumors of rebellion forced the secrecy of Alençon's visit, and when she had commanded silence regarding the visit and the marriage. Even without considering the particulars of Stubbs's book, its mere appearance at this would justifiably have offended the Queen.

That the language and contents of *A Gaping Gulf* were particularly provocative is undeniable, but before considering this, some regard needs to be given to the text's production and dissemination. As we have already seen, William Camden wrote Stubbs and *A Gaping Gulf* into the enduring history of puritan opposition to Elizabethan government.[14] Modern scholarship, however, indicates that Stubbs and William Page had associations with important people in the government, and while their interests may have been "oppositional," they were hardly government outsiders. Kenneth Barnes has convincingly demonstrated that Page, the "disperser" of copies, was William Page M.P., the gentleman servant to the 2nd Earl of Bedford, who enabled Page to be returned for Elizabeth's first four parliaments.[15] This association seen in light of remarks made by both the French Ambassador Mauvissière and the Venetian ambassador, Barnes argues, points to "Stubbe's tract forming part of a general propaganda exercise with high-level backing":

Mauvissière more or less puts this suspicion into the queen's mouth when he reports her as saying, speaking of the condemned men, that "elle conneust bien quils n'estoyer que les secretaires de plus méchans que eulx" who had put them up to it. In an earlier dispatch, before the trial, he had reported the rumour that some of the Council were privy to the launching of the pamphlet: "éstimoit l'on quil [i.e. the author] ne l'avoit faict sans le consentement de quelques ungs de ce conseil."[16]

The circumstances of Stubbs's later life and internal evidence from *A Gaping Gulf* offer convincing corroboration to Barnes's conclusion.

John Stubbs spent between fourteen and eighteen months in prison following the public punishment for writing *A Gaping Gulf*. Upon his release in 1581, he returned to his home in Thelveton in Norfolk. According to Simon Adams, Leicester procured for him the Stewardship of Yarmouth in 1585, a responsible position that Lloyd Berry points out "was always filled by some eminent lawyer."[17] The Stewardship brought Stubbs back to London where the corporation secured him rooms at the Grey Friars. At the same time, he served as secretary to Peregrine Bertie, Lord Willoughby de Eresby. In 1587 Burghley employed Stubbs to reply to Allen's attack on Burghley's *The Execution of Justice*,[18] and the same year he was made an Associate to the Bench of Lincoln's Inn. In 1588 following a trip with Lady Willoughby to the Low Countries, Stubbs was returned to Parliament as a member for Great Yarmouth. Once Parliament was dissolved in March 1589, he joined Willoughby's forces in France, which were aiding Henry of Navarre against the Catholic League.

Such public recognition and service goes a long way to support Barnes's conclusion; so too do suggestions in the book. *A Gaping Gulf* has long been reputed to be a vituperative text. Strype said it was a "violent book" against the Queen's proposed marriage, written in a "bitter scoffing style." Camden said it had "a stinking style."[19] Such estimations cloud the degree to which the text reflects a sophisticated political perspective[20] and, indeed, an insider's knowledge of international politics. *A Gaping Gulf* begins with a religious argument citing biblical precedents in Israel against bad and ill-conceived marriages with the unfaithful, but this is only a small part of the discussion that, for the most part, reflects many of the objections being raised at court. Stubbs maintains throughout that the French marriage threatens the Protestant Church of England. An important foundation for his argument is the degree to which France had been unfaithful to "the Church of Christ" in the vast cruelty of the St. Bartholomew's Day massacre. He returns to this several times as evidence of French unreliability and duplicity, particularly in matters regarding the Queen-mother Catherine de' Medici.

Besides offering religious arguments – both biblical and contemporary – *A Gaping Gulf* dissuades the match by presenting historical precedent, evidence from international politics, legal arguments about succession (both in France and England) and the status of foreign denizens in England, economic threats, and a dose of character assassination. Stubbs appears well versed in arguments favoring the French marriage as the means to achieving a balance of power in Europe, and answers these arguments by demonstrating that Alençon was relatively ineffectual in both Continental and French domestic affairs. Particularly interesting is Stubbs's use of Machiavelli, the chosen political philosopher of Europe's *politiques*, such as with regard to domestic affairs when Stubbs invokes his arguments about the importance of religion to the well-governed state:

Now to prove that any alteration in religion or expectation to have religion altered is a politic bile inflaming the peace of a settled and even state, I might have sufficient authority to some men out of Machiavelli. But I loathe once to take up his best texts, though they were written in golden letters of the fairest text hand. Hereon will I only rest for this point, that to alter our good religion or to give any permission to so wicked idolatry as is his takes away God's blessing from the state, whose providence it is whereby rulers reign and states do stand. And let him, pardie, that holds himself the best politic, hold this with me for a cornerstone and most lucky principle in policy, that, as to bring in and hold true religion procureth God's protection and worketh subjects' obedience of heart far above all other laws or fear of laws, so to put out God's gospel and to bring in idolatry or to enlarge Antichrist and straiten the passage of Christ doth shut all blessing from heaven, so as the Lord shall curse our counsel and cast us in our wisdom of overweening. (p. 39)

Stubbs must have gleaned his knowledge of Machiavelli's *Prince* and *Discourses* from one of those manuscripts in "fairest text hand" being circulated at the highest levels of government in sixteenth-century Europe.[21] Also telling is his use of the noun "politic" to refer to a statesman and "policy" for governing. Such allusions and sophistication point to the kind of "high-level backing" for Stubbs's writing posited by Barnes.

Although it can be argued that rumors may have spread information about the French marriage beyond the Court, Stubbs's highly specialized knowledge about arguments advanced in the Privy Council and events at Court points to backing from, or at least access to, high levels of government. *A Gaping Gulf*, as we have seen, belongs to the events of Summer 1579. Stubbs was obviously aware that plans were being made for Alençon's visit, and he knew when that secret visit had taken place. Furthermore, he demonstrates familiarity with both French–Scottish diplomatic relations and Sir James Fitzmaurice's invasion of Ireland during that same summer when he argues that France had been involved in plots against England:

For treason they are so imbrued in blood as they are like to assent into whatsoever plat [plot] never so barbarous. And this is also a device fit enough for such a soliciter as is that false Scot prelate Ross [John Leslie], mortal enemy hither, who is presently in France and, like enough, her [Mary, Queen of Scots] agent to procure this device. Yea, unless we ourselves close our own eyes, we may see that it is a very French Popish wooing to send hither smooth-tongued Simiers to gloss and glaver and hold talk of marriage, and yet, in the meanwhile, Jacques Fitzmaurice, who hath been in France and conversant with Ross and even now came immediately thence into Ireland to invade our Queen's dominion there . . . Is it possible for the breath of marriage well meant in England and war performed in Ireland to come out of one mouth? (pp. 79–80)[22]

Stubbs also alludes to factionalism at Court when he refers to the "present persuaders" to the marriage tending to "their own enriching and advancement, making no great reckoning of this matter" (p. 32). This hearkens to the Spanish Ambassador's comments about Burghley and Sussex supporting the marriage for self-advancement at Leicester's expense.[23] Furthermore, Stubbs identifies as political ingenues the marriage's supporters: "Those, therefore, that persuade this band of strange alliance must needs be such Englishmen as find themselves not advanced in this state according to that desert which they conceive in themselves and therefore disdain at others' good estate" (p. 67).

Stubbs being a political insider goes a long way to explain responses to his trial and punishment. The French Ambassador reported that the Queen did all that she could to have Stubbs and his fellow perpetrators die by the "law and justice," but that "law and justice" did not condemn them accordingly but sought to clear them, alleging that they had been motivated by the affection they bore their country.[24] Furthermore, the Ambassador said that when the men were taken prisoners, they had been advised by leaders in the kingdom that they had done nothing wrong.[25] This letter reflects the general sense that Stubbs, Page, and Singleton had acted in the country's best interests with the approval of important people in government. Even so, they were sentenced in open court.[26] Perplexed historians have mistaken Stubbs's actions on the scaffold when he received his punishment – whether by Camden's report that he removed his hat with his other hand and declared "God save the Queen," or by Harington's report that Stubbs said, "I ame sorie for the losse of my haund, and more sorie to lose it by judgment; but most of all with her Majesties indignation and evill opinion, whome I have soe highlie displeased."[27] History has attended more to the harshness of the punishment, the improper course of the legal action, or to Stubbs's inordinate charity toward the Queen than to the extraordinary circumstances of the whole affair – that is, that men acting with the support of important figures in the government should have had harsh measures taken against them for writing and publishing a book containing opinions shared by so many Englishmen and widely supported by members of the government – indeed for containing opinions that had been expressed before (unpunished) both in sermons and in print without sanctions.

A Gaping Gulf produced a stir not simply because it opposed the

Queen's marriage plans, or represented Alençon unfavorably, or reflected "puritan" interests. It provoked suppression and the prosecution of its perpetrators because not to do so would have jeopardized Elizabeth's foreign policy. Besides its pervasive attack on France, its rehearsal of the St. Bartholomew's Day massacre recalled France's cruel anti-Protestant policy that had brought an end to French/English marriage negotiations and caused an estrangement of relations that continued until 1579. For Stubbs the massacre was,

. . . very lamentable. A king falsified his sworn word; the marriage of a king's sister imbrued with blood; a king murdered his subjects; many noble and honorable gentlemen shamefully used; valiant men surprised by cowards in their beds; innocents put to death; women and children without pity tossed upon halberds and thrown down windows and into rivers; learned men killed by barbarous soldiers; the saints of god led to the shambles all the day long and all that week long by vile crocheteurs, or porters; the Church of Christ razed, the very nest egg broken as far as men's mischievous reasonable wit could reach; and, that at which was worst, those that lived were compelled to forswear their God . . . (pp. 26–7)

He strongly condemns the Queen-mother as the author of French anti-Protestant policy and the mastermind of French politics, and characterizes Alençon as his mother's puppet:

. . . the King, his brother, and his mother have some other meaning against the church, state, and person of our prince even to have an eye in the head of our Court if they can bring it to pass, and hand in the heart of this realm to work our ruin and their great hatreds, and that as the mother hath long time ruled and turned the wrong side outward of France, so she might have this land another while for her stage; she is dressing her Prologue to send him in; trust him not. The players be tragical, although he wear peaceable laurel on his head. (p. 85)

The attacks on Alençon's person pale by comparison to this. About his reputed licentiousness, Stubbs says he will dismiss gossip and "reckon reports and bruits as reports and bruits"; however, should "but the fourth part of that misrule bruited should be true, it must needs draw such punishment from God . . ." (p. 71). As character assassination this is relatively mild, particularly compared to his most vituperative disdain, which is expressed for Alençon's followers: the "needy, spent Frenchmen of Monsieur's train, being of contrary religion and who are the scum of the King's Court, which is the scum of all France, which is the scum of Europe" (p. 46).

Had Stubbs's pamphlet reached only the domestic reader, it may have been judged far less harshly. It had the misfortune, however, of being brought into international politics. On 29 September, the Spanish Ambassador reported to the King of Spain the Queen's proclamation, noting not only the rapidity and ceremony with which it was promulgated but its international implications: "Alençon is flattered by saying that it was through him that the Portuguese had been kept in France" (vol. II, p. 603). On 16 October he reported that the proclamation "instead of mitigating the public indignation against the French, has irritated it and fanned the flame" (vol. II, 606). Further, Stubbs's book was translated both into French (and printed in France) and into Italian, with a manuscript sent to the Pope.[28] Elizabeth's failure to suppress *A Gaping Gulf* would have implied that she approved its contents, and both she and England would have lost political credit abroad: ". . . if these kind of barbarous depravings of all men's actions . . . should be permitted, it might be doubted that it should breed a common loathing of the English name to all other nations of Christendom."[29] Furthermore, once she issued the proclamation, had she not proceeded by law against the libelers, she would have been perceived as ineffectual in domestic affairs. In taking the actions she did – suppressing the text with considerable fanfare and calling for the libelers' deaths when the statute under which they were prosecuted specified the loss of their hands – she dealt herself a hand full of trump cards for both domestic and international relations.

At home Elizabeth's actions spoke strongly against popular domestic unrest and conciliar opposition. The proclamation gives as a principal ground for suppressing the text that it "seditiously and rebelliously" stirred up "all estates of her majesty's subjects to fear their own utter ruin and change of government."[30] While this claim in the proclamation may be overstated, it was not unwarranted. The text does not advocate open rebellion (if it had, it would have been prosecutable under the treason statutes), but it does argue that the French marriage would alter government. The 1579 edition draws particular attention to this in the marginal glosses that call even the casual reader to attend to the warning:

Sin drawth mariage. (A34)
This mariage is sin. (A3v)
Conclusion against England (A7v)
The kings sin striketh the land. (A7v)
Alteration of government. (C2r)

Contrary religion. (C3r)
As the wife is subject to hir husband:
So is hir country to his hand. (D3v)

Such marginalia, absent in modern editions, clearly argue that the French marriage would be a sin for Elizabeth which would be visited on England in the form of altered government and religious conflict – a threat given some resonance by the religious wars in France. The judgment of history has long been that this pamphlet was far less seditious than its censorship suggests. The rumors of rebellion reported by the Spanish Ambassador throughout 1579, along with letters to the French Ambassador threatening rebellion,[31] offer some ground for Elizabeth's fears that were fed further by the above marginalia. Censoring the text may have been an overreaction, but by suppressing the text and proceeding at law against the libelers, Elizabeth sent a strong message to whatever councillors fostered this kind of opposition that this was not the way to proceed in opposing her.[32]

Suppressing this offensive text proved a good political investment both abroad and at home. Elizabeth's actions bought her credibility with the French that would serve her interest in achieving a French alliance whether or not the marriage proceeded. The proclamation itself established conditions for the marriage intended to allay the opposition's fears: that Francis be acceptable to the French Protestants, that he not require changes in English law in any matter, religious or otherwise. Furthermore, it made it clear that the marriage would not proceed without parliamentary, and hence national, approval: "Neither was there anything of moment that might concern the Crown or the nation of the realm that was ever demanded by this prince . . . otherwise than should be found meet to be confirmed by Parliament."[33]

These conditions effectively bought the Queen time to win over her councillors and the English people, and an "out" should she fail to do so. Once again the Queen appeared to be interested in the response of her Privy Council, and once again she summoned them to give their opinion of the marriage that less than a month before she had treated as a *fait accompli*, and on 16 October the Spanish Ambassador told the king of Spain that they reported to her that,

After having met and considered the subject on many occasions, they were of opinion that, for the security of her person, the tranquillity of her realm, and the preservation of her Crown, it was not fitting that she should marry any member of the House of France. They pointed out the many objections to the entrance of Frenchmen into the kingdom, they being ancient enemies; as well as the danger from the Scots who were the same. If she were to die, as might be feared if the French were to obtain control of her person, they should take possession of the country, with the aid they would get from Scotland, without the English being able to prevent it. They set forth also the other things that might occur, and showed how much opposed public opinion was to the marriage, although she had been so popular with her subjects in consequence of her actions during the years she had reigned, whilst on this matter they showed such bitter hatred . . . and they added afterwards that, in consequence of the general dislike of the people to the coming of the French, they thought Parliament should not be summoned yet, in order to avoid disturbance and sedition but should be delayed until later. If she still desired to marry, they should have time to persuade the people of the country to agree to it before Parliament was summoned. (vol. II, p. 606)

Elizabeth prorogued Parliament and prolonged the marriage negotiations. Her call for the libelers' heads was a nice piece of showman-
ship to convince the French that her intentions were earnest at the
same time that she was deferring at last to her councillors' opposition. Elizabeth could safely demand execution, knowing that the law
against seditious libel under which they were tried did not provide
for the death penalty.

Stubbs's *The Discovery of a Gaping Gulf* belongs to this extraordinary
spectacle of political gamesmanship where losing and winning were
often indistinguishable. Only from a post-enlightenment perspective
is there a clear loser: free expression was sacrificed to realpolitik –
national interest prevailed over individual rights. Stubbs and Page
paid a high price for expressing their views, but their voices of
opposition clearly got the Queen's attention, and her interest in the
French marriage never again seemed as determined as it had been
before. Leicester and Walsingham must have gained some political
credit since she became more willing to support Protestant efforts on
the Continent. Elizabeth maintained a strong bargaining position in
France and demonstrated at home that she both would and could
take strong repressive (and legal) action against stirrers of sedition
and rebellion, but she lost the kind of security for her throne and
posterity that an heir would have brought. A gossipy letter from de
Mendoza suggests that the Queen's loss in the matter was as personal
as Stubbs's and Page's hands:

Speaking to Walsingham about it she told him begone and that the only thing he was good for was a protector of heretics. Knollys who is a gret heretic and the treasurer of the household, married to her first cousin, asked her how she could think of marrying a Catholic, she having forbidden Protestants to do so. To this she replied that he might pay dearly for the zeal he was displaying in the cause of religion, and it was a fine way to show his attachment to her; who might desire, like others, to have children. (vol. II, p. 607)

CHAPTER 7

The review and reform of Holinshed's Chronicles
"reporte of matters of later yeers that concern the State"

The censorship and revision of both editions of Raphael Holinshed's *Chronicles of England, Scotland, and Ireland* looks different from the recall of Gascoigne's *Poesies* or the suppression of Stubbs's *A Gaping Gulf,* since for both the 1577 and the 1587 editions of the *Chronicles,* the Privy Council gave orders to stay their sales until "they shall be reviewed and reformyd."[1] That the texts were "reformyd" and not suppressed, even that the *Chronicles'* 1587 edition was printed under a royal privilege, suggests that they enjoyed a status quite different from other texts censored by Elizabeth's government, and further, that the offenses' kind and degree differed markedly from the offenses (or supposed offenses) of Gascoigne and Stubbs. The *Chronicles* enjoyed considerable status as cultural capital, and their censorship and revision – particularly of the 1587 edition – represents an effort on the part of the government to construct a favorable domestic and international image. This was not a wholesale propaganda effort, but rather, a response to specific materials that the government – or members of the government – felt would jeopardize England's international image. Their censorship argues that Elizabeth's government regarded them as instrumental in offering to an international audience an account of a national government in England respectful of justice and law, and of the sovereign rights of neighboring countries.

The 1577 edition of Holinshed's *Chronicles* appeared as part of a deliberate movement to elevate the stature of England, English letters, and English language through writing and publishing maps, histories, national epics, and theoretical works on English poetry – what in *Forms of Nationhood* Richard Helgerson refers to as "the Elizabethan writing of England."[2] The prominent London printer Reyner Wolfe, apparently with Lord Burghley's support, planned the *Chronicles* as a "universal Cosmographie" that would include histories and maps.[3] Wolfe's friend and assistant, Raphael Holinshed, at the behest of Wolfe's wife's will, ensured the completion of the Scottish, Irish, and English descriptions and histories when the "Cosmographie" was cut short by Wolfe's death.[4] Holinshed's dedication to Burghley makes it clear both that Burghley was familiar with his (and Wolfe's project) and that it enjoyed much the same status as Christopher Saxton's maps of England,[5] that enterprise of nation-making that Richard Helgerson suggests should be called "The Queen Elizabeth Atlas."[6] The 1587 edition of the *Chronicles*, continued through 1586 and substantially revised, likewise enjoyed a privileged status. On 30 December 1584, Henry Denham and Ralph Newbery entered in the Stationers' Register their assignment of Henry Bynneman's privilege to print "all dictionaries and chronicles whatsoever," including and specifically naming Holinshed's.[7] Holinshed's 1587 *Chronicles*, then, were duly printed *cum privilegio*, as the 1587 colophon states.[8]

Both editions of the *Chronicles* participated in some way with printing interests (royal privileges) that can best be described as "national," which distinguishes their discourse from Gascoigne's personal aspirations and Stubbs's factional opposition – though each is in its own way political. While the *Chronicles* vest their interest in building Englishness, theirs is not an exercise in government propaganda. Annabel Patterson argues convincingly in *Reading Holinshed's "Chronicles"* that they, like the printers who produced them, "were dedicated to the task of showing what it might mean to be 'all Englishmen' in full consciousness of the fundamental differences of opinion that drove Englishmen apart."[9] The review and reform of the *Chronicles* (both editions), as we shall see, offers some striking insights into how the government (or more specifically, how individual members of the Privy Council) viewed the representation of English national interests and what they regarded as threatening to that vision.

The 1577 edition of the *Chronicles* came to the Privy Council's attention in December 1577 with regard to Richard Stanyhurst's part of the "History of Ireland," "in which many thinges are falcelie recited and contrarie to the ancient records." The Council ordered the Bishop of London to stay the sales until the text could be reformed, and he called upon the Earl of Kildare to present Stanyhurst to the Council. On 13 January 1578 the Council ordered the Bishop to release the stay once he received notice from the Lord

Treasurer that the revisions Stanyhurst had agreed to make were completed.[10] While *STC* notes three cancels in the 1577 *Chronicles*, only the F7 gathering appears to contain significant changes. This section reports the rebellion led by the Earle of Ormonde against Gerald Fitzgerald, the Earl of Kildare during the reign of Henry VIII. The reformation toned down the strong bias in favor of Kildare and removed some disparaging remarks about Archbishop John Alen.[11] Apparently, when the Privy Council met with Stanyhurst they discovered far less that was offensive than they had expected. Although no records exist to suggest what led the Privy Council to suspect problems in the 1577 *Chronicles*, it looks like someone had complained to them about "many thinges" and when they met with Stanyhurst, they actually found few.

On 1 February 1587 the Privy Council sent a letter to the Archbishop of Canterbury requesting "the staye of furder sale and uttering" of a new edition of Holinshed's *Chronicles*,

until they shall be reviewed and reformyd; for the better examinacion of which thinges theyr Lordships wishe him to commytt and devide the volumes and partes of the said booke to the consideracion of Mr. Randolph and Mr. H. Killegrew, with Mr. Doctour Hammond . . . for the more speede to be used in the reformacion of the same.[12]

The censorship and reformation was carried out in three stages, and while each reflects different motivations and interests – most related in some way to English interest in Dutch and Scottish affairs – a concern for the representation of the administration of English justice appears throughout.[13] The reforms appeared in the continuations of the Scottish and English histories that extended the 1577 *Chronicles*, and the censors appear not to have reviewed other sections of the monumental chronicles. This is consistent with the Privy Council's letter which called for speedy reformation and gave as grounds for the recall that the *Chronicles* "conteyne reporte of matters of later yeers that concern the State."

The earliest state of the reformed text of the 1587 *Chronicles* is represented in a fragment taken from a broken copy once owned by the Book Club of California.[14] The Book Club fragment has from "The Historie of Scotland": five consecutive leaves from the 2Q gathering, containing a cancel page 421/424, and nine consecutive leaves from the 2R and 2S gatherings (pp. 429–52), containing the cancels 443/444 and 445/450. From "The Historie of England" the fragment has: the five-leaf 6M gathering containing the 6M3 cancel 1328/1330; six consecutive gatherings (6V–7E) of original leaves; a two-leaf cancel, FGHI, replacing the 7F–7I gatherings; the 7K gathering; the 7L gathering containing original leaves 1551/1552 and 1561/1562 and two cancels 7L2 (1553/1554) and 7L3; and the 7M gathering of original leaves.[15] The cancels in each of the reformations offer a written bridge to the remaining original text, so the narrative reads coherently.

The Book Club fragment, thus, reflects censorship and reformation at three sites in the "Historie of England" – in the 6M, the F–I, and in the 7L gatherings – and in "The Historie of Scotland."[16] A close consideration of the censored passages and cancels reveals that at the earliest stage of censorship the state's concerns principally had to do with English international involvement – either in Dutch or Scottish affairs, or with the Catholic missionaries from the Continent.

The first cancellation and reformation in the Book Club fragment's "Historie of England" appears at pages 1328–30.[17] The uncensored text is concerned with two events in 1582, the trial and execution for treason of the Jesuit Edmund Campion and the departure of "Monsieur duke of Anjou" (Alençon) from England for the Netherlands in 1582;[18] both events had far-reaching repercussions. This change appears to have been intended to position better Elizabeth's government in early 1587 to negotiate the difficult straits of both Anglo-Dutch relations and complex international and domestic response to the order for Mary's execution (for politics and not religion). Campion's trial and execution provoked a propaganda war that cut to the core of Catholic persecution and English justice, producing William Allen's *A Briefe Historie of the Glorious Martyrdom of XII. Reverend Priests, executed within these twelvemonethes for confession and defence of the Catholike Faith But under false pretence of Treason* (1582), Burghley's defense of English policy, *The Execution of Justice* (itself reprinted in Holinshed's *Chronicles*), and Allen's reply *A True, Sincere and Modest Defence* (1584).[19] The *Chronicles'* report of Campion's trial exposed both sides of the issue to public scrutiny.

Alençon, of course, had in 1579 been at the center of an equally provocative controversy, the French marriage, but he was also at the center of English policy in the Low Countries. His trip to England at the end of 1581, still in pursuit of marriage, met with a warm reception at the English court though the Queen's announced intent to marry still met with Leicester's, Hatton's, and Walsingham's opposition. Accompanied by a host of English nobility, his 1582 departure for Zeeland to assume sovereignty as the Duke of Brabant marked a change in English Continental policy. According to Wallace MacCaffrey, "The States had now formally thrown off their allegiance to Philip and were thus vesting the Duke with sovereignty. The English were at last giving their blessing to an act of rebellion and implicitly recognizing a new sovereign in the Low Countries."[20] Alençon's 1583 attempt to seize Antwerp (regarded by the Dutch as a betrayal)[21] and permanent return to France, marked a failure of Elizabeth's policy in the Low Countries to oppose Spain indirectly and build solidarity with France. Following his ignominious departure, the Dutch suffered both a series of defeats and the loss of their leader with the Prince of Orange's assassination in 1584. The Dutch appealed to Elizabeth for active English involvement. According to MacCaffrey,

the argument for intervention rested on familiar grounds, the longstanding "ill mind" of Philip towards England, going back to 1558 and based on "his mortal enmity against all persons not of the Romish religion." Once victorious in the Low Countries, with abundance of men and ships at his disposal, he would turn his resources against the Queen. War was inevitable; better to forestall it by acting now while Dutch resistance was alive . . .[22]

On 22 October 1585 Elizabeth issued a formal commission to Leicester to command English forces in the Low Countries, and he entered them with considerable show, promising greater triumphs than what followed. His military success amounted to holding Spanish advances in check, recovering Doesbury, and isolating Zutphen, but he lost Grave and Venlo. His political relations with Dutch leadership were fraught with tension and misunderstanding so that by late 1586 the Dutch Council was strongly asserting its political leadership. Leicester returned to England late in 1586 in part to defend his efforts and in part to appeal for greater support. In January 1587, one of his political protégés, Sir William Stanley, defected to Spain with his troops, badly affecting Leicester's and England's reputation in the Low Countries. In March Elizabeth sent Lord Buckhurst to negotiate a new arrangement between England and the Low Countries and to resolve conflicts among Dutch factions; at the same time that she was deliberating openly with the Dutch about granting further military and financial aid, she was attempting to reach a negotiated settlement with the Duke of Parma. Elizabeth returned Leicester to the Low Countries in

July 1587 after Buckhurst's embassy failed. Ultimately, Anglo-Dutch relations cooled, in part because of Leicester's defeats, in part because the Dutch feared her attempt to negotiate a peace with the Duke of Parma would betray them. Leicester left the Low Countries for good in December 1587.[23] Alençon's 1582 departure, marking as it did the shift in English policy toward Spain, was thus the first in a series of events that led domino-like first to Leicester's failure in the Low Countries and ultimately to open confrontation between England and Spain.

Leicester's return to England in late November 1586 came close on the heels of another crisis: the trials and executions of the Babington conspirators and Mary, Queen of Scots' treason trial in Parliament for her role in that conspiracy. By 1 February 1587, the date of the *Chronicles*' recall, the royal proclamation of Mary's death sentence had been issued, but Elizabeth, hearing appeals from France and Spain, was staying the actual execution order. Despite the support of most of her government for the execution, Burghley recognized that "the taking away of the Scots Queens liff" could not "be a preservative to the Queen, but contrary, for the offence that hir friends will conceive shall provoque them."[24] Events in the Low Countries and at home possess clear resonances with contents of the first reform site in the *Chronicles*.

In *Reading Holinshed's "Chronicles,"* Annabel Patterson has suggested that the expurgation of the materials related to the trial of Campion was "ordered . . . on the grounds that it contained a tactless account of the trial of Edmund Campion – indeed, that it was intended to erase the chroniclers own view: 'and yet this man forsooth (albeit notorious) died not for treason but for religion.' "[25] The offense, however, more likely lay in the relationship to the extensive propaganda war Campion's death provoked, and which focused the highly volatile debate on the treatment of Catholics in England.[26] Actually, the report of the trial begins several pages before the reformed section. It has testimony from the trial, including that of a "yeoman of hir majesties chamber" (an informer), who learned from a priest of a "horrible treason intended against hir majestie and the state":

That there should be levied a certeine companie of armed men, which on a sudden should enterprise a most monstruous attempt: a certeine companie of these armed men should be prepared against hir majestie, as manie against my L. of L. as manie gainst my L. T. as manie against S. F. W. and diverse other, whose names he dooth not well remember. The deaths of these noble personages should be presentlie fulfilled, and hir majestie used in such sort, as modestie nor dutie will not suffer a subject to rehearse: but this should be the generall crie everie where, Queene Marie, queene Marie.[27]

According to the informer, when he asked the priest how he could do anything so horrible, the priest replied that "the killing hir majestie was no offense to God" (p. 1324, A60–1). The *Chronicle* goes on to report that Campion and his fellow priests pleaded ignorance to these accusations of treason, bolstering "up one another with large protestations, railing words, and subtill surmises: affirming that they were not sent hither for anie such intent" (p. 1324, B14–17). Following this denial, a priest reports that in a Continental seminary sometime before there had been rumors "that shortlie there should be preests appointed for England, to win the people against the appointed time, when as a great armie should be readie to joine with them" (p. 1324, B21–4). The full report of the trial reiterates the insistence of Campion and the others that they came to England only "to get the sheepe into the fold which hath long run a straie" (p. 1324, B52–3). The chronicler concludes that in their insistence they showed that "they were so craftilie schooled" to conceal that "they themselves sought to accomplish hir majesties death":

This was manifestlie prooved by verie large and ample evidence, credible witnesses, and their owne confessions and writings: whereupon the jurie, having wiselie and discreetlie pondered and searched and seene into the depth of everie cause, worthilie and deservedlie gave them up all guiltie of the treasons whereof they were indicted and arreigned. (p. 1326, B53–9)

He notes the good reputation Campion enjoyed in England, and the conduct of the condemned men at the execution – including Campion's effort to retain good credit. The report concludes with the execution itself (by quartering): "according as it was appointed by justice" (p. 1329, A9–10, uncensored; p.1330, A9–10, *STC* 6M3v).

Patterson maintains that one of the protocols observed by the Holinshed chroniclers was the presentation of multiple historical perspectives, and that, in the case of the Campion conspiracy, censorship sought to silence the conspirators' voices.[28] Throughout the report of the trial, however, the pleas of innocence that led to Catholic outcries about English justice went uncensored. That outcry itself – even though it is phrased in the strongest terms of condemnation – was suppressed.

No sooner had justice given the blow of execution, and cut off the foresaid offendors from the earth; but certeine enimies of the state politike and ecclesiastike, greatlie favouring them, and their cause, which they falslie gave out to be religiion, dispersed abroad their libels of most impudent devise, tending to the justifieng of the malefactors innocencie, to the heinous and unrecompensable defamation of the course of justice and judgement against them commensed and finished: in so much that speaking of the daie whereon they died, they blushed not to intitle them martyrs . . . (p. 1329, A32–43, uncensored)

The text includes a Latin poem illustrating the kinds of "things not publishable" that were being spread abroad, and concludes, "Thus slanderouslie against the administration of justice scattered these vipers brood their lieng reports, therein to the skies advancing the children of iniquitie as spotlesse; yea forging most monstruous fables, put them in print" (p. 1329 A55–9, uncensored). It then goes on to tell the false rumors Campion's supporters spread:

. . . it was bruted abroad not by men, but brute beasts, that on the selfe same daie whereon Campion was executed, the river of Thams did neither eb nor flow, but stood still. O miracle! Whether this were a lie or not, as all the world may sweare it was no truth; this is certeine and undoubted, that there was found a facultie about Campion a little before his death, wherein authoritie was given him from the bishop of Rome Gregorie the thirteenth, to execute the sentence of the bull published by Pius Quintus against all the queens majesties subjects as heretiks, &c: and yet this man forsooth (albeit notorious) died not for treason but for religion, as with fowle mouths they are not ashamed to saie: *Relligio crimen non mala vita fuit.* (p. 1329, A63–B3, uncensored)[29]

Patterson may be right about the motives for censoring this passage. It is quite possible that the labored syntax of the passage led the censors to believe that the chronicler was supporting Campion's claims. The strategy, however, is to repeat the libels *and* repudiate them as "lieng reports" and then to present the truth, "certeine and undoubted," that a papal dispensation (facultie) from Pope Gregory XIII (1572–5) was found in Campion's possession giving him authority to execute the sentence of the 1570 papal bull against the "queens majesties subjects as heretiks." Despite this, these libelers are unashamed to say that "this man . . . died not for treason but for religion." The censored comments and the censored poem, like Alfield's censored pamphlet and Allen's *True, Sincere and Modest Defence*, say "things not publishable" – that Campion's death was precious to God, a death to bring eternal joy to him as a martyr. Of course, what the government most objected to in Alfield and Allen, perhaps more than their martyrology, was their attack on the English justice system – the attack so assiduously answered by propaganda included in the *Chronicles* that is invoked by the words: "Thus slanderouslie against the administration of justice scattered these vipers brood their lieng reports."[30] With the trial and execution of the Babington conspirators in October 1586, Mary's Parliamentary trial and death sentence published 4 December,[31] the French and Spanish appeals to the Queen for Mary's life, and Burghley's concern over retaliation by Mary's supporters, the English administration of justice was once more in January and early February 1587 (and even more than in 1582) an issue.[32] All in all, the censors cut forty-seven lines from over 1,078 lines of text about the Campion conspiracy and trial. The uncut version reports the "due process" of the English justice system; the cuts eliminate accusations of injustice.

Interest in the Earl of Leicester's reputation appears to have motivated the reformation of the account of Alençon's departure in 1582. Immediately following the Campion trial, the uncensored *Chronicles* contain fourteen and three-quarter pages on the Duke of Alençon commencing his government of the Low Countries – which the text makes clear received the enthusiastic support of Queen Elizabeth and her nobility. The censored text has over twelve and three-quarter pages, so slightly less than two pages were suppressed, the substance of which appears in the reformed passage:

. . . you shall understand that about this time Monsieur duke of Anjou, departing out of England, was accompanied with diverse lords, knights, and gentlemen of great traine, to the sea side, and imbarked sailed with prosperous wind and weather, arriving at the length at Flushing, where he was honorablie interteined, finding there all sorts of his officers: for his household and his gard of Swissers and Frenchmen, departing from Calis and Bullongne foure daies afore, were come to Middleborough, ther attendant and readie to doo him service. (p. 1330, A32–43, 6M3 cancel)

The uncensored text differs in detail and tone, principally with regard to the relationships between England and Alençon and between him and France. The censored text conceals Elizabeth's personal regard for Monsieur and her government's investment in Monsieur's Dutch enterprise. It commences with the Prince of Orange's summons of Alençon from England, "to shew unto him the exceeding great desire which all the people had to see his highnes,

for the present ratifieng of the former covenants that had passed
betwixt them." According to the report:

it was needful that he should passe over with all speed . . . Whereupon the
queene calling the lord Howard, commanded him . . . to take upon him the
charge of the admerals ship, and to go to Rochester, and there to choose
vessels meet for transporting of the monsieur & his traine, & to furnish them
with men of war, mariners, & all manner of necessaries as well of war as of
vittels . . . And for so much as the monsieur came into England
accompanied but with a few princes and lords . . . the queene determined
to give him a companie & traine meet for his greatnesse, taking his journie
about so great & noble exploit. (p. 1329, B24–50, uncensored)

Among the train "of an hundred gentlemen, and more than three
hundred servingmen" (p. 1330, A10–aa) that Elizabeth committed
were Lords Leicester, Hunsdon, and Howard "of whom the first two
were of hir privie councell, and all three were knights of the order of
the garter . . . whereunto the said lords obeied verie willinglie"
(p. 1329, B56–62). The revision of Alençon's departure effectively
distances England from him, and from what appeared later because
of his attack on Antwerp, a mission of French imperialism. Even
more important, the original passage with Alençon and Leicester
sailing together on the English ship *Discoverie* firmly associated him
and his French betrayal with Leicester, who by early 1587 had
himself become unpopular with the Dutch. By thus distancing
Leicester from Alençon, the reformation sought to aid the Earl, who
needed if not whatever favorable report, at least, any diminution of
negative aspersions.

The second site of censorship in the Book Club fragment, beginning on p. 1491, likewise serves Leicester's interests – here relating
indirectly to his 1585 entrance into the Low Countries. To understand the censorship again requires a clear picture of what precedes
it. Pages 1419–90 contain "A discourse of the earles of Leicester by
succession," an account of his 1585 departure for the Low Countries
and his lavish reception and entertainment there, "A placard
conteining the authoritie given by the states of the low countries,
unto the mightie prince, Robert earle of Leicester," his political
appointments, and a generally favorable report of the English war
enterprise, though with a few brief reports of failures. The Leicester
materials take up nearly sixteen pages (to p. 1434); a short paragraph
returns to English affairs – the February 1586 appointment to the
Privy Council of William Brooke, Lord Cobham, Thomas Sackville,

Lord Buckhurst and John Whitgift, Archbishop of Canterbury – and on pp. 1435–90 is Francis Thynne's history of the archbishops of Canterbury (largely an English translation of Matthew Parker's Latin *De antiquitate Britannicae ecclesiae & privilegiis ecclesiae Cantuariensis, cum archiepiscopis eiusdem 70* [1572–4]). Then in the Book Club fragment, two leaves 1491/1536 and 1537/38 replace pp. 1491–1538. This suppresses most of the history of Parker, the very short histories of Archbishops Edmund Grindal and Whitgift, the "Descent of the Lord Cobhams," and the "Catalogue of the Lords Warden of the Cinque Ports and the Constables of Dover Castle."

The occasion for inserting Thynne's history of the archbishops was Elizabeth's three appointments to the Privy Council. Even with its two-and-a-half pages on Whitgift, the uncensored Holinshed treats the appointees disproportionately. Cobham enjoys seventeen pages rehearsing his lineage and another nineteen pages on his tenure as Lord Warden of the Cinque Ports, but not a word is mentioned about Buckhurst. In the uncensored text, Leicester's prestige in the two-page "Discourse of the earles of Leicester" (pp. 1419–21) pales against Cobham's. Quantity alone, however, may not have provoked the excision. Cobham's and Buckhurst's appointments after Leicester departed for the Low Countries represented an effort to build support for Burghley's interest in negotiating peace in Continental matters. Indeed, Cobham so favored negotiation that he may even have pursued peace efforts independent of Burghley.[33] Reports of English peace negotiations with Parma undermined Leicester's credibility with the Dutch and would likely have further alienated him from Cobham. Furthermore, Elizabeth Story Donno suggests that social status may have been part of the motivation for eliminating Cobham's pedigree, his line being traceable back to the time of Henry III and Leicester's title being new.[34] Such a representation of disparity in status Leicester and his supporters must have regarded as demeaning, particularly given both the long-standing enmity between him and Cobham and recent dissatisfaction with Leicester's government in the Low Countries.[35] Retaining the lustrous report of Leicester's reception there while cutting the Cobham materials unquestionably serves to heighten Leicester's prestige. Whether this was a personal matter or a matter of state, however, is difficult to determine. According to F. G. Oosterhoff, one reason Leicester returned to England in November 1586 had been to work for increased personal support with the Queen and in

Parliament for greater financial and military resources for the provinces. united under the Dutch Council of State in the Low Countries.[36] A great deal was at stake for Leicester. One of the censors, Henry Killigrew,[37] himself a Leicester ally and client, would have understood well the importance of enhancing Leicester's reputation; he may have been representing his friend's personal interests as well.

The censors may also have cut the passages on Archbishop Parker partly out of loyalty to Leicester. Leicester, as Donno points out, "had frequently been at odds with Parker, who reported to Burghley on several occasions that the earl was offended and 'purposeth to undo' him."[38] While his personal sentiments may have been taken into account, the cut was more likely made in deference to the Queen because it eliminated passages on the early years of the Elizabethan Reformation.[39] The censored text refers to Parker's role in depriving existing nonconforming bishops and ordaining new ones, and the imprisoned Marian bishops were a sensitive issue with Elizabeth. During a 1564 visit to Cambridge University, a group of students provoked Elizabeth by performing a masque ridiculing the deprived bishops – a performance that the Queen curtailed with indignant words.[40] Further, only a decade later Parker's ordinations were labeled by radical Protestants as "disorderly orders."[41]

The third reformation in the Book Club fragment is by far the most complex because it cuts or condenses several different reports in the 7L gathering to a two-leaf cancel (1553/1554, 1555/1560).[42] The principal end of the censorship is the representation of English justice. (To accomplish the condensation, it also cuts three Latin poems praising Sir Henry Sidney and takes the opportunity to correct the report of Sir Philip Sidney and his death in the Low Countries in 1586.[43]) The five matters occupying pp. 1557–60 include the Lovelace libel, George Closse's sermons, the execution of two priests, Jone Cason's witchcraft trial, and the story of Foule of Rie, "hanged for robbing his wife." The Book Club fragment censors altogether the fifteen lines reporting the condemnation and execution of the two priests, William Tomason alias Blackeborne and Richard Lea alias Long – this time it looks much more like religion and not treason was their crime.[44] The reformation leaves intact reports of the witchcraft trial and the story of Foule of Rie. Accounts of the other two matters are reformed to eliminate parallels (however oblique) to the highly incendiary trials of Mary, Queen of Scots and the Babington conspirators and any suggestions that Elizabeth's government crafted both ingenious nets to trap traitors and disingenuous testimony to condemn them.

The first concerns Thomas Lovelace, who "trecherouslie sought to spoile his nearest kinsmen of their lives to have his lands . . ." (printed marginal gloss on 1557, uncensored). The page and a half report is condensed to a paragraph in the Book Club fragment:

About this time one Thomas Lovelace late of Staple inne gentleman, for counterfeiting of false and trecherous letters against his owne kinred, conteining most traitorous matter against hir majesties owne person, was judged in the Starchamber to be carried on horsse-backe about Westminster hall with his face to the horsse taile, and a paper on his backe declaring his offense; then to be set on the pillorie in the palace at Westminster, and there to have one of his eares cut off: then to ride in like sort into London, and in Cheapside to be set on the pillorie upon a market daie; after that to be conveied into Kent, where standing openlie on the pillorie in the place of assise as before, he should loose his other eare; and lastlie be set upon the pillorie one market daie in Canturburie, and another at Rochester; his offense and punishment in everie of the said places openlie read and published: which judiciall sentence was accordinglie executed. (pp. 1555/1560, B6o–A4, Book Club)

This retains the outline of the principal events but eliminates the means by which he was discovered: the craft of Privy Councillors Cobham and Burghley. The uncensored text reveals that letters implicating Richard Lovelace in treason came into the hands of Cobham, who referred the matter to the Lord Treasurer (Burghley). He summoned Richard Lovelace, was satisfied of his innocence, and dismissed him, and then summoned Thomas. Burghley had Thomas copy out a letter, and "the same slips & imperfections of orthographie" that had been in the original letters "did clearlie discover the workeman of this whole matter" (p. 1557, B53–4, uncensored). Of Cobham's intelligence network that intercepted the letters and Burghley's rather clever trap, the chronicler remarks: "how profitable it is to those countries & commonwealths, where the councellors doo rather seeke with sharpenesse of judgement to discerne and discover the qualities and causes, before they applie . . . the heavie burthen of laws . . ." (p. 1557, B62–7, uncensored). However celebratory the remarks, they still attributed to Burghley and Cobham the kind of craft and rigor in justice's administration from which Burghley was trying to distance himself. Furthermore, in the trials of

Mary and the Babington conspirators rumor was alleging that the state built its case on false letters and guileful discovery.

The issues of justice are even more complicated in the next reformed passage regarding the preacher George Closse. While the original text looks like it might have led to censoring because it relates to the silencing of a reform-minded preacher, the revisions point once again to the nature of justice. The Book Club fragment reports the event in one short paragraph:

Upon sundaie the sixt of March a preacher of London making a sermon at Paules crosse, wherein he reprooved the cheefe magistrate of the citie then and there present, and the same verie offensivelie taken; the said preacher was injoined to preach in the same place againe the seven and twentith of March following, and in his sermon to make his submission: wherein he so discharged himselfe, that he had the approbation and applause of the people. (p. 1560, A5–13)

According to the original text, Closse's sermon was on justice, and he "reprooved the maior of London particularlie being there present, for shuffling up a cause" (as he termed it) that came before him (p. 1558, B1–10, uncensored). ("Shuffling up a cause" echoes allegations in both the Lovelace and Babington cases.) Offended, the Lord Mayor complained to the Ecclesiastical Commission, which ordered that Closse preach a recantation sermon. This sermon was to the satisfaction of "thousands . . . gathered together of each age & sex" (p. 1559, A54–5, uncensored), and while they left "with general approbation and applause" (p. 1559, B1, uncensored), the discontented Mayor renewed his complaints to the Archbishop of Canterbury. Closse, however, had obtained from the Archbishop and the High Commission a certificate dismissing him "from further molestation" (p. 1559, B9–10, uncensored). Still unsatisfied, the Lord Mayor complained to the Privy Council, who appointed a special commission that after hearing the matter called for private reconciliation. The Lord Mayor refused and pressed his cause until "after some suspense of his request, at last he obteined of the bishop of London, & others of the temporall commissioners, a certificat to be made, and the matter was continued in suspense till his mayoraltie expired" (p. 1558, B35–9). This conclusion indicates that the Lord Mayor, through the privilege of his position, could prevail even when the system of justice – ecclesiastical and temporal – judged that Closse had satisfied its requirements. In the original text privilege prevailed over justice. In suppressing the Lord Mayor's continuing complaints and ambiguous satisfaction, the reformed text censors those matters that relate to the administration – or rather, the misadministration – of justice.

At the time the *Chronicles* were called in, England faced a much more important occasion of privilege prevailing over justice. Mary, Queen of Scots stood accused and convicted by Parliament of high treason. Despite this, Elizabeth protested her reluctance to execute Mary. In a speech on 12 November 1586, Elizabeth said to Parliament: "in this last act of parlement you have brought me unto a narrow streit, that I must give direction for hir death, which cannot bee to mee but a most greevous and irksome burthen" (p. 1583, A48–51). In her refusal to take immediate action she said: "But for as much as this matter is rare, weightie, and of great consequence, I thinke you doo not looke for anie present resolution" (p. 1583, B16–18). Her reluctance prevailed even after the 4 December royal proclamation, and when the Privy Council called for the *Chronicles*' review two months later, the sentence had still not been carried out. Mary was alive by virtue of royal privilege even though the English legal system had judged her guilty of treason and called for her execution.

The Book Club fragments from the English history argue that the two principal concerns of the censors (at least initially) were the representation of English justice and matters related – however obliquely – to Leicester and the Low Countries. Donno has established that Leicester, Sir Thomas Bromley, and Lord Burghley were the Privy Councillors concerned with the *Chronicles*' review and reform.[45] The kinds of materials censored and reformed in the Book Club fragment correlate both to their interests[46] and to the particular expertise of two of the censors the Privy Council had recommended in its order to the Archbishop of Canterbury. "Mr. H. Killigrew," as Donno has pointed out, was a "practiced diplomat, who served as an adviser to Leicester (who refers to him as 'little Hal') on the Dutch Council of State."[47] Moreover, according to his biographer Amos C. Miller, throughout his career Killigrew received Leicester's patronage and shared his political and religious views.[48] Besides supporting Protestant intervention in the Low Countries, when Killigrew represented English interests in Scotland between 1570 and 1575, he effectively secured the regency for Protestant Morton and worked diligently against French interests in Scotland. The second censor, "Mr Doctour Hammond" (John Hammond, LLD), according to Donno, "a notable exponent of civil law and member of the Court of High Commission,"[49] frequently was called upon by the Privy Council as a special commissioner in all kinds of unrelated legal matters: admiralty and trade, debt, piracy, and (probably most important here) treason. He had examined both Campion and Alexander Briant, who had been tried with Campion in 1581. Hammond's appointment must have been made with a clear interest in how the *Chronicles* represented English civil law. The third reviewer, Thomas Randolph, a good friend of Killigrew, replaced Killigrew in Scotland, and, according to Conyers Read, shared his puritan views.[50] Randolph served twice as an English envoy in France, but his principal service was in Scotland between 1570 and 1586 where his most recent negotiations had effected a league between Elizabeth and James by which in exchange for a pension from her, James agreed to give no aid to her enemies and to assist her with troops if England were attacked.[51] Such expertise on recent Scottish affairs suggests that the review and reformation of the "Historie of Scotland" coincided with the first review reflected in the Book Club fragment.

The "Historie of Scotland" was censored and reformed in three locations: pp. 422–4, 433–6, and 441–50. While several small but significant events appear in these passages, the principal object of the censorship was accounts reflecting English intervention in Scottish domestic affairs. Knowing as he did James's opposition to English military intervention in Scotland, Thomas Randolph had eliminated or radically reformed reports of the recent history of Scotland that in some way had engaged Elizabeth's government. The revisions, reflecting as they do the keen eye of a specialist in Scottish affairs, require some review of Scottish history in the late sixteenth century.

The persistent problem in Scottish politics between 1570 and 1585 was the vulnerability of the kingdom to the power of the nobility, with shifting coalitions of nobles gaining power over the young king.[52] These circumstances occasioned English intervention during Summer 1586 that culminated in a negotiated settlement between James and Elizabeth. For most of the 1570s the young James had been under the influence of the Protestant faction led by the Earl of Morton. A shift occurred in September 1579 when Guise interests represented by the Earl of Lennox effected a coup, and Morton was charged with the King's father's death. At this point Randolph was sent to Scotland to seek to discredit d'Aubigny and plead for Morton, and, if he failed, Randolph was to summon English troops

into Scotland to restore Morton by force. The Queen commissioned
Lord Hunsdon to command this force of 2,500. Randolph's negotiations were unsuccessful. However, he advised the Queen not to
invade, since James opposed it. Hunsdon disagreed with Randolph
and attempted to discredit him with the Queen. England did not
invade, but d'Aubigny had Morton executed as a traitor. This broke
off Anglo-Scottish diplomatic relations for more than a year.[53]

The first of the Scottish history's three censorship sites (pp. 422–4)
suppresses nearly two full pages of text recounting an early incident
during the factional strife between Lennox and Morton.[54] The
passage concerns English military raids into Scotland against
members of Lennox's faction. Here, Lord Hunsdon, acting on a
commission from Elizabeth

having a time appointed him accordinglie, and being in order set, well
furnished with men and munition . . . threatened spoile to manie places of
Scotland belonging to the borders, and burnt the houses of the lords there
inhabiting; if they joined themselves with the male-contents, as they had
fully deliberated for to doo. (p. 424, A1–8, uncensored)

This occurred when, according to the official reports of England's
current ambassador in Scotland, Robert Bowes, the armies had
come to terms.[55] Such a discrepancy, however, was probably not as
important as how English intervention on Morton's behalf looked
from the perspective of 1587 – when the previous summer England's
support for the Protestant faction had helped to effect a coup d'etat.
Randolph, too, may have taken his own partisan pleasure in suppressing a report of Hunsdon's successful military intervention, given
Hunsdon's efforts to discredit him for opposing later similar intervention.

At the Scottish history's second site (pp. 433–6), the censored
materials include notice of Randolph being sent ambassador to
Scotland following Morton's death, reports of James Stewart's ill-got
gain of the title of the Earl of Arran, the exchange of ambassadors
between France and Scotland, and the detention of a Scottish Jesuit
in England for plotting against the Queen. The cuts reflect a keen
knowledge of Scottish affairs and a diplomatic awareness of those
issues that may have been particularly sensitive at that time (but
which are not entirely clear today).[56] James Stewart had, of course,
led the coup against Morton, and the report of his acquisition of the
earldom may have been perceived as offensive to King James.[57]

Perhaps the logic lies in the changing fate of Arran and his place in the King's favor. The other cut reports England's detention and release of William Creighton, well known to English diplomats for his efforts to elicit the Pope's support for d'Aubigny as a means to achieving Catholic control of Scotland and ultimately England.[58] The *Chronicles* report Creighton's cooperation with Walsingham in providing evidence about a fellow prisoner, William Parry, and Creighton's expected liberty – obviously negotiated in exchange for the information. This account of realpolitik belies English claims of both noninvolvement in Scottish affairs and just treatment of priests and Jesuits.

The Scottish history's last site of censorship (pp. 441–50) is concerned with events that drastically affected diplomatic relations between England and Scotland. In 1583 after a Scottish court revolution in which the Earl of Arran had gained authority, two members of the pro-English party, the earls of Angus and Mar,[59] were dismissed from court and fled to England. In response, Elizabeth sent Edward Wooton as ambassador to Scotland to negotiate a new league. While he was in there, a border dispute led to the English Lord Russell's death, "much lamented of the English, and that especiallie sith his untimelie death so injuriouslie (by the erle of Arrane, as the common fame went) procured" (p. 444, A65–8, uncensored). According to Conyers Read, Arran was apprehended in Scotland for his role in the death but was later released by James, much to English dissatisfaction.[60] The Queen then demanded that he should deliver to her Fernehurst, who actually shot Russell, in exchange for Angus and Mar. When James refused, Angus and Mar returned to Scotland, but not as prisoners: within a week they took possession of the King and had Arran proclaimed a traitor. This coup brought Randolph back to Scotland to negotiate the 1586 league that finally cemented Anglo-Scot relationships. The reformation suppresses the efforts of the Scottish ambassador, Louis Bellenden ("Ballentine"), to secure from Elizabeth the redelivery of Angus and Mar for treason charges and the circumstances surrounding Russell's death. Furthermore, it radically reforms the report of Angus's and Mar's return to Scotland with their raising of an army of "others of the nobilitie to joine in one action, for the redresse of such government as was used by persons about the king, suspected to nuzzle him in the Romane religion" (p. 446, A1–6, uncensored). The force of their action is reduced to: ". . . the banished lords of Scotland remaining in England, entered their countrie: and after some abode theire, upon diverse meetings & consultations, at last gethered their powers . . ." (p. 443, B34–7, censored). The revised text also suppresses three columns reporting the course taken "for the redresse of . . . government" by which the "lords of religion" gained custody of the King and Arran fell. According to Read, this coup achieved a change in the government much more acceptable to England.[61] Elizabeth quickly sent William Knollys to James to disclaim any hand in the revolution; he accepted this and maintained his interest in establishing a league with England. Since Randolph negotiated that league, he would have been well aware that all the matters of the revolution may have well been sensitive issues, particularly since the original version in Holinshed suggests the enthusiasm with which it was received in England.

The suppression and reformation reflected in the Book Club fragment – with the exception of the Cobham materials – correspond to the matters set forth in the Privy Council's order. It appears to have been carried out rather precisely: events concerning the state and offensive to James were reformed in a timely manner. The timeliness is apparent in one cancel in "The Historie of Scotland" that refers to the "Now imprisoned queene of Scotland" (p. 443, A6–7). Since the page with this reference was reset, the initial review and reformation, including resetting the cancel leaves, must have taken place within a week of the initial order[62] as Mary was executed on 8 February. This may have been a mere oversight except throughout the text the chroniclers tended to treat matters of life and death with considerable care, such as Philip Sidney's death.

That this initial censorship seems to have received a fine tuning can be seen from a second state of the text that represents further censorship of Thynne's "The lives of the archbishops of Canturburie," already partially censored in the Book Club fragment. This state, represented by the Igoe copy[63] contains the same cancels as the Book Club fragment (1553/1554 and 1555/1560), but expands the censorship that began at p. 1491 (reflected by the Book Club cancel 1491/1536). The Igoe copy retains this cancel and adds two more, beginning its expurgation sooner – at p. 1432. Pages 1432–90 are replaced with two leaves 1431/1432 (signed ABCDE) and 1433/1490 (unsigned).[64] The cancel condenses Thynne's essay from fifty-six pages to twenty-three lines. I suspect that Archbishop Whitgift called for the suppression and may have offered the rationale that "this kind of discourse, being ecclesiasticall, is unproper for this secular historie" (p. 1490, B61, Igoe; *STC* ABCDEv). The replacement passage suggests what the censor sought in suppressing Thynne's history. Following an announcement of the appointments of Cobham, Buckhurst, and Whitgift to the Privy Council, the cancel reads:

And here, as in other places of these chronicles, where we have set downe certeine collections of right worthie personages in high calling and verie honourable office, we are lead by some reason to deliver a catalog of the names (at least) of such archbishops as have successively possessed the metropolitan see of Canturburie, therein implieng their antiquitie and authoritie, &c: and from thense proceed to saie somewhat of the lord Cobhams and lord wardens of the cinque ports, as a matter of some consequence, by means of the mutual advancement at one instant which hir highness of speciall grace vouchsafed them both. (p. 1490, B29–42, Igoe)

The chronicler goes on to list the names of the first twenty-nine Archbishops and to say that he would speak something of the deeds and times except for their impropriety in a history. The second censor apparently saw "The lives of the archbishops" differently from the first. The first appears to have been concerned with the representation of Elizabethan archbishops and offense to the Queen. The second, in the interest of preserving enough of the "Historie of the archbishops" to represent the office's authority and antiquity, shows concern for promoting pro-episcopal propaganda.

That Thynne's entire "Historie" may not have been regarded as achieving this end is suggested by another contemporary treatment of archbishops, a life of Archbishop Parker. This enjoyed a rather dubious status in the pamphlet war staged by radical Protestant reformers. *The life of the 70. Archbishopp off Canterbury presentlye Sittinge Englished, and to be added to the 69. largely Sett forth in Latin. The numbre off seventy is so compleat a number as it is great pitie ther shold be one more: but that as Augustin was the first, so Mathew might be the last* appeared in 1574 from a Continental press, the title reflecting the translator's bias. The biography is followed by an epistle, "To the Christian reader, peace in Christe, and warre with Ante-christ"[65] that attacks Matthew Parker's *De antiquitate Britannicae ecclesiae*, Thynne's principal source for his history. The epistle sees Parker's book as one "sett forth, to the hurte of Christian men" because it contained,

. . . certaine, Rapsodies, and shredes off olde forsworne storyes, allmost forgotten, had he not nowe latlye awakened them out of a dead sleape, and newly sewed them togither in one booke, printed, whose glorious title promiseth not mountaines off gold . . . but beareth Christ in the browe, and is honested with this title in the fronte. De antiquitate Britannicae Ecclesiae & privilegiis Ecclesiae Cantuariensis cum Archiepiscoppis eiusdem septuaginta. As thoughe it weer somme worthye monument, and rich hoorde, whearin had been honorablie buried, great heapes off the knowledge, and actes off the first Christian infancie of this church off England. And yett havinge rolled a waye that glorious gravestone, off that counterfaicte title, and setinge further into it, appereth a very painted sepulchre, gorgeouslye dected withe that outward onelie name, and whithin full off broken shankebones, and reliques off dead carcases, yea nothinge, but a very charnell howse, off brainlesse unleaned skulles, off suche men as wear wicked in their life, and not worthye any memorye being dead.[66]

Revealing as it did the lives and times of the archbishops, Thynne's history sometimes showed "men as wear wicked in their life." The problem that Thynne's history posed to the censor was not so much that "a survey pointing to England's long succession of bishops could be considered unduly provocative," but that it did not represent the archepiscopacy in an entirely favorable light.[67] As the reformed text suggests, the censor wanted a catalogue of the archbishops that would have shown the antiquity and authority of the office. Indeed, one longer and with more detail than the reformed passage actually contains may have been entirely acceptable, but as the reviser's use of "implieng" suggests, such propagandizing of antiquity and authority may not have interested the chroniclers enough to waste precious time, paper, or labor costs.

The *Chronicles'* final reformation reflects a careful attempt to influence international and domestic regard – though principally the first – for England in anticipation of both its efforts in late Spring 1587 to negotiate a settlement in the Low Countries and international response to Mary, Queen of Scots' execution. The state of the 1587 *Chronicles'* text noticed in the *STC* contains the expurgations and reformations represented in both the Book Club fragment and the Igoe copy but reflects further censorship in two places in the English history. At the first site, the final stage of censorship commences at p. 1419 (Book Club had begun at p. 1491, Igoe at p. 1432). It eliminates the 6V gathering and the Igoe cancels, 1431/1432 and 1433/1490, and replaces them with new cancels numbered 1419/1420 (signed 6V) and 1421/1490 (signed ABCDE).[68] This expurgation reforms material on Leicester's reception in the

Low Countries. The second site is between pages 1551 and 1574, which contained original leaves 1551/1552 and 1561/1562 and earlier cancels 1553/1554 and 1555/1560, which are discarded entirely and three new cancels 1551/1552, 1553/1554 and 1555/1575 replace pp. 1551–75.[69] The new cancels censor and revise further materials present in the Book Club and Igoe texts on the Sidney family, suppress entirely the passages on Jone Cason's witchcraft trial and Foule of Rie, and newly reform the report of the trial and execution of the Babington conspirators.[70]

The changes made between pages 1419 and 1433 consist of condensing slightly fewer than sixteen pages on the Earl of Leicester and his reception in the Low Countries between December 1585 and May 1586 to a little less than three and a half pages. The changes reveal that the censors were less interested in concealing events than in altering how participants in those events were represented.[71] The uncensored record of Leicester's arrival had depicted him as a glorious representative of English rule whose conduct earned him the admiration and respect of the Dutch. He found bonfires and the peel of bells in Flushing: "He was there feasted and lodged in the ambassadors house, where, according to his accustomed disposition, he demeaned himselfe so humblie . . . that he purchased to himselfe no lesse love & good liking than among the English" (p. 1424, B33–8, uncensored). At Middleborough he was accorded royal honors as the Queen's representative, and each successive city received the Earl more gloriously than its predecessor: "And it is to be noted, that the further the earle went up into Holland, the braver the countrie was, and the better his lordship was beloved, as appeared by his more excellent interteinment" (p. 1426, A30–3, censored).[72] At Donhage, the Dutch had compared Leicester to "Arthur of Britain" and at Leiden "himselfe with a canopie carried over his head was brought to his seat" at the stage's edge to view a play (p. 1427, A19–20, uncensored). His progress had culminated in the Dutch appointing him as the States' Governor General.

The revision still reports Leicester's progress through the Low Countries, including his appointment.[73] No city is neglected, but the activities and entertainments devised by the cities that reveal the degree to which Leicester's "person" was "answerable" disappear altogether from the censored text (along with the "Discourse of the earles of Leicester"). The military successes are likewise gone. Leicester is stripped of his glory.

The motivation for revising the Leicester/Low Country materials, Donno and Anne Castanien have found in Leicester's interest in his own reputation – particularly given the tension that had arisen with the Queen over his acceptance of the Governor Generalship – and both believe that he was instrumental in obtaining censorship of these materials.[74] That these revisions offer a far more modest account of Leicester's esteem and success counters their assessment. Indeed, I doubt that Leicester had anything to do with these revisions. Instead, they were motivated by a changed political climate in mid-February 1587 when the governorship was no longer a matter of contention between Leicester and the Queen.[75] Further, by then the Earl had retired from Court, and another matter arose regarding the Low Countries that more likely affected this censorship. Lord Buckhurst, who supported a negotiated peace in the Low Countries, was preparing for his departure to the Low Countries to negotiate further English involvement and the terms under which Leicester would return. He was a longtime opponent of Leicester, and, according to Oosterhoof, "revealed himself as Leicester's most outspoken critic" in the course of his embassy.[76] Buckhurst may have seen the *Chronicles'* adulation of Leicester as contrary to both the interests of his embassy and his own political views.

Such *raison d'état* presents a more seemly rationale for tinkering with Leicester's image than another possibility – that is, that it was the product of petty factionalism among the Privy Council, but this must not be ruled out altogether. The first stage of censorship had removed any traces of Thynne's two long discourses on his patron, Lord Cobham – even though a parallel discourse on the Lord Treasurer remained. As we have seen, Leicester and Cobham were at odds personally and politically. Suppressing the *Chronicles'* glorification of Leicester may have been Cobham's response to the earlier censorship. Such a supposition might appear preposterous except for two things. First, Francis Peck's index in *Desiderata Curiosa* of the papers of Abraham Fleming (the 1587 edition's corrector)[77] mentions one manuscript on the *Chronicles'* censorship identifying Leicester, Bromley, and Burghley's involvement, and another on "other censorsings of various men whose malevolence was only exceeded by their subtlety."[78] Retributive censorship by Cobham would fit this description. Second, the Leicester/Low Country materials did not go permanently censored. Stow included them in the 1592 edition of his *Annales,*[79] four years after Leicester's death and the year that

Cobham's attendance at the Privy Council became less and less frequent.

Privy Council rivalries serve likewise to explain other differences between the final state of censorship and the earlier Book Club/Igoe cancel 1552/1553. The new cancel 1551/1552 cuts further the adulation of the Sidney family that had survived the first cut. Donno has discussed this reformation in some detail but finds the "motivation for excising them puzzling," particularly from the perspective that Leicester was involved with the censorship.[80] This particular reformation is less puzzling if he is not regarded as being involved. The most substantial cuts here appear in the praises of Sir Henry Sidney and his son Philip.[81] Sidney had twice successfully served as governor in Ireland between 1565 and 1578; even so, his administration was fraught with problems raised by conflicts at the English court between Leicester and his opponents, Norfolk, Sussex, and Ormond. Sidney's administration in Ireland was vulnerable to factional efforts to unseat Leicester's control of Irish patronage, his reputation suffering most when Leicester was out of favor.[82] The final reformations do not suppress altogether Sir Henry's administration of Ireland, but they do omit the praises which are marginally glossed: "his skill far exceeded other men in knowledge & secrets of Ireland"; "He had seane and knowne more of Ireland than anie one, yea of that countrie birth"; and "The love & affection the Irishrie bare him, drew manie of them to civilitie," as well as "His service was subject to the eare and to the eie, whereby his vertues manie times were suppressed" (p. 1551–2, uncensored). The new 1551/1552 cancel similarly suppresses praises of Sir Philip (and his poetry), but retains the passages on his service and death in the Low Countries, though it omits the Dutch respect for his service. The Sidney reforms, like those that affected Leicester's image, though not exactly insulting to him, reflect court rivalry since they concern his brother-in-law and nephew.

All of the final stage's remaining cuts and revisions address the representation of English justice. While this concern had likewise motivated the earliest stage, this time text that had been acceptable in early February was now deemed objectionable. Two small matters overlooked by the initial censors – the stories of Foule of Rie and Jone Cason's witchcraft trial – offer a key to the *Chronicles'* remaining censorship. Cason's witchcraft trial, juxtaposed as it was with Foule of Rie (tried "at the mayors hastie proceedings" and executed for stealing from his wife), intimates that law and justice were not always the same thing.[83] Perhaps more important to the censors than the ambiguity, however, was the report of how Cason accepted the administration of her sentence:

> . . . she said in hir confession upon the gallowes (taking hir death that she died giltlesse herein) that the judgement of God was in such measure laid upon hir, and therewithall made so godlie and penitent an end, that manie now lamented hir death, which were (before) hir utter enemies. Yea some wished hir alive after she was hanged, that cried out for the hangman when she was alive . . . (p. 1561, A14–21, Book Club)[84]

The story relates the change of public sentiment for a woman falsely convicted for one crime but guilty of others who by dying a good death engages public sympathy and respect. This provoked complete suppression after the initial censorship order. On 8 February Mary, Queen of Scots was secretly executed at Fotheringay.[85] By 17 February Burghley had prepared "The state of the causes, as it ought to be concerned and reported concerning the execution done upon the Queen of Scots."[86] On 18 February Charles Arundel approached the Spanish Ambassador in Paris to inform him of Mary's execution.[87] On 27 February a license for a ballad entitled "An excellent dyttye made as a generall rejoycinge for the cutting of the Scottishe queene" was entered in the Stationers' Register, suggesting that it took from eighteen to twenty days for Mary's death to become common knowledge in London.[88] The *Chronicles'* final censorship and reformation, I believe, belongs to the period between Mary's execution and public knowledge of it. In wrestling with the advisability of Mary's execution, the strongest argument Burghley found against her death was "the offence that hir friends will conceive shall provoque them."[89] This stage of censorship seeks to control the offense to Mary's friends by reminding them (and the rest of the *Chronicles'* readers) that "The execution of Lawe, is injurious to no man,"[90] particularly in the case of the Babington conspiracy.[91]

The 1587 *Chronicles'* report of Mary's trial and conviction, Elizabeth's reluctance to sentence her to death, and the royal proclamation finally announcing Mary's sentence went uncensored. The censored text, however, vastly reforms the reports of the Babington conspiracy and of the trial and execution of the conspirators. While the record of the events goes unchanged, it reduces "in scale and colour" the writer's original rendering so aptly described by Patterson as "peculiarly barbarous."[92] The qualitative (and quantitative) transformation can best be seen in the alterations regarding the apprehension of the traitors and their trials and executions. The reformed passage on the first reads,

. . . order was taken for a verie strict inquirie and search universallie to be made for their apprehension, which was accordinglie executed, in so much that the conspirators distressed and succorless were put to verie hard shifts by this inquisition and pursute, and in ti[m]e[93] apprehended, to the great rejoicing of the citizens of London . . . (p. 1553, A73–B6, 7L2 cancel, *STC*)

This conceals the relentlessness with which the public officers pursued the conspirators, which continues for an entire page in the original (pp. 1563–5, B27–45, uncensored). There "such officers, as upon whome the charge was imposed, demeaned themselves so preciselie (and speciallie the constables of London, to their praise be it spoken) that they spared not their next neighbors houses, but indifferentlie and without parcialitie did search them . . ." They continued "daie and night" until finally when "double diligence was used in a further inquirie . . . that hedge and bush was so beaten, as at length some of those noisome birds were unnested and surprised." The original expends considerable effort disparaging the traitors ("O caitives most execrable, begotten and borne to miserie") and recounting the people's joy at their capture ("some wearied themselves with pulling at the bell ropes"; others built bonfires, sparing no wood "although wood was then at a sore extent of price").

The trials and executions of the Babington conspirators are likewise reformed to reflect an orderly legal process and to soften the chronicler's (and the people's) exultation in their executions. The censored text reads:

And now to resume our former rememberance of the conspirators, you shall understand, that after due examination had, & no rigor used either by torture or torment, the wicked wretches guiltie consciences driving them to voluntarie confession, on the seventh day of September, certeine of them were led from the Tower of London to Westminster by water, where they were indicted; first, for intending treason against the queens owne person; secondlie, for stirring civill wars within the realme; and thirdlie, for practising to bring in forren power to invade the land. Seven of them appeared at Westminster on the thirteenth daie of September, who all pleaded giltie, and therefore had no jurie, but were condemned, and had judgement on the next morrow. (p. 1555 A61, 7M cancel, *STC*)

The original text opens up the possibility that there may have been some "rigor" in the "winnowing out" of the treacheries. Further, the

Council's consideration of "rigor" allows that torture was a practice available to the administrators of justice.[94] Both the censored and uncensored texts report the execution individually of each conspirator and conclude that the executions ended "to the full satisfaction of the peoples expectation" (p. 1575, A51). Censorship, however, altogether suppresses the kind of cruelty reported in the conclusion to the first day's executions:

Now when these venemous vipers were thus hewne in peeces, their tigers hearts burned in the fire, and the sentence of law satisfied: their heads and quarters were conveied awaie in baskets, to be fixed upon poles and set over the gates of London . . . (p. 1574, A22–6, uncensored)

Between the report of the traitors' confessions and executions, the original text consists of nearly two pages excoriating traitors and treason that the censored text omits entirely. The contents differ little from the Church's homily on disobedience; their tone, however – of a jeremiad – makes treason into sin and English justice into damnation. Of these particular traitors,

who had woven the web of their owne wo, being now forlorne, as hated of heaven, and irksome to the earth, seeing no hope of life, but deserved death imminent and hanging over their heads, occupied their wits in dolorous devises bemoaning their miseries, of the like stampe to this here annexed, favouring more of prophane poetrie than christianitie of fansie than religion. (p. 1570, B35–43, uncensored)

The elegy of Chadiock Tichbourne, one of the conspirators, follows the Jeremiad.

Patterson believes that the censors' attention was directed principally at the elegy because it uttered a powerful appeal for popular sympathy.[95] Actually the jeremiad included it to argue that the traitors in their "prophane poetrie" showed more concern for their mortal woes than their eternal souls. The entire censored passage, rather than showing any compassion proclaims that the traitors "deserved a death of exquisit crueltie" (p. 1571, A29–30, uncensored). Such cruelty is justified "By the law of nature" that "men should doo as they would be doone unto" (p. 1571, A34–5, uncensored). There is no way of ascertaining whether or not the censor was so subtle as to recognize the problem here with the writer's logic, which rendered his justification of execution false – the Babington conspirators had not engaged in "exquisit crueltie." He does, however, appear to have recognized that the excesses in defense of English justice achieved the opposite effect. The rhetorical strategy of this section is to vindicate justice by denigrating the traitors and treason – that is, the vileness of treason and traitors is so extreme that extreme punishment – even eternal damnation – is warranted. Such excess was clearly antithetical to the official government position that "The execution of Lawe is injurious to no man."

The censors purged anything that exulted in the conspirators' suffering. Public support, as the uncensored chronicles show it, was squarely behind the government and vehemently against the conspirators. The uncensored passage looks rather like pro-government propaganda that was acceptable to members of the Privy Council and their agents *before* the order was given for Mary's execution. In the place of an almost rabid anti-papal nationalistic diatribe, the censored text fully represents the conspiracy, the trials, and the executions of the Babington conspirators; it cuts the narrator's moralizing and the English crowd's vindictiveness and hatred. It does, however, keep the sole expression of sorrow and sympathy that appeared in the assessment of the executions – that they were carried out,

to the full satisfaction of the peoples expectation; who neverthelesse . . . were inwardlie touched with passions ingendred by the deepe impressions of the present objects: but touched they were . . . as they were men, in whome humanitie should so have prevailed, as that they should rather have chosed losse of life & livelod, than to have intended the desolation of their native countrie, the deprivation of prince, the deposition of peeres, the destruction of people. (p. 1575, A51–62, all)

The representation of English justice motivated the *Chronicles'* censorship both in the early and the late stages, but the nature of that interest shifts. The first stage, in the Book Club and Igoe texts, reconstructed accounts of justice to insist that fair public officers administered trials and executions in England according to the due process of law. At the last stage, in the Babington section, the reformed text tempers justice, if not with mercy, at least with compassion.

I have argued that the *Chronicles* underwent three stages of censorship, most likely within a month. *STC*'s note that they underwent a second official recall raises the possibility that some censorship may belong to a period later than 1587, but I disagree. According to *STC* "On 3 Nov. 1590 the Queen sent word to Burghley of her disapproval of a passage, and perhaps this was the occasion for cancellation of pp. 1328–31."[96] According to Donno,

The second review took place at the end of 1590. On 3 November, Thomas

Windebank, Clerk of the Signet and a trusted individual admitted to secret councils by the queen, wrote to Burghley to report her disapproval of a "certain declaration" appearing in the *Chronicles* and of her command to have it called in, saying that she vehemently inveighed against it as being "fondly set out."[97]

Donno and *STC* have assumed that there was a second recall probably because they rely on the *Calendar of State Papers*' summary of Windebank's letter.[98] His letter, probably not a royal order, reports to Burghley a conversation with the Queen:

Whereas it appearith that the declaration mentioned in Mr Bowes letter be annexed to Mr Hollyngsheds Chronicle, her Magesty marvelleth that such a thing could escape to be supresed, And howsoever commanded that chronicle to be called in. Whereunto I answered that the which I thought could not be called in, the same being printed w[ith] licence and having [had] so long tyme recorse. But the declaration might be. Howbeit her majestie still insisteth upon the calling in both of the one & the other for she vehemently inveigheth against the Chronicle to be fondly sett out. And so in these kynd of matters her magesty wold have that they should remove any offense to the king of Scotland.[99]

Windebank discusses Scottish affairs reflected in letters from Bowes, the ambassador to Scotland. Given this, and Donno's evidence that Burghley and Bowes reached a settlement with James over the furor associated with matters related to a "certain declaration," that the declaration was never censored from the *Chronicles*, and that no evidence exists among Privy Council orders or Stationers' Court records indicating a recall, the book probably was not called in in 1590.[100]

  Whether or not the *Chronicles*' sales were stayed a second time, Windebank's letter underscores one of the most important aspects of its censorship – the question of offense to someone other than the ruling monarch of England. Seemingly similar offense was, as we have seen, an issue with regard to *A Gaping Gulf*, because it attacked the Duke of Alençon (Anjou) and his mother. Holinshed's *Chronicles*, however, do not attack James. The censored matters regarding Scottish affairs principally concern the representation of *English* interests in Scotland. They reflect both English support for Protestant factions in Scotland and active intervention on their behalf. In the case of the uncensored "certain declaration," James was unhappy about English anti-presbyterian, pro-episcopal meddling in Scotland – or at least that it came to the public's attention through print – and that it made him appear to oppose the Presbyterians in his own country. The desire to see the declaration suppressed reflects anxiety on his behalf about ruling his country; that is, it suggests that he feared the *Chronicles* would further feed the kind of factionalism that had destabilized his regency. Similar concerns about destabilization seem to have prompted the censorship of the Scottish history – but from Elizabeth's perspective. The 1586 coup led by Angus and Mar and supported by England had ultimately pressured James to accept the long-sought treaty that protected England from Scottish–Spanish and Scottish–French alliances. This censorship seems to suggest that Elizabeth feared the effect that public knowledge of English intervention might have on James's authority in Scotland – or upon England's ability to maintain the alliance finally forged with Scotland. The censorship of Anglo-Dutch matters (outside of that which derived from personal rivalry) reflects similar concern about the effect of how the representation of England's (and Leicester's) association with Alençon would sit with the Dutch – or of how the *Chronicles'* representation of Leicester would affect either Buckhurst's negotiations in the Low Countries or Leicester's interests both at home and in the Low Countries. The censorship of these particular kinds of "matters of later yeers that concern the State and are not therfore meete to be published in such sorte as they are"[101] indicates that the English "State" saw in the printed word – particularly in Holinshed's *Chronicles* – real power to influence the subtle realm of international diplomacy. This means that in particular the Privy Council (Walsingham, Leicester, Buckhurst) envisioned among the *Chronicles'* readers if not kings, at least their informants, and they understood the potential role of the book in forming a national image favorable to English diplomatic interests.[102]

Such a concern for image, as we have seen, likewise dictated the reformation of the *Chronicles'* representation of English justice. Here, the censors sought to make it consistent with the official position articulated in Burghley's *The Execution of Justice* that justified prosecuting Jesuits and seminary priests from the Continent who would not pledge allegiance to the Queen under treason laws. More was at stake here, though, than simply justifying how the missionaries were treated. Censored and uncensored, the *Chronicles* insist throughout that law is the foundation of English society. Patterson has suggested that the chroniclers' emphasis on law and trials reflected their interest in "the making of knowledgeable citizens and future

jurors."[103] That the censors preserved the *Chronicles'* reports of trials
– even of conflicting testimony – but censored charges that the
exercise of law was unjust *and* exultations in the law's harshness –
suggest that the chroniclers and the government shared faith in the
institution of English law. In the case of Mary, Queen of Scots,
however, even a just representation of the law of a Protestant nation
was not enough to make the state invulnerable to the machinations
of her friends. The Privy Council could not allow anything that
might suggest that Mary or the Babington conspirators – or any
other Catholic conspirators – were anything other than traitors *under
the statutory civil law* – particularly that they might be portrayed as
martyrs sacrificed at the altar of English Protestant zeal. The
censoring of the enthusiastic condemnation of the Babington conspirators reflects the Council's interest not so much in suppressing
written opposition but in containing the potentially volatile response
– both at home and abroad – to Mary's execution within a discourse
of law and government rather than retribution and damnation. Even
though image making is here related to domestic events, these events
held international ramifications since those friends of Mary that
Burghley feared were the same Catholic powers that he saw as a
threat to England.[104]

   Government control of the printed word in matters of such
international importance as treason and diplomacy, while they may
violate post-enlightenment ideals of a free press, look remarkably like
that area where even democratic governments today maintain their
right to control the press, "national security." What is remarkable is
that the *Chronicles* (both editions) were the only books the Privy
Council called in for review and revision. This, to a degree, lends
credence to Annabel Patterson's view that writers understood the
limits to their expression, and that censorship occurred when a writer
did not understand the code. In the *Chronicles*, however, the writers
made it very clear throughout that they understood the codes,
frequently commenting that they would refrain from certain topics
they knew were inappropriate, such as discussing a ruling monarch
or theology. The writers who compiled the continuation of Elizabeth's reign wrote in good faith of matters that may well have been
acceptable had the political climate not changed.

   But not all materials expurgated and reformed in Holinshed's
Chronicles had to do with policy and governance. Their censorship to
the modern eye looks arbitrary – what we expect from the author-

itarian Tudor state. Certainly altering matters about which the Queen was sensitive – her relationship with Alençon, the imprisoned Bishops – belong to Tudor authoritarianism, and they alone may have provided grounds for calling in the *Chronicles*, particularly at a time when the dignity of her person was a matter of political importance. If, however, it had not contained material that touched on sensitive diplomatic issues, it is not altogether clear that the remaining matters that were expurgated or reformed, *in and of themselves*, would have warranted (or indeed invoked) the recall. Admittedly, the reputation of the episcopacy was a matter of some concern to Whitgift in 1587, but Matthew Parker's *De antiquitate Britannicae ecclesiae*, which provided the basis for Thynne's "Lives of the archbishops," had long been in print. How Leicester looked in comparison to Cobham, or how much better Cobham and Buckhurst may have looked to their peers without written reminders of Leicester's glorious progress in the Low Countries had nothing to do with statutory libel, or even the kind of personal offense to Privy Councillors, that invoked government censorship on other occasions. Had personal image been the only issue with which the Council was concerned, the *Chronicles* may not have been censored at all – particularly given Windebank's later opinion that it "could not be called in, the same being printed w[ith] licence . . ."[105] Censorship in these matters of image, then, probably tells us more about the *Chronicles* than they do about censorship. Thomas Nashe may have believed that it was not in the power of "lay Chronigraphers" to "endowe . . . names with never dated glory,"[106] but clearly these Privy Councillors, Whitgift included, saw the *Chronicles* as an instrument of fame. Patterson may be correct in viewing this book as a kind of textual space for the middle class, but those reformations performed in the interest of fame suggest that "all Englishmen"[107] (not only the middle class of the chroniclers and their intended audience) expected some profit from the important piece of cultural capital known as Holinshed's *Chronicles*.

CHAPTER 8

Martin Marprelate and the puritan press
"as thou hast two eares, so use them both"

Between October 1588 and September 1589, relying on a secret (and movable) printing press, radical Protestant reformers brought their case against the English bishops and the established Church before the public in seven witty and satiric diatribes written under the pseudonym of Martin Marprelate. A royal proclamation issued in February 1589 ordered their suppression.[1] The Marprelate pamphlets have elicited a wider range of interest than other texts censored during the reign of Elizabeth. With a style so inventive and lively it created a new fashion among a generation of Oxford and Cambridge educated writers (the University Wits), the Marprelate pamphlets have engaged the interests of literary historians.[2] Frederick Siebert regards their tracts as politically important because they represented "the most notorious defiance of the Elizabethan printing regulations."[3] Patrick Collinson credits the activities of "Martin" and the Marprelate press with leading "directly to the uncovering of what had hitherto been a well-kept secret [the network of presbyterian classis], and exemplary prosecution of some of the leading ministers before the High Commissioners and in the Star Chamber, and the subsidence of the organized puritan movement."[4]

So highly visible and significant, the Marprelate pamphlets are often taken to epitomize Elizabethan censorship of the puritan press. From this perspective, their censorship belonged to a campaign initiated by Archbishop of Canterbury, John Whitgift, to silence the voice of dissent. His principal weapon was "his" 1586 Star Chamber Decrees. That the puritan and printer of the first four pamphlets, Robert Waldegrave, was forced to flee to Scotland was a measure of the campaign's success against the "puritan press."[5] The death sentences of John Udall and John Penry, both suspected of being Martin, along with the executions of separatist writers Henry Barrow and John Greenwood, demonstrated the campaign's cruelty and established a legacy of repression: "the precedent set by Martin Marprelate could not be dismissed."[6] With regard to the tracts this view is not entirely wrong – neither is it entirely right. The government engaged in a formidable effort to answer Martin's attack, to discover his identity, and to punish radical Protestant reformers whose names were identified with him. But Martin's case was not typical. Hundreds of tracts, treatises, admonitions, and sermons had issued from the presses of puritan printers during the 1570s and 1580s without invoking the ire of ecclesiastical and government authorities. Martin changed the terms of the debate, and did so in a highly provocative manner. He used the printed word, according to his own admission, for the "displaying" of the bishops "and their proceeding until they bee made as odious in our Churche and commonwealth, as they be thought of al sorts, unworthie to be harboured therein."[7] The "displaying" amounted to a highly personalized denunication of specific prelates for specific sins. Rather than provoking the people to reject the bishops, the means of Martin's "displaying" provoked government sanctions against Martin – whomever the government thought him to be. Martin Marprelate was not one of a flock of lambs sought by the wolves, but a young fox who inadvertently led the hounds to his own den.

Lamb or fox, Martin Marprelate belongs to the company of sixteenth-century religious reformers usually referred to as "puritans," and his publishers were members of the so-called "puritan press." Knowing who the "puritans" were, what status puritan printers enjoyed in the London printing trade, and how "puritans" employed the printed word to work for religious reform enables a clearer sense of how radical, confrontational, and provocative Martin's discourse truly was. Considering what constituted "puritanism" and the "puritan press" in late sixteenth-century England is not quite so easy as it once was since recent historiography became engaged in redefining "puritanism."[8] The Whig view of puritans as radical reformers of both the Church of England and English society, according to Peter Lake, leads to an understanding of Elizabethan puritanism as "a series of gestures against the Elizabethan settlement and the church."[9] From this perspective, the puritan press produced oppositional literature. Such a Whig view is implicit in Frederick Siebert's assessment of the puritan press:

Balked both in Convocation and Parliament, the Puritans discovered another avenue open to them – an appeal to the country through the medium of the press. The skill with which they conducted the campaign in spite of stringent regulations on printing and in spite of the opposition of both the crown and the ecclesiastical hierarchy demonstrated for the first time in English history the power of the press.[10]

While Collinson counters Siebert to some extent in recognizing that the early 1580s were "comparatively free years of puritan pub-lishing,"[11] he fails to clarify the degree to which puritan publishing resided within the printing establishment. His view that most works carrying the "puritan imprimatur" issued from Waldegrave's press, which was ultimately destroyed by the authorities, depends, like Siebert's, on an oppositional definition of puritanism.

Lake would replace such a negatively defined notion with a more positive one that takes into account the "positive evangelical protes-tant aims" that undergirded the critique of the Church. According to Lake, if the "godly" refused to conform to the liturgical forms of the English church, it was because these "crypto-popish" forms offended "those truly affected to the gospel" who sought instead " 'edifica-tion,' that process through which a true community of godly and properly self-conscious true believers were called together and sustained within the church."[12] For Lake, and for Nicholas Tyacke as well, the distinguishing feature of Elizabethan puritanism was Calvinism. According to them, the teachings of John Calvin, particu-larly with regard to predestination, pervaded the Church.[13] Puritan "moderates," according to Lake, were able to distinguish between "doctrine and discipline"; they argued for a true church validated by doctrine rather than by presbyterian polity.[14] Implicit in Lake and Tyacke is the notion that the English church could embrace within a "reformed consensus" some doctrinal variety, a view that Peter White articulates more fully in *Predestination, Policy, and Polemic*.[15] He, however, finds the Elizabethan church more closely aligned to the Protestantism of Edward VI's reign, which, besides holding moder-ately Calvinistic views on predestination, embraced the teachings of other Continental Protestant reformers. White points out that during the 1570s and 1580s changing political circumstances in France and Spain increased the polarities between Catholicism and the refor-mers, which led, in turn, to increased pressure among the Calvinists on doctrinal conformity. This posed a threat to the Church in England when an "active minority who were 'Calvinists' in the more literal sense of admiring Calvin and Beza as the founders of a church

polity," judged that polity to be "indispensable to a full reformation."[16] The notion of "full reformation" is more useful for coming
to terms with Elizabethan puritanism than Lake's discrimination
between doctrine (predestination) and polity (presbyterianism). As
White makes clear, polity for "literal Calvinists" was part of doctrine;
the Elizabethan settlement had initiated a reform of the Church that
would be complete only when it became a biblical church, that is,
when it contained only those offices and liturgical practices instituted
by Jesus and the twelve apostles. While the Elizabethan church could
"allow" the writings of Calvin and Beza (alongside other Protestant
reformers), literal Calvinists, unable to abide the state of the Church,
pressed for greater doctrinal (biblical) conformity.

White's understanding of Elizabethan Protestantism as doctrinally
broad helps to explain practices in the puritan press. Rather than
make a Whiggish discrimination between an establishment and an
oppositional "Puritan Press," it is more useful to designate a
constituency of "reform-minded" printers: those whose efforts
brought into print all kinds of literature (sermons, treatises, exhortations, devotional works, catechisms – and attacks) seeking further
reformation of the Church. These "puritan printers," most of whom
belonged to the printing establishment, appear to have been particularly astute at comprehending the limits of acceptable reform
advocacy. For the most part, they employed ecclesiastical authorization and Stationers' Company regulations to their best advantage;
they entered those titles in the Register, either with or without
ecclesiastical authorization that they judged most acceptable to the
Church hierarchy. Other titles – probably those that would jeopardize their authors in matters of conformity, but that posed little
problem for the printers themselves – the printers signed with their
own names and establishments but neither attributed authorship nor
entered in the Register. The most radical texts that both authors and
printers feared would provoke sanctions were printed outside of
London or on the Continent. Testimony to these practices appears
both in the bibliographic record of writings by radical reformers and
in the career of Waldegrave.

Two of the most important instances of radical Protestant dissent
during Elizabeth's reign were the Marprelate tracts and the texts in
the *Admonition* controversy. John Field, Thomas Wilcox, and Thomas
Cartwright were the Admonition controversy's principal reform
authors, and John Penry, John Udall, and Job Throckmorton are

most reliably associated with Marprelate.[17] All wrote extensively in the interest of puritan reform, but not all their works were printed illegally. Interestingly, Cartwright, whom Peter Lake identifies as a moderate puritan, had only one title printed legally in England during Elizabeth's reign: John Day printed *A very godly and learned treatise of the exercise of fasting* (1580), and subsequently assigned it to John Harrison the younger and Thomas Man. Most of Cartwright's writings issued from Geneva, where he resided for several years. Two of Field's three works (besides *Admonition*) printed during Elizabeth's reign received the Bishop of London's imprimatur, and the third was signed by the printer.[18] Of the ten works by Wilcox that appeared in print, six were entered in the Register (three with ecclesiastical authorization), and the other four were signed by the publisher, Man, and sometimes also the printer.[19] Of the Marprelate writers, only Throckmorton went unpublished in England. Waldegrave printed Throckmorton's *A Dialogue wherein is plainly laide open the tyrannical dealing of Lord Bishopps* and *Master Some Laid Open in His Coulers* in La Rochelle in 1589. Only one text by the Welsh minister Penry was printed legally in England; his anonymous *A treatise containing the aequity of an humble supplication* was printed in Oxford by Joseph Barnes, and sold by Toby Cooke in London (1587).[20] Waldegrave printed three more surreptitiously in England in 1588-9 – two from the traveling Marprelate press.[21] The remaining (six titles) were printed either on the Continent or in Edinburgh – most by Waldegrave.[22] While Penry's writings tended toward political activism to achieve religious reform, John Udall's writing was more theological in nature and included sermons and commentaries that were legally published by Thomas Man. (One Man entered in the Register; five others bore his name on the title page.)[23] Two of his works were censored: *Diotrephes* (printed secretly by Waldegrave, 1588)[24] and *Demonstration of Discipline* (printed secretly by Waldegrave at East Molesey, 1588).

The printing history of radical reformers' writing points to the success of puritan printers in bringing them into print (sometimes legally, sometimes not). (Outside of the *Admonition* and Marprelate tracts themselves, only two books, both by Udall, were actually suppressed.) This success not only bears testimony to the keen sense people such as Man and Waldegrave had of the limits of acceptability, it also belies claims that have been made (often by the reformers themselves) about the perils of the "puritan press." Some did exist for puritan printers, but, as the example of Waldegrave – the most visible of them – makes clear, the oppositional relationship between their printing and the establishment (the Stationers' Company and the government) has been overstated – particularly by Martin Marprelate.

An Epistle to the Terrible Priests of the Convocation House, the first of the Marprelate pamphlets (printed by Waldegrave in 1588), would have us believe that Waldegrave's "puritan press" was the object of relentless High Commission investigation and suppression ("Waldegrave dares not shew his face for the blood-thirstie desire you have for his life," Martin tells the bishops, p. 23). While some of the texts he printed indeed provoked the Commission, throughout his career he received protection from his fellow Stationers. Waldegrave was a member of the Stationers' Company, began printing in London in 1578, and by 1583 maintained two presses.[25] Between 1580 and 1589 he printed eighty-four texts still extant, seventy-three of which were in some respect "puritan" – either in their Calvinist theology or their interest in church reform.[26] Twenty of the latter, including the Marprelate tracts, Waldegrave printed without placing his name or press location on either the title page or colophon, making twenty-three percent of his printing "illegal." Waldegrave apparently felt no need, however, to conceal Dudley Fenner's *Counter-poyson, modestly written for the time* (1584), which answers Richard Cosin's reply to *An abstract of certain acts of parliament* (*An answer to the first two and principall treatises of a certeine factious libell* [1584]). The *Abstract,* which argued the illegality of the High Commission's proceedings by quoting from civil and ecclesiastical law, however, Waldegrave printed but did not sign. Since he was printing both signed and unsigned texts in the same years, his legal press probably produced "illegal" books, and some of them got Waldegrave into trouble with the Company, but not those that issued from his "secret" press. Sometime in 1583–4 the Company fined him for printing illegally against Seres's privilege.[27]

Waldegrave's trouble with the Archbishop of Canterbury came probably in 1586, if Martin Marprelate is to be believed, when ". . . his grace kept him 20. weekes together in the white lyon for printing the Complaint of the comminaltie, the Practize of prelats, A learned mans judgment."[28] Martin's recounting of the circumstances of this imprisonment and release suggests the curious position of Waldegrave as both an opponent of printing privileges and a printer of variously "illegal" books, and the High Commission's response. His friends apparently sought his release from the White Lyon by negotiating a bond, and according to *Hay any worke*:

> You must be bounde saith he, in a 100. pounds, to print no more books herafter, but such as shalbe authorized by hir Majesty or his grace, or such as were before lawfully authorized: wherunto he answered, that it was not possible for him to containe himsselfe within the compasse of that bond, neither should his consent ever go to the same . . . yet he would gladly have his libertie if he might lawfully. For saide he, I being a poore workeman to my companie, cannot possibly observe it. For many bookes heretofore printed, had *cum privilegio*, and yet were never authorized: and againe, that it were but a folly for him to sue to her Majestie, the office were very base and unfit for her. And he might be wel assured that Caiphas of Cant. would never authorize any thing for his behoofe, and so it fell out. (pp. 41–2)

None of the three books Martin mentioned was licensed by the Stationers' Company, entered in the Register, or printed "legally" with Waldegrave's name and press location, so the terms of the bond would have pledged him to the standard sought by the 1586 Star Chamber Decrees.[29] Waldegrave's response – that he could not financially afford licensing costs, especially in a market where privileged printers printed without them – ignores altogether "illegality" in terms of sedition or heresy. Indeed, the nature of the imprisonment and the bond suggest that he may not have been arrested for printing heretical or seditious texts at all – he would have been tried and, if found guilty, subjected to sanctions far severer than a bond.

Whatever measures the High Commissioners took in 1585 or 1586, Waldegrave risked printing *Diotrephes* without entrance, license, or authority, and suffered the loss of his press. Nothing in the Stationers' Company records indicates that the High Commission called in *Diotrephes*, but the *Dictionary of National Biography* says the Commission deemed the work seditious and ordered Waldegrave's press seized.[30] His culpability lay "onely for printing of bookes which toucheth the bishops Myters."[31] Waldegrave was brought before the Stationers' Company Court of Assistants for printing the book "without auchtority" and contrary to the recent Star Chamber Decrees for Order in Printing. Finding the claim valid, the Court "ordered & agreed by force of the said decrees & accordinge to the same. that the said books shalbe burnte and the said presse letters and printinge stuffe defaced and made unserviceable accordinge to the said Decrees."[32] Three months later Waldegrave was at work printing the Marprelate tracts, this time outside of London at a press both secret and portable.

These tracts offer the only extant record of the ongoing confrontation between Waldegrave and the bishops. These position him as the victim and them as the oppressors. Waldegrave's press undeniably mounted a spirited attack on the bishops (this, after all, was the intent of Marprelate), but judging the entire relationship between puritan printing and the Church upon Martin's evidence, however, seems unwise. His rhetoric, based as it is upon hyperbole and attack, depends upon the polarized position of Waldegrave and the bishops to achieve its ends. From his perspective Waldegrave experienced harassment from the bishops for information about any puritan printing; he suffered in prison and endured the destruction of his press, while his family was exposed to penury from his loss of earning power (his press being destroyed). Martin even accused Whitgift of obtaining the 1586 Star Chamber Decrees, under which authority Waldegrave's press was seized and destroyed, "onely for Waldegrave" who "never printed book . . . that contayneth eyther treason or impietie."[33]

Marprelate's account ignores several important factors. In printing against Seres's patent, Waldegrave involved himself in the dispute within the printing trade in the 1580s about both privileged printing and the Stationers' Company's authority. Despite this, the Stationers appear to have been surprisingly sympathetic to him. They ignored a long history of printing without the Company's license (or, at least, without entrance). When he did print against Seres's privilege, rather than having his press destroyed, he was either fined £40 (which he did not pay) or required to post a £40 bond. They lent him money and promised to protest his imprisonment. Twice in 1584 fellow Stationers' licenses were entered in the Register with the requirement that Waldegrave be the books' printer.[34] Some of his fellow Stationers may even have forewarned him of the pending search for *Diotrephes*, since he was able to spirit away a case of type. In many respects, it appears that Waldegrave's status as a Company member may have allowed him protection that he otherwise might not have enjoyed.

Scholarly opinions have concurred with Martin that Whitgift sought the 1586 Star Chamber Decrees for Order in Printing to put an end to the liberties taken by the "Puritan Press."[35] From this perspective, from the time that Whitgift became Archbishop of Canterbury, he engaged in an escalating campaign against the puritan press that culminated in the Star Chamber Decrees. His success after 1586 forced them underground and abroad. This view, following as it does Martin's account of Waldegrave, assumes that puritan printing centered in Waldegrave's efforts.[36] As long as Waldegrave was in England, a puritan press existed: when he left, so did puritan printing. Two problems exist with this view: it neither takes into account the differences in kind issuing from the presses of puritan printers, nor does it admit the depth of puritan interest among members of the printing trade. As we have seen, even the most radical reformers saw their writings legally printed, and not through Waldegrave's efforts alone. The writings of Wilcox, Field, Udall, and Penry represent a few chapters in an enormous book of puritan texts printed in England. Similarly Waldegrave was only one of many puritan printers. Several others were sought out by the publisher Thomas Man. In the 1580s Man published forty-four titles (seventeen after the Star Chamber Decrees) that reflected his interest in religious reform; the 1590s saw sixty-four printed texts by the puritan writers William Perkins, Phillip Stubbes, and the deprived ministers Henry Smith and George Gifford. Man generally entered his titles in the Stationers' Registers, most of these (not all of them – even after the 1586 Decrees) carry an ecclesiastical imprimatur. All of this suggests a religious establishment far less hostile to puritanism – even to debates about Church polity – than has previously been believed.

Some hostility, however, did exist. Waldegrave (and others) undeniably printed texts the bishops disliked that criticized episcopal polity – the texts issuing from the bishops answering these criticisms make their dislike apparent. Peter Milward's *Religious Controversies of the Elizabethan Age* offers a detailed record of the printed debate of what has come to be known as the *Admonition* (over twenty titles), the Subscription (twenty-nine titles), and the Marprelate controversies (over thirty-five titles not including those by separatists Henry Barrow and John Greenwood).[37] In each controversies, the authorities sought to suppress some of the texts, but their efforts often came late, as we have seen with *Admonition*, and had little effect in removing the books from circulation. The number of texts actually censored in the three controversies represents between one-quarter and one-third of those published on the radical reformers' side.[38]

Outside the controversies, hundreds of "puritan" texts went unmolested. It was clearly not the case, as Martin claimed to the bishops, that "any book . . . printed in the defence of Christs holy discipline, or for the detecting of your Antichristian dealings" warranted suppression.[39]

That circumstances surrounding the printing and the suppression of the Marprelate tracts have been misread to epitomize the confrontational relationship between religious and personal freedom and state authority does not diminish their significance for English ecclesiastical history. If Collinson's assertion is correct that their attack on the bishops unleashed a reaction that led to the discovery and devastation of the presbyterian classis movement in England, then their importance cannot be dismissed. If the tracts were not simply the victims of an ecclesiastical witch-hunt, as I have argued, then something in their rhetoric or allegations distinguished them from the hundreds of other sermons, treatises, and admonitions that likewise berated episcopacy and advocated presbyterian polity. To appreciate Marprelate's distinctive characteristics requires briefly reviewing the course of the religious debate during Elizabeth's reign.[40]

The central position of Protestant reformers was that the work begun by the Elizabethan settlement, while valuable in its own right, was insufficient to establishing Christ's church in England. The Church of Christ as it was instituted by the Apostles and defined by Holy Scripture should be centered in a ministry of the word (*edification*)[41] by a preaching ministry trained in biblical learning (*a learned ministry*). This ideal is best expressed in the words of *An Admonition to Parliament*, "The outward marks whereby a true christian church is knowne, are preaching of the woorde purely, ministring of the sacraments sincerely, and Ecclesiastical discipline which consisteth in admonition and correction of faults severely."[42] According to Thomas Wilcox, "None but Christ only hath full and sole authoritie to make lawes unto his Church,"[43] and scripture contained those laws. "A true report of our Examination and Conference" explains that the reformers "would goe forward to perfection" (1567, p. 32). Their goal was to reform the Church according to scripture by having in the church *only* those practices found in scripture: ". . . we wilbe tryed by the worde of God, which shall judge us all at the last day" (1567, p. 35).[44]

While referring to the reformers' uses of language in these matters as equivocation may be somewhat strong, to the literal Calvinists the words *edification, a learned ministry*, and *discipline* had precise meanings in regard to church polity that enabled them to advocate a radical presbyterian reform of the Church in terms that appealed to even the most conformity minded bishops. Few Church clergymen during the reign of Elizabeth would have objected to pure preaching of the Gospel, sincere ministering of the sacraments, or using the existing ministry and the Church courts to admonish and correct faults. Many, however, would have objected to the literal Calvinist agenda concealed by the *Admonitions'* words. For the word to be preached "purely" meant that it had to be preached by a scripturally appointed ministry – pastors or doctors "elected" by the people, educated in the Holy Word, and examined and ordained by "elders." The only sincerely administered sacraments were baptism and the Lord's supper. For baptism to be sincerely ministered it could not be done in private; no sign of the cross could mark the candidate's forehead; no godparents could speak on behalf of a child; and under no conditions, as the Book of Common Prayer admitted for an emergency, could a woman administer it. The Lord's Supper was sincere when no remnants of the papist mass were spoken, when bread rather than wafers were used, and when the bread and wine were distributed to a standing or sitting (not kneeling) congregation. Finally, only "elders" (the governors of the congregation), and not ecclesiastical courts or visiting bishops, could admonish and correct the Church.

The printing press provided the reformers with both an effective medium for edifying the emerging Church of Christ and an efficient disciplinary tool for admonishing and correcting "severely" the existing Church of England. The reform writers saw it their task to present both "a cleere glasse where may be seene the daungerous and desperate diseases of our English church" and " A CORASIVE of the wholesome hearbes of God his worde" (n.d., p. 55). The language here, relying as it does on scriptural metaphor, reflects the manner in which reform discourse proceeded. This example employs a principal New Testament metaphor for the Church. The Church is a body with Christ as its head, and the people and ministers are the body's "members." From a historical perspective Christ and the Apostles had left the Church a healthy body sustained by scripture. The Popes in usurping authority from the biblical Church had poisoned the body's health. Those vestiges of papacy that remained in the English Church – its "daungerous and desperate diseases" – had to be purged by the herbs of scripture that could restore the biblical Church. Dudley Fenner's *Counter-poyson* (1584) makes clear that the "discipline" – pastors, doctors, deacons, and elders – offered the only remedy to the ailing Church. While this metaphor afforded the literal Calvinists one of the best means to introduce the "wholesome hearbes" of the discipline, two others provided useful ways to define the role of reformers and to mirror existing errors in the Church. If the Church was the bride of Christ, then their task was "with godly jelousie to present the church and spouse of Christ under their charge, a pure Virgin to Christ her husband" (1570, p. 2). That papist relics sullied that bride, particularly in matters of dress, represents Catholic remnants if not more benignly at least more passively than another prevailing metaphor – the Church as a flock of lambs. This was widely employed to condemn practices in the English Church – particularly a nonresident and nonpreaching ministry – that starved Christ's lambs. It also served as an effective means to characterize the Church's vulnerability to ravenous predators – the Pope is the wolf ever outside the door, but hypocritical deceivers work their ways inside the fold. In 1570, looking back to Marian martyrs, Anthony Gilby could claim ". . . by Gods power we have fought with the Wolves, for these & such like Popishe chaffe, and God hath given the victorie: we hav[e] nowe to do with the Foxes, let us not feare" (1570, pp. 13–14). In 1588 reformers maintained that the English bishops "stop the mouth of the sheepheardes and set at liberty the ravaging wolves."[45] These threads embroidering sermons, treatises, admonitions, and exhortations kept the reformers' writings centered in the scriptural imperative for reform and lent to their discourse a kind of unity that enabled them to encode some of their more radical notions in language discernible principally to the "godly."

However much specific language could be used to conceal their more radical ends, puritans sought high visibility for the literature of reform. Title page after title page carried the legend from Luke, "I tell you that if these should holde their peace, the stones would crye" (19:40).[46] The reformers wrote to the end that they might be answered *in print* by the established church. Only a few months after *An Admonition to Parliament* appeared in print, *An Exhortation to the Bishops and their clergie* appeared from the same secret press and called for response:

. . . my desire is, & that for Israels sake, I meane the children and the churche of God, they which are the eyes of the churche, & are oure overseers to watche for our soules . . . wolde take this matter in hand, to debate the equitie and truth of the cause, by the scriptures and worde of God, which is the only food of oure soules . . .[47]

Implicit in the appeal for debate was the reformers' certainty that scripture supported their cause, but more important was their conviction that if their cause were rightly understood – by the people, by Parliament, by the bishops, or by the Queen – reform would proceed unobstructed. Such confidence is clear in Cartwright's 1574 translation of Walter Traver's work on discipline, *A full and plaine declaration of ecclesiastical discipline*:

This whole controversie is fullie and at large to be disputed of: that when they understand the goode cause that we have to reprive the one, and require the other, they maie joyne together with us in earnest praier unto god, and humble suite unto her Majestie. That this Popish tyrannie being at last utterlie abolished and cleane taken away, In place thereoff a better and more holie government of the churche according to Goddes worde maie be established.[48]

This confidence, maintained into the 1580s, is similarly reflected in Laurence Chaderton's *A fruitfull sermon . . . of the 12 Chapiter . . . to the Romanes*, "I perswade my selfe moreover that if her Majesty should heare and knowe, the grounds of this doctrine, we should not long pray for the reformation of the Church."[49]

While the Church willingly entered into debate – in print – with the reformers about most matters of reform, the issue of ecclesiastical polity was not discussed to the satisfaction of the literal Calvinists. In refusing to debate church polity, the English bishops became the principal obstacle to reform. In *Diotrephes* – a "conference" between a bishop, a papist, an innkeeper, and a godly preacher – the preacher Paule contended that Diotrephes (the bishop) misjudges the reformers' ends and appeals to the bishop to read:

Ecclesiastical Discipline: A lerned discourse of Ecclesiastical governement: The Counterpoyson: A Sermon upon the 12 to the Romanes, & M. *Cartwrites* last reply . . . some of which books have bene extant this dozen yeeres, and yet are none of them answered.[50]

Paule here takes umbrage at the bishop's ignorance and the Church's refusal to judge the discipline by scriptural standards. Earlier reformers had been able to use "bishop" and "pastor" interchangeably, but as *Diotrephes* makes clear, by 1588 the bishops had become the enemies, and removing them – the hierarchy that refused even to talk about scriptural standards for church polity – became the reformers' principal goal. Where *Diotrephes* had failed to shame the bishops into debate, Marprelate devised a fiery purgative to cure their chilling silence.

The motive for Martin's assault does not rest alone in printed controversy (or lack thereof). Confrontation between the Church hierarchy and religious reformers became increasingly politicized in the 1580s. Precisely when reformers were becoming more literal minded in their Calvinism, Whitgift, newly appointed Archbishop of Canterbury in 1583, initiated a campaign directed at both radical Protestants and Catholics to achieve greater conformity to the 1559 Church settlement. He required that ministers subscribe to a set of three articles, of which the most objectionable to the reformers was their required assent that the 1559 Book of Common Prayer contained nothing contrary to the word of God – objectionable for those who disliked vestiges of papist ceremonies, an intolerable position for those who opposed on biblical grounds the prayer book's ordination of ministers and bishops. Opposition to Whitgift's articles was so great that the Privy Council forced him to moderate his demands, which he did, but not before his efforts had aroused fierce passions.[51] Following J. E. Neale, Patrick Collinson has viewed puritan political efforts in parliamentary elections in 1584 and 1586, and the reform measures introduced in the 1586/7 Parliament as a reaction to Whitgift's conservatism. Diarmaid MacCulloch agrees that the reformers took advantage of the 1584 Parliament to launch a propaganda campaign pointing out the Church's defects, but cautions against seeing the parliamentary elections as a puritan landslide. According to MacCulloch, "Puritans certainly tried to array their forces in the Commons, but most of them were elected for boroughs with small electorates, often dominated by fellow-Puritan aristocrats: where they faced electorates numbering thousands in the shire elections, they had much less success."[52] The 1584 Parliament failed to produce any reforms in the Church. In the 1586/7 parliamentary elections, however, the reformers fared better, gaining a strong puritan showing. Poised to take advantage of this, they orchestrated a series of petitions to Parliament and the Privy Council, and prepared a sweeping program of Church reform. According to MacCulloch,

It was Anthony Cope, one of an intake of new MPs probably resulting from a Puritan election drive, who put forward the most sweeping programme of church restructuring ever presented to an Elizabethan Parliament . . . not only did it envisage a full Presbyterian system and Geneva service book, but in enacting clauses whose brevity was equalled only by their apparent naivety, forthwith abolished all existing legislation relating to church polity and liturgy. One cannot imagine that the group of Puritan gentry MPs backing Cope envisaged this inept measure as anything more than a shot across the bows of Whitgift and his supporters; it was a sensational way of holding the Commons' attention while they pursued the defects of the established Church in a series of set-piece speeches before Elizabeth could gather her wits and issue the inevitable ban on further proceedings.[53]

Leland Carlson has located the Marprelate pamphlets in the reformers' frustration following their 1587 parliamentary silencing.[54]

While Martin Marprelate may well have been born of the general frustrations Job Throckmorton and John Penry experienced in the 1587 Parliament,[55] the rhetoric of the tracts more directly responds to the orchestrated counterattack on the puritans that followed their parliamentary attacks on the church. According to MacCulloch, following the "Puritan parliamentary fiasco of 1586," Richard Bancroft and a group of conformist clerics, supported by Lord Chancellor Christopher Hatton (a "crypto-catholic"), took it upon themselves "to mount a counter-attack on the Presbyterians by making claims for the institution of episcopacy way beyond anything that Whitgift's generation had asserted in their defence of the Church polity."[56] This group countered the literal Calvinist claims that presbyterian polity was commanded by divine law by maintaining a scriptural foundation for episcopacy. John Bridges, Dean of Salisbury, wrote *A defence of the government established in the Church of England for ecclesiastical matters* (1587) to expound this view. MacCulloch's estimation that this went "beyond the aggression of Whitgift's drive for subscription" and attacked the Presbyterian reformers "on their own theological ground" helps to explain why the Marprelate pamphlets assumed a rhetorical strategy that departed from the extensive and cohesive reform literature that mirrored abuses and provided the corrosive of scripture. In *Diotrephes*, as we have seen, Paule complained that the Church had not answered the important statements of presbyterian polity by Travers, Cartwright, and Chaderton. Bridges answered them – but not to Marprelate's satisfaction, so the first two pamphlets took aim at him and fired a battery of attacks that repudiated any possible claims for a scripturally instituted episcopacy. No pastoral admonition or scriptural counter-poison here, Martin abandoned biblical metaphors and offered instead a detailed account of the bishops' individual sins and follies that argued that the usurping bishops, like the Pope, were "begate by the Divel."

To understand what so provoked Martin to alter the debate requires looking more closely at Bridges's *A defence of the government*. The title of it continues: *"against the Tetrarche that our Brethren would erect in every particular congregation, of Doctors, Pastors, Governors, and Deacons,"* which makes clear that this is the response the radical reformers had long demanded to their arguments for presbyterian polity. In their confidence that their vision of ecclesiastical discipline was scripturally ordained, they had not expected a response like Bridges's which emphasizes in its epistle "To the Christian reader" that it proceeds by the same premises as the arguments for the discipline. As the reformers appealed for indifferent judgement, Bridges says that he writes to correct their misconceptions because "the will of man must be perswaded, can not be compelled."[57] Like the reformers, he maintains scriptural authority for church polity – only he finds it for the episcopacy:

It is necessarie therefore, that (as God be praysed) we have the truth in doctrine, and defend it wel, not only by the authorities of the Magestrate, but by the words owne authoritie, openly in writing by the Ministers theroff, set foorth to the world, against all these resisters of the same. (¶v)

Bridges's position is that the reformers "pretend (for the reformation which they devise) prescription of gods word, practise of ancient churches & testimony of holy fathers & yet cannot prove either any cleare scripture, or produce of any ancient church, or cleare testimony of any holy Father" (pp. 35–6), and he proceeds by examining the scriptural foundations for each of the four parts of presbyterian polity.

Bridges's method – "to search the places, our selves, that are alledged" (p. 943) – puts the reformer's claims for presbyterian polity to the scriptural test. How it failed to produce the reformers' desired ends can be seen in his scrutiny of Romans 12. The arguments for presbyterian polity, epitomized by Chaderton's *A fruitfull sermon . . . of the 12 Chapiter to the Romanes*, cir Romans 12 as authority for doctors to teach, pastors to minister, and elders to admonish. Chaderton builds on verses 4–8 (from the Geneva Bible):

4. For we have many members in one bodie and all members have not one office,

5. So we being manie are one bodie in Christ, and everie one, one anothers members,

6 . . . let us prophecie according to the proportion of faith:

7. Or in office, let us waite on the office: or he that teacheth, on teaching:

8. Or he that exhorteth on exhortation . . .[58]

In Bridges's reexamination, he adds the preceding verse and the part of verse six that arguments for the discipline ignore. He thus considers the following (from the Bishops' Bible):

3. For I say, through the grace given unto me, to every man that is among you, that no man esteeme of himself more than he ought to esteeme: but so esteeme himself that he behave him selfe discreetely according as God hath dealt to every man the measure of faith.

4. For we have many members in one body, and all members have not one office:

5. So we, being many, are one body in Christ, and every one members one of another:

6. Seeing that we have divers giftes, according to the grace that is given unto us, either prophecie, after the measure of faith:

7. Either office, in administration: or he that teacheth in teaching:

8. Or he that exhorteth, in exhorting . . .[59]

Bridges says that these passages refer "not to the external orders of the church ecclesiastical government" but to the gifts Christ gave the Church and the "excellencie of Love and Charity" (pp. 61–5).

Bridges's use of this approach to exhaustively – and exhaustingly – dismantle the reformers' arguments lends considerable credence to his conclusion: "we finde not so much as any good probability, that is grounded on the Scriptures, but only the meere interpretations and sayings of some the chiefest persons in estimation on ther side . . ." (p. 13). Bridges did not go so far as later proponents of episcopacy would to claim its divine authority, but in the course of arguing against presbyterian polity, he found precedents in both scripture and patristic writings for the existing English ecclesiastical polity – bishops as overseers who ordained church ministers (sometimes called elders, sometimes ministers in scripture) and deacons – and governing regional bishops who oversaw the local city bishops (a precedent for the archbishops so hated by reformers). Like the reformers, Bridges maintained that the primitive church was corrupted by the Bishop of Rome's usurpation of authority over other regional bishops. Indeed, he lamented that the reformers parted company with the reformed English Church and chose to attack the English hierarchy rather than work with them, as in earlier days, to overthrow Antichrist. Bridges judged to be libellous the reformers' view that the English Church participated in "the tyrannical jurisdiction that Antichriste hath set up" (p. 1080).

This was not the response reformers expected or sought. Bridges's use of scripture – *the same scripture* – to justify episcopacy produced a stalemate that forced the reformers to take a new approach. The first Marprelate pamphlet, commonly called *An Epistle,*[60] departs entirely from the earlier conventions – very little effort is made to answer Bridges's book or argue the reformers' cause. Instead, under the auspices of presenting statements for disputation, it lashes out with personal assaults on members of the Church hierarchy. Marprelate challenges the Church to further debate and then offers each item for debate as the major premise of a syllogism; negative personal and particular examples form the syllogism's minor premise(s); and he closes the debate with the inevitable conclusion forced by the logically stated but not necessarily "true" premises:

Those that are pettie popes and pettie Antichrists, ought not to be maintained in anie Christian commonwealth. But everie Lord B. in England, as for ilsample, John of Cant. John of London, John Excetor, John Rochester, Thomas of Winchester. The B. of Lincolne, of Worcester of Peterborow and to be briefe all the Bb. in England, Wales, and Ireland, are pettie popes & pettie Antichristes . . . and therefore neither John of Cant. John of London, &c. are to be tollerated in any christian commonwealth. What say you now brother Bridges, is it good writing against puritanes. (p. 4)

Marprelate thus quits arguing for presbyterian polity and instead launches a personal attack on the existing Church hierarchy. With no holds barred, he openly commits the libel Bridges had lamented, and argues that the bishops are "pettie popes" because they usurp their authority – ecclesiastical and temporal.

Marprelate is particularly stringent in his attacks on the abuses he attributes to the Bishop of London (John Aylmer) and the Archbishop of Canterbury (John Whitgift). John of London engaged in "playne theft and horrible oppression" in confiscating cloth taken in a robbery in his district and not giving it to the dyers who claimed it. He kept cloth for liveries for his men and "to make quishions and coverings for tables" (p. 9). Further, the Bishop of London in his worldliness and corruption abused his sacred trust:

Who is a carnall defender of the breache of the Sabboth in all the places of his abode John London. Who forbiddeth men to humble themselves in fasting and prayer before the Lorde, and then can say unto the preachers, now you were best to tell the people, that we forbidd fastes? John London. Who goeth to bowles upon the Sabboth? Dumbe dunsticall John of good London, hath done all this. (pp. 19–20)

Martin's accusations against of the Archbishop of Canterbury extend from popery to treason. For his failure to prosecute allegedly Catholic printers, Martin remarks, "Is not he a very Pope in deed that thus hideth poperie and knavery?" (p. 14). Martin finds the Archbishop so entirely a papist that he says, "Wee need not fear (if we can keep him) the Spaniards and our other popish enemies, because our metropolitans religion and theirs differ not much" (p. 25). He finds him even more reprehensible in matters of governance, and accuses him of unjustly depriving a minister because his congregation falsely complained about him, of calling Penry before the High Commission on the grounds that he committed heresy in maintaining preaching essential to salvation, and of rejecting a minister patronized by Ambrose Dudley, the Earl of Warwick.

The strategy of Martin's conclusion – extorting the bishops' compliance with his demands – compounds the offense of his exposé. The *Epistle* concludes with Martin's "Conditions of Peace": If the bishops fail to promote preaching, refuse to admit godly ministers to the clergy, prevent the publication of Cartwright's answer to the Rhemish Testament,[61] continue to urge subscription for noncomformity, and persevere in "molesting" those who attend "assemblies" to hear the word duly preached and the sacraments sincerely administered – in short, if the bishops refuse to allow a presbyterian movement to emerge within the Church – or if they seek out Martin – he promises all their "dealings shall be knowen unto the world" that they will be "an example to all posterities" (p. 37). Martin claims that he knows all of the bishops' "knavery" and that "it may be he keepes a register of them." If the authorities violate his peace conditions, Martin assures them, the consequences will be dire:

. . . your learned brother Martin doth proclaime open war against you, and entendeth to worke your woe . . . First I will watch you at every half turne, and whatsoever you do amisse, I will presently publish it: you shall not call one honest man before you, but I will get his examination (and you thinke I shall knowe nothing of the oppression of your tenants by your briberie, &c.) and publish it . . . And rather then I will be disappointed of my purpose, I will place Martin in everie parish . . . Secondly, al the books that I have in stor already of your doings, shalbe published upon the breache of the former covenants or any of them. (p. 40)

Whether or not his extortion was extended sincerely or taken seriously probably has less to do with the furor the pamphlet caused among the authorities than his position that every charge the *Epistle* made against the bishops was true:

You will go about I know, to prove my booke to be a libell, but I have prevented you of that advantage in lawe, both in bringing in nothing but matters of fact, whiche may easily be prooved, if you dare denie them: and also in setting my name to my booke. (p. 40)

By naming the bishops and their victims, Martin lends considerable credibility to his claim of "matters of fact." But whether these are indeed factual matters rather than libels – and the accusations of popery the bishops certainly regarded as libels – could only be determined by law. Martin has here extended a double false dilemma. The first rests in the "peace": the bishops can deny their own authority and allow presbyterian polity to emerge, or they can maintain their authority only to have it marred by Martin's slanders. The second rests in their legal recourse: if they opt for his slanders, and seek to prosecute him in a court of law for libel, the libels will be proven true. The only genuine option for the bishops – the option Martin neglects – is for the bishops to proceed in a libel trial and have him proven a libeler. Even there, he holds the trump card. He has, after all, set his name to the book, so that they may proceed against him at law and at their risk, but Martin extended his offer under a pseudonym; he cannot be prosecuted unless he can be found. And he will not be found since he is protected by a veil of secrecy that, given the fates of Penry and Udall, the Martinists must have been sworn to protect at all costs.[62]

Given the clearly libelous nature of some of Martin's claims and his litigious taunt, it is not surprising that the authorities proceeded against him long before a royal proclamation censored the Marprelate tracts, or that one of the proclamation's principal goals was to secure information about the persons responsible for Martin Marprelate. On 14 November 1588, less than a month after the *Epistle* appeared, Hatton and Burghley urged Whitgift "by force of your Commission ecclesiastical or otherwise, to serch out the authors hereof and their Complices" and cause them to be apprehended that they might be tried by the Privy Council.[63] If Martin were found, trial could proceed, and the bishops could clear themselves. Their letter also makes their objections to the *Epistle* clear: "the Contentes of the book being principally, to move a mislyke of ye present government of this Church of England by the Bishoppes and other Ecclesiastical Governors and therewith also expressyng in a maliciouse manner sundry slanderous reports, ageynst your grace and the rest of the Bishoppes of the realme." Unlike countless other reform treatises and admonitions, Martin's *Epistle* risked an explicit attack on named individuals in the Anglican hierarchy, clearly invoking statutory slander and libel laws, to prove, as none of the general arguments against episcopacy had, that the bishops were against the law. Martin's "proof," unlike all the reformers' scriptural arguments, could not be confuted as "meere interpretation."

As the preface to the second Marprelate pamphlet, *Oh read over D. John Bridges*, commonly called *The Epitome*, makes clear, the authorities' pursuit broke Martin's conditions and invited this tract, which he begins with a direct attack on Whitgift:

John of Canterbury is a pettie pope . . . I am plaine, I must neede call a Spade a Spade, a Pope a Pope. I speake not against him, as he is a Councellor, but as he is an Archbishop and so Pope of Lambeth. (p. 2)

Outside of the preface and a few barbs against Bridges's writing style, the *Epitome* belongs more to the tradition of printed controversy.[64] The gist is the central difference Martin sees between Bridges's book and the presbyterian reformers:

For the Church governement is no more prescribed in the word (sayeth the deane) then the civill government is. You may see then, how headie and perverse these our brethren are, that had rather sticke unto a poore fisherman and Tentmaker, Peter and Paule, in a matter of trueth, then imbrace the manifest falsehood of so plaine an untrueth, with a fat deane, and all the brave spiritual Lordes in the lande. (C3v)

In some respects the characterization of Bridges's contents could be applied to Martin himself: "He speaketh every thing so fitly to the purpose, that he never toucheth the matter in question" (B1v). Bridges's principal point, ignored entirely in Martin's *Epitome*, had been that the reformers' arguments were "meere interpretations": the "matter of trueth" of "a poore fisherman and Tentmaker" was only partial truth. True to the disputation tradition, Martin excerpts sections of Bridges's argument, demonstrates their flaws, and counters with his own views. By taking the arguments out of context and juxtaposing statements from different contexts, Martin reduces them to nonsense. Furthermore, Martin combines this with the kind of *ad hominem* attack he had used so well in his *Epistle*. Calling Bridges a "dunse" for his interpretation of scripture (D2r), however, is not quite so insulting as his characterization of named bishops when he digresses to an unspecified book by Aylmer:

But unlesse you, and John of Excetor, with Thomas Winchester, who have beene in times past hypocrites as you have bene, leave off to hinder the word, and vex godly men, I will make you to be noble and famous bishops for ever. And might not a man wel judge you three to be the desperat Dicks, which you brother London, page 29. affirm to be good bishops in England . . . Whereas other bishops in the land, for the most, (onely John Canterburie excepted) lest they should one day answere for their proceedings unto her majestie, and gaine the evill will of the noble men, and gentlemen that favour the sinceritie of the gospell, will not seeme to bee such dealers as you 3. are, though they serve at an inche in their place, to maintaine his graces pride and cruelty, to stay the course of the gospell . . . But you three, like furious and senceles brute beasts dread no perill, looke no farther than your feete, spare none, but with tooth and nail, cry out, down with that side, that favoureth the gospel so. (E1r)

Martin's exasperation about the state of the debate is clear in his direct remarks to Bridges about the episcopacy: "In dignitie they are popes, in office proud prelates, and in ministerie plain dumb dogs for the most part. This is proved, hath bene prooved, and will be prooved, to the proudest of the Bishops teeth" (F4v–G1r). On the whole, the *Epitome* attacks less harshly than the *Epistle*, but together they expose the bishops on two grounds – their morals and their doctrine.

Leland Carlson believes that Martin would have stopped with *Epitome* if Thomas Cooper had not responded with *An Admonition to the People of England* (1589), providing new grist for Martin's mill.[65] Given his continued attack on specific bishops in the latter pamphlets, it is difficult to believe that Martin would have retired so quietly. Cooper simply gave Martin grounds for his most formal disputation. Actually his response to Cooper came first in a broadside, *Certaine Minerall, and Metaphisicall Schoolpoints*, and then in *Hay any worke for Cooper*. The broadside contained thirty-seven statements purportedly made by the church hierarchy – most taken out of context to reflect embarrassing contradictions and hypocrisy – and called for their authors, specifically named, to defend them. *Hay any worke* followed with an answer to Cooper's warnings about the dangers of presbyterian polity, most of which reiterates familiar arguments: a church of doctors, preachers, elders, and deacons is the perfect church because it is ordained by Christ; nothing may be added or taken away from the true and perfect Church; and since bishops are created or denied by the magistrate they are not perfect and do not belong to the perfect church. Further, *Hay any worke* answers Cooper's defense of the particular bishops' sins (enumerated in the *Epistle*) by recounting their errors and identifying new ones. The positions are not new, but in its language *Hay any worke* treads on dangerous ground. It libels the bishops as "traytors to God and his word, and also enemies unto hir Majestie" (p. 12), and nearly denies the Queen's ecclesiastical supremacy: "No civil magestrat may lawfully either maime or deforme the Body of Christ . . . but whosoever doth abollish any lawful church officer out of the church government, he doth either maime or deforme the church" (p. 6). Further it threatens her with God's wrath for exercising that supremacy: "He denounceth his wrath against all you, that thinke it lawfull for you, to maim or deform his church: he accounteth his Churche maimed, when those offices are therein placed, which hee hath not appointed" (p. 17). This, and Martin's parting words – "Farewell, farewell, farewell olde Martin, and keepe thee out of their handes for all that. For thou art a shrewd fellowe, thou wilt one day overthrow them Amen" (p. 48) – made good the claims against Marprelate's writings made in the February royal proclamation that they were "slanderous to the state" and dangerous because they sought "the overthrow, of her highness' lawful prerogative."[66]

In considering the Marprelate tracts, Patrick Collinson is particularly generous when he remarks,

It was the genius of Marprelate to see that the Achilles heel of the establishment was the vulnerability to ridicule which high ecclesiastical dignitaries have seldom lacked, and to recognize that this comic aspect of the bishops' enormities could be exploited to give them the widest currency. This was great satire, better than that of the professional wits of the day . . .[67]

The first three Marprelate tracts, as we have seen, do far more than ridicule the church hierarchy (though they do that as well). They tread on dangerous legal ground, and in their manner they taunt the law. Furthermore, they violate whatever good will the Church had demonstrated in participating in debate – in allowing people to hear with both ears. Lorna Hutson has suggested that it was not merely what Marprelate said that so offended the authorities, but how he said it. She suggests that by employing satire, a genre subversive by its nature, Marprelate quite literally added insult to injury.[68] To see satire as merely subversive, however, argues an oppositional relationship between the state and dissent that cannot accommodate evidence that at many levels the government and the Church adopted some aspects of reform and on other matters engaged in reasoned disputation with reformers. Martin engaged in a particular kind of satiric argument that violated the conventions of the dispute about reform. For example, Martin relied little on the biblical imagery that shaped so much of the reformers' discourse, using instead language with realistic immediacy, which makes his unfavorable representations of the bishops more lively and "real." His mode of argument is similarly immediate and direct – especially by contrast to Bridges who relied on long laborious arguments drawn from theologians to demonstrate the terms of his syllogisms. Martin parodies the use of the syllogism with blunt general assertions and minor premises full of personal attack. Martin fires the syllogisms so fast that the apparent logic of his argument, coupled with the "realistic" evidence overwhelms the reader. In some respects Martin creates his own epistemology, changing the ways in which he – and his readers – can know their world. He fragments and decontextualizes "reality" in a way that appeals to his readers' emotions at the same time that he replaces logical discourse with pseudo-logic. It was bad enough that Martin libeled the bishops. It was worse that his rhetoric did more than challenge their authority, it challenged epistemological conventions. (And he did it in print – a medium whose novelty already made it inherently suspicious.)[69]

On 13 February 1589 Sir Richard Knightley, John Hales, and Roger Wigston and his wife were arraigned before the Court of Star Chamber for harboring the Marprelate press. In April Waldegrave declined to print further Marprelate tracts and left England. According to Collinson, Waldegrave abandoned Martin because Martin's methods had offended all but a handful of reformers.[70] Even so, Martin wrote four more pamphlets – *More Worke for Cooper, Theses Martinianae* (or *Martin Junior*), *The Just Censure and Reproof of Martin Junior*, and *The Protestatyon of Martin Marprelate* – and found a new printer, John Hodgskin. *Theses Martinianae*, an exercise in bullet theology, lists 110 statements of Martin's beliefs, most of which had appeared in the earlier writings. Martin Junior's "Epilogue" continued the attack on the bishops, particularly Whitgift, who are characterized as "raised up out of the dust, and even from the very dounghill" (D3r). The *Theses*, hurriedly printed, were somewhat disorganized, and *The Just Censure* castigates Martin Junior for his work. The self-consciousness of *The Just Censure* gives it a delicious sense of irony that replaces the harsh invective of the earlier writings. Nevertheless it sustains the personal attack on the bishops – particularly on Whitgift. Martin characterizes him as a paranoid fool by giving him a dramatic monologue in which he orders pursuivants to search far and wide for Martin. That his obsession represents all that Martin has condemned the bishops for throughout the tracts is clear in Whitgift's parting words to the searchers:

To be breife, I have said enough unto you alreadie, but my meaning is, that you should give all the good her Majestie hath, or finde out Martin. Goe me to Devonshire, and to the North partes, where my Lords grace of Yorke also will direct his warrants by you, to seeke this traitour Martin. For I will have him, or else I wil no longer be archbishop of Canterburie. He die at the Groine, as they saie? Naie, heele be hanged ere heele die there. He is in some corner of England, lurking and doing mischiefe. I tel you true, I doe thinke him and his brood to be worse then the Jesuits . . . And therefore, either get him, or wee shall never staie their course. And I thinke I shall grow starke madde with you, unlesse you bring him. (A4v–B1v)

Whitgift is pictured as risking his sanity, his episcopal see, indeed all of England in his vindictive pursuit. In *The Just Censure* Martin and Whitgift personify what have become the irreconcilable opposites of a godly church and a corrupt regime. The confidence Martin expresses in both his own perseverance and his triumph in eluding the pursuivants leaves little question about whose side God is on.

Martin was perhaps a little too brazen in exulting in his own invulnerability in *The Just Censure*. In August 1589 Hodgskin and his two assistants, Valentine Simmes and Arthur Thomlin, were arrested while they were printing *More Worke for Cooper*.[71] In the final Marprelate pamphlet, *The Protestatyon*, Martin disdains the taking of these "poor men" and assures his readers that he cannot be deterred in his crusade against the "tyranny of our wicked priests" until "they be made as odious in our Church and commonwealth, as that they be thought by all sorts, unworthie to be harboured therein" (pp. 3, 9). To assure this end, he offers himself to the bishops, to dispute with them and prove "the cause of the church government" (p. 11).

Martin, of course, requires that he "be not delt with or molested, except thei overthrow me by the worde of God" (p. 11). Martin ends where *Diotrephes* began, complaining that all the learned discourses "whereby the corruption, and the unlawfulnes of the places, and proceedings of L. bishops, are shamefully laid open unto the world, are as yet unanswered" (p. 13). Because of this, Martin claims victory in the debate, but once again condemns the bishops, "herein their spoile and robberie is apparent . . . their tyrannie and blood-thirstie proceedings is unexscusable" (p. 21). However much he claims victory, *The Protestatyon* reveals if not a chastened Martin, at least an accountable Martin. He closes, "And here also I end this my protestation. Desiring thee (good reader) according unto thy place, to be carefull of the reliefe and deliverance of the distressed printers" (pp. 31–[2]). Such concern as is expressed for the consequences of his writings on the poor printers is likewise extended to one man suspected of being Martin – John Penry. In *The Just Censure* Martin had Whitgift call for the apprehension of Penry. In his final words ("for I protested unto thee without all fraud and ambiguitie, I was never as yet married in my life" [p. [32]) Martin tries to undo whatever damage that his brazenness may have done to Penry – a married man.[72]

Aside from the more subtle literary achievement of *The Just Censure*, the final Marprelate writings cover little ground not already seen in the first four pamphlets. Similarly, Martin's argument for presbyterian polity followed the same lines that had dominated reformers' writing throughout the 1580s. Others had even called the bishops "pettie popes" and ministers of Antichrist, but they had not invoked the kind of official ire that Martin did. It is wrong, however, to see him simply as the victim of an escalating campaign against puritan propagandists. He was not Whitgift's sacrificial lamb, nor was he a victim of political circumstances. Undeniably, Martin chose to exercise his attack on the episcopacy at the most inopportune moment. During Leicester's absence in 1586 fighting for the Protestant cause in the Low Countries, Burghley had effected a conservative coup by securing the appointments of Cobham and Buckhurst to the Privy Council, and in 1587 Christopher Hatton became Lord Chancellor. Opposed as they were to any kind of zealous international Protestantism, Cobham, Buckhurst, and Hatton were unlikely sympathizers to reform interests at home. Further, the cause of religious reform lost considerable support on the Council when

Leicester died in 1588. Also that Martin had chosen to launch his campaign in 1588 when a Spanish invasion threatened was particularly unwise. At the moment that Protestant England was preparing to defeat Spain's effort to win back England for the Catholic Church, Martin exposed the truth that even England's Protestants could not agree.

Although Hatton's and Burghley's response to Martin may have been intensified by current politics, he would probably have provoked the authorities even without the Spanish Armada. Martin openly and defiantly broke the statutory libel law making it a felony "that no man should be so hardye or contryve speacke or tele any false Newes lyes or other such lyke false things of Prelats."[73] Unlike other reformers that generally attacked the institution of episcopacy, Martin attacked persons, naming names and detailing crimes. Moreover, his false identity mocked the very legal recourse he called upon to disprove his libels. It is no coincidence that so many printers and aiders and abettors of the Martinist press who were arrested and even convicted were pardoned. The government wanted Martin as much to disprove the libels as to punish the libeler. And when he could not be found to serve the first end, the government settled for the second. Thus, it is also no coincidence that the government found a way to proceed against Greenwood, Barrow, Penry, and Udall – all suspected Martinists – for writing texts less objectionable than the Marprelate tracts. As Udall's trial made clear, Martin had changed conditions for them. Udall was sentenced to death for writing against the Queen in his *Demonstration of Discipline*; another man (one not suspected of being Martin) in his place, however, may not have not been judged so severely. In his counsel to Udall, the judge at the assize made this very clear:

Well Mr. Udall, you were best to submit your self to the Queen's Mercy, and leave these Courses; for I tell you, that your Book is most seditious and slanderous against her Majesty and the State; and yet I assure you, that your Book had been passed over, if there had not come forth presently after it such a number of slanderous Libels, as *Martin Mar-Prelate, Martin's Epitome, Martin Jun.* or *Theses Martinianae, Martin Sen.* and other such like; of which your Book was judged to be the Ring-leader.[74]

Udall died in prison awaiting the Queen's mercy. Greenwood, Barrow, and Penry, all convicted under 23 Eliz, ca. 2 for treasonous writing, suffered execution.[75]

The censorship of Martin Marprelate was not about suppressing dissent, nor was it about eliminating the dangers of satire. That Richard Bancroft recruited young men – not theologians – trained in the universities to respond in kind to Martin's attacks indicates that he understood the dimensions of the challenge, but it also tells what he did and did not fear most. That Bancroft called on writers to respond at all shows little fear in the disorder that came from dissent: he seems still to have agreed with Whitgift's charge to "Trie before thou trust: beleve not lightly every reporte: as thou has two eares, so use them both."[76] That the respondents employed Martin's literary methods indicates that his subversive discourse was not really the issue. Nor was it that Elizabeth could brook no criticism of her church. Naming prelates and peers and taunting the institution of law, however, violated the government's basic assumptions about English institutions. That the authorities tore up the countryside looking for Martin, and that Penry and Udall received death sentences argue that in violating libel laws, flaunting legal process, and seeking reformation by extortion, Martin had proven what most reformers had taken great pains to deny: radical religious reform endangered the state – and not merely because it sought to overthrow the religious establishment. Martin challenged civility and reason and denied the order of law.

CHAPTER 9

The 1599 bishops' ban
"shreud suspect of ill pretences"

In 1599 the Archbishop of Canterbury, John Whitgift, and the Bishop of London, Richard Bancroft, engaged in an act of censorship that was extraordinary because it affected both the London Stationers and literary works, and was apparently unmotivated by concerns about conformity or treason. On 1 June Whitgift and Bancroft issued an order to the Stationers calling in the books of Thomas Nashe and Gabriel Harvey and prohibiting any further printing of their works or of any satires and epigrams. It prohibited printing histories without Privy Council allowance or printing plays "excepte they bee allowed by suche as have aucthorytie." Further, the order specified that nine books, mostly epigrams and satires be seized and brought to the Bishop to be burned. The single documentary source for the Bishops' ban is the 1 June 1599 entry in the Stationers' Register.[1] An entry three days later records that the bishops' order was published to the Company and sent particularly to a group of specified Company members, and it notices the burning of seven of the nine works, plus the calling in of one more book, *Willoby's Avisa*.[2] The order resulted in the burning of John Marston's *Pygmalion* (1598) and *The scourge of vilanie* (1598), Edward Guilpin's *Skialetheia or A Shadowe of Truth*, (1598) Thomas Middleton's *Microcynicon* ("Snarlinge Satires") (1598),[3] John Davies's *Epigrames*, (n.d.), Ercole and Torquato Tasso's *Of Marriage and Wyvinge*, (1599), and *15 Joyes of marriage* (n.d.). Joseph Hall's *Virgidemiarum*, (1597, 1598) and Thomas Cutwode's *Caltha Poetarum* (1599), though initially called in, were reprieved.[4]

Lacking any documentary explanation for the bishops' order, scholars have usually followed G. G. Perry and Charles Gillett in accepting the works' "licentiousness" as grounds for justifiable ecclesiastical suppression. Perry asserts without qualification that "On 1 June 1599 an order signed by Whitgift, archbishop of Canterbury and

Bancroft, bishop of London, directed the Stationers' Company to
burn Hall's satires, together with books by Marston, Marlowe, and
others, on the ground of their licentiousness."[5] Likewise, Gillett, who
devoted an entire chapter entitled "Books which Offended against
Morality" to the satires, states that "in the years 1599 and 1600, a
number of writings were burned because of their offence against
morality."[6] More recently in looking at satire's use of homosexual
imagery, Bruce Smith has agreed about the motivation and suggests
that the ban was issued by the ecclesiastical authorities because they
"knew how easily scourges could be seduced by their sexual subjects
and how easily scourges could turn into scourges of moral
authority."[7] Lynda Boose argues that the ban sought to proscribe
"the pornographic pleasures of Aretino" that had become "Englished" in the satires.[8]

While the satires undeniably employ both sexualized discourse (in
satiric descriptions of both male and female prostitutes and their
customers) and explicit sexual epithets (in their vituperative attacks),
certain circumstances argue against sexual morality as the principal
motive for issuing the ban. First of all, two of the works that have
generally been regarded as the touchstones for sexual immorality, *Of
Marriage and Wyvinge* and *15 Joyes of marriage*, really do not offer
pornographic pleasures; they are instead blatantly misogynistic
tracts. *Of Marriage and Wyvinge* is a dialogue between Ercole and
Torquato Tasso. The first part argues against marriage by presenting
a compendium of classical and medieval evidence that "women are
most pernitious and ill" and ends in a compliment to Elizabeth for
being "a Virgine and Maiden Queene" (G3r, G3v). The second part,
a humanist praise of marriage, also ends in an ostensible praise to
her whose "matchlesse vertues" are like "an intricate laborinth,
wherein a man may sooner loose himselfe, then finde the end of the
same anyway" (L2r). With or without the pun on "loose," the closing
compliments to the Queen failed to contain the text's uncomplimen-
tary (at least to her) coupling of misogyny with praises of marriage. *15
Joyes of marriage*, if it was like the 1510 and 1603 versions (no edition
from the 1590s being extant), was likewise misogynistic, representing
feminine misrule in marriage.[9] Christopher Marlowe's translation of
selections from Ovid's *Elegies*, the most erotic of the five remaining
texts, was printed with Davies's *Epigrames*, but Davies's appears to
have been the offensive part of the book, since his is the only title
mentioned of the two in the order and 4 June notice of the burning.

Furthermore, it had probably been available for three years without provoking the authorities – illegally printed though it was. Of the remaining four, Marston's discourse in both of his books is by far the most sexualized. Smith observes that "Marston gives us a titillating, up-close view of Renaissance debauchery in which the pleasure is as much the poet's and the readers' as the subjects."[10] Marston's books present a particularly perplexing problem if, indeed, morality motivated the ban, since both had received ecclesiastical approval. *Pygmalion* was reviewed and approved by the Archbishop of Canterbury's secretary, Abraham Hartwell, *Scourge of vilany* by Samuel Harsnett. Actually, of the seven named satires censored, all but two had previously received ecclesiastical approval.[11] Further, *Nashes Lenten Stuffe* had received the Archbishop's own imprimatur in January 1599. Finally, as Smith has demonstrated, late Elizabethan satire drew upon classical models of Ovid, Juvenal, and Martial. The Latin sources had been widely available in England in the sixteenth century; indeed most were printed under royal patents and taught in the schools; all appeared in English translations. Either the Archbishop was singularly ineffective in conveying his moral standards to the ecclesiastical authorizers, or the moral climate changed rapidly and drastically in June 1599, or (and most likely) other concerns prompted suppressing previously approved texts.

Not everyone who has considered the so called "Bishops' Ban" has found its motivation in controlling sexual morality. Annabel Patterson regards it as part of the general "public surveillance" in which Elizabeth and her ministers engaged to assure "that the cultural forms of late Elizabethanism took the form they did because the queen and her ministers were watching."[12] Reading from the ban back to this culture, Patterson has suggested that "the writing of history was specifically included in the province of official censorship" because "the history of the realm belonged to the monarch."[13] Furthermore, satire was "a safe mode of self-expression" only as long as it remained private and unpublished.[14] The medium and not the message, then, was the problem. Lorna Hutson's study of Thomas Nashe relies on a similar sense of the offending medium: satire was inherently subversive.[15]

While both Patterson and Hutson offer a credible explanation for 1599 government interest in controlling cultural forms, particularly those deemed subversive neither takes into account the fact that forms previously acceptable – indeed officially approved – became in 1599 suddenly unacceptable. Richard McCabe argues that it was not the medium alone that provoked official censorship but its contents.

Verse satire, in short, was clearly one of the most popular forms of the day, and the epigram, its sister genre, shared in this new popularity – all of which might have been quite harmless were it not becoming increasingly obvious that the enthusiastic response of the reading public was prompted by an awareness that the new writers were beginning to realize the full potentials of their medium as a vehicle for social complaint.[16]

Noting that Joseph Hall's *Byting Satyres* (1598) attacked those responsible for enclosures, McCabe further remarks that "such pointed and articulate criticism in so popular a form must have given the authorities cause for concern" and "the authorities must have decided that satire had gone far enough."[17] McCabe correctly expands Patterson's and Hutson's understanding of the subversive nature of the genre to describe satire as subversive in its meanings as well as its modes, but like them, he subscribes to a kind of generalized discontent on the government's side – an inherent distrust, an accumulating anxiety – that ignores the immediacy of the official response. Nashe's and Harvey's satiric war occupied the early 1590s. The banned satires were written and authorized from 1596 to 1598. Whitgift himself approved Nashe's work as late as January 1599. All of these approved works contained articulate and pointed criticism of social practices, but appear, as Nashe remarked in *Pierce Penilesse* (1592), to have understood satire's limits: "The Court I dare not touch, but surely there (as in the Heavens) be many falling stars, and but one true Diana."[18] Rather than being an instance where existing transgressions against understood limits were suddenly recognized by the authorities, the 1599 bishops' ban was a response to political events that changed the ways in which the offending texts were read. Hutson has suggested that the prevailing official attitude was censorious – that officials engaged in an ongoing effort to find "new and ingenious forms of censorious interpretation resulting from a post-Marprelate sensitivity to the subversive potential" of printed texts.[19] If this were so, the bishops' actions in 1599 were an awfully long time coming.

Despite their roles as official licensers, the Bishop of London and the Archbishop of Canterbury appear to have been far less interested in censoring nonreligious texts than is generally believed. I have found only four instances during the reign of Elizabeth where either of

them or an ecclesiastical commission acted to suppress printed texts
not related in some way to religious issues: once in 1576 with
Gascoigne's *Posies* (along with two other works that were later
allowed); twice in 1599, first with John Hayward's *The first part of the
life and raigne of king Henrie the IIII* (1599), then in the 1599 bishops'
ban; and in 1600 with a surreptitious edition of Essex's *Apology, against
those which falsely taxe him to be the only hinderer of the peace* (n.d.).[20] These
three specific instances of censorship tell us something about the
bishops' action in 1599. Particularly, that these texts related in some
way to Robert Devereux, the Earl of Essex, suggests that censorship
was motivated less by prevailing attitudes than by particular interest
in deflecting criticism of the government during the crisis of 1599 –
the Earl of Essex's ill-fated war effort in Ireland.[21]

As we have seen, Gascoigne's *A Hundreth Sundrie Flowres* and *The
Posies* provoked if not censorship then certainly censure for its
scandal directed at "worthy personages." The interests of such
persons likewise influenced the censorship of Hayward's *Henry IV*,
which has recently received considerable attention, especially, like
the bishops' ban, as an exemplary case of Tudor hegemony and
censorship practices.[22] Hayward's book, which F. J. Levy has shown
reflects the emerging historiographic practice of "politic history,"[23]
was in itself probably rather innocuous. John Chamberlain, at the
end of a letter of 1 March 1599 to a friend, says that he encloses
"three or four toyes," one of which was Hayward's *Henry IV*:

The treatise of Henry the fourth is reasonablie well written, the author is a
younge man of Cambridge toward the civill lawe. here hath ben much
descanting about yt, why such a storie shold come out at this time, and
many exceptions taken, especially to the epistle which was a short thing in
Latin dedicated to the erle of Essex, and objected to him in goode earnest,
wherupon there was commaundment yt shold be cut out of the booke, yet I
have got you a transcript of yt that you may picke out the offence yf you
can; for my part i can find no such buggeswordes, but that every thinge is as
yt is taken.[24]

Not only did Archbishop Whitgift suppress the book's epistle to the
reader, but a second edition of the history was confiscated from the
printer and burned. A year later, after having scrutinized the work
for parallels between the monarchies of Richard II and Elizabeth
and between the ambitious Bolingbroke and the equally ambitious
Essex, Attorney General Edward Coke not only used *Henry IV* as part
of the evidence against Essex in his trial for misconduct in Ireland,

but he imprisoned Hayward.[25] In this matter Coke's notes on the book are especially instructive, particularly on Hayward's reports that Richard II met both with rebellion and ill success in Ireland, that he extracted money under the name of benevolence and borrowed of Londoners, that his councillors were corrupt, and that noblemen applauded his opponent, Bolingbroke. The endorsement for this document in the state papers, reads "Harsnet allowed it and passed the press, Wolfe persuaded him to dedicate to the earle to correct it the printer carried it so soon as it was printed; a month after, it was sent to the Earl, and the epistle taken out."[26] These notes appear in the State papers adjacent to depositions of Harsnett, *Henry IV*'s authorizer, and John Wolfe, its printer;[27] Chief Justice John Popham's interrogatories for the Essex trial; and the articles of accusation against Essex. He was to be charged with high treason for his conduct in Ireland, "namely that he plotted and practised with the Pope and king of Spain for the deposing and selling of himself as well the Crowne of England."[28] This could be proven by the proceedings of a Jesuit named Thomas Wright, a declaration regarding him, his confession, the rebellion in Ireland, the Earl's actions, and

his underhand permitting of that most treasonous booke of Henry the fourth to be printed and published being plainly deciphered not only by the matter, and by the Epistle itself, for what ende, and for whose behalf it was made, but also the Erle himself being so often present at the playing thereof, and with great applause giving countenance and lyking to the same.[29]

The examination of the printer gives a partial calendar of the events.[30] Hayward requested Wolfe to print the book, which he did in February 1599. It had no epistle dedicatory when Hayward brought the book in (Harsnett likewise claimed that there had been none when he authorized the book), so Wolfe and Hayward together agreed it should be dedicated to the Earl of Essex, "he being a martial man, and going to Ireland, and the book treating of Irish causes." When the book was printed Wolfe took a copy to the Earl at Whitehall, and three weeks later the Stationers' Company Wardens received an order from Whitgift that the epistle dedicated to the Earl should be cut, though 500 to 600 had already been sold: "no book ever sold beter." The remaining 500 or 600 copies sold shortly afterwards. Because of its popularity, Wolfe obtained a new edition from Hayward, "wherein many things were altered": the text was expanded and an apologetic epistle added. Printing commenced around Easter. Wolfe also took a copy of this "book" to Essex, at Richmond, where he went again three or four times to see what the Earl thought of it, but was always put off by some of his men: "his Lordship was much busied about his voyage to Ireland." Wolfe printed 1,500 copies which were almost finished in the Whitsun holidays. When they were printed, Wolfe presented them to the Bishop of London. Subsequently, all of that edition was burned at the Bishop's house, and Wolfe spent two weeks in prison.[31]

Using Wolfe's deposition and Chamberlain's letter, the schedule of events in 1599 is as follows:

Early February	*Henry IV* (first edition) printed; copy taken to Essex
Before 1 March	Whitgift ordered epistle removed
27 March	Essex departed for Ireland
Around 8 April (Easter)	Printing on second edition began
Around 28 May (Whitsunday)	Printing on second edition completed
After 28 May	Second edition confiscated and burned[32]

Since we know that Essex left London for Ireland on 27 March, the "book" Wolfe took to Essex, if indeed he took it, would have to have been a manuscript. Francis Bacon indicated that Essex wrote a formal letter to the Archbishop of Canterbury desiring him to call in Hayward's book a week after it had been published.[33] Since Essex was in Ireland at the time of the publication of the second edition, he must have written before he left for Ireland, which is unlikely since Bacon refers to publication, or Bacon must have conflated the February recall of the dedicatory epistle with the late May suppression of the second edition. Either way, Essex made some request for all or part of Hayward's book to be called in, and Whitgift acted, at least once, in response to Essex.

Whitgift's action is, I believe, important. Most studies of the censorship of Hayward's work have credited the Crown and Privy Council with suppressing it because of perceived historical parallels. Hayward, an unlikely traitor and a victim of "strong" reading, was brought before the Star Chamber and imprisoned. The timing, however, contradicts this, and so does the testimony of Bacon. Hayward's work did not receive much attention from the Queen or her Councillors until *after* Essex's catastrophic return from Ireland and subsequent fall from royal favor. Sometime in the late Fall of 1599 the Queen asked Bacon's opinion of the Hayward's book:

For her Majesty being mightily incensed with that booke which was dedicated to my Lord of *Essex*, beinge a storie of the first yeare of king *Henry the fourth*, thinking it a seditious prelude to put into the peoples heads boldnesse and faction, said she had good opinion that there was treason in it, and asked me if I could not find any places in it, that might be drawne within case of treason: whereunto I answered; for treason surely I found none, but for fellonie very many. And when her Majestie hastily asked wherein; I told her, the Author had committed very apparant theft, for he had taken most of the sentence of *Cornelius Tacitus*.[34]

In his *Apopothegmes New & Old*, Bacon retold the story but with the caveat that his comment on felony was "to take off the Queenes bitternesse with a jest."[35] In early 1600, probably February, Popham and Coke began looking closely at *Henry IV*, particularly, as the interrogatories Popham prepared reveal, to discover Hayward's motivations for writing it and who put him to the task.[36]

Hayward was interrogated in July 1600, at least seven months after the Queen's conversation with Bacon, when Essex's private hearing was held. Hayward was subsequently "conveyed" to the Tower, but of much greater importance was the use of his book in the case against Essex. Bacon reports how he was engaged to prosecute the matter during midsummer term 1600, after the decision was made to try Essex privately rather than publicly in the Court of Star Chamber:

. . . the next news that I heard, was, that we were all sent for againe, and that her Majesties pleasure was, we all should have parts in the businesse . . . it was allotted to me, that I should set foorth some undutifull carriage of my Lord, in giving occasion and countenance to a seditious Pamphlett, as it was tearmed, which was dedicated to him, which was the booke before mentioned of king *Henry* the fourth. Whereupon I replyed to that allotment, and said to their Lordships, that it was an old matter, and had no maner of coherence with the rest of the charge, being matters of *Ireland*, and therefore that I having bene wronged by bruites before, this wold expose me to them more; and it would be said, I gave in evidence mine owne tales. It was answered againe with good shew, that because it was considered how I stood tyed to my Lord of *Essex*, therefore that part was thought fittest for me which did him least hurt: for that whereas all the rest was matter of charge and accusation, this onely was but matter of caveat and admonition.[37]

Bacon's perception that he would be giving in evidence his "owne tales" in prosecuting the matter of *Henry IV*, as well as the Council's assurance that it was but a "matter of caveat and admonition," suggests the degree to which the book's sedition was a trumped-up charge.

At the time that *Henry IV* was suppressed, between February and 28 May 1599, Elizabeth, Whitgift, and other Privy Councillors would have had to have been remarkably prescient to see Essex as Bolingbroke, or if they had made such a connection, to have allowed Coke to proceed in drafting the legal patents for Essex's expedition (which were not completed to the Council's satisfaction until March 1599) would have been political folly. Preparations were in enough turmoil that given such a motive as the Earl's prospective treason, a number of the Councillors would have gladly called upon someone other than him to lead the English forces. Since Whitgift recalled Hayward's work at Essex's request, the maelstrom of events and his involvement in them, as well as his relationship with Whitgift, offers a better perspective for Whitgift's act (or possibly acts) of censorship than literary texts alone.

The most important political event of 1599 was Essex's expedition to Ireland. By August 1598, it became clear to Elizabeth and her advisors that they could no longer ignore Tyrone's rebellion in Ireland, which was being fed by Spain's interest in obtaining a Catholic foothold in the British Isles. At that time, Essex was absent from court because he had taken affront when the Queen had boxed his ears. With a crisis in Ireland imminent, he returned to Court and made a tenuous peace. Throughout the fall, amidst considerable faction, Essex emerged as the most likely candidate to lead an expedition. By early January, Essex clearly understood that the commission was his, though his relations with the Queen and Council were not mended, and letters patent were not issued. In early January, Essex wrote to his cousin, Fulke Greville:

> . . . in the eve of the last year the Queen having destined me to the hardest task that ever any gentleman was sent about, she hath yet [thought?] to ease her rebels in Ireland of some labour by breaking my heart [with her hardness] . . . For if I might with my death either quench the great fire of rebellion in Ireland, or divert those dangers with from foreign enemies are threatened, I should joy to be such a sacrifice. But how much soever her Majesty despiseth me she shall know she hath lost him who for her sake would have thought danger a sport and death a feast . . . And all the world shall witness that it is not the breath of me, which is but wind, or the love of the multitude, which burns as tinder, that I hunt after, but either to be valued by her above them that are of no value or to forget the world and be forgotten by it.[38]

In a letter of 4 January 1599 to Lord Willoughby, Essex makes clear his own political jeopardy:

Now for myself. Into Ireland I go. the Queen hath irrevocably decreed it; the Council do passionately urge it; and I am tied to my own reputation to use no tergiversation . . . I am not ignorant what are the disadvantages of absence; the opportunities of practising enemies when they are neither encountered nor overlooked.[39]

Willoughby's 21 January response concurs amidst plaudits to the Earl:

You have made already the conquest your own, you have encountered evil itself, subdued it to your virtuous self, the other conflicts are but light skirmishes, your trophy is already advanced, and death itself is fallen at your feet. Hanno is subdued alive, Hannibal from the senate throws his trifling enemy to the stairs' foot, Cato his poison ends himself, you victorious shall see these new acted. But glory and safety! Though Ireland calls you, Satyrs can hear that England cries out for you. Is peril present there in eye, it is here imminent in heart. But must you needs go, yet, noble lord, bestride us down, firm one foot there but rest the other here, that, when you step to us again, it may be without slipping.[40]

By the end of January, it was also clear that the Irish mission itself was encountering problems: funds were inadequate to pay for munitions; troops were hard to muster; commanders of English forces on the Continent complied with the call for forces by sending their "broken companies." By the beginning of March, still no letters patent appeared and Essex was overwrought. According to Chamberlain, "The Erle of Essex is crased, but whether more in body or mind is doubtfull . . . New difficulties arise daily about his commission . . . he is so litle satisfied that many times he makes it a question whether he go or not."[41]

Knowing both his own political vulnerability and the difficulty of raising the Irish mission, it is not at all surprising that Essex would not wish his name associated in any way with a history representing an English monarch's failure in Ireland. Furthermore, considering the factions at Court, any "press" for Essex could not escape being bad press, and that both for himself and for an Irish expedition would do little to mend his continuing poor relations with Elizabeth. Given these circumstances, that Essex would call upon his friend and ardent supporter Whitgift to recall Hayward's history in order to eliminate the association of his name with it would be quite plausible.

The question remains of why the second edition would be suppressed entirely, even though it lacked the epistle to Essex. Again, the Irish expedition offers some explanation. Even after Essex left London, faction continued. The Privy Council had refused to allow Sir Christopher Blount to accompany the expedition, and on 4 April Essex wrote to the Council to protest. Henry Howard's letter to Essex's friend, the Earl of Southampton, makes clear that earlier concerns about the peril at home were warranted:

> If you, too, have heard the manner of proceeding with my Lord [Essex] about Sir Christopher Blounte, you will then conceive whether I had reason, as well out of judgement as out of tenderness, to shrink in the behalf of my dearest and most worthy friend at the beginning of this enterprise. For this is only at the first *tentare patientiam* without any ground, and after, as advantage ariseth upon accident, to prove unconstancy. The body of the Court begins now to grow wholly and entirely into one part and that not the best.[42]

Furthermore, once Essex arrived in Ireland, progress was not as expected, and by late May Robert Cecil knew that he had marched on Munster despite the Irish Council's directives to confine his operations to Leinster. Sitting on the Privy Council, Whitgift certainly knew that Essex's enemies would welcome any further opportunity to think ill of him. Surely the further publication of a negative portrayal of Anglo-Irish affairs, particularly one with which the Earl's name was formerly associated, could afford such an opportunity. If Essex had called upon his friend once before to take advantage of whatever authority he exercised over the press and use it on his behalf, would not Whitgift, unbidden, exercise such authority to help his absent friend?

The friendship of Essex and Whitgift has never been raised with regards to censorship. Whitgift's action has always been seen within the purview of his role as "official censor." While the 1586 Star Chamber Decrees for Order in Printing had reiterated the authority of the Archbishop of Canterbury and the Bishop of London as the official authorizers appointed to assure that printed works did not oppose the authority of the Elizabethan church settlement, in the case of Essex, Whitgift seems to have extended his own authority according to the bonds of friendship. We learn something about their relationship from Whitgift's secretary, George Paule. Whitgift and Essex had been recommended to each other by the Queen's favor. Essex's efforts "to runne a course for Cleargie causes . . . and to cast off these Novelists" won him the Archbishop's "constancie and firmness" even in his "disgrace and trouble afterwards."[43] Whitgift's loyalty to Essex was so great that,

his misfortune drew upon the Archbishop the greatest discontentment, and severest reprehension from her Majestie, that he had ever before undergone in all his life. For after that the Earle began to fall upon courses displeasing, & distastefull unto her Majesty, neverthelesse such was the confidence the Archbishop had in the Earles loyaltie, and his owne stedfastnesse in that friendship, which he had formerly professed unto him, that he could not be drawne from being a continual intercessour for him; wherewith her Majestie was so highly displeased and so sharply rebuked him for the same, that the good olde Archbishop came sometimes home much grieved and perplexed. (p. 69)

That Elizabeth's "White Gift," as she affectionately referred to him, should have risked such disfavor, attests to a loyalty that would have empowered him not only to intercede on Essex's behalf but to intervene, bidden or unbidden, to suppress any printed "bruits." He had done so with *Henry IV*, and he would do so again with the *Apologie*.

On 10 May 1600, at Essex's request, Whitgift confiscated the *Apologie*, being printed surreptitiously. For it, a defense of Essex's use of force in Cadiz, to appear while he was under house arrest and awaiting trial for his conduct in Ireland, could have been used by his enemies. According to Richard Berkeley in a letter to Cecil, Essex protested,

himself free from all thought or purpose to have the book published either in writing or print, and that he was so far from giving copies of it as he charged his man that kept his papers not to let any of his friends see it but in his hand, or at least in his presence. He cannot guess how it should come abroad but by the corruption of some of his servants that had access to his chamber, who might take and write out his loose papers which lay ever sheet by sheet under his bed's head till he had leisure to finish the whole.[44]

In his own letter to the Privy Council, Essex protested that publication, like so many previous libels against him, was the work of his enemies:

Though I have been many times and deeply wounded by practising libellers, who since my commitment have shewed their intended mischief to me under pretended grief or passion for me, yet I have been silent till now that I hear that they do not only renew their former practices, but have conspired with a printer to set out a pamphlet in my name.[45]

Once again, Whitgift acted to spare his friend political repercussions from a printed work associated with Essex's name.

In summary, four circumstances in the swim of events in 1598–1600 emerge as significant for understanding the 1599 bishops' ban. First, while the Irish campaign was foremost in the minds of the English in 1598–9, the preparations were fraught with faction and conflict. Second, Essex himself, often at the center of Court controversy, was the object of malicious "bruits," as Willoughby had pointed out. Third, Essex called upon his loyal friend Whitgift to act on his behalf both in 1599 and in 1600 to suppress printed works damaging to him. Fourth, the suppression of the second edition of Hayward's *Henry IV* occurred within days of the 1599 bishops' ban. Against this background, it is difficult to envision the ban as unrelated to Essex. Surely its call for Privy Council authorization of histories was a direct consequence of Whitgift's experience with Hayward's history. And it is entirely possible that the 3 June calling in of *Willobie His Aviso* related more to the association between the title and the name of Essex's friend Lord Willoughby than to its innocuous contents. But what of the provisions for plays and satires? To answer this we need to look briefly at several of the banned works and the way in which they, and works like them, were received by contemporary audiences.

Guilpin's *Skialetheia* offers a good example of satirists' methods. It focuses on the "folly-soyled age" and begins with a group of epigrams addressed to particular names, presumably representing general groups of people. The particularity implicit in the direct address, however, invites "busie conjectures." This can be seen in two epigrams:

> *Of Metius.*　36
> Metius of late hath greatly cosend me,
> I tooke him for an earnest Catholike,
> He talk'd so much of almes and charity;
> But I was mightily deceav'd belike.
> 　He praiseth charity and almes, because
> 　He was made Barrister for almes, not lawes.

> *Of the same.*　37
> With what conscience can Metius sell law deare,
> When of meere almes he was made Barrister?[46]

They satirize both religion and law with Metius as a representative of both, but they particularity invite the reader to consider which Church lawyer or member of the Inns of Court could actually be Metius. Seven verse satires follow the epigrams. The first is a prelude on poetry and defends satires. Each of the following six attacks a particular vice: hypocrisy, cosmetics, inconstancy, jealousy, vanity, and the sway of opinion over reason. Like the epigrams, the satires personify vices in such a way that they invite speculation. In that on hypocrisy, the reader cannot help but wonder who Matho really is when he reads,

> Pale trembling *Matho* dies his milke-stained liver
> In colour of a discreet counsell-giver:
> And coole advisement: yet the world doth know,
> Hee's a rancke coward: but who dares tell him so.   (C3r)

Apparently, the allusions were veiled enough in 1598 not to arouse the ecclesiastical authorizer's concern even about a passage that has been widely read as satirizing the Earl of Essex:[47]

> For when great *Foelix* passing through the street,
> Vayleth his cap to each one he doth meet,
> And when no broome-man that will pray for him,
> Shall have lesse truage then his bonnets brim,
> Who would not thinke him perfect curtesie?
> Or the honny-suckle of humilitie?
> The devill he is as soone: he is the devill,
> Brightly accoustred to bemist his evill:
> Like Swartrutters hose his puffe thoughts swell,
> With yeastie ambition: *Signior Machiavell*
> Taught him this mumming trick, with curtesie
> T'entrench himselfe in popularitie,
> And for a writhen face, and bodies move,
> Be Barricadode in the peoples love.   (C3v)

The satirists were not unaware that their methods invited "busie conjecture." At the end of his prologue, Guilpin reminds the reader: "*Explicit* the Satyres flourish before his fencing" (C2r), which both calls upon the reader to unravel first the general meaning, then the barb, and reminds him or her that the satirist's meaning is "explicit." In his epilogue to *The scourge of vilany*, Marston is explicit about the reception of satire:

. . . I shall be much, much injuried by two sorts of readers: the one being ignorant, not knowing the nature of a Satyre, (which is under fained private names, to note generall vices,) will needes wrest each fayned name to a private unfained person. The other too subtile, bearing a private malice to some greater personage then hee dare in his owne person seeme to malingne, will strive by a forced application of my generall reproofes to broach his private hatred.[48]

Marston's remarks both invite conjecture and condemn it. Since his and Guilpin's comments belong to 1598 and appear in satires that received ecclesiastical approval, one can surmise that both authors and authorizers understood satire's potential for inviting conjectural reading, but until circumstances arose that provided analogies between the satires and some private hatred, these readings were not in themselves offensive.

A series of satiric pamphlets that appeared in 1601 confirm how in 1599 the satires had been read. John Weever's *The whipping of the Satyre*, among other things, charges the satirists with attacking specific people: "And verily you have greatly troubled your selfe in naming certaine particular persons. Such a one you call Fabius, and another, Felix, anon comes me Rufus and Clodius."[49] Nicholas Breton's *No whipping, nor tripping: but a kinde friendly Snipping*, speaking directly to justifications like Marston's that he was at the mercy of ignorant and malicious readers, confirms that whatever the satirists maintained, their readers perceived malicious (even seditious?) intent:

> Spend not your thoughts in spilling of your wits:
> Nor spoile your eies, in spying of offences.
> For howsoever you excuse your fittes
> They carry shreud suspect of ill pretences.[50]

However general the satirist might intend his attack, he was always suspected of libeling individuals. Suspicion, however, turned to conviction in the charged political climate of 1599 when events provided analogues to art.

How contemporary events alter reading can best be illustrated by considering one satire's presentation of the Prodigal.

> The will once prov'd, and he possest of all,
> Who then so gallant as young Prodigall?
> Mounted aloft on flattering *Fortunes* wings,
> Where like an Nightingale secure he sings:
> Floating on Seas of scarce prosperitie,
> In girt with pleasures sweet tranquilities.
> Sute upon sute, flatten too too base,
> Velvet laid on with gold and silver lace:

A meane man doth become, but yee must ride
In cloth of fyned gold, and by his side
Two footmen at the least, with choise of steeds,
Attired wher she rides in gorgeous weeds.
Zodon must have his Chariot gilded ore,
And when he triumphes, foure bare before,
In pure white Satten to usher out his way,
To make him glorious on his progresse day.
Vaile bonnet he that doth not passing by,
Admiring on that Sunne inriching skie,
Two dayes encag'd at least in strongest hold,
Storme he that list, he scornes to be controld.
What is it lawfull that a mounted beggar,
May uncontrolled this beare sway and swagger?

If I were to say that this appeared in Joseph Hall's 1596 *Virgidemiarum*, that it represented a general satire of pretension and vanity would be acceptable. Once we know that this is from the second satire in *Microcynicon* (B4r–B4v), which appeared in 1599, Zodon looks like Essex, a man who indulged in luxuries though beset by debts.[51] If this appeared after his departure for Ireland, "glorious on his progresse day" and "Two dayes encag'd at least in strongest hold" acquire a topicality impossible if the text appeared several years earlier. How the reading public would have read "he scornes to be controld" is unclear, but if Essex had shared Willoughby's warning with Whitgift ("Though Ireland calls you, Satyrs can hear that England cries out for you. Is peril present there in eye, it is here imminent in heart"), Whitgift, knowing of the conflict between Essex and the Irish council, may well have over-read the last few lines and found the entire passage disparaging of Essex. And all this, even though *Middleton*'s author may not have even considered Essex when he wrote it.

Of course since *Microcynicon* did appear in 1599,[52] it may well have been one of the texts that fed Whitgift's "shreud suspect of ill pretences." Cutwode's *Caltha Poetarum* and *Nashes Lenten Stuffe* also appeared in 1599. Cutwode's work has been read as primarily erotic.[53] The following passage appears to confirm this.

My child quoth she, & puls him by the chin
   And laies her other hard about his neck,
And with her lips she culls & kisses him,
   As she were charmd, from giving him a check,
Because the boy was alwaie at her beck

> The flattering queen knew how to curry favor
> Who woed the wanton boy with bold behaviour.[54]

But when this, along with the representation of a northern war and religious faction, is read in light of Essex's departure for Ireland, much of what initially looked erotic becomes political satire. *Caltha Poetarum* centers in a northern garden of state where "the princely red rose & the white as Chaircs of State" spring, and where Marygold shines like "a second Sun below" (B3r, B4r). One of the courtiers, a bee, raises an army, and establishes a new religion ("Calthanists" [C5r]) in honor of the Caltha flower (the Marygold). To which the rival queen, Venus, responds,

> And calling *Cupid*, this her pretie Squire,
>   quoth shee, lets to these Heretiques in hast,
> And burne the bees, and set their hives on fire,
>   And all their wax in superstitions wast,
>   And charme their Caltha there that is so chast:
>   And bring her cursed Cannons to their care
>   And plague her prelates with their prophane prayre . . . (C5r)

Although the volume was not ultimately banned, that it became object of scrutiny at all derives both from its mock heroic treatment of war and from a possible association with Essex that may have been unknown to Cutwode. A poem about the Earl's relationships at Court, "The bussin Bee's Complaint" – possibly by Essex – identifies him with a bee:

> Of all the griefs that most my patience grate
>   There's one that fretteth in the high'st degree;
> To see some Catterpillers bredd of late,
>   Cropping the flowers that should sustain the Bee.
>   Yet smyled I, for the wisest knowes
>   That mothes will eat the cloath, cankers the rose.[55]

Anyone at Court who had read or even knew of the apian fashioning – or self-fashioning – of Essex could justifiably suspect *Caltha Poetarum*'s author, Tailboys Dymock (the brother of Elizabeth's champion), of ill intent.

Even without suspicion of the bees, *Caltha Poetarum* makes the motives for war look as ridiculous as they do in *Nashes Lenten Stuffe* where the red herring – the king of the herrings – comes to his preeminence through a war effort. In Nashe's beast fable, the events through which "the Herring scrambled up to be King of all fishes" began when "a fauconer bringing over certaine hawkes out of Ireland, and airing them above hatches on ship-boord" lost a hawk to a shark when she went after a fish "mistaking it for a partrich."

The newes of this murderous act, carried by the Kings fisher to the eares of the land foules, there was nothing but arme, arme, arme, to se, to sea, swallow & titmouse, to take chasticement of that trespasse of bloud & death committed against a peere of their bloud royal. Preparation was made, the muster taken, the leaders allotted, and had their bils to take up pay; an old goshawke for gernral was appointed, for Marshall of the field, a Sparhawke, whom for no former desert they putte in office, but because it was one of their linage had sustained that wrong, and they thought they would be more implacable in condoling and commiserating.[56]

While the giants among the "fraternity of fishes" jeered at the ridiculous threat, "the lesser pigmeis & spawne of them thought it meete to provide for themselves betime, and elect a king amongs them," and "None woone the day in this but the Herring, whom their clamourous suffrages saluted with *Vive le roy*, God save the King, God save the King."[57] Lorna Hutson has argued that Nashe's satiric strategy – his diffuse Menippean method – sought to confound precisely the kind of reading that events in 1599 might have given to this – that is as an *à clef* to contemporary events.[58] No one, not even *Lenten Stuffe*'s authorizer, Whitgift, and least of all Nashe could have foreseen the fate of Essex's war effort that provoked the Archbishop to fear the kind of construction that texts like this one or Cutwode's might have received.

A speech by the Lord Keeper Sir Thomas Egerton confirms that the 1599 satires were associated with Essex. On 14 June 1600, in his annual Star Chamber address, Egerton admonished the country's justices to take particular care "against libellers who by tongue and pen did not spare to censure states, &c. And such of late had slandered her Majesty's officers by libels."[59] In a digression he recalls the events of 1599 when the Queen sent an army to Ireland "and to lead this army she made choice of a person such as none the like of him for that purpose was to be found in her kingdom." He then recounts her dissatisfaction with Essex's mission, which occasioned the libels of "gallants." Egerton digresses further to the proceedings against Essex and to an assessment of how touched everyone was by his humble submission to the Queen. When someone drew the Lord Keeper's attention to his digression, he blamed the libelers, and summarily concluded "with a sharp invective exhortary to see them punished." In the mind of Egerton, at least, libel was clearly associated with Essex and the Irish campaign, and with the efforts of the class of young men – gallants – who produced the satires banned in 1599.

On behalf of Essex and the Queen, in 1599 Whitgift had most certainly suspected ill pretences and, together with the Bishop of London, issued the 1599 edict to silence whatever the Satyrs heard (and told) of the "peril . . . imminent in heart" for Essex and for England. This was an extraordinary act of literary censorship, particularly since duly authorized texts – that Whitgift's own author- izers had previously judged to be free from sedition or heresy – were called in and burned. Placing the bishops' actions within the context of the eventful history of Essex, however, goes a long way towards explaining why after the initial flurry of action the ban was largely inconsequential. The Stationers did conform to the 1599 bishops' order and confiscated from booksellers' stalls any available copies of seven works (the other two were reprieved because, I believe, the author's were well connected politically) and burned them. No mention is made of burning works by Nashe and Harvey, and a year later Nashe's *Summers Last Will and Testament*, a play written in 1593 for Whitgift, was duly licensed and printed, though without the author's name. English histories continued to be published without Privy Council authorization, and plays were published without necessarily being "allowed by those that have authority." For instance, on 28 August 1599 the plays *Edward IIII and the Tanner of Tamworth* and *The history of the life and death of master SHORE and JANE SHORE his Wyfe* were entered in the Stationers' Register. Sonybanck, one of the ecclesiastical authorizers, and not a member of the Privy Council, is identified as the official authorizer of the history, *The life and Deathe of THOMAS WOOLSEY Cardinal* (entered 7 September 1599). Despite the ban against satires and epigrams, Zachariah Pasfield authorized *The letting of Humors blood in the Head-vaine* (16 October 1600) and Mr. Vycars authorized *A mery metinge or tis mery when knaves mete* (2 September 1600) – both by Samuel Rowlands – which were subse- quently burned by a Stationers' Court order on 6 October 1600, along with "other Popishe books & things that were lately taken." Even this action did not put an end to satire, as Greg observes,

Apparently the burning of this book was a sufficient advertisement to make it worth reprinting, for on 4 Mar. 1601 and again on 1 Mar. 1602 Stationers were fined 2^s 6^d a piece "for their disorders in buyinge of the books of humours letting blood in the vayne being newe printed after yt was first forbydden and burnt" (Arber, II. 832-3). In all twenty-nine booksellers were fined . . .[60]

In 1601 the two pamphlets, Weever's *The whipping of the Satyre* and Guilpin's *The Whipper of the Satyre*, both duly authorized, were published without consequence. Furthermore, satiric drama dominated the London stage – and printed versions of the same were "sufficiently authorized." And after the death of Elizabeth (and Whitgift), epigrams regularly appeared in the Register as well as numerous satiric pamphlets. All in all, the eventful history of Essex, censorship, and the 1599 bishops' ban produced rather uneventful literary consequences.

The ban and the censorship of *Henry IV* have long served to epitomize the "whole machinery of censorship and control" Glynn Wickham envisioned in the Tudor state. The events related to these acts of censorship can be read as a litany of Tudor abuses: Hayward was imprisoned, apparently without a formal trial; previously issued licenses were not honored; books were burned on suspicions alone – and unstated suspicions at that. Legally delegated authority to authorize "according to her Majesty's Injunctions" was extended to apparently arbitrary book burning. All of this looks like the picture of Tudor censorship that has been perpetuated by Wickham, Siebert, and even, to some degree, Patterson. To remove these abusive acts from the specific political contexts of the troubled years of 1599–1601 and generalize them to Elizabethan – even early modern – cultural practice is, however, to engage in a reading of cultural practice as anachronistic and fallacious as finding references to Essex's 1601 rebellion in Hayward's 1599 history. The cultural practice of literary censorship seen through the fixed window of 1599 looks less like an efficient government system, stringently enforced and compliantly followed, than an improvisational play of competing personal interests acted out on stage of perceived national emergency. The 1599 bishops' ban represents an undeniable instance of Elizabethan literary censorship. That the ban is representative of a widespread, long term, and efficient cultural practice the singular affairs of Essex, Whitgift, and the Irish campaign belie. Indeed, the ban and the censorship of *Henry IV* might justifiably be called one of "those famous puzzling incidents" of censorship.

CHAPTER 10

Conclusion
"That libertie Poets of late . . . have exceeded"[1]

Pervasive government censorship of the press in early modern England has long stood as an unquestioned assumption in historical, literary, and cultural studies. An important way in which authority has been understood to manifest itself is censorship; indeed, in the post-enlightenment West, censorship has become a litmus test of political and social control. New historicists and cultural materialists are only recent subscribers to the paradigm of repressive Tudor and Stuart monarchy in which Whig historians invested heavily for the high yields of liberalism. Ecclesiastical historians have framed their martyrologies, as well as their testimonies to progressive toleration, in early modern suppression of religious debate. The roots of the assumptions are deep. They appear earliest in the writings of religious reformers – Catholic and Protestant – whose identification with early Christian martyrs both fed their faith and their propaganda assaults on the status quo: in Allen, in Field and Wilcox, in Martin Marprelate. They appear in the literary anxieties of writers like George Gascoigne, Edmund Spenser, Fulke Greville, and Ben Jonson hungry for royal patronage. And they make their way into the modern and postmodern political consciousness by way of John Milton and other champions of free expression. John Stubbs's bloody hand waves across the centuries, one of the "broken bodies" testifying "to the overwhelming truth represented by the queen."[2] In the process of constructing their narratives about censorship (or the fragments of their narratives that regard censorship), historians (political, cultural, and literary) have generalized from the hand of Stubbs to the pens of poets. They have accepted uncritically the claims of religious propaganda, and they have misread opinions as facts – like reading the letter from Burghley to Walsingham opining that Allen's *Admonition to the Nobility* ought to be declared treasonous as the government edict itself. What has come to be known about censorship – what, indeed, has come to serve as a basic assumption for constructing theories of literature and culture and for reading texts – is a curious amalgam of historical evidence, decontextualized facts, overgeneralization, and half-truths. By examining the theory and practice of censorship in England during the reign of Elizabeth, we have seen that each of the statements italicized below tells some truth – but only a partial truth – about press censorship. Reading these fragments within the complex narrative of sixteenth-century religion, politics, and economics challenges us to reconsider the cultural hegemony of the Elizabethan state.

Like other Tudor monarchs, Elizabeth's government had considerable interest in controlling the forms of culture, particularly the printed word. Tudor monarchs did, indeed, take interest in exercising control over the press, but not all their actions were repressive. Their governments took action first to encourage Continental printers to establish presses in England, and later, when the English print trade became self-sustaining to protect it from foreign competition. Tudor monarchs established what were essentially government printing houses by extending monopolies to royal printers, and they extended to private printers privileges that protected their right to print and sell particular texts. The governments' interest in restricting or suppressing the contents of printed texts derived principally from their interest in controlling religious and political opposition to their regimes – but in these matters the kinds and degrees of control and suppression varied significantly from monarch to monarch and responded to the immediate political and religious pressures their governments experienced.

To achieve this control, the Tudor monarchs instituted pre-print censorship. Such pre-print censorship, or licensing, was instituted by Tudor governments beginning with Henry VIII. Licensing requirements were variously instituted by statute, by royal proclamation, and by decree of courts of law; their effectiveness varied both with their means of institution and with the sanctions instituted to ensure their compliance. Licensing provisions variously required review by anyone from minor clerics to the monarchs themselves – the effect and effectiveness of royal control inevitably varying depending both on whom the official licensers were and on the access members of the printing trade had to the official licensers. The burgeoning of print culture at the end of the sixteenth century posed serious practical challenges to any theoretical designs for efficient pre-print censorship.

The mechanism for pre-print control (licensing) was efficiently in place throughout Elizabeth's reign (instituted by the 1559 Royal Injunctions), and all texts were licensed prior to print. While the 1559 Injunctions have been widely regarded as the central means by which Elizabeth established pervasive press censorship, the licensing provision was but one of fifty-three items in a document whose principal end was securing her religious settlement. These injunctions placed printing within the jurisdiction of the Ecclesiastical Commission convened in accordance with the Act of Supremacy "to visite, reforme, redressse, order, correct and amend all such errors, heresies, schismes, abuses, offences, contempts and enormities whatsoever, which by any maner Spiritual or Ecclesiasticall power, authority or jurisdiction, can or may lawfully be reformed, ordered, redressed, corrected, restrained or amended," and the heads of the Commission served as the principal licensers for the press. The licensing established by the injunctions was certainly ecclesiastical in its administration and likely ecclesiastical in its intent.

To further ensure control of the press, the government placed all printing in the hands of the London Stationers' Company, and its officials, serving as agents of the Crown, ensured that texts were approved before printing and engaged in searches for illegal (transgressive) texts. Queen Mary granted a royal charter to the London Company of Stationers in 1557 as a "suitable remedy" to seditious and heretical printing against the Catholic Church; two years later Elizabeth confirmed the charter – without changing its clear intent of controlling Protestant printing. Whatever ends Mary may have sought by this charter, she created in the Stationers' Company an entity that functioned with considerable independence from the Crown and whose principal interest was in securing exclusively for its members the economic benefits of a growing market. To accomplish this, the Company issued licenses to its members giving them exclusive publishing rights to titles they registered with it. Its licenses were issued for texts not officially authorized, though the Company Master and Wardens apparently required official approval for certain classes of books: those in foreign languages, translations, and those with religious or political contents. The kind of "illegal printing" that most concerned Stationers' Company officials was printing either outside the Company or printing by a member against the license of another member. The Stationers' Company employed its searchers to discover printing they regarded as "illegal." On some occasions, notably after the government had helped the Stationers secure court orders that protected the trade, its searchers served the government to discover texts the government regarded as transgressive. Far more regularly, the government employed its own pursuivants to discover offensive texts. *"Transgressive" texts were those that were printed without authorization (either at home or abroad) and that, hence, did not comply with the official version of culture.* A sense of what the government regarded as "transgressive" is far less clear than previous studies have suggested. Clearly works that violated statutory prohibitions – against treasonous writing, writing on the succession, and libel – were transgressive, and action was taken against their authors and printers (if these were English) in the law courts. Few of the books printed in England that were unlicensed by the Stationers or unscrutinized by official reviewers were actually treated as transgressive by the state. Even many Continental books – clearly unlicensed and unauthorized – were neither confiscated nor suppressed. On the other hand, several licensed and authorized books came to be regarded as transgressive after they were approved. That is, reception, far more than regulation, determined whether or not a particular text was transgressive.

When transgressive texts did manage to appear, the government actively suppressed them and subjected their authors and printers to rigorous sanctions. When texts violated statutory prohibitions, the government took whatever recourse against their authors, printers, publishers, and booksellers that the law allowed. In these matters the response was largely situational; that is, the written material would have to attract attention either by directly attacking the government or by being associated with some offensive event. Elizabeth's government does not appear to have policed the bookstands looking for writing against the statutes. It did, however, police ports and private residences for evidence of illegal Catholic practices, and popish books were seized regularly as evidence – though prosecutions rarely proceeded for these books alone. Every effort was taken, however, to prevent the importation and distribution of Catholic texts that "treated of the State and the Queen's majesty." Royal proclamations bear testimony to the government's effort to restrain their sale and dissemination, but because the authors were safely protected by the sea, sanctions against them and their publishers were unavailable and sanctions against their owners were rarely taken. There exists a surprisingly small number of texts written and printed in England that the government deemed transgressive which locate press censorship during the reign of Elizabeth quite precisely in the politics of personality, patronage, and national interest. These texts are small figures on an expansive (and expanding) landscape of print culture, but they cast long shadows because they appear at the moments of crisis attendant upon the rising or the setting of some political sun. A history of press censorship during her reign is a history of critical moments in the Elizabethan state. Press censorship was less a part of the routine machinery of an authoritarian state than an *ad hoc* response – albeit authoritarian – to *particular* texts that the state perceived to endanger the exercise of its legitimate and necessary authority.

While the theory of press censorship in Elizabethan England may have been religious, the practice was, in the fullest sense of the word, political. The object was texts that treated of the affairs of either state or statesmen and stateswomen; it was effected by political institutions. It is a mistake however to see political press censorship as illustrative of the kind of cultural hegemony posited by Foucault that assumes the interdependence of knowledge and power. This denies entirely the possibility of any kind of press unsanctioned by authority. This was simply not the case in late sixteenth-century England, where, as we have seen, countless unlicensed texts appeared – few of which were suppressed. Jürgen Habermas has located the emergence of a public sphere that sought to influence the decisions of state authority in eighteenth-century Britain.[3] Elizabeth, however, was not insensitive to her "public" (as evidenced in the events surrounding *A Gaping Gulf* and the French marriage). Neither, as the reformation of Holinshed's *Chronicles* demonstrates, was she indifferent to the ability of the printed work to affect opinions of government. The emerging print culture of late sixteenth-century England, while it may not have generated a truly public sphere, mediated the exercise of power by requiring that it be self-conscious of its practices. No government, however, is ever invulnerable in its exercise of power, and Elizabeth's government was particularly vulnerable in matters relating to the succession, the treatment of Jesuits and Catholic priests, its efforts against international Catholicism in the Low Countries and Ireland, and radical Protestantism at home. That printed texts which called attention to these vulnerabilities became vulnerable bears witness as much to the perceived power of the printed word as the practiced power of the Crown.

In identifying censorship with suppression and finding the locus of suppression in politics, I am effectively denying a condition of writing in early modern England best described as "repressive" that has long been assumed. From this perspective, the imaginative writer worked under precisely the same constraints as the Catholic apologist or the religious reformer. Since, as we have seen, the treason statutes, the religious settlement, and libel laws were the principal dictates of those constraints, the imaginative writer must have enjoyed considerably more freedom than has heretofore been allowed. Reports of literary censorship exist, but in nearly every instance, the condition of repressive writing is vastly overstated. John Harington's *Metamorphosis of Ajax* (1596), for example, has from the eighteenth century been regarded as having been denied a license on the basis that he had written "Seen and disallowed" on the copy he dedicated to Thomas Markham. This conclusion was undoubtedly fed by contemporary letters indicating the Queen's displeasure at Harington over alleged barbs at Leicester. Based on Richard Bancroft's imprimatur on a manuscript of *Ajax*, however, Elizabeth Story Donno justifiably rejects the idea that a license was refused.[4] Similarly, based largely on a comment in Thomas Middleton's *Father Hubburds Tales* (1604), Spenser's "Mother Hubberds Tale" has long been regarded as having been called in.[5] While Richard S. Peterson has found a letter dated March 1591 that appears to confirm this,[6] contemporary references suggest that whatever concern Spenser's tale elicited, it was mitigated shortly after. In a discussion of censorship in *Strange News* (1592), Thomas Nashe refers to the "sparkes of displeasure" regarding "Mother Hubberd" "that were quenched."[7] Even that notorious instance of self-censorship – Fulke Greville's destruction of his plays *Antony* and *Cleopatra* because they were "apt enough to be construed, or strained to a personating of vices in the present Governors, and government" – is less an illustration of a culture of literary repression than further proof that literature became vulnerable to censorship when poets with "invectives" exceeded their liberty and went where it was "not lawfull for a poynado . . . to intermeddle."[8] Even when poets exceeded their liberty, censure was not censorship. Being denied the court as Harington was for translating an offensive canto of Ariosto, or Sidney was for writing a letter opposing the French marriage, differs significantly from the sanctions for libel, seditious writing, or treason. It was not merely for writing poetry that the poet Bonfont in Book V of Spenser's *Faerie Queene* had his tongue nailed to a post; it was for libeling the Queen ("For that therewith he falsely did revyle, And foule blaspheme that Queene for forged guyle").[9] This is not to deny the possibility of literary censorship, but rather, to suggest that literature became the object of scrutiny when poets exceeded their liberty or when the conditions of reading drew a literary text into the political domain.

Notes

The place of publication is London unless otherwise stated.

I PRIVILEGE, LICENSE, AND AUTHORITY: THE CROWN AND THE PRESS

1 John Harington, *Nugae Antiquae: Being a Miscellaneous Collection of Original Papers*, ed. Henry Harington, 3 vols. (1779), vol. III, p. 279.
2 Glynn Wickham, *Early English Stages, 1300–1576*, 3 vols. (1959–81), vol. II, p. 94.
3 Frederick Siebert, *Freedom of the Press in England, 1476–1776* (Chicago, 1952), p. 2.
4 Annabel Patterson, *Censorship and Interpretation* (Madison, 1984), p. 16.
5 Philip Finkelpearl, "The Comedian's Liberty," *English Literary Renaissance*, 16 (1986), 134.
6 Richard Dutton, *Mastering the Revels* (Iowa City, 1991) and Richard Burt, *Licensed by Authority* (Ithaca and London, 1993).
7 Sheila Lambert, "The Printers and the Government, 1604–1637," in *Aspects of Printing from 1600*, ed. Robin Myers (1987), pp. 1–29.
8 A. B. Worden, "Literature and Political Censorship in Early Modern England," in *Too Mighty to be Free*, ed. A. C. Duke and C. Tamse (Zutfen, 1988), p. 48.
9 William Faques printed the earliest extant printed proclamation, 5 July 1504, on English currency and coins (*STC* 7760.4). (A. W. Pollard and G. R. Redgrave, *A Short-Title Catalogue of Books Printed in England, Scotland, & Ireland, 1575–1640*, 2nd edn., rev. and enlarged, begun by W. A. Jackson and F. S. Ferguson, completed by Katharine F. Pantzer (1976–1991), vol. I, p. 356). (Hereafter cited as *STC* in both the text and the notes).
10 1 Richard III, ca. 9. *Statutes of the Realm*, 9 vols. (1810–22), vol. II, pp. 489–93. My citations of statutes come from this edition, but for ease of reference all statutes will be identified, as above, by regnal year, monarch, and chapter.
11 On the conciliar courts, see G. R. Elton, *The Tudor Constitution* (Cambridge, 1960), pp. 87–93 and 158–94.

12 Ibid., p. 18.
13 The Privy Seal could enact administrative orders from the king's officers, issue writs of summons, and seal promises on bonds. The signet could authorize payments from the Household treasuries and direct administrative orders. On the procedures established in the fifteenth century for enacting government orders through the seals, see Elton, *Tudor Constitution*, chapter 3.
14 *Calendar of the Patent Rolls, Elizabeth I*, 9 vols. (1939–86), vol. VII, 2340. (Hereafter cited as *CPR, Eliz.*)
15 *STC* 7760.4, 16257l, 9357 respectively; *STC*, vol. III, p. 61.
16 *STC* 9266, 16179.
17 Richard Pynson received an annuity of £4 on 27 September 1515 retroactive to the previous Michaelmas after which time payments appear regularly, *(Letters and Papers, Foreign and Domestic of the Reign of Henry VIII*, 21 vols. [1864–1920], vol. II, p. 954).
18 Thomas Berthelet received £117 0s. 6½d. in 1543 on royal warrant for documents he printed for the state. A detailed accounting appears in Edward Arber, *A Transcript of the Registers of the Company of Stationers of London*, 5 vols. (London and Birmingham, 1875–94), vol. II, pp. 50–60. (Hereafter cited as "Arber" in both the text and the notes).
19 *Calendar of the Patent Rolls, Edward VI*, 6 vols. (1924–29), vol. I, p. 187. (Hereafter cited as *CPR, Edward VI.*) Berthelet had succeeded Pynson by an official grant of royal privilege under the Privy Seal. According to Siebert this patent (21 Henry VIII, p. 2, m. 17) is the earliest patent to survive. Technically, Pynson's grants of annuity are patents, but this is in clear recognition of Berthelet's appointment as King's printer. The text of the patent is given in Siebert, *Freedom of the Press*, p. 33.
20 *Calendar of the Patent Rolls, Philip & Mary*, 4 vols. (1937–39), vol. I, p. 53. (Hereafter cited as *CPR, Phil. & Mary.*)
21 *CPR, Eliz.*, vol. II, pp. 92–3.
22 *Letters and Papers, Henry VIII*, vol. XVIII(I), item 100(31); Paul L. Hughes and James F. Larkin, *Tudor Royal Proclamations*, 3 vols. (New Haven and London, 1969), vol. I, p. 353. (Hereafter cited as "Hughes & Larkin" in both the text and notes.)
23 *Letters and Papers, Henry VIII*, vol. XIV(I), item 1329.
24 If this practice was commonplace, it would explain why grants do not appear among the official grant records at the time that so many books were being printed *cum privilegio*.
25 Statistics taken from an on-line search of the *English Short Title Catalogue*, 3–5 June 1994, at the Huntington Library, San Marino, California.
26 *Letters and Papers, Henry VIII*, vol. VI, item 480.
27 Hughes & Larkin, vol. I, pp. 270–6.
28 See Siebert, *Freedom of the Press*, p. 37; Graham Pollard, *Shakespeare's Fight with the Pirates* (Cambridge, 1920); and W. W. Greg, *"Ad Imprimendum Solum,"* in *Collected Papers*, ed. J. C. Maxwell, (Oxford, 1966), pp. 407–12.

29 Hughes & Larkin, vol. 1, p. 270. For a discussion of the particular events out of which this proclamation was born, see Edmund G. Hamann, "The Clarification of Some Obscurities Surrounding the Imprisonment of Richard Grafton in 1541 and 1543," *Papers of the Bibliographical Society of America*, 52 (1958), 262–82.

30 The Latin of *ad imprimendum solum* is particularly problematic. *Imprimendum* as the gerund accusative form of *imprimere* means "printing"; and *solum* (the accusative of *solus*) agrees with it. The translation, then, would be "with privilege for printing only." Latin usage, however, was not always precise. The polyglot dictionary in use throughout the fifteenth and sixteenth centuries, *Sex linguaru, Latine, Teuthonice, Gallice, Hispanice, Italice, Anglice* (multiple editions from Continental and English presses), curiously categorizes all words with an *um* ending as participials rather than gerunds. If the proclamation's language was following this pattern of usage, however incorrect, *ad imprimendum solum* may have been intended to restrict privilege only to what was printed – that is, not to additions.

31 Grafton and Whitchurch's books were printed under their seven-year privilege for the sole printing of service books (see p. 8). The primer was authorized by royal proclamation 6 May 1545, and another proclamation on 28 May 1545 announced that Grafton and Whitchurch had the patent privilege. The *STC* lists eleven editions printed in 1545–6.

32 Greg, *"Ad Imprimendum Solum,"* pp. 407–8.

33 For a full discussion see chapter 2.

34 *CPR, Eliz.*, vol. 1, p. 11.

35 The printed patent in *The Cosmographicall Glasse* reads,
AN EXTRACTE OF THE QUENES
highnes gracious Priviledge, & Licence.

ELIZABETH by the grace of God Quene of Englande, Fraunce, and Irelande, defendour of the faith &c.

To all maner of Printers, Bookesellers, and other our Officers, Ministers and subjectes: greatyng. We do want you to understand, that of our grace especiall, we have graunted, & geven priviledge and licence: And by these presentes for us, our heyres, and successors do graunt and gyve Priviledge and Lycence, unto our wellbeloued subject John Day, of the citie of London, Printer, and Stationer, and to his assignes for the terme of his life, to Imprint, or cause to be Imprinted, as well the Cosmographicall Glasse, compiled by William Cuningham Doctor in Physicke, as also durynge the tyme of vii. yeares, all suche Bookes, and workes, as he hath Imprinted, or herafter shall Imprint, being divised, compiled, or set out by any learned man, at the procurement, costes, & charge, only of the said John Day. Straitly forbiddyng and commaunding by these presentes, all and singuler our subjectes, as well Printers, & Bookesellers, as all other persons within our Realmes & Dominions, whatsoever they be, in any maner of wise, to Imprint, or cause to be Imprinted, any of the aforesaid Bookes, that the said John Day shall by authoritie of this our licence, imprint, or cause to be imprinted, or any part of them: But onely the said John Day, and his assignes, vpon payne of our hyghe indignation. And that every offendor therin shall forfaite to our use fourtie shillinges of lawfull money of Englande, for every such Book or Bookes, at any time so Printed contrary to the true meanyng of this oure present Licence, and Priviledge: Over and besides all suche Booke, or Bookes so Printed, to be forfayted to whom so ever shall sustayne the charges, & sue the sayd forfaiture in our behalfe. &c. (T3r)

36 *CPR, Eliz.*, vol. I, p. 54.

37 Ibid., vol. V, item 2126.

38 Ibid., vol. I, p. 62.

39 Ibid., vol. IV, item 675.

40 Ibid., vol. VI, item 1181.

41 Ibid., vol. VII, item 2891.

42 Ibid., vol. V, item 2445.

43 Ibid., vol. VI, item 1445.

44 Ibid., vol. VIII, item 1593.

45 Ibid., vol. II, p. 218.

46 *The Dictionary of National Biography* describes Day as a zealous reformer who found a patron in Archbishop Parker. Parker, according to John Strype, had a "particular kindness" for Day (ed. Leslie Stephen and Sidney Lee, 53 vols. [1885–1900], vol. XII, pp. 233–5). (Hereafter cited as *DNB* in both the text and the notes.)

47 *CPR, Eliz.*, vol. I, pp. 54, 62–3. Tottell had printed law books under privilege since 1553, and perhaps Elizabeth's government found it suspect in 1559 that he had survived the Marian purges under which Day and William Seres had suffered.

48 George Unwin, *Gilds and Companies of London* (1925), chapter 15.

49 Arber, vol. I, p. xxi.

50 Frances Reynold [Regnauld] apparently used incorrect English. The letter further requested Cromwell to grant Reynold, a license to sell his current stock, with the concession that he will "print no more in English without having some learned Englishman to be his corrector" (*Letters and Papers, Henry VIII*, vol. XIII(2), item 336).

51 Cyprian Blagden suggests that the ordinance issued at an unknown date before 1557 "made it an offence for a Stationer to put out a book before he had shown it to the Wardens and had entered in the register" (*The Stationers' Company* [1960], p. 33). Blagden includes no citation for the source of this ordinance, and it appears from his list of documents in manuscript and print relating to the Stationer's Company (which does not include ordinances before 1577) that he assumes such an ordinance existed in the now lost Red Book of Ordinances. Evidently, it also required presentation of copy to the wardens before printing since in 1555 a master Wallye was fined 20s. "for conselying of the pryntynge of *a breafe Cronacle* contrary to our ordenances before he Ded presente the Copye to the wardyns" (Arber, vol. I, p. 45).

52 Some insight can be gained into the importance of a trade being

formally recognized as a guild or company, if we remember that for anyone not of the nobility or a nobleman's household to be a citizen of London, city ordinances required that he be either free of a London company or an apprentice.

53 Blagden gives a fuller description of the Company and its composition in *The Stationers' Company*, chapter 2.

54 According to Blagden these ordinances
were approved by the Lord Treasurer and the two Chief Justices in 1562. These were written into what was known as the Red Book and were added to from time to time; though the Red Book disappeared, probably during the confusion of the Civil War, it is possible to piece together, from references to their being invoked, some plan of the ground the ordinances covered (*The Stationers' Company*, p. 39).

55 Arber, vol. I, pp. 100–1.

56 Elizabeth also required government licensing in her 1559 Injunctions: see chapter 2.

57 1558; Arber, vol. I, p. 32.

58 Ibid., vol. II, p. 347.

59 Ibid., vol. II, p. 116.

60 Ibid., vol. II, p. 516.

61 Peter Blayney, "Exeunt Pirates," March 1993 version, unpublished MS, pp. 6–7. I am indebted to Peter for giving me a copy of this paper.

62 Arber, vol. I, p. 94.

63 MS 1138, Lambeth Palace Library.

64 These statistics derive from my computer database containing all entries in the Stationers' Registers. My record has been collated against the *STC*. Further, counts of extant books by decade have been made using the on-line *English Short Title Catalogue*, 18 July, 1994, at the Huntington Library. I have determined rate of entrance by comparing entries in the Stationers' Registers (excluding ballads) to total extant copies according to the on-line *ESTC*. Since ballads and other broadsides were so highly ephemeral, I have omitted them from my counts, which increases reliability. Furthermore, I have excluded assignments unless the assigned work was reprinted as a new edition. While the *ESTC* is not complete, it does contain nearly all records of the early English books on University Microfilms, that is, most first editions of extant early printed books, with the exception of some Bibles and official documents of Church and state. Admittedly such entrance rates can only be approximate, but the relative relationships should be fairly constant since there is no reason to believe that more texts would have disappeared from one decade than from another.

65 Blayney, "Exeunt Pirates," p. 6.

66 Respectively, Wickham, *Early English Stages*, vol. II, p. 74; E. K. Chambers, *The Elizabethan Stage*, 4 vols. (Oxford, 1923), vol. III, pp. 160–1; and Blagden, *The Stationers' Company*, p. 33.

67 Arber, vol. I, pp. xxvi, xxvii.
68 Further, Mary's charter to the Company included in its allowance of searches to enforce the Company's regulations the right "to seize, take, hold, burn . . . all and several those books and things which are or shall be printed contrary to the form of any statute, act, or proclamation" (Arber, vol. I, pp. xxviii–xxxii).
69 Blagden, *The Stationers' Company*, p. 28.
70 Ibid.
71 Jennifer Loach, "The Marian Establishment and the Printing Press," *English Historical Review*, 101 (1986), 137.
72 Arber, vol. I, p. xxxiv.
73 *CPR, Phil. & Mary*, vol. III, pp. 480–1.
74 Ibid., p. 481.
75 Arber, vol. I, p. xxxi.
76 Ibid.
77 Ibid., p. xxxii.
78 *CPR, Eliz.*, vol. I, p. 118.
79 Arber, vol. I, p. xxviii.
80 *DNB*, vol. LXII, p. 304.
81 *Letters and Papers, Henry VIII*, vol. VIII, item 6304.
82 E. W. Ives, *Anne Boleyn* (Oxford, 1986), pp. 306–7.
83 In *The Bookshops in Paul's Cross Churchyard* (1990), Peter Blayney observes that "during the second half of the sixteenth century, Paul's Cross Churchyard became the unrivalled centre of retail bookselling in London, and consequently in England" (p. 5), and Wolfe's was one of the more substantial establishments.
84 Quoted in *DNB*, vol. LXII, p. 304.
85 Blayney, *Bookshops in Paul's Cross Churchyard*, p. 19.
86 *CPR, Edward VI*, vol. I, p. 187.
87 *CPR, Phil. & Mary*, vol. III, p. 463.
88 Ibid. pp. 483–4.
89 *CPR, Eliz.*, vol. I, p. 417.
90 See Siebert, *Freedom of the Press*, p. 42.
91 David Loades, *Politics, Censorship and the English Reformation* (London and New York, 1991), pp. 97–8.
92 The 1529 proclamation gave the bishops the responsibility for seeing that offenders were arrested and held until they recanted, but the 1530 one placed implementation in the hands of civil authorities. See Hughes & Larkin, vol. I, pp. 181–6, 193–7.
93 While Henry VIII's defense of the Catholic Church was undoubtedly sincere, at least initially, the escalation of prohibitions and heresy prosecutions associated with these proclamations corresponds to his campaign across Europe to obtain papal sanction for his divorce from Queen Catherine.
94 See John Guy, *Tudor England* (Oxford, 1988), chapters 5 and 6.

95 Ibid., p. 178.

96 Ibid., p. 183.

97 The Proclamation was a political maneuver as well since it ensured that Cromwell's reforms would not entirely be stifled. While the conservatives were working against a Bible in English, the licensing provision for scripture (stated separately from the general licensing) – by the King, *one* of his Privy Council, or *one* bishop of the realm – in essence allowed Cromwell to proceed in his efforts to get one printed.

98 Siebert, *Freedom of the Press*, p. 48.

99 Elton, *Tudor Constitution*, p. 229. According to Elton, Parliamentary statute by the fifteenth century "had long been regarded as the highest expression of law in the realm," holding precedence over royal proclamations which, although they held legal authority within English common law practice, posed enforcement problems (p.22).

100 31 Henry VIII, ca. 14.

101 34, 35 Henry VIII, ca. 1.

102 The objection can well be raised that Henrician press control sought to suppress opposition to the King, and to the degree that religious reform opposed the King's authority, this is true. That the primary end of press control was quelling political opposition is, however, questionable. The treason laws, of course, included in their description treason "by wordes or writynge" (26 Henry VIII, ca. 13), but beyond this, took little note of printing and print control.

103 1 Edward VI, ca. 12. "Writinge pryntinge payntinge carvinge or gravinge" were, however, part of Edward's treason statute (5 & 6 Edward VI, ca. 11).

104 Hughes & Larkin, vol. 1, p. 517.

105 Guy, *Tudor England*, pp. 219–29. Whether or not the Proclamation had considerable effect is difficult to judge. The *STC* has over 250 titles for extant works printed in 1550, and this falls to 150 in 1552. While printing controls may account for some of the decline, so might a market saturated by the high printing levels of 1548 and 1549.

106 1 & 2 Phil. & Mar, ca. 3. This statute, retained by Elizabeth, provided that offenders should have their right hand "stricken off" in "some Market place." John Stubbs and William Page were convicted under this statute for writing and publishing *A Gaping Gulf* (see chapter 6).

107 Hughes & Larkin, vol. ii, pp. 5–8. "Freedom of conscience" extended protection to English Catholics.

108 Ibid., p. 59.

109 *CPR, Phil. & Mary*, vol. iii, pp. 24–5.

110 Hughes & Larkin, vol. ii, pp. 90–1.

111 Guy, *Tudor England*, p. 238.

2 ELIZABETHAN PRESS CONTROLS: "IN A MORE CALME AND QUIET REIGNE"

1   1 Edward, ca. 12.
2   She was so praised by pageants staged throughout London in honor of her entry into the city. Holinshed's *Chronicles* (1577) contains one of the earliest records of the entry celebrations. More recently they have received the attention of Sidney Anglo in *Spectacle, Pageantry, and Early Tudor Policy* (Oxford, 1969).
3   The nature of Elizabeth's religious "settlement," whose compromise has long been a textbook commonplace, continues to prompt historical debate. J. E. Neale defined the compromise as "conservative and comprehensive," yet unsatisfactory both to the religiously conservative Queen and her zealous subjects schooled on the Continent by a more radical kind of reform (*Elizabeth I and her Parliaments, 1559–1581* [1953], pp. 33–84). More recently, Norman L. Jones described Elizabeth as "a convinced Protestant" for whom "beyond the basic issues of faith and grace there were only 'adiaphora' – things which she could regulate in accord with the needs of the nation" ("Elizabeth's First Year," in *The Reign of Elizabeth I*, ed. Christopher Haigh [London and Hampshire, 1984], p. 28).
4   An anonymous draft of a speech to oppose the Stationers' effort to secure trade regulation reveals that certain parties, probably puritan, sought greater restraints on printing, but preferred them on moral rather than trade grounds. The draft also makes it clear that the speaker acknowledged statuatory restriction on "bokes sclanderous to the stat" (W. W. Greg, *Companion to Arber* [Oxford, 1967], p. 141).
5   1 Eliz., ca. 1.
6   The Act's sanctions were the loss of property or imprisonment if property was not worth twenty pounds for a first offense, praemunire for a second, and high treason for a third.
7   1 Eliz., ca. 5.
8   13 Eliz., ca. 1. A first offense invoked precedents of praemunire for treasonous acts and a second became high treason.
9   It was treason to print, bind, sell, or otherwise publish books or scrolls declaring that anyone other than Elizabeth "is or ought to be the right Heire & Successor."
10   1 & 2 Phil & Mar., ca. 3. See chapter 6.
11   23 Eliz., ca. 2.
12   John Gilbert Bellamy, *Tudor Law of Treason* (Toronto, 1979), pp. 110–25.
13   "Oyer" and "terminer" are from Anglo French, "to hear and determine."
14   Ibid. See particularly my discussion in chapter 4 of Burghley's *Execution of English Justice* and Allen's *A True, Sincere and Modest Defence*, and in chapter 7 of Campion's trial.

15 See pp. 93, 236, 253 n. 38.
16 Greg, *Companion to Arber*, p. 20.
17 Probably under 23 Eliz., ca. 2. 23 April 1584, Domestic State Papers, 12/120, fo. 48, London Public Record Office; Judgment Roll, Queen's Bench, 26 & 27 Eliz., roll 37, London Public Record Office.
18 *DNB*, vol. I, p. 282.
19 Ibid., vol. XXIII, p. 421.
20 Barrow was subsequently arrested and indicted for high treason, to which he pleaded guilty for maintaining that the Queen was not the queen: he was hanged (*DNB*, vol. XXIII, p. 421).
21 See chapter 8.
22 Libel, however, was still a serious matter throughout Elizabeth's reign. Slander and libel belonged to ecclesiastical moral law, and many cases were tried in the Church courts. According to Martin Ingram in *Church Courts, Sex, and Marriage in England 1570–1640* (Cambridge and New York, 1987), libel was the single most prevalent cause tried in Elizabethan England, but these were not brought by the church against individuals, but by those libeled against the libelee. Libel cases were also heard in the common-law courts, and many of these had to do with "lewd words" against the government or nobility. Between 1558 and 1603, the Privy Council addressed reports of such slander, usually by remanding investigation to local officials and with most cases being heard in the common-law courts. Press control does not appear to have been the issue in any of these actions. Suppression of rumor and libel, constituting as it does a kind of censorship, requires independent consideration beyond the scope of this book.
23 *A Letter*, essentially printed "privately" in a press run of one hundred (many of which Hall circulated), treated a violent confrontation between Hall and Mallerie over a card game and the subsequent battery and libel suits. The matter came before Parliament when Hall, claiming parliamentary immunity, refused to pay a judgment. In attempting to vindicate himself in print, Hall attacked other members of Parliament. According to Simonds D'Ewes, a motion to the House said that the book was "greatly reproachful against some particular good Member of this House of great Credit, but also very much slanderous and derogatory to the genral Authority, Power and State of this House, and prejudicial to the validity of the proceedings of the same, in making and establishing Laws" (*Journal of All the Parliaments during the Reign of Queen Elizabeth* (1682), p. 291). Hall was effectively tried before Commons and committed to the Tower until he recanted. The House condemned the book as a slanderous libel. See *DNB*, vol. XXIV, pp. 56–8, and Neale, *Elizabeth I and her Parliaments, 1559–1581*, pp. 333–45.
24 See pp. 58–9 n. 4.
25 J. E. Neale, *Elizabeth I and her Parliaments, 1584–1601* (1957), pp. 94–5.

26 See above n. 4. Greg, *Companion to Arber*, p. 142. The language of the
    speaker's celebration of printing – "that hath advanced & spread the
    kingdom of the gospell & battered the kyngdom of antechrist" – places
    the speaker's rhetoric within the tradition of religious reform rather
    than political control. Indeed, the speech is reminiscent of the language
    in the Edwardian proclamation calling for licensing.

27 Arber (vol. ii, p. 75) identifies the W. Lambarde who drafted this act
    with the William Lambarde who authored *Perambulation of Kent* and was
    an antiquarian and lawyer, served as Justice of the Peace in Kent and
    wrote four books on the English justice system, but was not a member
    of Parliament. Why he would have written drafts of parliamentary acts
    is not altogether clear, especially since in the 1570s his principal
    interests appear to have been English topography and an almshouse he
    founded. In April 1580 Lambarde assumed his responsibilities as Justice
    of the Peace in Kent. (A William Lambert did serve in Parliament for
    Yorkshire at this time.)

        According to Retha M. Warnicke (*William Lambarde, Elizabethan
    Antiquary 1536–1601* [1973] pp. 17–22), due to orthographical variants,
    William Lambarde of Kent is often confused with William Lambert.
    The latter "helped foment a constitutional crisis" in 1566 when he gave
    a "learned oration" for reiterating the suit to the Queen to limit the
    succession and name a Protestant heir (p.17). Warnicke suggests that
    this Lambert, clearly committed to Protestant causes, was likely to have
    been the Lambert who wrote to Lord Burghley on 16 July 1585,
    advocating military support for the Protestant cause in the Low
    Countries (p. 21). This William Lambert with his alignment to more
    radical protestant causes seems a more likely candidate for the author
    of the "Acte to restrain licentious printing."

28 According to Siebert, "Since the combined efforts of government
    officials, ecclesiastical licensers, and Stationers' Company searchers
    were insufficient to keep the writing of critics of the government and
    the established religion from finding their way into print, William
    Lambard [of Kent], the eminent jurist, was commissioned in 1577 to
    draw up an act which would accomplish the desired results" (*Freedom of
    the Press*, p. 60). According to Greg, Lambarde was responsible not for
    the 1577 draft but the 1580 draft, which substantially revised the earlier
    one (*Companion to Arber*, p. 20). The 1580 draft sought to place press
    control in the hands of the "Governours of the Inglishe Printe," a body
    composed of members of the Inns of Court, the Deans of the Arches
    and the churches of St. Peter and St. Paul. The 1577 draft includes the
    Archbishop of Canterbury as a principal authorizer, but he is excluded
    in the 1580 draft (though his authorization is not invalidated), which
    may have been prompted by the growing dissatisfaction of religious
    reformers with the episcopal hierarchy.

29 Arber, vol. ii, p. 751.

30 The *Journals* of both the House of Lords and the House of Commons make no mention of bills for press licensing being read during the reign of Elizabeth. Nor does Neale (*Elizabeth and her Parliaments 1559–1581* and *1584–1601*) or G. R. Elton (*The Parliament of England 1559–1581* [Cambridge, 1986]) refer to any such measure. Had the government inititated the bill, it probably would have been read. Being unread suggests it was promoted by special rather than government interests.

31 1 Eliz., ca. 2.

32 Jones, "Elizabeth's First Year," p. 50.

33 1 Eliz, ca. 1.

34 *CPR, Eliz.*, vol. 1, p. 118.

35 1 Eliz., ca. 1.

36 *Injunctions geven by the quenes majestie* (1559), B3r. (Further references appear parenthetically in the text.)

37 They also admonish "ecclesiastical persons not to "haunt or resort to Taverns or Alehouses" other "than for theyr honeste necessities" (A3v) and call for "quiet attendaunce, to heare, make and understande that is read, preached, and mynistred" of every man, woman, and child during religious services (C3r).

38 51. Item because there is a great abuse in the printers of bokes, which for covetousnes cheifle regard not what thei print, so thei may have gaine, whereby arriseth great dysorder by publicatyon of unfrutefull, vayne and infamous bokes and papers: The Quenes majestie straitly chargethe and commaundeth, that no manner of person, shal print any manner of boke or paper, of what sort, nature, or in what language soever it be, excepte the same be first licenced by her majestie by expresse wordes in writynge, or by .vi. of her privy counsel, or be perused and licensed by the archbyshops of Cantorbury and Yorke, the bishop London, the chauncelours of both unyversities, the bishop beyng ordinary, and the Archdeacon also of the place where any suche shalbe printed, or by two of them, wherof the ordinary of the place to be alwaies one. And that the names of such as shal allowe the same, to be added in thende of every such worke, for a testymonye of the allowaunce therof. And bycause many pampheletes, playes and balettes, be often times printed, wherein regard wold be had that nothing therin should be either heretical, sedicious, or unsemely for Christyan eares: Her majestie likewyse commaundeth, that no manner of person, shall enterprise to print any such, except the same be to him lycenced by suche her majesties commyssyoners, or iii. of them, as be appoynted in the citye of London to here, and determine divers causes ecclesiasticall, tending to the execution of certayne statutes, made the last parliament for uniformitye of order in relygion. And yf any shal sell or utter, any manner of bokes or papers, beynge not licensed as is abovesaid: That the same party shalbe punyshed by order of the sayde commyssyoners, as to the qualitie of the faulte shalbe thought mete. And touchinge all other bokes of matters of religyon, or polycye, or governaunce, that hathe ben prynted, eitheir on thisside the Seas, or on thother side, bycause the dyversitie of them is great, and that there nedeth good consideration to be had of the perticularyties therof: her majestye referreth the prohibition, or permission therof, to thorder whyche her sayde commyssyoners within the Cytie of London shall take, and notifye. Accordynge to the whyche,

her majestye straightly commaundeth al maner her subjectes, and specially the wardens and company of Stacyoners, to be obedyent.

Provyded that these orders do not extend to anye prophane aucthours, and workes in any language, that hath ben heretofore commonly receyved or allowed in any the unyversities or Scoles: But the same may be prynted and used as by good order they were accustomed. (Dɪr–Dɪv)

39 Arber, vol. ɪ, p. xxx–x.

40 See Chambers, *Elizabethan Stage*, vol. ɪɪɪ, pp. 161–4; W. W. Greg, *Some Aspects of London Publishing between 1550–1640* (Oxford, 1956), pp. 5–6; and Siebert, *Freedom of the Press*, pp. 56–9.

41 Siebert, *Freedom of the Press*, p. 56.

42 Ibid., p. 57.

43 While an English monarch might issue a commandment ("her majestye straightly commaundeth") by royal proclamation, prosecuting the disobedient was only as effective as the proclamation's provisions of san- ctions. As Elton points out, "Issuing as they did from king and Council, proclamations had no force in the courts of common law. It was left to the Council, sitting as a court in Star Chamber, to do what it could to make a reality of the policy enunciated in them" (*Tudor Constitution*, p. 22). With regard to book licensing, then, we would have to look to the Council for any enforcement the High Commission did not achieve.

44 1 Eliz., ca. 1.

45 Roland Usher, *The Rise and Fall of the High Commission* (1913), p. 7. This book is, according to Philip Tyler, "a work of pioneer scholarship" which "has remained the standard work on the subject for more than half a century ("Introduction," to reprint, [1968], p. i).

46 According to Tyler,

Usher's difficulty was caused by his failure to recognize that there were features common to the ecclesiastical commissions of both Richard II and Henry VIII. Broadly speaking, these were similar royal authorization, mixed clerical and lay membership, judicial powers and the ability to inflict secular penalties. Perhaps Usher was misled by this tendency to draw an unreal distinction between a "commission" and a "court" and by his mistaken belief that the "irregular" procedure of the early Tudor commissions ruled out any connection between them and the a late medieval heresy commissions. ("Introduction," Usher, *Rise and Fall*, p. xxi)

In this Tyler distinguishes his position from the caesaropapal position that it was not until after Henry VIII's breach with Rome that the English monarchy assumed spiritual authority previously belonging to the Pope, and also that the Court of High Commission would assume the authority as the highest court of ecclesiastical appeal.

47 Tyler, "Introduction," Usher, *Rise and Fall*, pp. xxviii–xxix. "Criminal" distinguishes a court where the government served as the plaintiff and the accused as the defendant from a court in which one subject could bring suit against another.

48 Guy, *Tudor England*, pp. 292–3.
49 Richard Cosin, *An apologie: of and for sundrie proceedings by jurisdiction ecclesiastical* (1591), p. 19.
50 Ibid., pp. 109–10.
51 The distinction in jurisdiction between the High Commission and other Church courts receives confirmation from several other early modern sources. Lambeth MS 2026 contains an entire collection of writings "shewenge what jurisdiction the clergie hath heretofore lawfully used and may lawfully use in the realme of England" (c. 1590) as does Lambeth MS 1371 (texts from the late sixteenth and early seventeenth centuries). Edward Coke devotes *The fourth part of the Institutes of the Lawes of England* (1664) to the jurisdiction of the common law courts and the Church courts, and he too distinguishes between the regular Church courts and the High Commission, to which he assigns jurisdiction over heresy. What becomes clear from all of these – and even John Burn's *The High Commission: Notice of the Court, and its Proceedings* (1865) – is that the High Commission's jurisdiction was in matters of heresy and conformity to the established Church.
52 *Acts of the Privy Council of England*, ed. John Roche Dasent, 46 vols. (1890–1964), vol. VIII, p. 331. (Hereafter cited as *APC* in both the text and the notes.)
53 Right honourable the master of the Requestes, D. Lewis, told me that your Lordship thoughte it meete we should not middell with any matters by vertue of the commission, but things as concerned religion, wherein I argue not your Lordship in iudgmente, as by whom I have ever desired to be directed and will be still, if it please you to graunte me that favour & that I four your wisdom, zeale, experience, learning & godliness. (I thanke God), I attempt to be such and my selfe in all things, that I woulde think my selfe happ to be directyd by you. And therefore my good Lordship to but suche points know your pleasure, And by God . . . I shallbe as readie to complie with it as any howsoever . . . (John Aylmer to Lord Burghley, 15 December 1581, Lansdowne MS 33, fo. 27, British Library)
   While Burghley's wishes may have stayed the High Commission's hand in nonreligious matters during the reign of Elizabeth – or at least until his death – once James I came to the throne its interest in matters regarding books and print increased. In 1613 by letters patent James granted the Ecclesiastical Commissioners the authority to "enquire and search" for all schismatic and seditious books and to take action against the offenders (George W. Prothero, *Select Statutes and Other Constitutional Documents* [Oxford, 1894], pp. 427–8). In "Changes in the Mechanism and Procedure for Control of the London Press, 1625–1637" (Unpublished B.Litt. thesis, Oxford University, 1976), P. M. Olander argues that even with this patent, the High Commission did not really consolidate its authority over the press until the 1637 Star Chamber Decree, despite several attempts to vindicate its own authority over printing offenses in the late 1620s (p. 91).

54 *APC,* vol. VIII, pp. 235–6.
55 With regard to the reliability of the Registers, Greg concludes from Richard Robinson's "Eupolemia," which contains a detailed record of the authorization and entrance of his nineteen printed works, that "failure on the part of the Clerk to mention by whom the license [authorization] was granted does not imply an absence of license" ("Richard Robinson and the Stationers' Register," in Maxwell, *Collected Papers,* ed. Maxwell, p. 421). Actually, for the seven titles that were entered in the Stationers' Registers only one received an ecclesiastical authorization that went unrecorded. (Another without notice of ecclesiatical authorization was actually an anomalous entry: Henry Denham printed Robinson's translation of Melancthon's prayers *cum privilegio* under William Seres's patent, so entry was not required.) Even if one were to generalize from Robinson's slim evidence that one in seven entries omitted the ecclesiastical authorization – and I do not think it appropriate to do so since he has errors about printers and other matters in his ledger – between 1560 and 1580 less than twenty and fifty percent respectively would have received official authorization.
56 A facsimile is reprinted on plate XII in Cyprian Blagden's "Book Trade Control in 1566," *Library,* 5th ser., 13 (1958), 287–92.
57 Bladgen, "Book Trade Control," p. 289. He speaks with the full benefit of hindsight even though few circumstances in 1566 suggest the assault on the Company and privileged printing that was to come between 1577 and 1586. Admittedly, in 1560 the High Commission had called upon the Master and Wardens of the Stationers' Company to punish those responsible for infringing William Seres's privilege for printing primers and Psalters (Arber, vol. II, p. 62). This indicates the commission's interest in ensuring one kind of "legal" printing, but it appears to have been a singular occurrence.
58 Greg, *Companion to Arber,* pp. 114–15.
59 For details of the "Great Controversy," see A. C. Southern, *Elizabethan Recusant Prose, 1559–1582* (1949), pp. 59–67, 542–4 and Peter Milward, *Religious Controversies of the Elizabethan Age* (1977).
60 Arber, vol. I, p. 421.
61 *Ibid.,* p. 347. Siebert concurs: "The two inquisitors after receiving written authority and a grant of five pounds for the year ending July, 1567, proceeded to visit the London printing houses, catching six culprits, and then went to the provinces where they discovered that Thomas Marshe, John Wight, and Gerard Dewes were the principal dealers in prohibited Catholic books" (*Freedom of the Press,* p. 83). Actually, the payment to Purfoot and Singleton was not a grant prior to their search, nor was the fine imposed on six London Stationers entirely distinct from the provincial search. The 1566–7 receipts include a separate notice of fines levied in relation to the Purfoot–Singleton

search: three were to members of the Company (Thomas Marshe, Garrad [Gerard] Dewes, and Humphrey Toye); two were to booksellers, free of the Drapers' Company (Master Whyte [John Wight] and Abraham Vele); and one to Anthonye Kydson (who is not listed in the records of printers and booksellers for the period) (Arber, vol. 1, p. 348). Marshe, Dewes, and Wight were all implicated by the "provincial" search (Robert Davies, *A Memoir of the York Press* [1868], pp. 30–3). The payment was made at the end of 1567 after the company account had already closed. The London Stationers (Wight and Dewes were booksellers, Marshe a printer) provided texts to the provincial booksellers.

62 Davies, *Memoir of the York Press*, p. 31.
63 Ibid., pp. 30–3.
64 They did, however, unlike three of the others fined from the Purfoot–Singleton search, pay their fines. See Arber, vol. 1, pp. 348, 368, 369, 391.
65 Arber, vol. 1, p. 346.
66 Both entered works in the register near to a work dated 25 November 1566, and Purfoot printed *Description of a rare and monstrous fish taken on the east coast of Holland the xvii of November*, which was entered in the Register. Furthermore, in November 1566 Purfoot bound William Hodgeson as an apprentice (Arber, vol. 1, p. 323).
67 Purfoot presented Nicholas Crowche as an apprentice in April or May 1567, probably May since he was in York in May (Arber, vol. 1, p. 325).
68 Arber, vol. 1, pp. 392, 421.
69 Ibid., p. 466. See below on the 1586 Star Chamber Decrees.
70 Printed books the High Commission regarded as "illegal" (oppositional) were usually issued from presses that were "illegal" in the sense that they were not operated by members of the Stationers' Company, or after 1586, not authorized by the Archbishop of Canterbury. Notably, the High Commission employed the Stationers to seek out the *Admonition* and the Marprelate presses once the their issue was deemed illegal. The High Commission, however, did not employ Company searchers to canvas the bookstalls for texts that might be oppositional.
71 See Alan Haynes, *Invisible Power: The Elizabethan Secret Services 1570–1603* (New York, 1992).
72 It is important to distinguish between oppositional reform texts, which were often (though not always) suppressed, and "puritan" writing, which was rarely suppressed. See chapter 8 for a full discussion of the "puritan press."
73 Records of the York High Commission are extant, and while invaluable for establishing procedural matters, it is unwise to generalize from them to the London High Commission both because printing was centered in London and because the York and London Commissions

appear to have had philosophical differences. According to Ronald A. Marchant, the High Commission at York between 1560 and 1603 was not "particularly vigilant in seeking out anything but the most radical acts of non-conformity," and, indeed, "men with moderate or radical Puritan views could usually escape with little more than a reprimand for nonconformity." Even the leading puritans Christopher Shute and Edmund Burney were members of the York High Commission (*The Puritans and the Church Courts in the Diocese of York, 1560–1642* [1960], pp. 24–7).

74 The two most influential studies in this respect have been Edward Arber's *An Introductory Sketch to the Martin Marprelate Controversy* (London, 1895) and William Pierce's *An introduction to the Marprelate Tracts: A Chapter in the Evolution of Religious and Civil Liberty in England 1588–1590* (1908). See also Patrick Collinson's *The Elizabethan Puritan Movement* (Berkeley and Los Angeles, 1967). See chapter 8 for a discussion of recent revisions in this perspective. For my choice of a lower case "p" for "puritanism," see p. 274 n. 8.

75 Martin Marprelate, *An Epistle* (1588), p. 23, in *The Marprelate Tracts [1588–1589]: A Scolar Press Facsimile* (Menston, England, 1970).

76 Leona Rostenberg, *The Minority Press and the English Crown* (Nieuwkoop, 1971), p. 170. According to the *STC*, Crowley probably did not print the texts that bore his name.

77 W. W. Greg, *Licensers for the Press, &c. to 1640* (Oxford, 1962), p. 28.

78 Collinson, *Elizabethan Puritan Movement*, p. 75. In January 1565 the Queen wrote a letter to Archbishop Parker expressing alarm at the increasing "diversity of opinions and specially in the external, decent, and lawful rites and ceremonies to be used in the churches" (ibid., p. 69). Parker and his fellow commissioners were called upon to ensure order and conformity in external rites and ceremonies. In response the Archbishop issued new visitation articles which called for use of the surplice in services and customary clerical outdoor dress. A large group of London ministers refused to conform to such "popish ceremonies." For a full discussion of this controversy and Crowley's role in it, see Collinson, *Elizabethan Puritan Movement*, Part II, chapter 2.

79 *DNB*, vol. III, p. 242.

80 Some sources credit Crowley with full authorship of the tract, but Collinson, after John Stow, says that its materials were supplied by "a whole multitude of London ministers, every one of them giving their advice in writing," with Crowley putting the tract in its final order (*Elizabethan Puritan Movement*, p. 77).

81 Arber, vol. I, p. 316.

82 Manuscript quoted in *The Seconde Parte of a Register*, ed. Albert Peel (Cambridge, 1915), a calendar to the puritan manuscripts of 1570 to 1590 (vol. I, pp. 87–8).

83 In *Puritan Manifestoes* ed. W. H. Frere and C. E. Douglas, (1907), p. xiii.

Parker's "we" could, refer to the High Commission or to his own staff. Further, this indicates that searchers, even for secret presses, were not necessarily the Stationers' Company.

84 *Puritan Manifestoes*, ed. Frere and Douglas, p. xiii.

85 Arber, vol. I, p. 467. The Stationers' Warden's Accounts for 1573–4 contain detailed expenses of this transaction, which have been misread as the record of a "Company" search, with John Harrison the elder serving as the searcher. Only the Stationers' Company had the right to seize a press, and in this instance they were called upon to do so, presumably by Archbishop Parker. His pursuivant must have carried a warrant for the printers' arrest, who were then brought up to London by the local constabulary. The press would be sold to the benefit of the Crown and the Stationers, and one of the Stationers, Bynnemann, paid 15s. for Stroud's type.

86 A report of this interview appears in "Strowd's Trouble," *Seconde Parte of a Register*, ed. Peele, vol. I, pp. 112–14. Subsequent quotations in the text are from this volume.

87 Stroud's troubles over conformity did not end there. In January 1574 he was questioned by a "Dr. Nevesonne," regarding *Ecclesiastica disciplina* (Walter Traver's blueprint for presbyterian reform), which according to "Nevesonne," was full of "treason, rebelion, and heresie." ("Nevesonne" is, I believe, Stephen Nevynson, prebendary of Canterbury, who was commissioned by Archbishop Parker to "examine such petty canons and vicars-choral as were suspect in religion" [*DNB*, vol. XL, p. 309]). When Stroud admitted that the book belonged to him, Nevynson had the bailiff arrest him, and the next day took the matter to the Bishop of Rochester, who prohibited Stroud from teaching or preaching "within the parish of Yaldinge or elswhere," and banned him from the diocese. Stroud clearly felt Nevynson's actions violated usual procedures since he requested "suretyes, to answer to my lord of Canterb., or to the high commissioners," which he was denied, although the Bishop of Rochester allowed him back to his ministry under the bishop's license until the matter might be "decided and ended." Shortly thereafter, Stroud, his church wardens, and members of his congregation were summoned to the diocesan court at Rochester, ostensibly to answer regarding parish baptismal practices (a conformity matter), but really to obtain information about his conformity. Stroud was then called to take an oath, which he refused as, "these things belonge to the queenes Majesties Commissioners, and not to him, and therefore I ought not to anwere them unto him."

Two years later, as letters on his behalf attest, Stroud was called before the Archbishop of Canterbury, charged as "a sower of errour in doctrine and of sedition in lyvinge, and consequently to be a disturber of the peace of the church and an enimie to the tranquillity of the realme." In his defense, numerous parishioners attested that Stroud's doctrine was sound, and "he hath given faithfull promise to forbeare the handlinge of any one question concerninge the policye of the church, and we thinke in our conscience that he hath truly perfomed it" ("Strowd's Trouble," in *Seconde Parte of a Register*, ed. Peele, pp. 108–12.)

88 See Collinson, *Elizabethan Puritan Movement*, p. 152.

89 See chapter 8.

90 *Records of the Court of the Stationers' Company 1576 1602*, ed. W. W. Greg and E. Boswell (1930), pp. 86–7. See my chapter 5.

91 Ibid., pp. 29–30.

92 Siebert, *Freedom of the Press*, pp. 60, 61

93 Collinson, *Elizabethan Puritan Movement*, p. 74. John Strype, *Life and Acts of Archbishop Whitgift* (1822), vol. i, pp. 422–3. Strype bases his claim that Whitgift initiated the Decrees on his identification of its being in the hand of Abraham Hartwell, Whitgift's secretary. The copy to which Strype must be referring is Lansdowne MS 905, fos. 280–1, and while the very careful secretary hand is quite close to Hartwell's, some orthographic differences exist when it is compared to his imprimatur. Further, the Stationers' Company paid for four copies to be made of the decrees, with Whitgift receiving one. See Collinson, *Elizabethan Puritan Movement*, pp. 274–5.

94 Even Whitgift's secretary George Paule's 1612 *The Life of the Most Reverend and Religious Prelate John Whitgift* makes no mention of Whitgift's involvement with the 1586 Decrees, though it discusses in some detail his confrontation with Cartwright and avid censorship of the Marprelate tracts.

95 One article proscribes that "no bookes be printed being not before perused and allowed under the handes of the Archbishop of Canterbury or Bishopp of London," that printers be restrained from printing editions of the Bible other than those allowed, and that "like order be taken for such treatises" that address the "state of the realme or the church" (Domestic State Papers, 12/163, fo. 31; London Public Record Office).

96 The cover letter to the Queen makes it clear that the measures were directed against Catholics:

> That it may please your majesty to give strait order, that the Lawes late made against the recusants may be putt in more due execusion: considering the Benefits that hath grown unto the church thereby, where they have been so executed and the encouragement which they and other doe receive by romishe Executing thereof. (Domestic State Papers, 12/163, fo. 31)

97 Elton, *Tudor Constitution*, p. 163.

98 Ibid., pp. 167–9.

99 Ibid., p. 170.

100 Ellesmere MSS 2652, 2768, Huntington Library. According to John

Guy, these summaries were prepared by the clerical staff of the Court of Star Chamber for the consideration of the Chancellor and ". . . were collected as much as anything in the quest for precedents affirming Star Chamber's jurisdiction, which Egerton was anxious to defend" (*The Court of Star Chamber and its records to the reign of Elizabeth I* [PRO Handbooks, No. 21, 1985], p. 89, n. 66).

101 Greg, *Companion to Arber*, pp. 123–5.

102 Wolfe served as an apprentice to a Stationers' Company member, John Day (1562–72), though he did not complete his apprenticeship. For full account of this assault, see Harry R. Hoppe, "John Wolfe, Printer and Publisher, 1579–1601," *Library*, 4th series, 5.14 (1933), 241–74. For further information about Wolfe's position in the London book trade, see Clifford Chalmers Huffman, *Elizabethan Impressions: John Wolfe and His Press* (New York, 1988).

103 Later on, Wolfe made further demands of Barker, insisting upon work, a loan, and an allowance of apprentices beyond the Stationers' Company's usual allotment of one to three, and while Barker agreed to help him, they still did not reach an agreement.

104 According to Hoppe, this appeal is distinct from one filed by the journeyman printers concurrently and he also notes that "An appeal was also sent to Sir Francis Walsingham, probably at the same time, asking for the liberation of their apprentices, and a hearing of their bill of complaint previously sent to the Star Chamber" ("John Wolfe," p. 249).

105 Wolfe and his cohorts opposed the compromise on the grounds that "they were freemen, and might print all lawfull bokes notwithstanding any commaundement of the Quene, and the Quenes comaundementes in this case were no lawe, nor warranted by law," a position that, according to Thomas Norton (one of the commissioners) directly opposed the Queen "in denyeng her whole prerogatiue for preuiledge of bokes which her progenitors haue allwaye vsed, and which all Christian princes do vse, and which in president of othr her prohibitions toucheth her royal dignite" (Arber, vol. II, p. 775).

106 Arber, vol. II, p. 780.

107 *APC*, vol. VII, pp. 188–9, 277–8.

108 Arber, vol. II, p. 753.

109 Ibid., pp. 790–804.

110 Greg, *Companion to Arber*, pp. 126–33.

111 Ibid., p. 33.

112 The 1586 Decrees set forth nine ordinances governing printing and placed their execution in the hands of the "Archebysshop of *CANTER-BURY* and the righte honorable the lordes and others of her highenes pryvye councell" (Arber, vol. I, p. 807). Eight items sought to remedy the above-mentioned problems in printing-trade relations. Items one and two required that anyone involved in printing register with the

Master and Wardens of the Stationers' Company, and restricted printing to London and the university presses at Cambridge and Oxford. Items six and seven reiterated the Stationers' right to search for illegal books and presses and authorized officials of the Stationers' Company to seize and deface presses engaged in illegal printing, giving them recourse against non-Company printers who had been violating copyrights and privileges. Item 3 prevented new presses from printing "tyll the excessive multytude of Prynters hauinge presses already sett up, be abated," at which time, printers who desired to establish presses had to gain the approval of the Court of Assistants and the High Commission. Only one item (4) may be construed as relating to content censorship, but that also protected the printing establishment:

No person or persons shall ymnprynt or cawse to by ymprinted . . . any booke, work, coppye, matter, or thinge whatsoever, Except the same book, woork, coppye, matter, or any other thinge, hath been heeretofore allowed, or hereafter shall be allowed before the ymprintinge thereof, according to th[e] order appoynted by the Queenes maiesties *Iniunctyons*, And been first seen and pervsed by the Archbishop of CANTERBURY and Bishop of LONDON . . . Nor shall ymprynt or cause to by ymprinted any book, work or coppie against the fourme and meaninge of any Restraynt or ordannaunce conteyned or to be conteyned in any statute or lawes of this Realme, or in any Iniunctyon made, or sett foorth by her maiestie, or her highnes pryvye Councell, or against the true intent and meaninge of any Letters patentes, Commissions or prohibicons vnder the great seale of England, or contrary to any allowed ordynaunce sett Downe for the good governaunce of the Cumpany of Staconers within the Cyttie of London. (Arber, vol. II, p. 810)

While the wording "seen and pervsed by the Archbishop" suggests pervasive censorship of contents, "according to th[e] order appoynted by the Queenes maiesties *Iniunctyons*" centers licensing interests in controlling heretical and seditious texts. Besides placing "allowance" under the Archbishop of Canterbury's control, this item largely reiterates the 1566 Injunctions invoked by the Star Chamber cases to protect the Stationers' rights with regard to royal patents and copy protection through entrance in the Stationers' Register.

113 Elton, *Tudor Constitution*, p. 171.
114 In 1582–3 a dispute had arisen between the London Stationers and Cambridge University, because the university proposed to establish a printing press in Cambridge under a license issued under 26 Henry VIII and appointed Thomas Thomas as printer to the University. In May 1582 Stationers' Company Wardens petitioned Bishop Aylmer on behalf of the Company to move Burghley and the Vice-Chancellor John Bell to stay the proceedings (Arber, vol. I, pp. 247–8). In June Company Wardens seized Thomas's press (set up in London). The University (and Thomas) regarded the seizure as an effort by the London Stationers to eliminate printing at the University, while the Stationers regarded Thomas's appointment as invalid in London. Bell

appealed to Burghley to resolve the matter on Thomas's behalf (Arber, vol. II, pp. 282–3).
115 Ian Archer, "The London Lobbies in the Later Sixteenth Century," *Historical Journal*, 31, 1 (1988), 17.
116 Ibid., p. 34.
117 Ibid., pp. 19–21.
118 Archer ("London Lobbies") demonstrates that success in Parliament for the livery companies was not unusual because of both the diverse interests represented in Parliament and the precedence government interests took in parliamentary matters. His insights about parliamentary processes suggest that statutory press control was not mandated by the Crown or it would have received greater parliamentary consideration, neither was repressive moral censorship the government's end – though sentiments existed within the population generally for such censorship.
119 *Records of the Court*, ed. Greg and Boswell.
120 According to Sheila Lambert, the 1586 Decrees were not altogether effective in regulating labor practices within the Stationers' Company. Despite the restrictions, the number of presses continued to grow until in 1615 the master printers, this time among themselves, agreed to limit again the number of presses and printing houses. Furthermore, both the number of journeymen and apprentices in the Company increased, leading to widespread dissatisfaction over underemployment. While the Company issued an order in 1613 to restrict the number of apprentices, the apprentices and journeymen persisted in their discontent, until their repeated petitions and complaints led to a new set of orders in 1635 and then to another decree in Star Chamber in 1637. See Lambert, "The Printers and the Government" pp. 11–13, 16–17.
121 In 1587 they suppressed John Knox's *The first booke of the history of the reformation of religion within the realm of Scotland* (1587). Later by warrant of "his grace and other high commissioners" dated 2 December 1594 "one barrell and ii firkins of books of Alexander Humes' Doing" were ordered seized (Arber, vol. II, p. 40); Hume was a Scottish poet and radical puritan.
122 *APC*, vol. XIV, p. 311.
123 Four were "Thesaurus Principium," "Ministromachia" (by Cardinal Stanislaus Rescius; Cologne, 1592), "Rosseus de re publica" (by William Rainolds, *De justa Republicae Chrestianae*, Douay, 1590, Antwerp, 1592), "Little French bookes in 8 and Surius Chronicle" (by Laurentius Surius, probably his hagiographical history, Cologne, 1572) (Arber, vol. II, p. 40). Religio-political interests were probably the motivation since the Rosseus book addressed the English succession.
124 See chapter 7 for a detailed discussion of the censorship of Holinshed's *Chronicles* and chapter 9 for Hayward's *Henry IV* and the satires.
125 An entry on 3 June 1588 in the Stationers' Court Book reads: "The

names of certen Preachers [& others] whome the Archbishop of Canterbury hathe made Choyse of to haue the pusinge and alowing of Copies. Any one of these settinge his hand to copie, to be suffycient Warrant for thalowance of the same to entringe into the hall books & so to be proceded with all to printinge." Whitgift's panel of authorizers included: "Doctor Cosin, Doctor Stallard [or Staller], Doctor Wood, Mr. Hartwll, Mr. Gravet, Mr. Crowley, Mr. Cotten, Mr. Hutchenson" as senior members and "Mr. Judsoin, Mr. Trippe, Mr. Cole, Mr. Dickens" as juniors (*Records of the Court*, ed. Greg and Boswell, pp. 28–9). According to Greg, the distinction between junior and senior licensers was not observed (*Licensers for the Press*, p. 2).

126 "Books" here is intentional. Because licensing requirements for ballads were highly irregular, and because so few ballads and broadsheets are extant, I have excluded them from my statistical analysis. See p. 229 n. 64.

127 Arber, vol. II, p. 536.

128 Ponsonby entered Spenser's *Complaintes conteyningbe sondrye smalle Poemes of the worldes vanity*, which included "Mother Hubberd's Tale," in the Register on 19 December 1590 with Thomas Staller's official authorization. This entry lends considerable credence to Jean R. Brink's contention: "There is no evidence that 'Mother Hubberds Tale' was printed in 1579 or at any time before 1591 . . . If the poem was not in circulation, it cannot have been called in." Had the poem been in print in 1579, entrance would have been unnecessary in 1591. Furthermore, given the heightened authorization requirements after the 1586 Decree, it is difficult to imagine that a member of the official panel of authorizers would have allowed a text formerly recalled. Brink continues that "After it was printed in 1591, 'Mother Hubberds Tale' was interpreted as an attack on Burghley," and, she contends, its censorship was more a matter of rumor than of official action. See "Who Fashioned Edmund Spenser? The Textual History of 'Complaints,'" *Studies in Philology*, 87 (1991) 153–68.

129 Olander, "Changes in the Mechanism and Procedure," pp. 111–39.

130 Greg, *Licensers for the Press*, p. 45.

131 Domestic State Papers 12, 275, f 31; London Public Record Office. This is reprinted in full in W. W. Greg, "Samuel Harsnett and Hayward's 'Henry IV,'" *Library*, 5th ser., 11 (1956), 4–5.Subsequent quotations in the text are to this essay. While I concur with Greg's conclusion that "it is nevertheless impossible to avoid the impression that at the end of Elizabeth's reign ecclesiastical licensing for the press was more casual and less effective than the authorities can have intended or perhaps realized" (p. 8), I understand the circumstances of *Henry IV*'s suppression differently: see chapter 9.

132 Greg rightly observes that Stationers frequently sought authorizations as well ("Samuel Harsnett," p. 6).

133 Greg, "Samuel Harsnett," p. 7.
134 Daniel Featly, *Cygnea Cantio* (1628), p. 5.
135 Ibid., p. 3.
136 Arber, vol. II, pp. 590, 595, 598, 624, 629, 643.
137 Ibid., vol. III, p. 89.
138 Perhaps the most interesting aspect of religious publishing in England throughout Elizabeth's reign was that legal or not, oppositional views received thoughtfully articulated printed response, and often the official response restated, even reprinted, the initial text, e.g. Whitgift's response to the *Admonition* (see p. 107).

3 ELIZABETHAN CENSORHIP PROCLAMATIONS: "TO CONSERVE HER REALM IN AN UNIVERSAL GOOD PEACE"

1 Elton, *Tudor Constitution*, p. 22.
2 Hughes & Larkin, vol. I, p. xxvi.
3 I rely on Hughes & Larkin's dating, sources, and texts of the proclamations.
4 Hughes & Larkin, vol. II, pp. 312–13.
5 The man who posted the papal bull, John Felton, was tried for treason and hanged.
6 Hughes & Larkin, vol. II, pp. 312–13, This refers to manuscripts of a scroll written by William Allen and to copies of the excommunication bull. Allen's scroll, ostensibly a work of Catholic edification directed to the English Catholic as a bulwark against Protestant claims, asserted papal supremacy and denied unequivocally the Church's claims to continuity with Apostolic Christianity. It was finally printed three times in the mid-1570s – twice on the Continent in Catholic apologetics, and once in England as part of William Fulke's *Two Treatises* (1577), in which he also answers it. See Southern, *Elizabethan Recusant Prose*, pp. 519–23.
7 Hughes & Larkin, vol. II, p. 347.
8 Ibid.
9 This proclamation was clearly a precursor to later recusancy statutes that provided a legal foundation for proceeding against those who harbored Jesuits and seminary priests.
10 Hughes & Larkin, vol. II, pp. 376–7.
11 (Louvain, 1572), *STC* 7601.
12 Hughes & Larkin, vol. II, p. 377.
13 Ibid., pp. 506–8.
14 John Leslie's *A treatise towching the right of the Most excellent Princesse Marie* (Rouen, 1584) and [*Leicester's Commonwealth*] *The copie of a leter, wryten by a master of arte of Cambrige to his friend in London* (Paris, 1584) (Hughes & Larkin, vol. I, pp. 506–8).
15 Hughes & Larkin, vol. III, pp. 13–17.
16 Ibid.

17 Southern, *Elizabethan Recusant Prose*, p. 36.
18 See chapter 8.
19 Hughes & Larkin, vol. III, p. 446.
20 *John Stubbs's "Gaping Gulf" with Letters and Other Relevant Documents*, ed. Lloyd E. Berry (Charlottesville, 1968), p. xxviii.
21 Hughes & Larkin, vol. II, pp. 375–6.
22 See Collinson, *Elizabethan Puritan Movement*, pp. 146–7.
23 Hughes & Larkin, vol. III, p. 376.
24 Collinson, *Elizabethan Puritan Movement*, p. 149.
25 Hughes & Larkin, vol. II, p. 474.
26 Ibid., p. 475.
27 The offending texts go unidentified; they are simply those "set forth by Robert Browne and Richard [Robert] Harrison fled out of the realm as seditious persons." Browne and Harrison opposed the episcopacy and royal ecclesiastical supremacy, but their most dangerous position was in privileging individual conscience over royal and parliamentary authority in religious matters (Hughes & Larkin, p. 501 n. 1).
28 Hughes & Larkin, vol. II, p. 502.
29 Ibid., vol. III, p. 34.
30 Ibid., vol. III, pp. 34–5.
31 Collinson, *Elizabethan Puritan Movement*, p. 397.
32 Hughes & Larkin, vol. III, pp. 34–5.
33 Collinson, *Elizabethan Puritan Movement*, p. 393.
34 In legal use as late as the eighteenth century, "mark" was used in stating the amount of a fine. Its value was fixed at 160d. or $\frac{2}{3}$ of the pound sterling.
35 William Henry Hart, *Index Expurgatorius Anglicanus* (1872–8), pp. 18–19.
36 James Larkin and Paul Hughes, *Stuart Royal Proclamation* (Oxford, 1973), vol. I, p. 243.

4 CATHOLIC PROPAGANDISTS: "CONCERNING THE QUEEN'S MAJESTY OR THE REALM WITHOUT LICENCE"

1 In 1581 the trial and execution for treason of two English priests, Edmund Campion and Alexander Briant, crystallized the irreconcilable positions of the Catholic propagandists and the English government. The Catholics maintained that the justice system was persecuting Catholics for their faith and their consciences; the government maintained that Jesuits and priests under the cover of religion were seeking to overthrow Elizabeth's rule and bring in a Catholic monarch. With regard to the press, Catholics maintained that the books they sought to distribute that the English government censored were books of prayers and spiritual exercises and meditations; the English authorities maintained that "*none have bene tormented for other matter then treason.*"
2 Rostenberg's *Minority Press and the English Crown*, p. 50 concentrates on

the Catholic press and efforts to suppress it. Haynes's *Invisible Power* considers the English secret service with a focus on its interest in Catholics.

3 Historical Manuscript Commission, *Calendar of the Manuscripts of the Marquis of Salisbury* (1883–1976), vol. x, p. 186. (Hereafter cited as HMC, *Salisbury*.)

4 HMC, *Salisbury*, vol. iv, p. 217.

5 Although Southwell was executed in February 1595 for treason under the laws exiling Jesuits, three volumes of his poetry were legitimately published with entrance in the Stationers' Registers. The first, *Mary Magdalen's Funeral Tears* (1591), was authorized by the Archbishop of Canterbury; the second, *St. Peters Complaint* (1595), received the imprimatur of Hartwell. *Mœniæ* (1595) was entered without notice of an authorizer.

6 See James E. Phillips, *Images of a Queen* (Berkeley and Los Angeles, 1964).

7 Ibid., p. 88.

8 Leslie, *A treatise concerning the defence of the honour of Marie of Scotland* ([Louvain], 1571) 5v; *Defence of the Honour* (London in Flete Ftrete [Rheims], 1569), 54v; *Treatise* (1584) D1r.

9 Leslie, *Defence of the Honour*, 51r; *Treatise* (1571), 2v; *Treatise* (1584) B6r.

10 Phillips suggests that the later versions increasingly oppose Elizabeth because they appeal to the Catholic princes of Europe: "in the hope that, moved by pity for the plight of a suffering coreligionist, they will come to the aid with either political or military pressures, or preferably both" (*Images of a Queen*, p. 104). He misreads Leslie's appeal to the Catholic princes, which actually asks that they come to Mary's aid "that she be not defeated of her right," and to this end publishes his defense of her rights that they might know the "full discourse of the whole cause" (*Treatise* [1584], A4r).

11 Phillips is, however, correct in distinguishing a difference between the 1569 *Defence of the Honour* and later versions in its treatment of Elizabeth. Although the later texts do not go so far as to repudiate her right to rule, they omit the complimentary address and references such as this:

our moste dreade Sovereigne Elizabeth dothe and hathe fitt in the royall seate with suche peace, quietnes, and tranquilitie amonge all her subjects hitherto, that we have greate cawse to render to God almighty our moste hartie thancks for the same: and to crave of him like continuance, wherof the singular fruite & benefitt, as longe as it shall please God to perserve her to us . . . (*Defence of the Honour*, 52v)

Even the statements of Mary's claim present in all the versions, originally carried the same kind of compliment:

We saye then and affirme that the right heire and Successor apparente unto the crowne of this realme of Englande next after our Sovereigne Ladie Quene Elizabethe and her issue, is suche a one as for the excellente giftes of God and nature in her most princlie appearinge . . . I meane the right excellente Ladie, Ladie Marie Quene of Scotlande . . . (*Defence of the Honour*, 54r–54v)

12 The 1569 editions of *Defence of the Honour* are a bibliographical muddle. *STC* lists the first edition, of which only one fragmentary copy is extant, and assigns it a Paris printing location, and the second edition, carrying a false London imprint, *STC* assigns to Rheims: previously these two editions were collapsed into one. In *A Bibliography of Books Relating to Mary, Queen of Scots* (Publications of the Edinburgh Bibliographical Society, II, 1896), John Scott identifies only one 1569 edition – with the false London imprint – and suggests it was probably printed in London since in a letter in the winter of 1569/70 Cecil wrote that he seized a book whose printing Alexander Hervey, a servant of the Bishop of Ross, had done secretly (ibid., p. 21). Scott fails to take into account Cecil's claim that they had intelligence of the printing before eight leaves could be printed, and seems to assume that the book seized was complete. Phillips gives a rather fanciful account of a single 1569 edition in *Images of a Queen*:

The 1569 edition of the *Defence* bears a London imprint, and a few of its pages may have been printed there. But the printing in London had no sooner begun than government agents raided the press and seized what had been started of the work. The book in its final form was probably produced on a Catholic press in Rheims and smuggled back into England. (p. 89)

It is highly unlikely that pages from the interrupted English printing would be carried to the Continent. Once the London printing was stayed, Hervey, may have managed to get a manuscript to the Continent. The second edition identified with Rheims was more likely printed entirely there, but when is not altogether clear. There is an alternative scenario. Leslie was detained at the Bishop of London's house between early February 1569/70 and May 1570 and Hervey was imprisioned for his role in procuring the London printing on 26 April 1570. In his examination by the authorities Hervey says he received the manuscript from Leslie around Easter 1569, and made the acquaintance of the printer during that summer (*Calendar of State Papers, Scotland 1547–1603*, 13 vols. [Edinburgh, 1898–1969], vol. III, p. 114. Hereafter cited as *Calendar of Scottish Papers*). When Leslie was questioned in May 1570, he clearly referred to it as already printed. Further, his examiners suggest that rumours existed on the contents. Although London printers generally used the new year from January onwards on their imprints, a London printing of the *Defence of the Honour* prior to 31 March might have used 1569, while a Continental printer would have more likely used 1570 – and this assumes that the printing was actually accomplished while Ross was detained. But this raises the possibility that a complete edition of the *Defence of the Honour* was printed in 1569, on the Continent, or possibly in London. Objections to it may not have arisen until after the scheme to marry Norfolk to Mary saw the Queen's full wrath in late Summer and early Fall 1569. Thus the stayed

London printing of Winter 1569/70 may have been a second edition, when Cecil was already fully aware of the potential danger of the contents. While any reordering of the 1569 editions is purely speculative, the fact remains that there were two editions dated 1569.

13 *Calendar of Scottish Papers*, vol. iv, p. 88. The smuggled books to which Phillips refers (see preceding note) were probably not the 1569 edition. His evidence is the copies in Bally's portmanteau, printed at "Lorayne." In 1571 another edition, *A Treatise concerning the defence*, has the imprint "Leodii, ap.G. Morberium, 1571," which the *STC* identifies as Louvain, printed by J. Fowler. The closeness of Cecil's "Lorayne" to Louvain suggests that Bally was bringing in this edition.

14 *Defence of the Honour*, 85v–86r.

15 Ibid., p. 87.

16 *Calendar of Scottish Papers*, vol. iii, pp. 134–5. In a 26 April 1570 letter to Cecil, the Bishop of Ross tells of sending "the principal copy" of his *Defence of the Honour*, "in which I am assured there is nothing to offend her majesty" to "the Queen's majesty to be 'considerit.'"

17 *Calendar of Scottish Papers*, vol. iii, p. 82.

18 Ibid., vol. iii, p. 158.

19 Ibid., p. 160.

20 Ibid., p. 181.

21 See the examination of Hervey, *Calendar of Scottish Papers*, vol. iii, pp. 114–15.

22 HMC, *Salisbury*, vol. iv, p. 498.

23 12 June 1595, Domestic State Papers, 12/253; London Public Record Office. This letter referring to Robert Parsons as the author identifies it as *Conference about the Next Succession*.

24 Domestic State Papers, 12/255, fo. 76. London Public Record Office.

25 See ibid., 12/253, fo. 28, London Public Record Office. Also, for means of excluding objectionable printed books see ibid., 12/261, fo. 94. I can find no corroboration in *Statutes of the Realm* or parliamentary journals, however, for the *DNB*'s claim in the article on Robert Parsons that "Parliament made it high treason for any one to have a copy in his house" (vol. xliii, p. 415). No treason statutes were passed after 1581, and Parliament did not meet between 1593 and 1597. It appears that the *DNB* misread M. A. Tierney's notes to *Dodd's Church History of England* (1839–43, vol. iii, p. xcv) that mention high treason in relation to *Conference about the Next Succession*. Actually, the book was at the center of the fierce division of English Catholics during the Appellant or Archpriest Controversy; one faction supported the Jesuits and their interest in securing a Spanish monarchy, and the other James's claim in exchange for religious toleration. Tierney's note makes it clear that the pro-James faction accused the Spanish faction of high treason in writing the *Conference*. See also T. G. Law, *Jesuits and Seculars in the Reign of Elizabeth* (1889).

26 Domestic State Papers, 12/271, fo. 29, London Public Record Office.
27 Ibid.
28 R. Doleman, *A conference about the next succession to the crowne of Ingland. Where unto is added a genealogie.* Published by R. Doleman [R. Parsons, R. Rowlands, and others]. Imprinted at N. [Antwerp, A Conincx], 1594 [1595], Part II, pp. 61–2. (Hereafter part and page numbers from this edition are cited in the text.)
29 While pretending to objectivity by tracing the York claim that Richard had an Act of Succession passed in Parliament in favor of Edmund Mortimer, heir to the Duke of Clarence through his daughter, Parsons dismisses the legitimacy of this claim of the nephew over the uncle by rehearsing the instances favoring the uncle.
30 *Elizabeth I and her Parliaments, 1584–1601*, p. 262.
31 Domestic State Papers, 12/255, fo. 76, London Public Record Office.
32 Elizabeth objected as well to Peter Wentworth's *A Pithie Exhortation to Her Majestie for Establishing her Successor* (published in 1598 in Scotland along with his *A Discourse of the True and Lawfull Successor*, written in response to Parsons's *Conference about the Next Succession*). Writing on the succession, even when Parliament was in session, got Wentworth a prison sentence. After his death, Waldegrave printed the book to vindicate his friend. On Elizabeth's behalf, Cecil sought to have Scottish authorities detain the printer, but their efforts were half-hearted and he fled. See *Calendar of Scottish Papers*, vol. II, p. 799. Wentworth's views apparently conformed to those of many English officials, including the Queen, but even so, writing on the succession was still illegal.
33 See Milward, *Religious Controversies of the Elizabethan Age*, p. 108. For a full (though biased) consideration of *Treatise of Treasons*, see Thomas H. Clancy's *Papist Pamphleteers* (Chicago, 1964), chapters 1 and 2. He subscribes to its condemnation of Burghley as the author of Elizabethan policy.
34 Hughes & Larkin, vol. II, pp. 377–8.
35 *A Treatise of Treasons*, 84v.
36 Apparently there were two 1572 editions, one printed in Paris and the other in Lyon, both without place of imprint.
37 Lansdowne MS 28, fo. 81, British Library. This is printed in Arber, vol. II, pp. 749–50. (My transcription differs from Arber's in punctuation, and where I read "furnishe," he reads "signifye.") This incident is rather telling about the mechanisms of censorship. Carter was apparently brought before the High Commission, but since he refused to take the oath, they could not proceed against him. Aylmer referred the matter to Burghley, who together with other Privy Councillors could take action in the Star Chamber to enforce the 1572 proclamation against Carter, which had only ordered destroying objectionable books.

38 Aylmer further tells Burghley: "I will send to you the wardens, which will enforme you further of an other Booke, which is abrode wherein her maiestie is touched" (see preceding note). Both Greg and Arber assume that the other book is Gregory Martin's *Treatise of Schism* (see pp. 33, 93–4). They infer that the Wardens' information derived from the same search of Carter's house. Had the *Treatise of Schism* been discovered in the same search, it is unlikely that he would have been treated so leniently – unless, of course, its objectionable passages were not objectionable in 1579 (Greg, *Companion to Arber*, p. 20).

39 Hughes & Larkin, vol. II, pp. 506–7. The letter (dated 20 or 26? June 1585) is published in D. C. Peck's edition of *Leicester's Commonwealth* (Athens, OH and London, 1985), pp. 282–4. (Hereafter page numbers from this edition are cited in the text.)

40 Ibid., p. 31.On the question of authorship, see ibid., pp. 25–32. Peck ascribes the principal authorship to Charles Arundell, but in his forthcoming book on the Earl of Oxford, Alan H. Nelson finds the style uncharacteristic of Arundell, and settles for a corporate authorship by the Paris circle.

41 Letter from Walsingham to Leicester, 29 September 1584, *Leicester's Common wealth*, ed. Peck, p. 285.

42 Milward, *Religious Controversies of the Elizabethan Age*, pp. 50–1.

43 [William Allen], *A True, Sincere and Modest Defence, of English Catholiques that suffer for their faith* ([Rouen, Fr. Parsons' Press, 1584]), A5v.

44 Gregory Martin, *A Treatise of Schism* (Duaci, ap.J. Foulerum [London, W. Carter,], 1578), D2r.

45 Ibid., D2v.

46 Southern, *Elizabethan Recusant Prose*, p. 353.

47 *DNB*, vol. LVI, p. 328. See also Wallace MacCaffrey, *Elizabeth I*, (1993), pp. 341–2.

48 The handwritten title-page inscription of the copy in the Bridgewater Library collection acquired by Henry Huntington from the Egerton family in 1917. The Bridgewater Library, containing books and manuscripts belonging to the Egerton family, was begun by Thomas Egerton, who served as solicitor general (1581–92), attorney general (1592–4), Master of the Rolls (1594–1603), Lord Keeper (1596–1603), and Lord Chancellor (1603–17). Among other important books and documents are the Ellesmere papers, official and semi-official papers relating to government offices held by members of the Egerton family, particularly Lord Chancellor Egerton. Though no records exist of the collection's early years, I suspect that this copy of Allen's book may have been part of Thomas Egerton's library. See also p. 97.

49 MacCaffrey, *Elizabeth I*, p. 330. For a more thorough consideration of Campion and the charges against him, see chapter 7.

50 The title was entered in the Stationers' Register on 2 January 1584.

51 [William Cecil, Baron Burghley] *The execution of justice in England* (1584), A3r.
52 Ibid., A3v, A4r–A4v, B3r–B3v.
53 Allen, *A True, Sincere, and Modest Defence*, *3v.
54 Milward, *Religious Controversies of the Elizabethan Age*, p. 69.
55 MacCaffrey, *Elizabeth I*, p. 332.
56 Most marginalia include the *nota bene* hand found in medieval manuscripts with the finger pointing to the relevant passage.
57 Allen, *A True, Sincere and Modest Defence*, pp. 191–2 (M7v–M7r).
58 It is not difficult to envision how a legal officer might make use of a text marked in such a fashion – as a touchstone for measuring the political views of seminary priests and recusants. If they subscribed to Allen's views then they committed if not treason, at least sedition.
59 String 1 at page 87 (F4) is torn out; the marginal annotation reads "[n.b.] ye Latern Counsel."
60 St. 2, p. 93 (F7) [n.b. toward p. 94].
61 St. 3, p. 103 (G4) [n.b. pointing to next page, appears to be indicating "continue"]. The bracketed words were added to transform the meaning of the words printed in the margin.
62 Allen, *A True, Sincere and Modest Defence*, p. 104.
63 Ibid.
64 St. 4, p. 107 (G6r).
65 St. 5, pp. 111–12 (G8).
66 Allen, *A True, Sincere and Modest Defence*, pp. 111–12.
67 St. 6, p. 114 (H1v).
68 Allen, *A True, Sincere and Modest Defence*, p. 115 (H2r).
69 The last string marks passages that reflect further on the nature of the argument and on Allen. Opposite string 7 (p. 191, M7v) the annotator comments, "th^{is} trato^r hathe a vile cõceit" regarding statements on Elizabeth's virginity: ". . . the Q. Maiesty her self, telleth us she is A MAYDEN QUEENE; seing that with the Protestants it is no great merite nor praise to be a virgin . . . And would God in stead of her Maiesties virginities (so that it had stood with Gods wil & hers) we might rather have had for the Realmes safety, issue of her bodie in honorable wedlocke" (p. 190). Still marked by the same string but at p. 191 (M8r), referring to Allen's opinion of the Stuart succession ("being now offred by God and nature in the sweetest and (doubtles) both indifferent sort that can be: and in two persons, Mother and Sonne"), the annotator comments, "here hee fishethe for a Cardenalls hatt." Further on the same page, "here hee woorkethe for hys pencyo^n" comments on Allen's description of Mary and James:
the one for approved prudence, vertue, patience, constancie, courage in adversitie, and equal love of both the Countries: the other for the rarest towardlines in al Princelie partes, of anie of his age in al Christendome: both of our flesh and blood, and the neerest of al the beloved race of *Herie* the 7.

70 Allen, *Admonition to the Nobility and People of England and Ireland*, (Hv).
71 Ibid., D5v.
72 The *Declaration* is reprinted in *Dodd's Church History of England*, ed. Tierny, vol. III, pp. xliv–xlviii.
73 *Calendar of State Papers, Domestic*, 1581–90, p. 466. The document is Domestic State Papers 12/211, fo. 15, London Public Record Office.
74 Ibid., vol. II, p. 211.
75 Domestic State Papers 12/211, fo. 67, London Public Record Office.
76 See p. 70.
77 Allen, *Admonition to the Nobility*, A3r.
78 Ibid., A4r.
79 Rostenberg, *Minority Press and the English Crown*, p. 50.
80 Ibid.
81 Ibid.

5 GEORGE GASCOIGNE AND THE RHETORIC OF CENSORHIP: *A HUNDRETH SUNDRIE FLOWRES* (1573) AND *THE POSIES* (1575)

1 George Gascoigne, *The Posies* (1575), ¶Hr. (Hereafter cited in the text.)
2 C. T. Prouty, *George Gascoigne, Elizabethan Courtier, Soldier, and Poet* (New York, 1942) p. 79. Among those who concur is Richard McCoy ("Gascoigne's 'Poëmata castrata': The Wages of Courtly Success," *Criticism*, 27 [1985], 29–55), who concludes,
Although the scanty records of the court of High Commission offer no evidence of a case against Gascoigne, Prouty suspects that "the Reverend Divines" were members of that ecclesiastical court which had the power of censorship. Whatever their source, the attacks on *A Hundreth Sundrie Flowres* must have been harsh and damaging as Gascoigne's defensive tone indicates . . . (p.43)
3 See Adrian Weiss, "Shared Printing, Printers Copy and the Text(s) of Gascoigne's *A Hundreth Sundrie Flowres*," *Studies in Bibliography*, 45 (1992), 71–104.
4 The word used so often by Gascoigne in the *Flowres* to designate a literary composition.
5 *Records of the Court*, ed. Greg and Boswell, p. 187.
6 George Gascoigne, *A Hundreth sundrie Flowres bound vp in one small Posie* (1573), A3r, p. 205; A2v, p. 204. (Hereafter cited in the text, with both gatherings and page numbers given, as the gatherings are repeated.) This letter, though signed A1, appears at p. 201.

Throughout this chapter I use the 1573 and 1575 editions, since modern editors have made decisions that significantly alter the text. The best modern edition of *Flowres* is B. M. Ward and C. T. Prouty's 1970 facsimile of the 1573 edition. See also C. T. Prouty's *George Gascoigne's "A Hundreth Sundrie Flowres"* (Columbia, MO, 1942). John W. Cunliffe's *Complete Works of George Gascoigne*, 2 vols. (Cambridge, 1907–10), is the only complete edition, and it favors *The Posies* as the revised text.

7 "The Printer to the Reader" appears after the title page entirely apart from Aı.

8 William C. Hazlitt, *The Complete Poems of George Gascoigne* (1869), vol. ı, p. ix.

9 *DNB*, vol. xxı, p. 37.

10 Ibid., p. 96. According to Weiss,
The fact that the manuscript junctions, as indicated by the bibliographical evidence, correspond exactly to textual divisions cannot be attributed to mere coincidence. When placed in the context of the long delays between sections and the minimum production time of eight months, the segmentation of printer's copy clearly indicates that the composition of the editorial frame and the "F. J." narrative, and the organization of previously written materials into the editorial frame, occurred during the January–August period after Smith undertook the publication of the project. ("Shared Printing," p. 97)

11 Prouty contends that Gascoigne returned to England in Fall 1572 and remained until 19 March 1573, and *Flowres* was printed rapidly in March 1573 (*Gascoigne's "Flowres,"* pp. 15–16). Of this view, Weiss remarks:
Prouty's conjecture that Gascoigne returned to England during the fall of 1572 seems certain, but that he remained until 19 March 1572/73 is contradicted by the printing and textual evidence. This date is clearly false in that context. Beyond that, the specificity of the date is quite extraordinary in a poem, and even more so because of Gascoigne's emphatic avowal "that cannot I forget." If he indeed was under threat of an investigation by the Privy Council (see Prouty, p. 16) and fled, it would have been of legal importance to publish the claim that he did not sail for Holland until 19 March . . . Flight to avoid investigation and possible prosecution is a prima facie admission of guilt. He had been jailed before for debt (see Prouty, p. 17) and could probably have expected to be again. The published date would serve as testimony that he had been in England all the while even though the Privy Council's agents could not find him. ("Shared Printing," p. 97n.)

12 Weiss, "Shared Printing," p. 99.

13 Ibid., p. 92. Weiss further speculates that,
"Dan Bartholmew" had originally been intended to stand alone, but appeared as the fourth part of the "Flowres" because when Gascoigne abandoned the composition of "Dan," it could no longer stand alone as an independent text. So he attached it to "F. J.," "The devises," and "devises of Master Gascoigne" through the simple expedient of G.T.'s quite short transitional editorial link (2E2v: 8–12). As delivered to Smith, "Dan Bartholmew" is a sub-text with its title embedded in G.T.'s editorial frame. (ibid., p. 101)

14 Ibid., p. 104.

15 Prouty, *Gascoigne's "Flowres,"* p. 19.

16 McCoy, "Wages of Courtly Success," p. 40. According to McCoy,
Gascoigne's text was one of the first published works to realize the rich literary potential of the codes of courtly discourse . . . By publishing *A Hundreth Sundrie Flowres*, Gascoigne sought to advertise his own considerable skills in these areas to a larger audience. Its "divers discourses & verses" show that he can write on any subject, and either woo or moralize on demand . . . Yet even as he presents

his wit for hire to such patrons as Lord Grey, he still retains what Jane Hedly calls the "poet's prerogative," for his work eludes the constraints of simple orthodoxy and plain truisms even as it incorporates and exploits them. He achieves a level of poetic freedom and sophistication impossible in more conventional literature. (ibid., pp. 41–2)

17 Ibid., p. 42.
18 Prouty, *Gascoigne, Courtier*, p. 80.
19 McCoy, "Wages of Courtly Success," pp. 43–4.
20 Prouty, *Gascoigne, Courtier*, p. 93.
21 *Records of the Court*, ed. Greg & Boswell, pp. 86–7.
22 These objections, McCoy says, "Gascoigne dismisses" by pointing out the contradictory nature of the conjectures, "hoping thereby to damp down the speculation he had once deliberately stirred up" ("Wages of Courtly Success," p. 42). McCoy accepts the dismissal and takes far more seriously (as Gascoigne undoubtedly intended his readers should) the charges of "wanton . . . and lascivious" (ibid.).
23 Lorna Hutson, "Sex and Credit in Shakespeare," a paper read at the Huntington Library, 28 February 1995.
24 She tells,
I dreamt this night that I was in a pleasaunt meadow alone, where I met with a tall Gentleman, apparelled in a night gowne of silke all embroadered about with a gard of naked swords, and when he came towardes me I seemed to be afraide of him, but he recomforted me saying, be not afrayd fayre Lady, for I use this garment onely for myne own defence . . . (E4v, p. 240)
25 Shrewsbury Papers, 24, printed in Edmund Lodge, *Illustrations of British History*, 3 vols. (1791), vol. ii, pp. 17–18.
26 Eric St. John Brooks, *Sir Christopher Hatton* (1946), p. 83.
27 *DNB*, vol. xxv, pp. 149–60.
28 Brooks, *Sir Christopher Hatton*, p. 107.
29 Ibid., p. 109.
30 *Leicester's Commonwealth*, ed. Peck, pp. 49–50.
31 *Calendar of State Papers Spanish, 1558–1603*. 3 vols. (London, 1894), vol. i, p. 491. (Hereafter *CSP, Spanish*.)
32 Prouty, *Gascoigne, Courtier*, p. 193.
33 Arthur Collins, *Historical Collections of the Noble Families of Cavendish, Holles, Vere, Harley and Ogle* (1752), pp. 77–8. In Holles's version of the events at Belvoir Castle, the beautiful Douglas Sheffield (who is a woman) is seduced by Leicester, who writes in a letter his plans for them to be together. The letter is revealed to Lord Sheffield, by the sister, Holles, and the husband vows revenge. From here on the stories differ since, according to Holles, Leicester poisoned Lord Sheffield. The sister Holles was the narrator Holles's aunt.
34 Although Holles used *Leicester's Commonwealth* as part of his source (for the incident itself), the details of the seduction and discovery derive from pure gossip:
I have been the longer and more punctual in this Relation, because it is known

to few, yet a certain truth . . . Mr. *Holles* says, he received the before mentioned Relation from a person of credit then living in the family, who gave him an Account of the Share his Aunt Holles had in it. (Collins, *Historical Collections*, pp. 77–8)

35 *Records of the Court*, ed. Greg and Boswell, p. 87. At 528 pages, *The Posies* would have required considerable time for typesetting and printing. The project would not have been economically feasible for Smith and Bynneman had they not produced a fairly large run, probably 1,000.

36 *CSP, Spanish*, vol. II, p. 511. The Countess of Essex, Lettice Knollys, who had been present at the Kenilworth festivities without her husband, married Leicester in 1578 after he died.

37 Hughes & Larkin, vol. II, p. 400.

38 *STC*, vol. I, p. 515.

39 *CPR, Eliz.*, vol. VI, 3238.

40 Blayney, *Bookshops in Paul's Cross Churchyard*, map.

41 Patterson, *Censorship and Interpretation*, p. 18.

42 Ibid., p. 17.

43 Ibid., p. 45.

44 Ibid., p. 57.

6 JOHN STUBBS'S *THE DISCOVERY OF A GAPING GULF* AND REALPOLITIK: "THE KINGS SIN STRIKETH THE LAND" BUT "GOD SAVE THE QUEEN"

1 Hughes & Larkin, vol. II, p. 446.

2 Page is usually regarded as its publisher, but this is an error. See p. 259.

3 See pp. 121–2.

4 Siebert, *Freedom of the Press*, p. 91.

5 J. A. Froude, *History of England from the Fall of Wolsey to the Defeat of the Spanish Armada*, 12 vols. (1862–70), vol. X, pp. 501–2.

6 William Camden, *Annales* (1625), book III, pp. 14–15. Book 3 begins with the year 1581, so Camden's report in misplaced.

7 Ibid., p. 16.

8 Despite Camden's association of Stubbs with the puritans, opposition to the French marriage was broad based, driven by antipapal and anti-French sentiment.

9 *John Stubbs's "Gaping Gulf,"* ed. Berry, p. 77. (Hereafter cited in the text by page numbers.)

10 Guy, *Tudor England*, pp. 282–3. See also MacCaffrey, *Elizabeth I*, chapter 16.

11 Camden, *Annales*, Book II, p. 391, Book III, p. 14.

12 One must recognize that the Spanish Ambassador's access to information was both through his own spies and through diplomatic sources – both undoubtedly often planned misinformation. While this may mar the quality of evidence, such gossip records fairly accurately sentiments

and responses. All citations of Bernardo de Mendoza's letters are from the *Calendar of Letters and State Papers, Spanish,* vol. II (1568–79) and vol. III (1580–6). (Hereafter cited as *CSP, Spanish* in the notes, and by volume and document number in the text.)

13 Ordered by the Queen-mother Catherine de Medici, the general massacre of the Huguenots began in Paris on 24 August, on the occasion of the wedding of Margaret of Valois to Henry of Navarre, attended by the Huguenot nobility. An estimated 3,000 people were killed in Paris and 70,000 in all France.

14 Camden, however, may have misread some of the circumstances of production since he places all of the events surrounding *A Gaping Gulf* in 1581, the time of the second Alençon visit (*Annales*, Book III, p. 14).

15 Rather then "publishing" *A Gaping Gulf* (as some have asserted), Page sent to Sir Richard Grenville, probably with Bedford's knowledge, fifty copies for circulation. See Kenneth Barnes, "John Stubbe, 1579, the French Ambassador's Account," *Historical Research* 64 (1991), 421–6.

16 Barnes, "John Stubbe," p. 423.

17 *John Stubbs's "Gaping Gulf,"* ed. Berry, p. xli. I am indebted to Blair Worden for the evidence from Adams's doctoral thesis about Leicester (p.30), as well as for directing me to Barnes's essay in *Historical Research.*

18 *John Stubbs's "Gaping Gulf,"* ed. Berry, pp. xliii–xliv. Berry concludes that though Stubbs's response was written and approved by Dr. Thomas Byng, Regius Professor of Civil Law and Master of Clare College, Cambridge, and Dr. John Hammond, the work apparently was not printed.

19 *John Stubbs's "Gaping Gulf,"* ed. Berry, p. xxxix, from Strype's *The Life and Acts of Matthew Parker* (Oxford, 1821), vol. II, p. 418.

20 Its recognition of arguments favoring the marriage as well as those opposing coincide with a memorandum in Burghley's hand in the state papers, dated 29 March 1579 (*Calendar of State Papers, Foreign, 1578–79,* [1903], 635). (Hereafter *CSP, Foreign.*)

21 Neither book was available in print in England until 1584 when John Wolfe printed Italian texts. Printed editions from the Continent were likewise unavailable, since they were on the Catholic Church's list of forbidden books.

22 Fitzmaurice, with French support, invaded Ireland at the end of June 1579. By 15 August the Irish Earl of Desmond rebelled and joined his forces. Elizabeth received report of Fitzmaurice's death on 5 September. This lends further support for *A Gaping Gulf* being written sometime during July and August.

23 *CSP, Spanish,* vol. II, 565:
   Lord Burleigh is not so much opposed to it as formerly, but I cannot discover whether Sussex and Burleigh have changed their minds, because they think that they may thus bring about the fall of Leicester, and avenge themselves upon him for old grievances, and for having advanced to the Office of

Chancellor, which Sussex wants, an enemy of Sussex and Burleigh. Their reason may, however, be perhaps the hope that if Frenchmen should come hither the country may rise, in which case, it is believed, Sussex would take a great position.

24 The letter cited in full in Barnes's essay says:
le dicte royne a faict tout ce quelle a peu pour les faire mourir par la loy et par la justice qui ne les ont condamnez qu'à cela encores quilz ayent cherchez tous les moyens de les apsouldre alleguant que s'etoit les affections et le coeur quilz avoyent à leur patrie qui les avoyent meu à faire le livre ("John Stubbs," p. 425)

25 "Lors quilz fuerent mis prisonniers ils ont este / conseillez par des premiers du royaume et de plusiers entroicts, les asseurant quilz n'auroyent poinct de mal, mais au contraire seroyent deliverez avec honneur" (Barnes, "John Stubbs," p. 425).

26 "Ilz ont estez condennez par ung jugement fort solennel" (ibid.). Cotgrave's *A Dictionarie of the French and English Tongues* (1611) explains my translation of "Solennel" as "open court." "Solennel: Solemne (not altogether as we doe commonly understand it, but) annuall, yearelie, or ordinarie, woont, used, accustomed, done publickly, and at a certaine time." The point, then, is that the legal procedure was very regular rather than that the judgment was harsh.

27 Harington, *Nugae Antiquae*, vol. III, p. 279.

28 *CSP, Foreign*, 1579–80, 73, letter from Poulet to Walsingham, dated 26 October 1579.

29 Hughes & Larkin, vol. II, p. 448.

30 Ibid., p. 446.

31 The French Ambassador reported that he and Simier had received letters requesting that they lobby for pardon for the libelers. One had promised a reward; another that by doing so they would gain the hearts of Englishmen, otherwise there was danger of popular rebellion. See (Barnes, "John Stubbs," p. 425)

32 The French Ambassador's letter about the incident curiously reports that when Elizabeth's pardon was sought for the libelers (principally by those that favored the marriage), she became obdurate and responded that she would rather lose her own hands, and further that they were only secretaries to others more base than they. See Barnes, "John Stubbs," p. 425. Their fault and punishment is here linked to the conduct of those more base.

33 Hughes & Larkin, vol. II, p. 449.

7 THE REVIEW AND REFORM OF HOLINSHED'S *CHRONICLES*: "REPORTE OF MATTERS OF LATER YEERS THAT CONCERN THE STATE"

1 *APC*, vol. XIV, pp 311–12. The Privy Council used the now obsolete sense of reform: "to correct, emend (a book, writing, chart, etc.), to recast, improve by revision and alteration" (*Oxford English Dictionary*

[2nd edn., 1989], vol. XIII, p. 480). While bibliographical usage may refer to alteration through censorship as "castration," the obsolete sense of "reform" employed by the Privy Council, together with "review," describes more precisely the process that Holinshed's *Chronicles* underwent. I adopt the Council's linguistic precision here.

2 Richard Helgerson, *Forms of Nationhood* (Chicago and London, 1992).

3 Raphael Holinshed, *The Chronicles of England, Scotland and Ireland* (1587), vol. III, A2r. He dedicated the *Chronicles* to Lord Burghley, with the personal acknowledgment that he was "ever so especiall good Lord to Maister Wolfe," and with an apology for the book's limitations not in relation to the patron's knowledge and capabilities (a conventional approach) but to his expectations based on his understanding of Wolfe's original conception. Annabel Patterson reads Holinshed's explanation in his dedication to Burghley of his own employment in the project, "although the cause that moved me thereto hath (in part) yer this beene signified unto your good Lordship," as evidence that Burghley had not commissioned the project (*Reading Holinshed's "Chronicles"* [Chicago, 1994], p. 280 n. 20). While this may indicate that Burghley was not paying all of the current (expensive) publication's costs, it has no bearing on whether or not he was interested in the project – indeed whether or not he commissioned it or offered financial assistance to Wolfe. Wolfe did, after all, hold the office of Queen's printer which granted him a 26s. 8d. yearly wage and protection for all Latin, Greek, and Hebrew texts, "also charts and maps useful to the king and his countries" with the proviso that the printer should print such works upon the monarch's request. (See *CPR, Edward VI*, vol. I, p. 187 and *CPR, Eliz.*, vol. VI, 1556.)

4 Henry Robert Plomer, *Abstracts from the Wills of English Printers* (1903), p. 22. When Wolfe died in 1573 he willed his entire establishment to his wife Jone, who died a year later. Her will provided for the *Chronicles'* publication; its compiler, publishers, and printer were either beneficiaries under her will or were related in some other way to the family business.

5 Holinshed, in a gesture of nationalistic *esprit de corps*, reconciled himself to omitting the maps Burghley expected since Thomas Seckford would see the mapping of England completed:

> . . . understanding of the great charges and notable enterprice of that worthie Gentleman maister Thomas Sackforde in procuring the Chartes of the severall provinces of this Realme to be sett forth, wee are in hope that in time he will delineate this whole land so perfectly, as shal be comparable or beyonde anie deliniation heretofore made of any other region, and therfore leave that to his well deserved prayse. If any well willer will imitate him in so worthie a work for the two other regions, we will be gladde to further his endevour with all the helpes we may. (¶2r)

Master of Requests Seckford paid Saxton for his atlas of England, and Burghley received a proof copy of it. Burghley (or Seckford) probably provided maps from the uncompleted atlas to William Harrison, the author of the *Chronicles*' "Description of England."

6 Helgerson, *Forms of Nationhood*, p. 109. See Ifor M. Evans and Heather Lawrence, *Christopher Saxton Elizabethan Map Maker* (1979), pp. 66–8. Helgerson sees the Saxton maps as "a project conceived, financed, and all but executed at court, a project that could fairly be said to have been authored by the queen and her government" (*Forms of Nationhood*, p. 131).

7 In 1580 the Queen extended a patent for all dictionaries and histories to Bynneman, the printer of the 1577 *Chronicles* (*CPR, Elizabeth*, vol. VIII, 1594). In their position as Bynneman's assignees, Denham and Newbery, 1584 "by ye queenes majesties graunte," paid sixpence each for the license to print "*Imprimis* Holingsheddes Chronicle in folio and all other Chronicles in ye said volume of folio," all Stow's *Chronicles* in quarto, octavo, and decimo-sexto, as well as all other chronicles in these formats, all dictionaries in Latin and Greek, all quarto dictionaries, all French–English quarto dictionaries and all Italian–English quarto dictionaries (Arber, vol. II, p. 438). This superseded an earlier entry (6 October 1584) by Company Warden George Bishop and Newbery, together with Denham and Thomas Woodcock, for a license to print only Holinshed's *Chronicles*; this is not a double entry, but rather notice of change enabled by Denham and Newbery acquiring Bynneman's patent.

8 Elizabeth Story Donno correctly observes that the title page of the censored 1587 edition carried the motto "*Historiae placeant nostrates ac pergrinae*" in place of the original issue's "*cum privilegio regiae majestatis*" ("Some Aspects of Shakespeare's Holinshed," *Huntington Library Quarterly*, 50 [1987], 238). This change suggests that the book's privilege was somehow withdrawn, but this is not the case: the notice of privilege could appear on the colophon or the title page. That the *Chronicles* were printed with privilege counters Patterson's notion that its publication suggested "if not scofflawry, at least a degree of circumvention of the regulations" (*Reading Holinshed*, p.11). Patterson believed that by entering the *Chronicles* in the Stationers' Register in 1584 when the publishers planned the edition, rather than in 1587, upon completion, they avoided review of those revisions made between 1584 and 1587 "and it was precisely the most recent materials that should have been reviewed before a license was granted" (ibid., p. 12). Printed as it was under a royal privilege that did not require either ecclesiastical or government review, it is unlikely that *any part* of the 1587 edition received pre-print scrutiny prior to the 1 February 1587 Privy Council Order. Indeed, given the way the review and reform proceeded, the entire book appears to have been completed and on sale when the Order was issued. Furthermore, the October 1584 entry was made by the Company Wardens (both of whom were among the publishers) without any notice of official authorization.

9 Patterson, *Reading Holinshed*, p. 23. This is the central argument of her book, and though I agree with her that the *Chronicles* represent the printers' interests in constructing a particular vision of national govern-ment – good monarchs responsible to good laws – and of the people's obligation to know about and understand that government's history, I do not agree that the *Chronicles* were intended by their authors as opposition, nor that they were censored by a government that feared this opposition.

10 *APC*, vol. x, pp. 114–15, 142.

11 Cardinal Wolsey appointed Alen as vice-legate for Ireland 1 June 1529. Alen was later fined for offenses in exercising this legatine authority (Steven G. Ellis, *Tudor Ireland* [1985], p. 120).

12 *APC*, vol. xiv, pp. 311–12.

13 The earliest state of the text is represented in the Book Club of California fragment, which contains original leaves not present in the Igoe copy (see below n. 63), and both of them contain leaves not present in most copies of the censored text noticed in the *STC*, which suggests this order for the appearance of the states: (1) Book Club of California fragment, (2) Igoe copy, and (3) the censored text with cancels noted in *STC*. I will refer to these as Book Club, Igoe, and *STC* texts. This order is supported by the cancels that both retain and reform further the text of the prior cancels. For further bibliographical argument see my *The peaceable and prosperous regiment of blessed Queene Elisabeth: A Facsimile from Holinshed's "Chronicles" (1587)* (San Marino, CA, 1997).

14 Stephen Booth discovered these leaves in a broken copy the Book Club of California was dismantling so that it could put authentic 1587 leaves in special copies of Booth's own *A Book Called Holinshed's Chronicles* (San Francisco, 1968). This state of the text goes unnoticed in *STC*, and Booth recognized its unique quality, and had the fragment placed in the Huntington Library. Without a census of the 1587 edition, it is impossible to suggest how prevalent such copies are. I know of two copies, at Yale University's Beinecke Library and in a private collec-tion, that contain the Book Club fragment's unique cancels in the 7L gathering and their associated original leaves.

15 Booth believes that pages 1561–74 "did not survive accidentally but as the purposed result of a special job of printing" subsequent to the other cancels. According to him, "We must assume, therefore, that at the time the three unique replacement pages in the Book Club copy were printed their substance was no longer forbidden; Denham and his partners would not otherwise have taken the risk" (*A Book Called Holinshed's Chronicles*, p. 59). But these leaves were not the product of a special later printing, as they match in setting and watermarks the British Library copy (674.l.5–8), as do p. 1419–90.

16 Since the Scottish history invariably appears in a volume separate from the English history, it is not possible to establish that the Scottish

history leaves in the Book Club fragment, identical as they are to other censored copies, belong to a different censorship/printing stage, particularly since only four of the twelve censored pages appear in the Book Club fragment. The 1587 *Chronicles* were printed in three volumes, each paginated separately, but often bound into two books, with volumes I and II – (the description of England and English history up to the Conquest, the description and history of Ireland, and the description and history of Scotland) together, and volume III (the history of England from 1066) as the second. Since volumes were not necessarily sold together in the sixteenth century, any extant copy may contain volumes which were originally sold at different stages of the censorship and reformation process. It is thus possible that an extant copy may contain a pre-censorship Scottish history, and a post-censorship English history, or vice versa. To further complicate the matter, either volume might contain original leaves overlooked by the censors together with variant cancels. For books in post-eighteenth-century bindings, eighteenth-century reprints of cancelled pages (very good print facsimiles that may go unrecognized by the untrained eye) may be sophisticated in.

17 This cancel is retained in later states of the text without further changes.

18 *STC* (vol. II, p. 591) indicates that this expurgation may actually belong to a later censorship order (see pp. 165–6). Given the method of censorship – that only unsold copies were called in – it seems unlikely that it could belong to the 1591 order and also appear in the earliest state of the text represented by the Book Club fragment.

19 Allen's *A Briefe Historie* incorporated the priest Thomas Alfield's original account of Campion's trial and execution, *A true report of the death and martyrdome of M. Campion Iesuite and preiste* (1582). Alfield was tried and convicted of treason in 1585 for disseminating Allen's *True, Sincere and Modest Defence*. For more on the competing publications, see Southern, *Elizabethan Recusant Prose*, pp. 279–83, 376–87.

20 MacCaffrey, *Elizabeth I*, p. 209.

21 A letter to Walsingham, dated 13/23 January 1583, reported that the "common people" hated Alençon and that his attempt on Antwerp was widely regarded as a French/Spanish plot to overthrow the religion (*CSP, Foreign*, January–June 1583[1913], 31). Another of 4 February 1583 from the Prince of Orange to Elizabeth indicates how betrayed the Dutch Felt:

But after Brabant, Flanders, and all the provinces in general had received the Prince [Alençon] with joy, and promised themselves that by God's grace they were now about to be victorious over the Spanish, and to enjoy tranquility . . . which led them to look for that kindly treatment to be expected from a father, defender, and saviour of the country. In spite of this Monsieur summoned from France a very large detachment of cavalry and infantry, and a regiment of about four thousand Swiss, which he massed in the suburbs of Antwerp, and on the 17th of January, about one o'clock in the afternoon, he seized the Kipdorp gate . . . The gate was seized, its guards cut to pieces, the flanking walls occupied, and the main streets, almost as far as the market place, to the cry of "Long live the mass; slay, slay, slay; city taken, city taken." (*CSP, Venetian*, 38 vols. [1864–1940], vol. VIII, 124)

22 MacCaffrey, *Elizabeth I*, p. 222.

23 For a detailed account of these events, MacCaffrey, *Elizabeth I*, chapter 17, and F. G. Oosterhoff, *Leicester and the Netherlands 1586–1587* (Utrecht, 1988).

24 *HMC, Salisbury*, vol. III, p. 206.

25 Patterson, *Reading Holinshed*, p. 130.

26 See chapter 4.

27 Hollinshed's *Chronicles*, vol. III, p. 1326, B53–9. Hereafter page, column (A or B), and line numbers from this edition are cited in the text. When citation is taken from a variant state, the copy designation will follow (Book Club, Igoe, or *STC*, with *STC* referring to cancels identified in *STC* (2nd edn., vol. I, p. 591). When cancels exist and I cite the uncancelled state, the citation will designate it as "uncensored."

28 Patterson, *Reading Holinshed*, pp. 37–40, 130.

29 Translated from Gregory Nazian Zene by Allen as "not for their faithe, but as malefactors" (*A True, Sincere and Modest Defence*, p. 73). The *Chronicles'* use of the exact Latin quotation reflects the writer's familiarity with Allen's text. My uncensored Holinshed citation is from one of the three eighteenth-century reproductions of the censored leaves. These reproductions are often sophisticated into copies of the 1587 *Chronicles*, though the Huntington Library has a bound 1587 edition without title page (originally part of the Bridgewater library), which contains a set of leaves identifiable by their "S" watermark as printed by Bateman and Cowse (Keith I. Maslen, "Three Eighteenth-Century Reprints," *Library*, 5th ser., 13 [1958], 122). All three sets of these leaves are print facsimiles of the original, hence my citations that indicate "uncensored" apply equally to any of these or to copies with original pages (one in the British Library and one in the University Library, Cambridge).

30 The words "the administration of justice" invoke Burghley's, *The Execution of Justice*, which incidentally carries, as its running head "Execution for Treason, and not for Religion" and prints the papal "Facultates" found in Campion's possession (C1r).The reference here is clearly to Allen's *True, Sincere and Modest Defence*.

31 The proclamation, dated 2 December, was published 4 December 1586.

32 That the *Chronicles'* censorship is somehow related to the trial and execution of Mary, Queen of Scots was suggested by Francis Peck, who in 1722 had access to the papers on the censorship of Abraham Fleming, the *Chronicles'* learned corrector. At the end of vol. I of his *Desiderata Curiosa*, (1722), Peck published a prospectus for vol. II that was

to include Fleming's papers and other papers on matters of importance during the reign of Elizabeth. (Vol. I contained material related to Lord Burghley.) Vol. II's projected Book IV (Liber IV) listed twenty items curiously configured: seven related to the censorship of Holinshed's 1587 *Chronicles* and thirteen to the death of Mary, Queen of Scots. Unfortunately it was never printed, and the manuscripts about the censorship have disappeared. Judging from the way Peck organized the other books – the contents of each on a related topic – the lost materials must have indicated a relationship between Mary's death and the *Chronicles'* censorship. Though cryptic, the table of contents offers some clues about the censorship. Of particular interest are four items: Item II is a Fleming manuscript about the castrations ("De castratione quae Raphaelis Holinshedi nuncapantur")and the subtitle indicates that it was particularly concerned with the censorship by Leicester, Chancellor Bromley, and Burghley: "Et imprimis de eorunden Censuris quando Comit. Leicestriae D. Thomae Bromley Cancellario & D. Guil Cecil Thesaurio ablutai." Item III is another Fleming manuscript on other censorings in the *Chronicles* by various men whose malevolence is exceeded only by their subtlety ("Censurae aliae diversorum Hominum malevolentium sed simium subtilium in eadem Chronica"). Peck's listing thus indicates two separate manuscripts that if they do not confirm two stages of censorship, at least distinguish two sets of motives – the first, official (suggested by the use of official titles), and the second, personal and motivated by subtlety and ill will. A third item (v), Whitgift's letter to Randolph, Killigrew, and Hammond on censoring the *Chronicles*, confirms that they performed the official review. Finally, Item IV, Fleming's brief and true relation of the mode of reforming the *Chronicles* ("Abrahami Flemingi (qui praeerat Typis & Praelo) de modo castrandi, Reformandiq[ue] Chronica praedicta brevis & vera Relatio"), suggests that he performed the actual cancellation and reformation. For a discussion of Fleming's role in the *Chronicles*, see Elizabeth Story Donno's "Abraham Fleming: A Learned Corrector 1586–7," *Studies in Bibliography*, 42 (1989), 200–11.

33 Conyers Read, *Mr. Secretary Walsingham and the policy of Queen Elizabeth*, 3 vols. (Cambridge, 1925), vol. III, pp. 146–7.

34 For this and other matters related to Cobham and Leicester, see Donno, "Shakespeare's Holinshed," p. 241.

35 See G. W. Parry, *A Protestant Vision* (Cambridge, 1987), pp. 142–4.

36 Oosterhoff, *Leicester and the Netherlands*, p. 132. Evidently Leicester had some success in defending his activities with the Queen since Oosterhoff reports that she complained to a Dutch delegation on 5 February 1587 about their ill treatment of him (ibid., p. 162).

37 See above n. 32, p. 152.

38 Donno, "Shakespeare's Holinshed," p. 240.

39 The Book Club reformations keep intact the beginning of the section

on Parker (about one-third of p. 1489 and all of p. 1490) through the early years of Elizabeth's Reformation.

40 See *Cambridge Plays, Records of Early English Drama*, ed. Alan H. Nelson, 2 vols. (Toronto, 1989) for the letter from Guzman de Silva to the Duchess of Parma that reports the event (vol. 1, pp. 242–3):

. . . entraron los representantes, en habitos de Algunos de los obispos que estan presos, fue el premero, el de Londres, llevando en las manos un cordero [lamb], com que le yua comiendo, y otros con otras devisas, y uno en figura de perro, con una hostia en la boca La Reyna se enojo tanto segun escriven que se entro, a priesa en su camara, diziendo malas palabras,y los que tenian las hachas, que era de noche, los desaron a escuras, y assi cése la Inconsiderada y desvergoncàda representacíon.

For a text of the masque, see Marion Colthorpe, "Anti-Catholic Masques Performed Before Queen Elizabeth I," *Notes and Queries* (1986), 316–18. (I am indebted to Alan Nelson for bringing this event to my attention.) Of the Queen's response to the masque, Froude comments:

Elizabeth could have better pardoned the worst insolence to herself: she rose, and with a few indignant words left the room; the lights were extinguished, and the discomfited players had to find their way out of the house in the dark, and blunder back to Cambridge. It was but a light matter, yet it served to irritate Elizabeth's sensitivity. It exposed the dead men's bones which lay beneath the whited surface of University good order; and she went back to London with a heart as heavy as she carried away from it. (*History of England*, vol. VII, pp. 205–6)

41 In 1574 an English translation of the life of Parker written by someone in Parker's household and intended to be appended to his treatise on the Archbishops of Canterbury (that did not include himself) was printed on the continent with a radical Protestant epistle to the reader and a table of Parker's bishops (*The life off the 70. archbishopp off Canterbury* [Zurich]). The epistle states the effect of the table "is to shewe what a creator of Bishopes he hath been / and how many he hath consecreted in his dayes," revealing in these appointments "disorderly orders" (F7r). See also pp. 157–8.

42 It retains 1551/1552 and 1561/1562 from the original.

43 Both the original text and the cancels pay tribute to Sir Henry Sidney, his wife Mary, and his son Philip, occasioned by their deaths. The uncensored text contains a paragraph about the world's expectations for Sir Philip, followed awkwardly by an inset reporting his death and apologizing for the previous paragraph, and then reports his activities up to and including his death as Lord Governor of Flushing under (and appointed by) Leicester. The Book Club cancel contains the full report but omits the paragraph on expectations and the awkward apology and substitutes a paragraph comparing Sidney pere and fils. It stops short, "And here to end the memorie of them, it shall not be amisse, to record an epitaph made and published, for the perpetuating of the name of sir Henrie Sidneie, never sufficiently commended" (p. 1556, A45–8, uncensored).

44 Tomason had been made "priest at Reims in France by the authoritie of the bishop of Rome": his crime was "remaining within this realme after the terme of fortie daies after the session of the last parlement" and was so "condemned of treason." Lea had been ordained in France, and received the same sentence. They were convicted under the recent parliamentary statutes exiling seminary priests and Jesuits (p. 1559, B64–75, uncensored).

45 Donno, "Shakespeare's Holinshed," p. 238.

46 Leicester's particular interest in February 1587 was in gaining moral and financial support for English involvement in the Low Countries. As Lord Chancellor, Bromley prosecuted Babington and presided over the treason trial of Mary, Queen of Scots. He presented to Elizabeth Parliament's appeal for Mary's execution, and, as head of the law, took the chief burden for the execution. According to *DNB* (vol. vi, pp. 400–3), in his passion for equity, Bromley tried to soften the legal treatment of heretics. Burghley was instrumental in forging the official position on the administration of English justice in the propaganda war following Campion's trial and execution (see note 30).

47 Donno, "Shakespeare's Holinshed," p. 232.

48 Amos C. Miller, *Sir Henry Killigrew* (Leicester, 1963), pp. 199–201.

49 Donno, "Shakespeare's Holinshed," p. 232.

50 Read, *Walsingham*, vol. ii, p. 261. On Randolph and Killigrew's friendship, see Miller, *Killigrew*, p. 183.

51 Read, *Walsingham*, vol. ii, p. 256.

52 Read, *Walsingham*, vol. ii, p. 120.

53 Ibid., pp. 144–72.

54 This reformation suppresses a full half page marginally cited as being from " 'The tragicall histoire of the civill warres in the low countries', li. 4.fo.31. Churchyard's choice" that recounts the engagement of a Scottish company under the leadership of Matthew Stewart, Earl of Lennox, in 1578. Objections may have been on two grounds: the first, this military engagement must have been at a time when any Scottish or English military presence was unofficial, and when the Queen's vacillation on whether or not she would commit money and troops to the Prince of Orange produced a considerable strain on relations with the Dutch States. The *Chronicles* describe the forces as a "puissant armie of all such nations as were there in service with them as English, Scots, Germans, and their owne countriemen" (p. 422, B43–6, uncensored). In the encounter with the forces of Don Juan,
the English brought themselves betwixt the enimie and the Scots, who mistaking the companie, and supposing them to be thier enimies, gave them from the hedge, where they laie such a volee of shot, that it made them to loose more ground than ever the enimie could have done. (p. 422, B66–72, uncensored)
The second ground may have been that it reflected poorly on Anglo-

Scots relations – which would be consistent with the other censorship. Also objectionable may have been the chronicler's disparaging remark about the English and Scots leaders after recounting the successes of their forces.

55 For a full explanation of Anglo-Scots relations at this time, see Read, *Walsingham*, vol. II, pp. 151–3.

56 A long Latin commendation of the English Duke of "Summerset" was drastically cut in the interest of space, made vulnerable, no doubt, by the chronicler's confession that he did not "greeve" to set down so much both because he "would not maime the author in telling his owne tale, and would a little recreat the reader by the obscuritie of the stile of Roger Wall," even though "they belong not, and be utterlie impertinent to the matters of Scotland" (p. 434, B69–71, uncensored).

57 The old earle of Arrane (the duke of Chaterleraults eldest sonne being lunatike, and first committed to the custodie of his said brother the lord of Arbroth) was after taken from that his tutor, and set over to James Steward to have the oversight of his person . . . Which James Steward being by nature and experience subtill witted, and by authoritie and the kings favor in great credit; found meanes partlie by policie, partlie by persuasaion, and partlie by flatterie, to wring from the lunatike earle of Arrane, a grant and departure of his right and title, and honor to the earledome of Arrane. (p. 433, R17–36, uncensored)

58 See Read, *Walsingham*, vol. II, pp. 374–5.

59 Respectively Archibald Douglas and John Erskine.

60 Read, *Walsingham*, vol. II, p. 245.

61 Ibid., p. 251.

62 Based on Philip Gaskell's output figures for compositors and presses, using only one compositor and one press, the production time for five sheets (the total number of cancels in the first stage of censorship) would have been six days. Denham's printing operation, however, had two compositors and two presses, and the cancels could have been printed in three days. See Gaskell's *A New Introduction to Bibliography* (Oxford, 1972), pp. 54–5, 132.

63 This copy according to Bernard Quaritch "Catalogue 1150,"
Both volumes of this copy bear the bookplate of Lady Elizabeth Germain (1680–1769), second daughter of Charles, second Earl of Berkely . . . After the death of her husband, she lived in an apartment at Knole, and left her library to George Sackvill, third son of the Duke of Dorset . . . [it] passed in to the library of Sir Walter W. Greg, the great bibliographer, and more recently in to the collection of Dr. B. E. Juel-Jensen. (p. 55)
I am indebted to H. E. Igoe, who acquired this copy, for making it available to me.

64 Since *STC* does not notice states of the text represented by the Book Club fragment or the Igoe copy, I suspect few are extant, and that few may have been circulated in 1587, further that for both, the cuts were made and the reformed text printed and gathered but only a few copies sold before still more changes were made. Since the Igoe

text cuts only one long section consisting of five gatherings on one subject, this reformation, consisting of a single sheet, could have been printed in a matter of days. Indeed, the second censorship may have taken place before the order staying the sale was rescinded, particularly since most extant copies reflect the full censorship.

65 *The life of 70. Archbishopp off Canterbury*, "To the Christian reader," ([Zurich], 1574), C4r.

66 Ibid., C4v–C5r.

67 Donno, "Shakespeare's Holinshed," p. 240.

68 The Igoe cancel also signed ABCDE. In the new cancel, the pagination abuts with the Book Club cancel 1491/1536.

69 This is somewhat confusing because pp. 1551/1552 and 1553/1554 correspond to earlier pagination. The text, however, differs significantly.

70 That Yale University's copy of the 1587 *Chronicles* contains the cancels 6V (1419/1420) and ABCDE (1421/1490) and not the STC 7L1, &l2, and 7M cancels suggests that the final reformation may have been two discrete events. Since it also contains all the original leaves in the 6M gathering, however, it is equally possible that the copy reflects incomplete castration.

71 That the events were not in and of themselves objectionable is indicated by the publication of T[homas] D[igges]'s *A briefe report of militarie services done in the Low Countries by the Erle of Leicester*, printed by A. Hatfield for G. Seton, 1587 (its signed title page indicating it was printed neither surreptitiously nor illegally). Had the representation of events been the matter of concern, it is unlikely that this pamphlet would have gone unnoticed.

72 I have discussed the nature of the entertainments in "Which Holinshed? Holinshed's *Chronicles* at the Huntington library," *Huntington Library Quarterly*, 55 (1992), 559–77. In accepting Booth's identification of the Book Club fragment as subsequent to the Leicester/Low Country reformation, like Donno and AnneCastanien (see n. 67), I misattributed the reformation to Leicester's concern for his reputation.

73 Knowing, as we do, that Elizabeth was incensed that Leicester accepted the Dutch offer to become governor (see MacCaffery, *Elizabeth I*, p. 226), the suggestion that he may himself have procured the censorship of his almost royal procession to avoid offending her is not unreasonable – except that the censored text retains *all* the details of the ceremony installing Leicester as governor and the full text of "A placard conteining the authoritie" (see p. 337).

74 Donno, "Shakespeare's Holinshed," pp. 239–40; Anne Castanien, "Censorship and Historiography in Elizabethan England: the Expurgation of Holinshed's *Chronicles*," Ph.D. thesis, University of California, Davis (1970), pp. 271–2. Castanien further suggests that Leicester sought this reformation to make himself appear more efficient and

responsible as a military commander by reducing the emphasis on entertainment, but the passages that would glorify his military prowess are cut entirely. The chronicler, at the conclusion of the Leicester/Low Country section, addresses directly the military cuts and suggests other motives for censorship and guidelines for reform:

To prosecute the sumptuousnesse, statelinesse, and varietie of devises in service at this banket, [St. George's Day] requireth a discourse of manie lines, and therefore leaving it to the imagination of the reader (having relation to the former) we will heare surcease; remembring thus much to the honour of the lord lieutenant, that sundrie militarie exploits or stratagems were with no lesse magnanimitie attempted, than with felicitie atchieved against the enimie, during the time of his abode in those countries, which it were better utterlie to omit, than not with convenient dignity record . . . (p. 1490, A69–B6, censored)

The total number of lines of any revision was a matter of some importance in producing a timely and economically feasible reformation. That the chronicler chose to omit military materials in this case, however, rather than condense them appears to run counter to the demands placed on him by the censor.

75 MacCaffery, *Elizabeth I*, p. 229. Further, the Queen eventually agreed to Leicester retaining the title (ibid., p. 226).

76 Oosterhoof, *Leicester and the Netherlands*, p. 164.

77 See note 32.

78 Peck, *Desiderata Curiosa*, end papers.

79 John Stow, *The Annales of England* (1592), pp. 1203–17.

80 Donno, "Shakespeare's Holinshed," p. 242.

81 The censored text cuts altogether pages 1551/1552 that remained from the original in the Book Club/Igoe texts and condenses one column in the earlier cancel 1553/1554 to a half a column on the new 1551/1552 cancel. A telling comment about Sir Henry Sidney's response to his critics that survived the first reformation gives some insight into that latter cut: " . . . for the more they contended to suppresse him, the more (like the camomill being foiled and trodden) his vertues rose up and appered, and their malice was both unfolded and controlled" (p. 1553, A1–4, Book Club).

82 See Steven G. Ellis, *Tudor Ireland, Crown, Community and the Conflict of Cultures, 1470–1603* (London and New York, 1985), pp. 249, 250, 253, 260, 268.

83 The jury acquitted Cason of witchcraft but found her guilty of a lesser charge for which the judge sentenced her to coming to sermons more frequently. His mercy was quickly condemned by a lawyer who pointed out that this charge also warranted a sentence of death. As she awaited her sentence, "sundrie preachers" pleaded with her to confess and ask for mercy, but Jone maintained that her only crime was adultery and a lewd life, though she accepted her punishment as justice for that life (pp. 1560–1, A5–A29, uncensored).

84 Annabel Patterson gives considerable weight to the presence of Jone

Cason's witchcraft trial in the uncensored *Chronicles* as evidence both of the chronicler's attack on English justice and of his interest in women. She finds this as part of the *Chronicles'* oppositional agenda critiquing English justice, and from this perspective, the grounds for censorship would rest in suppressing opposition. See *Reading Holinshed*, pp. 228–31, 161.

85 Regarding the secrecy, see Walsingham's notes, dated 2 February 1587, on preparations for Mary's execution. Reported in the *HMC, Salisbury*, vol. III, p. 471.

86 *HMC, Salisbury*, vol. III, pp. 223–4. Furthermore, *A Defence of the Honorable sentence and execution of the Queen of Scots*, was printed in London by John Windet in 1587. *STC* identifies this title with an 11 February entry in the Stationers' Register to Windet for "An Analogie or resemblance between Johane Queene of Naples and Marye Queene of Scotland," authorized by the Bishop of London and licensed by Stationers' Company Warden Henry Denham (the printer of Holinshed's 1587 *Chronicles*). The first chapter of *Defence of the Honorable sentence and execution* consists of "An Analogie or resemblance betweene Ione queene of Naples and Marie queene of Scotland." Since Mary's execution was not yet known on 11 February, I suspect that the entry was not for the *Defence* but for the "Analogie," and that the carefully argued defense was printed sometime later under the license granted for "Analogie." A transcript of "A defence of the Honorable sentence" (Yelverton 48,027 fo. 586, British Library) carries the inscription "It was comenly thought that this booke was made by Tho. Martin a Doctor of the Civile Lawe and being printed the bookes were supressed by the ArchB of Cant." I can find no evidence that the book printed by Windet was suppressed, but it would be consistent with the Holinshed censorship for "An Analogie" to have been stayed until the government could arrange damage control. The Privy Council's occasional dealings with Dr. Thomas Martin (including a royal commission) lead me to suspect his *Defence of the Honorable sentence and execution* to be government propaganda, and, thus, an unlikely candidate for supression.

87 *CSP, Spanish*, vol. III, 28. The French archival date is 28 February, but at this time the English calendar preceded the Continental by ten days. (Arundell was a member of the community of English Catholics in Paris, who maintained loyalty to Elizabeth as Queen but not as Head of the Church.)

88 Newsworthy events found their way into ballads and broadsides very quickly, especially for something so important. A Stationers' Company license was issued for a ballad on the "Joye for the takinge of the traitours" (authorized by Hartwell) on 27 August 1586, just days after the Babington conspirators were apprehended. Aldee entered his license on 6 December for two ballads on Mary's death sentence; the

proclamation had been published on 4 December. It took two men one day to set and print a broadside, so a single-sheet ballad could appear within a day of the license.

89 *HMC, Salisbury*, vol. III, p. 435.

90 Legend on the title page of *A Defence of the Honorable sentence and execution*.

91 The principal motivation for the extensive revision of the Babington/ Mary materials was, according to Castanien, offense to James, but since, as Booth observed, more survived in the censored text than was cut, this appears unlikely ("Censorship and Historiography," pp. 296–7). One passage that well may have offended him, however, was suppressed entirely in this stage: a reflection on those kings of Scotland with the name of James (pp. 1562–3, B15–A66, uncensored) (though the chronicler says, "The king himselfe we omit as touching his post be it as it is" [p. 1562, B19–20]), many of whom were scoundrels and villains.

92 Patterson, *Reading Holinshed*, p. 257. The reformation occupies *STC* cancels 1553/1554 and 1555/1574.

93 Printed as 'tine.' I depend here on the cancel present in the Huntington Library's Bridgewater copy.

94 . . . the honorable lords of the councell . . . did now enter into the discussing and winnowing out of such unnaturall treacheries . . . Wherein although the offendors had capitallie transgressed, and in a degree so eminent as none above, and therefore deserved what rigor (were it never so sharpe) might be thought upon, or used: yet not so much as falling into a conceipt of anie such proceeding, they so dealt with the conspirators by clemencie, circumspection, & persuasion; that whatsoever concerned their attempt in that heinous kind, they discovered . . . By which their voluntarie confession they satisfied the examinants . . . whereupon a preacher at Pauls crosse was commanded from authoritie, to deliver some notice to the assemblie, answerable to the knowledge which he himself received by eare at the best hand; namelie, that diverse of the traitors were apprehended, and without anie torture or torment confessed . . . (p. 1569, A72–B29, uncensored)

95 Patterson, *Reading Holinshed*, pp. 257–8.

96 *STC*, vol. I, p. 591.

97 Donno, "Shakespeare's Holinshed," p. 233.

98 *CSP, Domestic* 1581–90, p. 697.

99 Domestic State Papers 12/235, 3, fo. 5, London Public Record Office.

100 Patterson, following *STC*, says that the *Chronicles* were called in in 1590 "on the grounds that they contained a tactless account of the trial and execution of Edmund Campion" (*Reading Holinshed*, p. 131). She compounded the understandable *STC* assumption that the 6M cancel was made late, by ignoring Donno's work on "A Certain Declaration" ("Shakespeare's Holinshed," pp. 233–8). Patterson appears to assign a motive for the "1590 censorship" from her own reading of the passage.

101 *APC*, vol. XIV, pp. 311–12.

102 That men like Leicester, Walsingham, and Buckhurst were sensitive to issues of professional diplomacy – and that the Privy Council should

have appointed a professional diplomat like Randolph to reform the *Chronicles* in the interest of image making – is consistent with recent scholarship on Elizabethan diplomacy. See particularly the work of Gary M. Bell: "Elizabethan Diplomacy: The Subtle Revolution" in *Politics, Religion & Diplomacy in Early Modern Europe*, ed. Malcolm R. Thorp and Arthur J. Slavin (Kirksville, MO, 1994), pp. 267–88 and *A Handlist of British Diplomatic Representatives, 1509–1688* (1990).

103 Patterson, *Reading Holinshed*, p. 182.
104 See Malcolm R. Thorp, "William Cecil and Antichrist," in *Politics, Religion & Diplomacy*, ed. Thorp and Slavin, pp. 289–305.
105 Blatant attacks on the episcopacy and the royal supremacy or libels of ministers, even in a licensed book, would have been censorable, but these matters of image making did not concern attacks or libels.
106 Thomas Nashe, "Pierce Penilesse His Supplication to the Divell," in *Works*, ed. Ronald B. McKerrow (1905), vol. 1, p. 194.
107 Patterson, *Reading Holinshed*, pp. 16, 23.

8   MARTIN MARPRELATE AND THE PURITAN PRESS: "AS THOU HAST TWO EARES, SO USE THEM BOTH"

1 See pp. 73–5.
2 See Margaret Drabble, *Oxford Companion to English Literature* (Oxford, 1983); Ian Ousby, *Cambridge Companion to Literature in English* (Cambridge, 1993); and Oscar James Campbell, *Comicall Satire in Shakespeare's "Troilus and Cressida"* (San Marino, CA, 1938).
3 Siebert, *Freedom of the Press*, p. 98. They challenged the control the government had regained in 1573 following the destruction of John Stroud's presses.
4 Collinson, *Elizabethan Puritan Movement*, p. 396.
5 See ibid., pp. 274–5.
6 Lorna Hutson, *Thomas Nashe in Context* (Oxford, 1989), p. 198. See also pp. 66, 200–1. She relies on Siebert for her understanding of the mechanisms of press censorship.
7 Martin Marprelate, *The Protestatyon of Martin Marprelate* (1589), p. 9; in *The Marprelate Tracts [1588–1589]: A Scolar Press Facsimile* (Menston, England, 1970). All citations in notes and text refer to the original editions and to these facsimiles: some appear as page and some as signature references.
8 One aspect of this redefinition is to change the punctuation. Puritanism with a capital "P" has become a usage associated with the Whig view; with a small "p" it can refer to any who would bring the Reformation further than the terms of the Elizabethan settlement. I opt for the small "p" – though I generally attempt to prefer finer discriminations like presbyterian, literal Calvinist, radical reformers (that may or may not be presbyterian), or Separatist – all of which I define in the course of

my discussion. Although a presbyterian and not a separatist, Martin provoked the distrust of prominent "puritans."

9 Peter Lake, *Moderate Puritans and the Elizabethan Church* (Cambridge, 1982), p. 1.

10 Siebert, *Freedom of the Press in England*, p. 95.

11 Collinson, *Elizabethan Puritan Movement*, p. 274.

12 Lake, *Moderate Puritans*, p. 2.

13 In addition to Lake's *Moderate Puritans*, see Nicholas Tyacke's "Puritanism, Arminianism and Counter Revolution," in *The Origins of the English Civil War*, ed. C. Russell (1973), pp. 119–43; *Anti-Calvinists: The Rise of English Arminianism c. 1590–1640* (Oxford, 1987); and "Debate: The Rise of Arminianism Reconsidered," *Past and Present*, 115 (1987) 201–16.

14 Lake, *Moderate Puritans*, p. 115.

15 Peter White, *Predestination, Policy, and Polemic* (Cambridge, 1992).

16 Ibid., pp. 95–7.

17 Martin's authors, printers, and publishers effectively concealed his identity. See Donald McGinn's *John Penry and the Marprelate Controversy* (New Brunswick, 1966) and Leland Carlson's *Martin Marprelate Gentleman* (San Marino, CA, 1981) for their arguments for Penry and Throckmorton as Martin, though Carlson admits to some collaboration. Collinson offers a concise review of speculations about Martin's identity, and adds his own, that George Carleton may have been Martin (*Elizabethan Puritan Movement*, pp. 393–6).

18 *A Caveat for Parsons Howlett*, dedicated to the Earl of Leicester and printed by Waldegrave, was entered to Thomas Man and T. Smith, 11 August 1583, and *Godly Prayers and Meditations* (not printed until 1601) was entered 12 April 1583 to John Harrison – both were authorized by the Bishop of London. *A godly exhortation by occasion of the late judgement of God at Parris garden* Waldegrave printed in two editions in 1583, and both were signed by the printer (neither was entered).

19 The authorized works were *A Christian and learned exposition upon . . . 8 Romans* (Waldegrave f. Thomas Man, entered 11 June 1587); *A forme of preparation to the Lordes Supper [Master Wilcox's Catechism]* (Waldegrave f. Man 11 June 1587); and *Unfolding of sundry untruths & absurde propositions* (Thomas Dawson f. Thomas Man, 9 May 1581). Those not authorized but entered were *Exposition uppon the booke of Canticles* (entered 28 June 1585 to Thomas Man and printed though not signed by Waldegrave); *A glasse for gamesters* (Kyngston f. Thomas Man, 20 December 1580); and *A right godly & Learned exposition upon thw hole book of psalmes* (7 February 1586 to Thomas Man and printed though not signed by Dawson). The title pages of the above carried "T.W." rather than Wilcox's name. Man published the rest without entering them in the Register: *Large letters . . . for . . . distressed in conscience* (printed by Roger Ward, 1589); *A profitable and confortable letter for afflicted consciences written in 1582* (anon.,

printed by Waldegrave [1584]); *A short, yet sound commentatie written on the Proverbes* (T. Orwin, [1589]); and *The summe of a sermon preached at Southwell* (Widow Orwin, 1597).

20 Penry later maintained that this book calling for a learned ministry in Wales was presented in Parliament without objection, but was later seized by the Stationers, and Penry imprisoned. I can find no other testimony that the book was censored. Its treatment is quite mild, particularly in comparison to other contemporary appeals. Barnes had a few conflicts with London Stationers falsely using his imprint, and they with him for pirating their copies, so it is entirely possible that the Stationers seized Penry's book for trade matters. His imprisonment is consistent with High Commission practices of detaining a reportedly nonconforming minister until he could be questioned. Once Penry was questioned, he was released. For his account, see *Th' appelation of John Penry, unto the highe courte of Parliament* (R. Waldegrave, [La Rochelle], 1589).

21 *An exhortation unto the governours and people of Wales* [1588]; *A Defence of that which hath bin written in the questions of the ignorant ministerie and the communicating with them* [East Molesey, 1588]; and *A view of some part of such publike wants and disorders as are in the service of God, within Wales* [Coventry, 1589].

22 *Th' appelation of John Penry; A Briefe discovery of the untruthes and slanders contained in a sermon, preached the 8 of Februarie 1588 by D. Bancroft* [anon., R. Waldegrave, Edinburgh, 1590]; *A treatise wherein is manifestly proved, that reformation and those that favor the same, are unjustly cyharged to be enemies, unto hir majestie* [R. Waldegrave, Edinburgh], 1590); *An humble motion with submision unto the Privie Counsell. that ecclesiastical discipline [be] reformed after the worde of God* ([By J. Penry. R. Waldegrave, Edinburgh], 1590); *I John Penry doo heare . . . set downe the whole truth which I hold in regard of my faith towards my God and dread soveraigne queene Elizabeth* [printed abroad, 1593]; *To my beloved wife Helener Penry* [printed abroad? 1593] (*STC*, vol. II, p. 225).

23 The legal title was: *The true Remedie against famine and wars* (R. Waldegrave f. T Man a. T Gakes, entered 6 March 1588). The others were: *Amendment of Life: 3 Sermons* (W. B[rome] a. N. L[ing] for T. Man, 1584; anr. ed. Waldegrave f. Man a. Gubbins, 1588); *Combatt betwixt Christ and the devill. Foure sermons* (Waldegrave f. T Man [1588]); *Commentarie upon the Lamentations of Jeremy* (Widdow Orwin f. T. Man, 1593); *Obedience to the gospell. Two sermons* ([T. Windet?] f. Thomas Man, 1584); and *Peter's Fall* (Windet & Judson f. Lynd, 1584; anr. [Waldegrave] f. T. Man [1587]).

24 While sixteenth-century sources refer to the book as *Diotrephes*, its actual title was *The State of the Church of England, laide open betweene "Diotrephes" a Byshop, "Tertullus" a Papist, "Demetrius" an usurer, "Pandocheus" an Innekeeper, and "Paule" a preacher of the worde of God.*

25 Press Return, May 1583 (Arber, vol. I, p. 248).

26 *ESTC*, 8 July 1994.
27 The 1583–4 Wardens' Accounts notes: "Item an Obligacon of Robert waldegraue of xl£ to the Companie Concerninge not printinge of any thinge in master Seres pryvyledge" (Arber, vol. i, p. 507). See p. 177.
28 Martin Marprelate, *Hay any worke for Cooper*, p. 41. The works are *A lamentable complaint to the commonalty, by way of supplication to Parliament, for a learned ministery* ([1585](*STC* 7739), *The unlawful practises of prelates against godly ministers* ([1584?] *STC* 20201), and *The judgement of a most reuerent and learned man from beyond the seas, concerning a threefold order of bishops* ([c. 1585] *STC* 2021), written by Beza and translated by John Field, but published anonymously. Two of the texts Martin mentions were printed in 1585, so the imprisonment could not have come any earlier than 1585. I think it more likely belongs to 1586 since in 1585 Waldegrave's press was unusually active, printing at least twenty-three titles. The 1584 text, (*The unlawful practises of prelates*) recounts events that took place in June 1584 (see Collinson, *Elizabethan Puritan Movement*, pp. 263–4), and so was probably published in late 1584. (Collinson places the imprisonment in 1585 [ibid., p. 274].)

DNB erroneously puts the twenty-week sentence in Autumn 1588, subsequent to the initital Marprelate tracts' publication (vol. LIX, p. 21). But Ronald McKerrow says that Waldegrave was imprisoned in 1584, probably for printing *A brief declaration concerning the desires of all those faithfull ministers*, *A dialogue concerning the strife of our Church*, and *A declaration of some such monstrous abuses as our Bishops have not been ashamed to foster* (*Dictionary of Printers and Booksellers* [1910], p. 278). McKerrow too, is relying on *Hay any worke* which says his grace
violated his promise, in that he told the wardens of the stacioners, that if Walde-grave would come quietly to him & cease printing of seditious bookes, he would pardon what was past, & the wardens promised his wife, that if he were committed, they would lye at his graces gate til he ware released, and for al this, yet he was committed to the white Lyon, where he laye sixe weekes. (p.68)
McKerrow's date is probably based on a 1584 warrant for Waldegrave, that he found in the Stationers' Company records, and he chooses the troublesome works from that date. The only 1584 record concerning Waldegrave that appears among the Register and Court Book in the matter of printing against Seres's patent (see preceding note). It is possible that Waldegrave was temporarily imprisoned for this, since in a similar case of patent violation, Roger Ward was (*APC*, vol. xiv, pp. 82–3).
29 Article Four required allowance according to her Majesty's Injunctions and specified the penalty of six months in prison for printing without ecclesiastical authorization.
30 *DNB*, vol. LIII, p. 4.
31 Marprelate, *An Epistle*, p. 23.
32 13 May 1588, *Records of the Court*, ed. Greg and Boswell, pp. 27–8.

33 Marprelate, *An Epistle*, pp. 24–5.
34 For Timothie Rider's *Widowes Treasorer*, 6 April 1584 and John Harrison's *The Coat armorer of a Christian*, 22 September 1584 (Arber, vol. II, pp. 430, 435).
35 See pp. 55 and 242, n. 93.
36 Martin says in *Hay any worke*:
    For as soon as any book is printed in the defence of Christs holy discipline, or for the detecting of your Antichristian dealings, but your ravening purcivantes flye citie and countrie to seeke for Walde-grave, as though he were bound by statute unto you, either to make known who printed seditious books against my L. Face, or to go to prison himsselfe, and threatened with the racke. (p.67)
37 Milward, *Religious Controversies of the Elizabethan Age*, pp. 77–96.
38 Based on Milward's bibliography, forty texts issued from the puritan side; the seven Marprelate pamphlets and three *Admonition* pamphlets were clearly censored. Penry maintained that his *Treatise Containing the aequity* was seized by the Stationers, but see n. 20. Waldegrave's press was seized and destroyed for printing *Diotrephes*, and the Stationers' Court ordered the copies burned and the press destroyed (*Records of the Court*, ed. Greg and Boswell, pp. 26–7). I can find no record outside of Martin Marprelate's testimony that *The unlawful practises*, *A lamentable complaint*, or *The iudgement of a most reverent and learned man* were suppressed, though the High Commission may have detained Waldegrave to discover the authors.
39 Marprelate, *Hay any worke*, p. 41.
40 My principal concern here is the language and argument of the reform tracts – a topic that deserves far greater consideration than the constraints of this book allow.
41 Diarmaid MacCulloch explains that edification, the building of a community upon the foundation of Christ and the apostles, is an attempt to translate into English idiosyncratic Greek centered on the idea of buildings and building. Its use in scripture is metaphorical and allows Paul to refer to the community as "God's building" and the process of building as all of those things that relate to strengthening that community (*The Later Reformation in England* [New York, 1990], pp. 85–6).
42 *An Admonition to Parliament* (1572), A2v.
43 *A parte of a register* ([Edinburgh], 1593), p. 69. Though *STC* does not identify Edinburgh, the text is signed in Waldegrave's manner. *A parte of a register* was compiled by John Field and in reprinting texts central to the Puritan movement offers a historical record not only of the arguments for reformation but of the transformation in the rhetoric in which the argument was phrased. (Further citations by with the date of the selection and page number in the text.)
44 The distinction between the reformers and the Church, is that the established Church required those practices required by scripture,

denied practices prohibited by scripture, and judged everything else as "indifferent." The latter could be instituted by the monarch and Church councils. For example, using the sign of the cross in baptism was neither admitted nor prohibited by scripture; since its origin was not scriptural, the reformers objected to the practice. Since it was not prohibited, the Church found this unjustified.

45 John Udall, *Diotrephes*, (1588) V3r.
46 *A parte of a register*, title page. This depends on the Geneva Bible.
47 "An Exhortation to the Bishops II," in *Puritan Manifestoes*, ed. W. H. Frere and C. E. Douglas (1954), p. 70.
48 Walter Travers, *A full and plaine declaration of ecclesiastical discipline* (Heidelberg, 1574) p. 5. Collinson says that this book is often confused with the Book of Discipline being drafted and subscribed to by members of the classis movement in the 1580s (*Elizabethan Puritan Movement*, p. 294). Such confusion is undoubtedly prompted by the frequency with which the pamphleteers refer to Traver's work as a defining text of their movement.
49 [Laurence Chaderton], *A fruitfull sermon . . . of the 12 chapiter of the epistle of S. Paul to the Romanes* (1584), p. 52. Printed by Waldegrave and entered in the Stationers' Register, it appeared in three editions by 1586. Though published without authorial attribution, this seminal sermon has generally been attributed to Chaderton.
50 Udall, *Diotrephes*, B4v. The books to which Paule refers are: Travers's *A full and plaine declaration of ecclesiastical discipline*, Fenner's *Counterpoyson*, Chaderton's *A fruitfull sermon . . . of the 12. chapiter . . . to the Romanes*, and Cartwright's *The rest of the second replie agaynst maister Vuhitgifts Second answer* (Basle, 1577). *A lerned discourse of Ecclesiastical governement* may refer to Travers's *A defence of the ecclesiastical discipline ordayned of God to be used in his church* ([Middelburg], 1588).
51 See MacCulloch, *Later Reformation*, pp. 48–51, and Collinson, *Elizabethan Puritan Movement*, pp. 243–62.
52 MacCulloch, *Later Reformation*, p. 51.
53 Ibid., p. 54.
54 Carlson, *Martin Marprelate Gentleman*, pp. 6–8.
55 According to Carlson, one "immediate cause for the launching of the Marprelate attack was a fortuitous concurrence of events affecting Throckmorton, John Penry, Robert Waldegrave, and John Udall" (*Martin Marprelate Gentleman*, p. 6): Throckmorton was censured for speaking in Parliament against English foreign policy in the Low Countries, and escaped the Tower by fleeing to his home; Penry was summoned before the High Commission in relation to writing *Treatise containing the aequity*, which was presented in the same Parliament; Waldegrave's press was seized for illegally printing *Diotrephes*; Udall had been deprived of his ministry at Kingston-upon-Thames for nonconformity.

56 MacCulloch, *Later Reformation*, p. 55.
57 John Bridges, *A defence of government* (1587), ¶v. (Hereafter cited in the text.)
58 Quotations are taken from the 1576 Edinburgh edition.
59 Bishops' Bible (1574). The problem of theological dispute was undoubtedly complicated by the reformers' use of the Geneva Bible. While this did not affect the arguments regarding church polity with regards to Romans 12, the differences between the versions of verse 3 suggest how problems may have arisen.

> 3. For I say through the grace that is given unto me, to everie one that is among you, that no man presume to understand above that which is mete to understand but that he understand according to sobrietie, as God hathe dealt to everie man the measure of faith. (Geneva)

60 The first two Marprelate pamphlets are both entitled *Oh read over D. John Bridges, for it is a worthy worke: Or an epitome of the fyrste Booke of that right worshipfull volume written against the Puritanes*. The so-called *Epistle*, on p. 2. of the first tract, reads "To the right puisante, and terrible Priests, my cleargie masters of the Confocation house . . .," and the running head is "An Epistle to the terrible Priests of the Confocation house." The so-called *Epitome* begins with a letter from "Martin Marprelate gentleman . . . To all the Cleargie masters . . ."; this is followed by "The second Epistle to the terrible Priests" and then begins with the text preceded by the title "The Epitome of the first booke . . ." Scholars generally refer to them as *Epistle* and *Epitome*, though this is by mo means consistent.
61 In 1583, Leicester and Walsingham gave their patronage to Cartwright to write a response to a Catholic version of the New Testament published in Rheims. According to *DNB*, Whitgift discouraged the project, and Cartwright's *Confutation* was not published until 1618 in Leiden. (*DNB* relies on Martin's *Epistle* as evidence that Whitgift prevented the publication.) See Collinson, *Elizabethan Puritan Movement*, pp. 235, 237 and *DNB*, vol. IX, pp. 228–9.
62 The penultimate pamphlet, *The Just censure and reproof of Martin Junior*, (1589) gives a clear sense of how important Martin regarded secrecy to be:

> Well boy, to drawe to an ende, notwithstanding they small defecteds, perswade they selfe, that I love thee: doubt not that. And here before we part, take this one grave lesson of thy elder brother: Be silent, and close, heare manie, conferre with few. And in this point doe as I doe; know not thy father though thou mayest. For I tell tee, if I should meete him in the streete, I woule never ask him blessing: walk smoothely and circumspectly, and if anie offer to talke with thee of Martin, talke thou straite of the voyage into Portugal . . . (D4r–D4v)

(Martin shifts his persona in the course of the pamphlets, from Martin Marprelate in the first four, to Martin's younger son in the fifth, and to Martin's elder in this one.)

63 Arber, *Introductory Sketch to the Marprelate Controversy*, pp. 107–8.

64 Included in the *Epitome*'s barbs are Martin's justifiable complaints of the book's length ("very comprehended in a portable booke, if your horse be not too weake") and Bridges's style ("there be not 3. whole periods for every page in the book") (Bir, Biv).

65 Carlson, *Martin Marprelate Gentleman*, p. 12.

66 Hughes and Larkin, vol. iii, p. 34.

67 Collinson, *Elizabethan Puritan Movement*, p. 392.

68 Hutson, *Nashe in Context*, pp. 200–1.

69 Even though printing was a hundred years old, during the 1570s and 1580s the popular press gained tremendous momentum in London. In some respects this "boom" parallels the late twentieth century growth of television which has contributed to replacing a linear rational epistemology grounded in print culture with one grounded in images. For Marprelate to have violated the few ground rules that had become accepted for printed discourse confirmed the suspected dangers of the medium.

70 Collinson, *Elizabethan Puritan Movement*, p. 393.

71 Apparently the assistants were questioned and released, but, based on their testimony, Hodgskin was tried for under 23 Eliz, ca. 1 for printing seditious writing. Although a death sentence was proclaimed, Carlson in *Martin Marprelate Gentleman* concludes that he must have submitted since he received the Queen's mercy and was released.

72 If, indeed, McGinn's *John Penry* is correct and Penry was Martin, this is a gesture of self-protection. I am better persuaded by Carlson's argument in *Martin Marprelate Gentleman* for Throckmorton, but certainty is impossible.

73 1 Eliz, ca. 6, reaffirming the statute against libel 1 and 2 Phil. & Mary, ca. 3, opens by reiterating the Westminster statutes 1 and 2 Richard II, ca. 5 and ca. 11 that defined libeling "Prelats Dukes Earles Barons and other Nobles and Peares of the Realme" as felonious.

74 *State Trials* (1730), vol. i, p. 170. Udall was questioned in January and again in July 1589/90 by the Privy Council about the Marprelate pamphlets, but maintained his innocence (*DNB*, vol. lviii, pp. 4–5). On 24 July 1590 he was tried before the Judge of the Assize for writing *Demonstration of Discipline*, which a court had already determined to be felonious writing. Though the jury decided that Udall was the author, thereby convicting him of a felony, no sentence was issued. He appeared before the assizes, where, neither affirming nor denying authorship of the *Demonstration of Discipline*, he maintained his views on the necessity of reformation (Carlson, *Martin Marprelate Gentleman*, pp. 84–5). The court quibbled with Udall about the intention of his statements related to reformation not tarrying for the magistrate and on that basis found him guilty of treasonous writing.

Judge. Nay, the meaning is, That if the Queen will not, yet you say, it shall come in; for so the Words are, *That it must prevail, maugre the Heads of all that stand against it.*

Udall. Nay my Lords, the Words are, Maugre the Malice of all that stand aginst it. For there are many Heads that are not maliciously bent against it: There is great difference between Malice and Heads; for some are gainst the Cause, through Ignorance.

Judge. It is all one in effect. (*State Trials*, p. 170)

Barrow and Greenwood, founders of a Separatist church, were in recurring trouble with the High Commission for their views that the Church of England was unlawful. In 1593 they with three other members of a newly organized Separatist church were tried by a special commission. Barrow was convicted under 23 Eliz, ca. 2, for writing *The Discovery of the False Church* that, among other things, denied the Queen's authority to make laws regarding religion. Greenwood was convicted for writing *A Collection of Certain Letters* that maintained all the laws of the English Church were false. Collinson credits Whitgift with hastening their execution "out of malice for the Commons, or so it was said at the time" for defeating a piece of legislation against puritan sectaries (*Elizabethan Puritan Movement*, p. 428). See also, Leland Carlson's *The Writings of John Greenwood and Henry Barrow, 1591–1593* (1970).

After Thomas Nashe's *The Almond for a Parratt* (1590) named Penry as Marprelate, he escaped to Edinburgh where his ministry was well received. In 1590 in Scotland, Waldegrave printed John Penry's *Reformation No Enemie*. According to Carlson:

This book was an incisive defiance of the rulers of England, who were stigmatized as a "multitude of conspirators against God, against His truth, against the building of His house." The hierarchy and clergy were reviled as a "troup of bloody foule murtherers, sacrilegious church robbers, and such as have made themselves fat with the bloude of mens soules, and the utter ruine of the church . . ." Even the Privy Council, which allegedly delighted in the "violent oppression of Gods saincts," was warned that God would afflict it "with an heavy plague." (*Martin Marprelate Gentleman*, p. 86)

In 1592 Penry returned to England; he joined Greenwood's Separatist Church, and was among the members who were imprisoned and brought before the High Commission. Penry subsequently was tried before the King's Bench under the statute against treasonous writing (23 Eliz, ca. 23) for *Reformation No Enemie*. He was convicted, and hanged.

These four were all ministers. Throckmorton was not, and he escaped harsh sanctions. In Summer 1590 he was indicted for "making certaine scorneful and satyricall libells under the name of Martin" (*Martin Marprelate Gentleman*, p. 112). The case was referred to Westminster, and in Easter term 1591 Throckmorton appeared in Westminster to answer the bill of indictment that among other things charged him with slandering the Queen and libeling the clergy. When his case was deferred to Trinity term the proceedings came to an end on a legal technicality. Carlson judges that Throckmorton's submissions and appeals of friends gained him favor and the Queen's clemency (*Martin Marprelate Gentleman*, pp. 116–28).

75 While the 1581 Parliament had mandated the pillory and losing one's ears (or a fine) for "false, seditious, and slanderous newes, rumours, sayings, or tale against our said most natural soveraigne," the devising, writing, printing, or setting forth "any manner of Booke, Rime, Ballade, Letter or Writing . . . containing any false, seditious, and slanderous matter to the defamation of the Queenes Maiesty" was deemed a felony that brought the death penalty (23 Eliz, ca. 2).

76 John Whitgift, *An answere to a certen libel intituled An Admonition* (1572), a2r.

9 THE 1599 BISHOPS' BAN: "SHREUD SUSPECT OF ILL
PRETENCES"

1 Arber, vol. III, pp. 677–8.
2 Ibid., p. 678.
3 *The Complete Works of Thomas Middleton*, ed. Gary Taylor (Oxford, forthcoming) attributes this to Middleton.
4 Joseph Hall's father, John Hall, was deputy to the Earl of Huntingdon, president of the north. *STC* says Tailboys Dymoke, younger brother to the Queen's Champion, wrote under the name of Cutwode (vol. I, p. 276).
5 *DNB*, vol. XXIV, p. 75.
6 Charles Gillett, *Burned Books*, 2 vols. (New York, 1932), vol. I, p. 90.
7 Bruce Smith, *Homosexual Desire in Shakespeare's England* (Chicago, 1991), p. 164. See chapter 5 for a discussion of satirists' use of classical models, including Roman homophobia.
8 Lynda Boose, "The 1599 Bishops' Ban, Elizabethan Pornography, and the Sexualization of the Jacobean State," in *Enclosure Acts: Sexuality, Property, and Culture in Early Modern England*, ed. Richard Burt and John Michael Archer (Ithaca, 1994), pp. 185–200.
9 *15 Joyes* appeared in 1603 as *The Batchelars Banquet* and went through three editions.
10 Smith, *Homosexual Desire*, p. 179.
11 Neither Davies's *Epigrames* nor Middleton's *Microcynicon* was entered in the Registers, and thus presumably neither was authorized.
12 Annabel Patterson, *Shakespeare and the Popular Voice* (1989), p. 81.
13 Patterson, *Censorship and Interpretation*, pp. 47, 129.
14 Ibid., p. 92.
15 Hutson, *Thomas Nashe in Context*, p. 66.
16 Richard McCabe, "Elizabethan Satire and the Bishops' Ban of 1599," *Yearbook of English Studies*, 11 (1981), 191.
17 Ibid., pp. 191–2.

18 Nashe, *Works*, ed. McKerrow, vol. I, p. 216.

19 Hutson, *Thomas Nashe in Context*, p. 68.

20 Serving as a liaison between the Privy Council and the Stationers, however, the Archbishop of Canterbury called in both editions of Holinshed's *Chronicles*. One or the other may have called upon the Stationers to call in and burn Samuel Rowland's *The Letting of Humors Blood in the Head vaine* (see pp. 216–17), but no record of such an intervention exists.

21 Richard Dutton has obliquely considered the relationship between the Bishops' ban and the Earl of Essex when he discusses Hayward's history of *Henry IV* and its relationship to Essex, but he does not see any connection between the condemnation of the satires and Essex's fortunes ("Buggeswordes: Samuel Harsnett and the Licensing, Suppression and Afterlife of Dr. John Hayward's *The first part of the life and reign of King Henry IV*," *Criticism*, 35 [1993], 309).

22 See particularly Dutton's "Buggeswordes" and Leeds Barroll's "A New History for Shakespeare and his Time," *Shakespeare Quarterly*, 39 (1988), 441–64. Both consider in some detail the circumstances of *Henry IV*'s supression. Dutton shares my conviction that Essex was related to the censorship, but he sees as the motive the authorities' sensitivity to Essex's popularity (p. 309).

23 According to F. J. Levy, "Hayward's book was the first realization in England of a history in which the causes of events were seen in terms of the interrelationship of politics and character rather than in terms of the working out of God's providence" ("Hayward, Daniel, and the Beginnings of Politic History in England," *Huntington Library Quarterly*, 50 [1987], 2–3).

24 Domestic State Papers, 12/270, fo. 48; London Public Record Office. It was published in *Letters Written by John Chamberlain*, ed. Sarah Williams (1861) pp. 46–8.

25 See Dutton, "Buggeswordes," pp. 311–13. He is more convinced than I am that the authorities genuinely suspected Essex of modeling himself on Henry Bolingbroke and thus permitting Hayward's book and that the book "stood on a par with negotiating with Jesuits and Irish rebels" in the minds of the authorities (p. 314).

26 Domestic State Papers, 12/275, fo. 25; London Public Record Office.

27 Although the title page identified Wolfe as the printer, E. Allde and F. Judson actually printed the text (*STC*, vol. I, p. 568).

28 22 July 1600, Domestic State Papers, 12/275, fo. 33; London Public Record Office. This treason charge, related to Essex's conduct in Ireland, is independent of charges made after the 1601 rebellion.

29 Domestic State Papers, 12/275, fo. 33; London Public Record Office.

30 July 1600, Domestic State Papers, 12/275, fo. 28; London Public Record Office, is the source of quotations in this paragraph.

31 Dutton suggests that the burning "in private" was "of questionable

legality" since neither the author nor the printer had been accused of the offense ("Buggeswordes," p. 309).

32 Dates for holidays derive from Gabriel Frendes's *An Almanack and Prognostication* (1599).

33 *DNB*, vol. xxv, p. 311.

34 Francis Bacon, *Sir Francis Bacon His Apologie, In Certaine imputations concerning the late Earle of Essex* (1604), pp. 36–7. While Bacon's loyalties to Essex certainly vacillated, his record of the Crown's heavy "correction" of his *A declaration of the practises & treasons committed by Robert late earle of Essex* (1601) suggests the pressures that affected his loyalties. While the *Bacon His Apologie* is certainly an exercise in self-justification, the materials on Hayward appear to have little relationship to this end; hence they may be taken at face value, particularly since the dates, at least, conform to those set forth by Wolfe and Harsnett.

35 Francis Bacon, *Apopothegmes New & Old* (1626), pp. 76–7..

36 Margaret Dowling's "Sir John Hayward's Troubles Over His Life of Henry IV" (*Library*, ser. 4, 11 [1930], 212–24) mistakenly associates Coke's and Popham's papers in vol. cclxxiv of the *State Papers* with the "trial" of Hayward in January 1601, but Hayward's confession belongs to his questioning in July 1600. Dowling is correct in concluding that his troubles apparently increased concerns about Essex, since on 26 July 1600 Dudley Carlton wrote to John Chamberlain that Essex remained a prisoner "at his owne custody. the Queen had given him liberty to go into the cuntrie, but recalled it againe upon the taking of Doctor Haywood who for writing Henry the forth was committed to the tower." She does not, however, link this to his July interrogation. On 22 January 1601 Hayward was further interrogated in the Tower, where he appears to have been detained until after Elizabeth's death. Hayward's remarks from vol. cclxxviii that Dowling calls his "confession" belongs correctly to this interrogation, though his responses hardly constitute a confession. Although Hayward was imprisoned, no indictment exists, nor does he appear to have been tried under laws against treasonous writing. Unfortunately, Dowling's account has misled scholars.

37 Bacon, *Bacon His Apologie*, pp. 48–50.

38 HMC, *Salisbury*, vol. ix, p. 4.

39 Ibid., p. 10.

40 Ibid., p. 35.

41 Domestic State Papers, 12/270, fo. 48; London Public Record Office.

42 HMC, *Salisbury*, vol. ix, p. 125.

43 George Paule, *The Life of the Most Reverend and Religious Prelate John Whitgift* (1612), pp. 56–7. (Hereafter cited in the text.) The "Novelists" are the radical church reformers including Barrow, Greenwood, Penry, and the authors of the Marprelate tracts.

44 HMC, *Salisbury*, vol. x, p. 142.

45 Ibid., pp. 141–2.

46 Edward Guilpin, *Skialetheia* (1598), B1r–B1v. (Hereafter cited in the text.)
47 McCabe, "Elizabethan Satire," p. 192.
48 John Marston, *The scourge of villanie* (1598), I3r.
49 John Weever, *The Whipping of the Satyre* (1601), A3v.
50 Nicolas Breton, *No whipping, nor tripping* (1601), A6r.
51 Early in Essex's career, Bacon had written to him warning of the dangers of his prodigal habits.
52 There is no way of ascertaining when in 1599 it appeared since it was not entered in the Register.
53 See McCabe, "Elizabethan Satire," p. 189.
54 Thomas Cutwode, *Caltha Poetarum* (1599), B5v. (Hereafter cited in the text.)
55 Steven May, *The Elizabethan Courtier Poets* (Columbia and London, 1991), pp. 266–9. In *A Catalogue of Early English Literature at Bridgewater House* (1837), J. Payne Collier comments on Essex's literary effort in this poem of fifteen six-line stanzas:

> The Earl of Essex was a poet, and, though none of his verses have been printed, some are preserved in manuscripts of the time. The most interesting of these relates to himself, and appears to have been written when he was banished by Queen Elizabeth from the Court: in the copy preserved among the Ashmole MSS. at Oxford it is called "The bussin Bee's Complaint"; but in a more authentic copy, subscribed "R. Devereux. Essex," it is headed "*Honi soit qui mal y pense.*" (p. 241)

Collier makes no mention of the source of the "more authentic copy." Based on a copy in the British Library (Harleian MS 6947, fos. 230r–231v), May categorizes the poem as "possibly by Essex" and gives the title as "A Poem made on the Earle of Essex (being in disgrace with Queene Eliz): by mr henry Cuffe his Secretary" (*Elizabethan Courtier Poets*, p. 264).
56 Nashe, *Works*, ed. McKerrow, vol. III, p. 201.
57 Ibid., p. 203.
58 Hutson, *Nashe in Context*, especially pp. 127–51.
59 HMC *Salisbury*, vol. X, pp. 182–4.
60 *Records of the Court*, ed. Greg and Boswell, pp. lviii, 79, 81. It is not entirely coincidental that the *State Papers* (12/275) contain several appeals from Essex to the Queen for favor during October 1600, and that his plight is the subject of letters between Dudley Carleton and John Chamberlain in the same volume.

10 CONCLUSION: "THAT LIBERTIE POETS OF LATE . . . HAVE EXCEEDED"

1 "*That libertie Poets of late in their invectives have exceeded,* they have borne their sword up, where it is not lawfull for a poynado, that is but the page of prowesse, to intermeddle." Thomas Nashe, "Strange Newes" (1592) in *Works*, vol. I, p. 281.

2 Jonathan Goldberg, *James I and the Politics of Literature* (Baltimore, 1983), p. 2.

3 Jürgen Habermas, *The Structural Transformation of the Public Sphere*, trans. Thomas Burger (Cambridge, MA, 1989), pp. 27–33.

4 *Harington's Metamorphosis of Ajax*, ed. Elizabeth Story Donno (1962), pp. 42–3.

5 See p. 246 n. 128.

6 Richard S. Peterson, "Laurel Crown and Ape's Tail," *Spenser Studies* (forthcoming) cited in *Greene's Groatsworth of Wit*, ed. D. Allen Carroll (New York, 1994), p. 107.

7 Nashe, *Works*, ed. McKerrow, vol. I, p. 281.

8 Fulke Greville, *The Life of the Renowned Sr. Philip Sidney* (1652), p. 178. It is particularly telling that Greville's destruction of his plays is associated in his mind with circumstances surrounding the contribution of libel to the destruction of Essex:

> And again in the practice of the world, seeing the like instance not poetically, but really fashioned in the Earle of *Essex* then falling; and ever till then worthily beloved, both of *Queen*, and people: This sudden descent of such greatnesse, together with the quality of the Actors in every Scene, stir'd up the Authors second thoughts, to bee carefull (in his owne case) of leaving faire weather behind him. And accordingly, under the same cloud, his enemies took audacity to cast Libels abroad in his name against the State, made by themselves; set papers upon posts, to bring his innocent friends in question. (ibid., pp. 179–80)

9 Edmund Spenser, *The Faerie Queene*, ed. A. C. Hamilton (New York, 1977), Book V, Canto IX, stanzas 25–6.

Index